Classic
JEWISH
HUMOR
in
AMERICA

ALSO BY HENRY D. SPALDING

Encyclopedia of Black Folklore and Humor

Encyclopedia of Jewish Humor: From Biblical Times to the Modern Age

Joys of Irish Humor

Joys of Italian Humor and Folklore

Joys of Jewish Humor

Classic JEWISH HUMOR *in* AMERICA

Henry D. Spalding

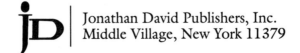
Jonathan David Publishers, Inc.
Middle Village, New York 11379

CLASSIC JEWISH HUMOR IN AMERICA

Copyright © 1995
by
Henry D. Spalding

Jonathan David Publishers, Inc.
68-22 Eliot Avenue
Middle Village, New York 11379

This is a revised and abridged edition of the author's *Treasure-Trove of American Jewish Humor,* first issued in 1976. Copyright © by Henry D. Spalding. All rights reserved.

2 4 6 8 9 7 5 3 1

Library of Congress Cataloging in Publication Data

Jewish humor in America / [compiled by] Henry D. Spalding.
    p.   cm.
Abridgement/revision of: Treasure-Trove of American Jewish humor.
Includes bibliographical references.
ISBN 0-8246-0383-4 (hardcover)
1. Jewish wit and humor. 2. Jews—United States—Humor.
I. Spalding, Henry D. II. Joys of Jewish humor.
PN6231.J5J465 1995
808.87'935203924—dc20

Printed in the United States of America

Acknowledgments

My sincere thanks go to Dorothy H. Rochmis, former editor of *Israel Today*, Los Angeles, for her gracious permission to use the many Yiddish, Hebrew and Russian words and phrases which appear in the glossary of this book, many of which were originally prepared for the *Encyclopedia of Jewish Humor*. I have added a number of new items to the glossary and, of course, if there are any errors in interpretation they are mine, not Dorothy's.

My deep thanks are also conveyed to a considerate and dedicated gentleman, Leopold Fechtner, author and Curator of the Museum of Humor, Kew Gardens, New York, for his kind permission to quote from his book, *American Wit and Gags*, and for his continued interest in this work.

Literally, scores of other people—far too many to mention here—gave unstintingly of their knowledge, time and effort, and their contributions will be found on many of these pages. In fact, all parts of this book which do not meet with your approval may be attributed to them.

HENRY D. SPALDING

Contents

Preface

In the past two decades since Henry D. Spalding selected the humorous stories and anecdotes that appear in this volume, the American-Jewish community has experienced significant changes. The East European immigrant has made way for an acculturated American Jew whose own children would have only a 50-50 chance of "marrying Jewish." Instead of shopkeepers and textile factory workers, almost everybody's son—and daughter, too—is a doctor, dentist, or lawyer. The canasta game and mahjongg have become casualties of the liberated woman. The Borscht Belt has become a casualty as well, and Yiddish has become a "new" language to learn.

Humor is the signature of a people. It is not static. As the culture changes, so too do the jokes and stories one finds funny. This volume of classics is a retrospective of the best of American-Jewish humor over the years. Although some of the stories might seem corny, they nonetheless are artifacts of their times and are representative of at least a century of American-Jewish humor. And they are wonderfully funny and familiar.

Many of our readers may not know Yiddish. A glossary is provided for those who have no *bobeh* or *zayde* to provide translations of the Yiddish words within.

BETTE ROTH YOUNG

Introduction

Just as man has always devised new schemes on the graves of a thousand disappointments, many Old World Jewish jokes emitted their sparks of wit on the flintstone of tragedy. In America, however, with past agonies receding from memory, the people's humor assumed a new and vibrant quality that mirrored the pulsating energy of what was to them, quite literally, the Land of Liberty that had for so long filled their dreams. This humor cannot yet be termed a uniquely American art form, carrying, as it does, the still-fertile seeds of its European origins—seeds which were brought to our shores by hundreds of thousands of bright-eyed immigrants in the present and past centuries. However, it is clearly in the process of evolution and there will come a time when it will be recognized as distinctly native to the United States.

American Jewish humor began with the early colonial settlers, the Sephardic Jews who first arrived in New Amsterdam (now New York) from Brazil in 1654, aboard the *St. Charles*, otherwise known as the Jewish *Mayflower*. Not generally realized, their descendants, multiplied by later-arriving Sephardim, constituted a majority of the Jewish citizenry in the Northern Continent of this hemisphere for more than 200 years. To them we attribute the Oriental mystique, the subtle artistry of expression, the continuity of the ancient exempla and even the Moorish influence of the fables which are still evident in American Jewish humor.

The influx of German Jewish newcomers was next to exert its influence upon the people's humor in the United States. This tide began as early as 1815, but it was not until 1848, when the liberal rebellion in Germany was crushed and the oppression of Jews in that country was resumed, that they joined in a concerted flight to the New World. That human flow did not abate until thirty years later, in 1880. The German Jewish contribution to the humor of their coreligionists in America was an urbanity and worldliness that differed markedly from the more traditional type that existed here. Yet, in time, the sophistication of the German Jews and the gentle wisdom of the earlier Sephardim coalesced into a rare form of humor that was at once intellectual, progressive and reverent—

a far cry from the caricatures of Jewish humor carried in the press of that day.

But the most durable and certainly the most pervasive influence upon American Jewish humor began with the immense wave of immigration from Russia during the last third of the 19th century. There, the familiar pattern of persecution rose to new and vicious heights under the reign of Tsar Alexander III, who promulgated the infamous "May Laws" and encouraged widespread terrorism against the Jews. The frequent *pogroms* and the anti-Jewish riots of 1881 resulted in a mass exodus of Russian Jews to America. Between 1881 and 1900, some 600,000 Jews of Eastern Europe, including the oppressed of Poland, Rumania, Hungary, Lithuania and other countries in that region, found a haven of refuse in the United States. But the persecutions did not cease. In Russia, especially, violent *pogroms* followed one upon the other, taking their heavy toll in Jewish lives and added misery for the survivors. Then followed the massacres by the "Black Hundreds,"* and the Russian Revolution, precipitating the flight of nearly a million more Jews to the hospitable shores of the United States.

The 200,000 Jews of Sephardic and German origins who had arrived earlier were now completely inundated by the two million of their brethren from Eastern Europe. This was the era of "melting pot" America, symbolized by the Statue of Liberty and which was inscribed with the immortal sonnet by Emma Lazarus:

> Give me your tired, your poor,
> Your huddled masses yearning to breathe free,
> The wretched refuse of your teeming shore,
> Send these, the homeless, tempest-tost to me.
> I lift my lamp beside the golden door!

Why have I delved into this seemingly irrelevant background of agony suffered by the Russian and other Jews of Eastern Europe? Because therein lies the paradox! Those harried, persecuted and plundered people, whose beginnings in this country were marked by the direst poverty, gave to American Jewish humor its warmth, its deep compassion and its joyful optimism. And these lovely and loving qualities, added to and diffused with those of the Sephardic and German Jews, formed the bedrock of the robust humor we know today.

American Jewish humor is a social documentation of the people's history in the United States, characterized by its playful ob-

---

*Bands of ruffians organized by the Tsarists government to perpetrate new *pogroms* upon the Jews.

servation of past events as well as a comic view of the present. Most history, however, is autopsy. But Jewish humor is vivisection, its razor-sharp edges honed on the whetstone of stark reality. Yet, it is not all sardonic and trenchant. As we shall see, most Jews do not spend their lives in somber thought, using their wit as a cloak to hide a "message" or "moral." They also know how to laugh for the sake of good, earthy laughter itself. It is that lighthearted, sunny nature which is the essence of this book.

You will meet here such diverse characters as Bret Harte, Henrietta Szold, Rabbi Stephen M. Wise, David Sarnoff, Bernard Baruch, Felix Frankfurter, Gertrude Stein, Albert Einstein and many others, some of whom are not usually associated with humor. Most of these older, true anecdotes are published here for the first time, and I must again thank the families and descendants of these historical personalities for their painstaking and time-consuming research of names, locales and dates, all of which immeasurably strengthened and speeded the preparation of my original manuscript.

There is yet another mirthful surprise in store for the reader who believes that slapstick comedy was invented in Hollywood or that zany antics are the exclusive property of modern youth. In these pages you will find a number of uproarious adventures by such stalwart figures as Hayman Levy, the largest fur trader in all the American colonies; Mrs. Rebecca Hayes and her son, Lt. David Hayes, who served under General Washington, and which may well be the first *Yiddishe* mama joke in the United States; Mordecai Manual (Major) Noah, the writer-statesman who attempted to establish a City of Refuge in the United States for the world's oppressed Jews. And here too are such famous families of early Judaica Americana as the Seixas, the Mendozas, the Franks of Philadelphia and the Sheftalls of Georgia. These and many other Jews played an important role in the shaping of America's destiny, and they now reach out across the centuries in a symbolic clasping of hands, bridging the past with the present, a merry twinkle in their eyes and a smile upon their lips.

A word about the preparation of this volume:

No one knows precisely when the first Jewish book of humor came into being. The *Book of Delight*, issued in the year 1200 by Joseph Zabara, believed to have been a physician of Barcelona, and the *Ma'aseh Book*, a 16th century collection of fables, legends and myths, are early examples of the people's fun-loving nature. In recent times, a number of works devoted to Jewish humor of all nations appeared, including my own *Encyclopedia of Jewish Humor* (1969). However, for reasons which I cannot fathom, no single volume devoted solely to the humor of *American* Jews had ever been published until the issuance of this present book. Consequently, as with any pioneering effort, I had no guidelines to indicate the content or direction that would be most entertaining to the reader and still fulfill the requirements of serious authorship.

For example, what do we mean by authentic *American* Jewish humor? Is it enough to say that it comprises those humorous anecdotes and witticisms which are told by Jews to other Jews and which revolve around Jewish subject matter? But what is meant by Jewish subject matter? And what of the use of accented English? Should dialect jokes by deleted altogether? These and other perplexing questions are discussed in the introductions to each of the following chapters, but it is only fair to confess that any author's opinion is subjective—no matter what he may say publicly. In my case, this book represents the offspring of a not-too-clandestine love affair with my people, and like any father, I hope to be forgiven for all lapses of objectivity.

The original manuscript of this volume contained 71 categories and 119 sub-classifications—far too unwieldy for a single work. Subsequently, these were consolidated into the present 28 chapters, each bearing up on a distinctive facet of Jewish life or upon qualities of character or personality. The jokes and quips which were translated from the *Yiddish* are so indicated, but the reader will note that I have included the *Yiddish* terms and expressions in many of the stories exactly as they were related to me in the first place—some when I was a boy, and just beginning to collect examples of Jewish folklore and humor. The adults who attended evening classes at Cooper Union, Workmen's Circle or citizen education groups did not speak like Harvard professors, and, if for nothing else than authenticity and the preservation of its *Yiddishkeit*, I thought it best to write as closely to their original telling as possible. For those not familiar with the language employed, I have appended a glossary of the *Yiddish*, Hebrew, Russian, Polish and other words and phrases used throughout this book, prepared, let me hasten to add, by the knowledgeable Dorothy Rochmis. The glossary is an expanded version of the one she compiled for *Encyclopedia of Jewish Humor*.

This volume, obviously, is by no means confined to the turn-of-the-century inhabitants of New York's East Side. As to the *krechtz*, or groan, which permeated much of Old World wit, American Jewish humor may be delivered in a minor key but it has long since discarded its hair-shirt and is anything but a lamentation. I do not deny, of course, that many of the newcomers were bottled up in their tenement-prisons—as effectively pickled in their ghetto environment as a cucumber in brine. Nevertheless, there were times when the ghetto-dweller stood on the tiptoe of expectation as he dreamed and planned of entering that "other" America which he knew existed "out there." The jokes they told echoed those yearnings and ambitions, and many of their mirthful stories remain as cheerful remembrances that have not lost their appeal to this day.

Not all humor evokes laughter; sometimes it produces a wry and occasionally a bitter smile. Through their lore, the Jewish people reveal themselves in a sort of musical pattern adorned with the secret pangs and passions of their innermost selves. But there are times when the music is a cacophony formed by dark memories of their past. These thoughts are the dogs that bark within their Jewish hearts. And it is these which they have seized by their tails and made to dance to the tune of an old Italian's hurdy-gurdy on Orchard Street. Sometimes the music cannot be gentled because the barking chaos of racial remembrance will not be crushed into silence and yelps its agony like a gutter mongrel hit by a speeding taxi. A few of these momentary gasps are presented here, but on the whole, the music is joyous, lilting and filled with bubbling delight. The reason is clear enough: Down through history the Jew has always managed to find the medicine of humor within the mist and swirl of pain and become the merriest hypochondriac who ever danced the Charleston on Parnassus. It was that ability which helped to prevent him from becoming a jacketed and trousered neurosis.

To its credit, Jewish jokes and witticisms are usually told or written in simple language, without the abstruse stories or intellectual crossword puzzles that are unintelligible to those who do their thinking in plain English. And this is where the author parts company with the academic folklorists, the professional joke-analyzers and the psychologists who are bound hand and foot, tongue and mind, to the mumbo-jumbo of motifs, leitmotifs, patterns and other esoteric jargon which they have inherited from past generations of dryasdusts. What they fail to see is that humor is a social *problem* that calls for the psychiatrist's couch. Humor which is studied under a Freudian microscope is humor without laughter.

In this rather extensive collection I have tried to include only those jokes and flashes of wit which I believed to be genuinely funny, which do not insult your intelligence, and which are truly representative of America's Jewish people. But whether the attempt merits a *kaddish* or a *mazel tov* is your decision to make.

Shalom!

HENRY D. SPALDING

1

Hearts and Flowers and Fiddle Music

Introduction

Someone once said, quite correctly, that humor is no laughing matter. The same might also be said for love.

What brooding secrets are hidden in the hearts and minds of lovers—and in our case, Jewish lovers? What secret yearnings haunt their dreams and drive their primitive passions?

No matter how one turns and twists his words or thoughts, one conclusion is inevitable: Love is love; and Jewish love is the same as gentile love—only more so. When a man finally decides to take that fateful step into matrimony, it is not always at a time of romantic fervor under a bower of roses.

The Jewish man or woman sees love from its practical as well as its esoteric side. A Yiddish maxim tells us, "Love tastes sweet, but only with bread." Another solemnly declares, "A heart without love is like a pocket without money." And, in 1831, Disraeli said, "Where we do not respect, we do not love." Sometimes, the sayings get a little out of hand. One enthusiastic biblical sage made the rather startling declaration, "Love covers all transgressions." Bluebeard might have taken that passage literally, but, then, look what it got him. And he wasn't even Jewish.

But, if Jewish love can be practical, it can also soar on the wings of gossamer beauty. It tells the world that the magic of first love lies in believing that it will never end. "Every goose is a swan in the eyes of a lover," states the Talmud. "You are not loved when you are lovely, but when you are loved, you are found to be lovely," wrote the romantic Boern in 1824. Today, it seems, many of us appear more anxious to hide our love than our hate.

The gifted poet, Louis Ginsberg, understood the need for tender expression. In his poem, "Song," published in *The Liberator* (1930), Ginsberg cautioned the undemonstrative lover with this quatrain:

> Love that is hoarded, moulds at last,
> Until we know, someday,
> The only thing we ever have,
> Is what we gave away.

The most enduring love is the love that laughs, as George Jean Nathan once pointed out. Had I been one of the early settlers in the New World, I would not have chronicled the experiences of the long voyage across the uncharted ocean or even the later privation of the colonists. Instead, I would have written a romantic novel, *The Shenandoah Shammes and his Shayneh Shikseleh*, the story of how pious Pincus the Pilgrim pursued and proposed to pretty Pocahantas between Purim and Passover and proudly produced the first *parve* papoose on Pitkin Avenue.

Or, as Samson murmured ecstatically to Delilah while she gave him a non-union haircut, "Love-shmove—as long as you really care!"

H.D.S.

While we're on the subject, let us bear in mind that true love can come to us no matter what our age might be. For example, eighty-five-year-old Mr. Becker fell in love with a grandmotherly lady of seventy-five. They decided to marry.

"Do you take this woman for your bride?" the rabbi asked the faltering groom.

Replied Mr. Becker: "I should only live so long."

For those loving hearts who prefer all their music integrated in one "swell foop," we are pleased to pass along a new trend in Reform Jewish marriage ceremonies, as reported in the *Zion Chronicle*:

"Cantor Shamir Baumgarten's wedding was absolutely beautiful and quite traditional, except for the fact that the cantor himself sang 'I Love You Truly' to his blushing bride, while the organ played some Strauss waltzes."

We're not thoroughly convinced that this was merely a writing error and not a peculiar papa, but here's another news items from *Zion Chronicle*:

"The bride was given away by her father wearing a white satin gown with a long train."

Poetry time again, dear young lovers:

> A romantic Jewish young Mr.
> Had a girl and he often Kr.
> But he asked her to wed,
> And she solemnly said:
> "I can never be more than a Sr."

"My boyfriend's name is Dorfman, but I call him Draftsman," explained the girl with a trace of annoyance in her voice. "Every time I mention marriage he draws the line."

He was debonair, he was handsome, he was rich. He approached the lady's table and bowed.

"Madam," he said in a cultured voice, "may I join you?"

"*Join* me!" she screeched in maidenly horror. "Am I coming apart?"

World-shaking Events Department: This is to advise our readers that there is no substance to the gossip concerning Moshe Dayan and Zza Zza Gabor.

But, as the man said when the boarding house blew up, "Roomers are flying."

He was a persistent suitor and very anxious to marry the girl. For the tenth time he proposed to her, but, to be painfully frank about it, she couldn't stand the man.

"Sweetheart," he said ardently, "I would go to the ends of the earth for you."

"That's what you say now," snapped the girl, "but what guarantee do I have that you'd stay there?"

When Gimpel the grocer arrived at his lodge meeting on Saturday evening, his best buddy quickly noticed his sad expression.

"How come you're looking so downhearted, Gimp?" asked the friend.

"I lost my girl," said Gimpel.

"I'm sorry to hear that," said the friend sympathetically. "And I'm surprised, too. I thought she was interested in you."

"So did I," answered Gimpel sorrowfully. "But, last night, I told her I'd lost my capital, and right off she lost her interest."

After repeatedly warding off her date's amorous advances throughout the evening, the pretty young thing decided to put her foot down.

"See here," she demanded, "this is positively the last time I'm going to tell you 'no.'"

"Fine!" enthused her date. "Now, maybe we can start making a little progress."

". . . and as far as I'm concerned, *Mister* Oscar Kaplan, you won't be needing a fan this summer—I'm giving you the air."

Clara was simply ecstatic as her suitor, on his knees, proposed marriage. Never had he or anyone else spoken so beautifully to her. His voice was like a tender caress, his words as delicate as rose petals.

"Oh darling," she breathed, "I wish this would never end. But I'm still not sure. Let me hear that part again where you realize you're not half good enough for me."

Julius: How many Cammandments are there?
Julia: Ten.
Julius: What would happen if you—er—well—you know—if you broke one of them?
Julia (encouragingly): So, there'd be nine.

Raleigh Rosenbloom, the romantic young bachelor of Palm Beach, who was also a big spender, telephoned the girl he had just met the night before. She was not only gorgeous, but had also proved to be a real swinger. He wanted another date. To his surprise, however, she turned him down.

"How come you're refusing to go out with me tonight?" he demanded. "Only yesterday you said there was something about me you adored."

"There was, baby," she crooned in her husky voice, "but you spent it!"

Barney the Bagel King had trouble spending the interest on his money. Among his treasures were a palatial home in Palm Springs, California, a townhouse in New York, a yacht and—his most cherished possession—Bubbles Bernstein of Beverly Hills. He was really in love with her.

Then, the bottom dropped out of the stock market, and overnight all of Barney's wealth disappeared. The ex-millionaire was broke.

Sadly, he called at her apartment to break the depressing news.

"I lost everything," he told her mournfully. No bank account, no stocks, no yacht, no house—nothing! I haven't got a dime left."

She kissed him sweetly and murmured, "You may have lost everything else, darling, but not my love."

"You really mean that?" he exclaimed in an ecstasy of joy.

"Of course, dear. And I want you to know I'll always remember you with affection."

It was Selma's birthday and she was watching the six o'clock news on television while her room-mate, Maxine, was thumbing through a magazine. Suddenly, it occurred to Maxine that Selma had not been invited out for this gala occasion.

"Don't you have a date this evening?" she asked.

"No," answered Selma sadly. "I'm afraid I lost my boyfriend."

"What happened?"

"Someone told him that I had an affair with another man before I met him. He just stopped calling me."

"Don't let that worry you," counseled Maxine. "You just go to him in a perfectly straightforward, honest way, and lie about the whole thing!"

There are very few humorous stories about promiscuity among Jewish girls of past generations. Here is one of those rarities, circa 1930:

Rabbi Isaacs was quite fond of the Shapiro family whose members were longtime congregants of his Temple. So it was understandable that he would react sympathetically when they asked him to have a serious talk with their daughter, Rachel, who was unmarried, but pregnant again for the third time.

He confronted the young lady on the following evening.

"I can't understand how a nice Jewish girl could allow such a disgraceful thing to happen," he began severely. "Three times yet! I suppose the babies all have different fathers?"

"Oh, no!" said Rachel. "It's the same fellow."

"He's single, this man?"

"Certainly. You think I'd go with a married man?"

"Then why don't you marry him?"" demanded the rabbi.

"Well, frankly," Rachel answered with complete candor, "he doesn't appeal to me."

Last line heard on a bus:

". . . so I said good-bye to him with a permanent wave."

After one year of marital bliss:

She: Whenever I talk to you, it's like a dog barking. You never answer me.

He: It's not true! When's the last time you barked and I didn't answer?

It had been three years since Morris left for the battlefields of Europe during World War II. Most of the time, he had been stationed in France. And now that he had returned home, he could hardly wait to display his newly-acquired French vocabulary to Jennie, his best girl.

The autumn evening had turned chilly, but inside the apartment the lights were low and the hi-fi was playing soft music. If the room was a bit drafty, neither of them noticed. Morris turned to Jennie.

"*Djhonveeyev*," he murmured caressingly, coming as near to the French pronunciation of "Genevieve" as he was able. "*Je t'adore.*"

"Why, you lazy thing," snapped Jennie. "Shut it yourself!"

Velvel was aghast to learn that his sister, Odelia, had decided to marry Al Scharf, a nightclub comic.

"You call that guy a comic?" Velvel demanded. "Believe me, you can get more laughs watching a guy fix a flat tire. He's an arrogant, pushy slob—the type who gets into a revolving door behind you and comes out first on the other side. He's not for you, Sis. That character couldn't cheer up a laughing hyena."

"You're just jealous because he's a self-made man," Odelia retorted.

"Well, if that's what he told you, I gotta hand it to him," acknowledged Velvel grudgingly. "At least he's taking all the blame!"

Karl the Knaidel King of Kansas City had everything in life that a man could ask for, except for one thing—he wanted a grandson to carry on the family name, to say nothing of the family business. So, he was understandably happy when his bachelor son told him, one evening, that he had fallen love and was planning to marry.

"It's a smart thing you're doing," advised Karl. "Until a man marries he's incomplete."

He pondered the wisdom of his own statement for a moment or two and then added solemnly, "He's not only complete—he's finished!"

2

Martial Relations

Introduction

Marriage, in the traditional Jewish view, is a better prescription for what ails a person than chicken soup—and chicken soup has a time-tasted reputation. It might not be a real cure, but chances are pretty good that it will help. This analysis is especially applicable to the *nahr*—the foolish one—when it comes to setting his life straight. ("What! That *shlemiel*? Better he should marry!")

If a man is already married, it is pro-forma evidence of his wisdom. After all, look how many times Solomon stood under the *chuppeh*. This faith of the Jew in the curative powers of the marriage canopy is international, and has persisted since the earliest times, even though no one has ever discovered a simpleton who became a sage after the knot was tied.

This way of life—this attitude—is ingrained in the Jew. It is expressed at the strangest times. You may recall the historic visit of United Nations mediator Dag Hammarskjold to Israel at the time of the Suez blockade. The UN, as usual, was marching to the drumbeat of Egypt rather than that of Israel. Hammarskjold flew to Israel and went to see Prime Minister David Ben-Gurion and there he met B.G.'s wife, a woman who was more frank than diplomatic. "Listen, you are a nice man," said Paula to Hammarskjold, "so why don't you get married and leave Israel alone?"

Jewish wit being what it is, marriage was an easy solution, and Jewish literature abounds in cynical proverbs and caustic commentaries about wedlock. The Talmud ruefully states, "When love was strong, we could have made our bed on a sword's blade; now, when it has become weak, a bed of 60 cubits is not large enough for us." The sages were not above mixing a little humor with their declamations. Wrote one Talmudist: "A great man should not disdain to serve as best man to one of minor position. The Holy One, Blessed-be-He, was best man at Adam's wedding."

It is no secret that humor serves as a cloak for anger and indignation. We express our hostility indirectly—often with a derisive quip or a funny anecdote. And the smile or the laughter it evokes gives us a sense of vengeance fulfilled. We have gotten even! We have struck back! The feeling gives us more relief than Alka Seltzer.

If we are to believe the psychologists, and I suppose we should—as long as we don't make a habit of it—they tell us that even Sholem Aleichem reflected a degree of hostility in his humor: He once said: "I ask you, my friend: Who started all this business of marriage and wives?" This was his way of striking back. It also explains why Disraeli made the wry comment, "I have always thought that every woman should marry—and no man." He voiced his resentment with a smile, but Gloria Steinem would never have voted for him.

Considering all the marriages that were made in heaven and that culminated in the other place, they must be doing a big export business up there. We have entered the age of the gay divorcee and the unshackled, uninhibited ex-hubby. It is also the era of the liberated housewife. This means that her loving spouse is now entitled to change the baby's diapers and wish the dishes, but it does not necessarily mean that she need ever take out the garbage. As a liberated woman, she can now hang her stockings, pantyhose and other frillies on the shower-curtain rod, with the cold drip-drip tattooing hubby's bare bottom when he tries to sneak into the tub. But, if *he* is so thoughtless as to hang his underwear on the bedroom door-knob so he can find it in the morning, he is a male chauvinist (you-should-pardon-the-expression) "pig." He is just like *his* family. He is not *neat*! He is a *slob*! That's what happens when a decent, well-brought-up *Litvak* girl marries one of those *Galitzianers*! Sound familiar? Go make a joke and get it out of your system. Then kiss your wife—if she'll let you.

But, is all this really hostility, or is it simply good-natured *kibitzing*? Don't ask your friendly neighborhood marriage counselor. There are more divorced marriage counselors than there are divorced actors. Whatever the marital expert happens to know about connubial bliss, he learned from reading this chapter.

All this hostility hoopla has gone too far. There are undoubtedly times when we are hostile, but as a rule we are simply and innocently amused.

As an example, the New Testament tells us, "It is better to marry than to burn." In response, Jewish wit slides off at a tangent and retorts, "So what else is new?" But, the Jew is just as quick to read a funny meaning into his own literature. Take the "Palestine Bridal Song" as an illustration: "The bride: no powder, no rouge, no hair-do, yet a graceful gazelle." It is really a lovely phrase, but that impish sense of humor flashes a question in our mind: "If all brides are so beautiful, then why do they always wind up looking like Mrs. Khrushchev?"

H.D.S.

Hymie, the henpecked hubby of Houston Street, hoisted a hefty hooker of holiday happiness at "Herbie's Hangout," and tearfully told a tippler of his trials and tribulations with his spouse, Tillie.

"My wife doesn't understand me," moaned Hymie, who happened to be a linguistic innovator.

"Why don't you just assert yourself?" suggested the drinking companion curtly. "What are you, a man or a mouse?"

"I must be a man," sighed Hymie. "Tillie's afraid of mice."

The newspapers carried a number of stories about the nation's most beautiful actresses and the insignificant men they sometimes choose as husbands.

"I'll never be able to understand why the biggest *shnooks* always get the prettiest women," sighed the very-much-married Moishe.

"Why, darling," exclaimed the pleased and surprised wife, "what a very sweet compliment!"

"Rose, explain me something," said the girl's sister. "Your husband's name is Gedalia. So why do you always call him 'Abie'?"

"Because it fits him," sighed Rose. "He's everything I used to dream about—from A to B."

Joan and Jake were having another of their interminable arguments. This time it was about Jake's annoying habit of criticizing her family, and at the same time praising his own. The accusations grew so barbed that Joan burst into tears. Jake knew he had gone too far, and was immediately contrite.

"I'm sorry, honey," he said abjectly, "I really didn't mean all those nasty things I said about your family. In fact, if you want to know the honest truth, I like your mother-in-law much better than I do mine."

A TIFFANY TEEYATER PRESENTATION

The Distinguished Cast

Eve ....Pat Hand
Adam...Paris Franz

Scene
The Garden of Eden

(Adam is speaking while Eve knits baby-booties)
Adam: We had plums, we had oranges, we had pineapples, bananas, figs, pomegranates, nectarines, watermelons, cantaloupes, peaches—but no, *you* wanted an apple!

"What is a wife?" asks Oren, the oracle of Orchard Street, who likes to answer his own questions.

"A wife is a woman who stands by her husband through all the *tsuris* he wouldn't have had if he'd stayed single in the first place.

"Generally speaking, she's generally speaking," observes Oren. "She spends more time mending your ways than your socks. She's a dish-jockey who never has anything to wear, and has four closets to keep it in. She can dish it out, but she can't cook it.

"Still and all, she's never still at all, but make no mistake about it—a wife is a thing of beauty and a jaw forever!"

Feivel the furrier was talking to his partner over a cup of coffee.

"Tomorrow my wife leaves for two weeks to visit her mother on the West Coast."

"How about your own vacation?" queried the partner. "When

does that start?"

"I just told you," explained Feivel. "Tomorrow!"

Schoenberg, the silk manufacturer, who had been married for twenty-five years, took council with one of his bachelor friends.

"It seems to me," he complained, "that my domestic affairs are slipping into a rut. I'm afraid my wife is getting bored with me. There doesn't seem to be any of the old romance left that we had in our early married life. I wish I knew what the problem could be."

"I can make a guess," said his confidant. "Do you still pay your wife those little attentions that you once did when you were courting her?"

"Well, no," confessed Schoenberg. "I can't say that I do."

"I thought as much," replied the friend. "Now this is my advice to you: Turn over a new leaf. Start this very day. Begin paying your wife some attention. Fuss over her just like you used to do when you first got engaged. Try to be a sweetheart to her instead of just a husband."

"Say, that's pretty good advice!" exclaimed Schoenberg. "Take my word, I'll do it!"

That evening, when he burst into the house, his arms laden with parcels, he planted a warm kiss upon the cheek of the astonished Mrs. Schoenberg and, in tones of well worked-up enthusiasm, he cried out: "This is going to be a big night for us, baby! Here's a five-pound box of candy for you and here's a dozen American Beauty roses. Now, I want you to slip into your best gown. I reserved a table at the Ritz-Carlton for dinner, and I ordered two seats for the concert at Carnegie Hall."

He stopped short and stared at his wife. Her face was pale and her lips were beginning to tremble. "What's the matter?" he asked.

"Well, to start with," she answered, "our daughter told me today she's interested in a *shaigetz*. Your aunt Clara arrived unexpectedly this morning for a visit. Our little Sammy was sent home from school with a bad cold. I lost an earring someplace while I was shopping, and now—now —" she burst into tears—"and now you have to come home drunk!"

We've heard of many optimists in our time, but Hollywood's Oren Opatashu is the mostest with the bestest. He went down to City Hall to find out when his marriage license expires.

"I love you truly."
"Only me?"
"Baby, I said *truly*, not *only*!"

Mrs. Silver and Mrs. Gold were gossiping over the back fence as they hung out the wash.

"My husband—ahh, such a faithful man," boasted Mrs. Silver. "He never even looks at another woman."

"The same with my husband," said Mrs. Gold. "He never chases after women either. He's too fine, too decent—too old!"

Phil Bernstein, the Bronx furniture retailer, was walking along Fordham Road when he encountered a woman who appeared vaguely familiar to him. He nodded his head in greeting.

"You're Mrs. Kovacs, aren't you?" he asked.

"That's me, in person," she replied.

"Aren't you a member of Hadassah?"

"For a good twenty years."

"Were you at the executive meeting today?"

"Certainly. Why are you asking?"

"Well, my wife was there also. She'll tell me all about it when I get home this evening, but I'd like to know now if she was one of the speakers."

"Hmm, I don't know your wife, but there was one short, stout lady who got up . . ."

"Yes-yes, that must have been my wife. Go on."

"She got up and said she couldn't find the words to express her feelings."

"No," said Bernstein, shaking his head, "that couldn't have been my wife!"

Wifey: I'm wearing my new dresses shorter this year.
Hubby: I'd like it better if you wore the old ones a little longer.

The butcher and the milkman were discussing the pros and cons of married life. "Do you really believe it's better than being single?" demanded Weiss, the butcher.

"In a way," said the milkman, who was fond of philosophizing. "After all, if it weren't for marriage, we'd have to do all our fighting with strangers."

"My wife deserted me," moaned the unhappy husband. "She took the car and ran off with a traveling salesman."

"Why, that's terrible!" exclaimed his friend, aghast. "Your brand new car!"

"You ungrateful loafer! I gave you the best years of my life," screamed the wife.

"Now just a minute!" retorted the husband. "In the first place, who made them the best years of your life? And in the second place, what do you want—a receipt?"

"Happy birthday, darling," gushed the young wife. "Have I got a surprise for you!"

"Why, thank you, sweetie-pie," said the pleased husband. "I can hardly wait to see it."

"Wait just a minute," she cried enthusiastically, "and I'll try it on for you."

". . . and so Myron and Sybil were married and they lived happily forever after for several months."

Weeping plaintiff: Believe me, your honor, when she ran her fingers through my hair, she was after my scalp!

Frieda was listening to some music on the stereo system while

Freddie was reading a newspaper article concerning the population explosion.

"It says here," remarked Freddie, "that nine out of ten people were caused by accidents."

"Terrible, terrible," responded Frieda. "But such a big accident rate wouldn't happen if people didn't drive so fast."

"What annoys me most about my mother-in-law," observed Herman the hair stylist, "is that she thinks I'm effeminate. And yet, compared to her," he added after a moment of reflection, "I guess I am."

"I'm convinced that there would be more happy marriages if couples would go out at least once a week for dining, dancing or a movie," said Barney, the Beau Brummel of Broadway. "My wife and I always make it a point to doll up and paint the town red. She goes on Fridays and I go on Saturdays."

Down at the shop, Izzy had just finished talking to his wife on the telephone. When he finally hung up, his partner remarked, "You certainly must love your wife very much to call her 'Angel' all the time."

"It isn't that," explained Izzy. "I call her 'Angel' because she's always up in the air and harping about something or other."

Morris and Millie were taking a Sunday walk along Wilshire Boulevard when a gorgeous woman crossed their path.

"Boy," exclaimed Morris rapturously, "she looks like a million!"

"Well, I don't think she's quite that old," responded Millie coldly, "but you're close."

3

Yiddishe Mamas

Introduction

One of the distinctive characteristics of Jewish humor is the tendency to satirize whatever is most dear and closest to one's heart. The narrator or writer will employ irony, sarcasm, travesty and ridicule—to deride or expose what he considers to be vice or folly. Nothing is sacrosanct. But the difference—and this is what makes Jewish humor unique—is that the "derision" is aimed at the *quality* of weakness, seldom at the weak *person*; it denounces human frailty, not the human being. There are obvious exceptions, of course. Hitler may be cast as a buffoon in a Jewish joke, but the expression of hostility towards him and his likes is quite understandable.

The "Jewish mother" joke may burlesque, jibe and scoff, but, at its core, there is profound compassion and deep affection. She may be the subject of the story, and is not always presented in an admirable light, but she is still *mamenyu*—dear mother. The conclusion or punch line of the joke arouses a feeling of compassionate understanding, a desire to implant a kiss upon the cheek of the hapless Yiddishe mama.

Turn-of-the-century European Jews told very few Yiddishe Mama jokes. The Yiddishe Mama joke is a strictly *American*-Jewish phenomenon.

Many Jewish comedians have excelled in the Jewish mother type story. These include George Jessel, Joey Bishop, Zero Mostel and Buddy Hackett, to name a few. Their humorous tales often mirrored their own life experiences—tragic as well as pleasant. Thus, from the treasure-trove of personal remembrances, they were able to weave their funny, fanciful jokes, mostly fiction, to be sure, but with just enough sprinkling of fact to nudge our own memories.

And, now, before we get to the meat of the matter, let us resolve never to forget the ancient Yiddish saying, "God could not be everywhere, so he created mothers."

H.D.S.

For several months, Esther the hairdresser had urged her mother to have her hair styled, but each time she was met with a firm refusal.

"But, mama, how does it look for a successful hair stylist to have a mother who needs her hair done? It's a shame and a disgrace!"

The daughter's persistence finally wore her mother down. "All right. Just don't make me I should look like a heepie."

"Listen, mama, you'll look perfectly marvelous," Esther gushed. "When I get through with your hair-do, your best friends won't recognize you. Even your own family won't know you."

It took almost two hours, but finally mama's new hair-style was finished. "Now go look in the mirror over there," said the daughter, "while I wait on this other customer."

In a few minutes, Esther returned to the same spot where she had left her mother.

"Yes, madam," she said courteously to the old lady, "can I help you?"

Zero Mostel was fond of telling the story about his mother's worried insistence that he start a savings account. "Show me a bankbook with $10,000 and I'll be satisfied," she would constantly tell him. The day finally came when he proudly displayed his bankbook showing a total deposit of $10,000. She shrugged, and murmured, "You call that a lot of money?"

Sadie Greenspan was running for the office of secretary of the local PTA. But, although the other parents and teachers liked her and recognized her good qualities, she was making little progress against Sally Blum, her rival candidate. The reason was obvious:

Sadie was a shy, soft-spoken Yiddishe mama type, while Sally Blum was a fast-talking, quick-thinking, glib young woman.

One of the teachers drew Sadie aside.

"Look, Mrs. Greenspan, it's all right to be reserved and to display such commendable humility but, if you expect to win the election, you'll have to be more outspoken. Let the members know how smart you really are. Do a little bragging about yourself the way Mrs. Blum does."

Sadie shook her head. "That I won't do," she said firmly. "By me it's a question of principles. I'm very proud to be so humble."

Joey Bishop's quip: Back in 1942, I said, "Mama, I'm going into the Army." And she told me, "All right, but don't come home late."

The young man had just landed a job as a census taker, but he returned home quite despondent after making his first day's rounds.

"I thought you liked your new job," said his mother. "What's the matter you're so sad?"

"I just can't get any cooperation," answered her son. "The women simply refuse to give me their right age."

"That's not the way to learn a woman's age," said the mother reprovingly. "You have to do what I do."

"What do you do?"

"When I want to find out how old a woman is, I just ask her sister-in-law."

A rabbi said to six-year-old Bobby: "So your mother says your prayers for you each night. Very commendable. What does she say?" And Bobby replied: "Thank God he's in bed!"

Two ladies were in the beauty parlor, sitting under the hairdryers, and with obvious difficulty, were discussing their families.

"Do you mean to tell me that your son and daughter-in-law were married six months ago, and you haven't visited them yet?"

exclaimed the first lady. "I'm shocked!"

"What's to be shocked?" demanded the second lady. "I'm waiting until they have their first baby. Everybody knows that a grandma is always more welcome than a mother-in-law."

"Mama," asked the young bride, "is it true that the way to a man's heart is through his stomach?"

"Well," replied mama thoughtfully, "that depends on what he's hungry for."

Thirteen-year-old Tessie came home in tears.

"What's the matter, dear?" asked her mother.

"Oh, mama, my best boyfriend left me for another girl," she sobbed, throwing herself full-length on the bed as she had seen Barbara Stanwyck do in a late-late TV movie. "Oh, the agony of it all! Why must we women suffer like this!"

"Tessie, you really want to forget all that agony and suffering?" asked her mother calmly. "Try wearing tight shoes for a few days."

A "sushel" worker was making a visit to a poor widow on the East Side. The woman's four little boys all wore glasses.

"What a pity!" exclaimed the visitor sympathetically. "I'm sorry that all your children have eye trouble."

"Trouble? What trouble?" demanded the mother. "Their eyes are perfect, *Gott sie dank!*"

"Then, why in the world do you make them wear glasses?"

The mother stared at the social worker in amazement. "Tell me the truth," she said carefully, as though speaking to a retarded child, "You ever in your life saw a doctor or a lawyer *without* glasses?"

It was an embarrassing moment for both mother and daughter, but there was no putting it off.

"Now that you're getting married, it's time I should give you a little advice," said mama, trying hard to sound casual.

"Oh, mother, *please,* it really isn't necessary," protested the sophisticated daughter. "That's so old-fashioned!"

"Old-fashioned, new-fashioned, it makes no difference. A good Jewish mother gives her daughter advice when she marries, and that's all there is to it," declared the older woman flatly.

The daughter gave a resigned shrug. "All right, I'm listening."

"The first thing I have to warn you about," said mama, choosing her words carefully, "is that you should never line the closet shelves with newspapers. If you do, everybody will know when you last gave the house a good cleaning!"

Marvin went to Boy Scout camp for the first time. During the required inspection, the scoutmaster found an umbrella neatly placed inside Marvin's bedroll.

"Now look here," reproved the scoutmaster, "you know perfectly well that an umbrella is not listed as a necessary item."

Marvin, echoing the sentiments of untold millions of other Jewish boys, replied wearily, "Sir, did you ever have a mother?"

"*Oy,* doctor, have I got *tsuris* with my son," wept the lady. "All day long he's doing nothing but blowing bubbles. From soap suds he's making the bubbles and he's blowing them out from a clay pipe."

"Really, madam, there's no reason for you to be concerned," said the psychiatrist, smiling indulgently. "Lots of sons blow bubbles."

"Well, I think it looks funny," insisted the woman, "and so does his wife."

The young mother, not long in the United States, and still unaccustomed to American ways, diffidently entered a photographer's studio.

"How much it costs, please, for children's pictures?" she asked.

"Ten dollars for six," replied the photographer.

The mother's face fell. "Oh, I'm sorry, but I'll have to wait," she cried, her voice full of disappointment. "So far, I only got two."

The young woman, her children in tow, was visiting her mother.

"You look tired," said the elderly grandmother to her daughter.

"I am," said the daughter. "Mama, isn't there any way at all for a housewife to get a few precious minutes to herself?"

"Yes," said the old lady sadly, "just start doing the dishes."

✧ ✧ ✧

There is an amusing folk tale which illustrates the fact that the traditional Yiddishe mama was much in evidence during colonial times and the Revolutionary War period. The story revolves around the real-life David Hays, his younger brother, Michael, and their strong-willed mother.

David Hays was the Jewish patriot in the War of Independence who accomplished the singular feat of driving cattle from his Westchester farm, through the British lines, to the hungry Colonial troops. In reprisal, British forces visited his farm while he was away serving in Washington's army and burned his house down. Defiantly, he returned to the farm under the very noses of the enemy and, with his brother, Michael, rebuilt the house. Again, David left home to fight under Washington's command.

Back at the farm, David's mother was at the water-well in the front yard when a Colonial officer approached her. He pointed to a plow team in the adjacent field and asked:

"Are those your horses?"

"Yes," she replied, thinking of all the cattle they had furnished the army, "and that big strong man at the plow is my son Michael. So don't make trouble."

"I'm sorry, madam," the officer said politely, "but the army is badly in need of horses. I'm afraid I'll have to confiscate them in the name of the government. You'll be reimbursed after the war, of course."

"Who is your commanding officer?" demanded Mrs. Hays.

"Captain David Hays," replied the army man.

"Oh, it's Captain David Hays, is it?" she exclaimed, a smile softening her hitherto stern features. "Well, you go right back and tell him his mama said he can't have her horses!"

4

Yiddishe Papas

Introduction

The Bible and the Talmud are replete with references to fathers—some humorous, but mostly philosophical. Aside from the sage guidance found in the Book of Proverbs, the Talmud contains many passages of this type: "He who brings up, not he who begets, is the father"—which might be interpreted as meaning that many mothers are fathers. Dear old dad seems to have gotten the worst of it in a number of Talmudic sayings! As for example this one: "A father's love is for his children; the children's love is for *their* children." One would think that having given all that love, the law of compensation would take effect, and the weary father might expect a little something in return for his efforts. But here we are confronted with another proverb: "One father willingly maintains ten children, but ten children are unwilling to maintain one father." Such ingratitude!

Franz Kafka, the Austrian novelist, gave the needle another gratuitous push when he observed, "Parents who expect gratitude from their children (there are even some who insist on it) are like usurers who gladly risk their capital if only they receive interest." With that statement, Kafka arouses the anger of his Jewish brethren everywhere. All *Litvak* parents castigated him as "that *Galitzianer*." All *Galitzianers* scorned him as "that *Litvak*." The Russian Jews, from their lofty perch on the Judaic totem pole, coldly accused him of being both—and of being improperly potty-trained as well. Retorted Kafka: "*Bopkes!*" Damn clever, these Austrians.

The modern male parent is no longer called a "Yiddishe papa." We now refer to him as a Jewish father—and often even the

"Jewish" is omitted. Yet, like the Yiddishe mama, he displays many of the traditional responses of the older generations, modified in the context of today's culture. He may be humming his favorite tune from *Fiddler on the Roof*, but listen more closely and you will hear the faint echo of *Eli, Eli*. Moreover, the people's bond with the past also extends to each other as individuals. That is why a Jew finds it easy to identify with the concerned father who sighs, "Young man, you can't afford my daughter—but then, neither can I." And he understands the acidity with which a suspicious father addresses his daughter's suitor: "My Goldie tells me you have that certain something, but I wish you had that something certain."

Still, could not these wry jokes be gentile just as well? Here, we run into that intangible Jewish sense of humor. *Schmaltz* on "wry" is the appetizer in nearly all Jewish jokes. Without the *schmaltz* they would lack the innate sentimentality that makes them distinctively Jewish, and without the wryness they would be devoid of that sharp Jewish tongue that can clip a hedge. Honey and acid—a strange combination for humor! Attribute it to all the "begats."

The bond between father and son has evoked countless expressions of admiration in ancient and modern literature. This continuity of the father-son relationship was well expressed by Abraham Mendelssohn, son of Moses Mendelssohn and father of Felix. He observed: "Formerly I was my father's son, now I am my son's father." That close tie exists today, vibrant as ever, although the rhetoric may be in breezy, contemporary language. An embarrassed father will shrug off your sentimental and flattering reference to the subject with the quip: "Whenever you hear it said that there is a beautiful tie between father and son, the son is probably wearing it." It may take several minutes to realize that he is saying "thank you" for a nice comment, but that is precisely what he is doing.

Yes, but is the quip *Jewish*? You will be interested to know that, aside from the obvious Hebraic origins of the ancient sayings, every joke used in this introduction was first heard some forty years ago on New York's East Side, and *all* have been translated from the Yiddish! There is one that I especially remember hearing around 1927 or so—a sweet little story, also translated from Yiddish to English—about a boy who proudly said to his mother, "Daddy never went past the sixth grade in school, but I think he's just as smart as if he went to the seventh."

In this chapter, we fondly offer that grand old man of ours his honorary diploma. He earned it!

H.D.S.

Among the first things that a Jewish boy learns is the Biblical injunction, "Honor thy father and mother"—or else! Herschel, age six, was reminded of the admonition the day his father came home and announced that he had decided to buy a car—the first his family had ever owned.

The father was in high spirits. "Imagine! We're in this country only a few years and soon we'll own a new car," he said proudly. "I can just see us riding around in Central Park. In the front I'm steering, and sitting next to me is mama. And in the back is our little Herschel."

Mama nodded, smiling her approval. "So when you're planning to buy the car?" she asked.

"In two weeks, a month maybe. No later."

The pleasant interlude was suddenly shattered by Herschel's mournful cry: "I don't wanna sit in the back. I wanna sit in the front and help steer."

"Only one steerer we need in this family," the father reminded his son. "In the front sits mama. In the back sits you."

"If I hafta sit in the back I'll bang my head on the wall, you'll see," wailed Herschel. He ran to the wall and assumed a threatening pose, ready to give action to his words. "Mama is sitting in the back. *I'm* sitting in the front!"

"No, Herschel, you're in the back," said the father sternly.

"In the front!"

"In the back!"

Herschel's voice rose to a shrill screech. "I ain't gonna sit in the back."

Father, his manner grim, extended his arm and pointed a commanding finger.

"Herschel," he said coldly, "get out of my car!"

Goldberg was reminiscing about his boyhood in Russia.

"I was born in Minsk," he said, "but actually I went to school right here in Brooklyn."

"Wow!" exclaimed his son. "That's what I call *busing*!"

It was getting on toward the close of business hours and Sanford Siegel was in an expansive mood. He lit a cigar, leaned back in his chair and reflected on his good fortune. The Siegel Clothing Company was flourishing, he had a loving wife, and his infant son was handsome and alert. Yes, some day that boy would be a partner. Sanford could visualize the new sign over the display window: *Siegel and Son.*

The telephone rang suddenly, jarring him from his pleasant contemplations. It was his wife, breathless with excitement.

"Oh, have I got news for you!" she cried. "The baby just spoke his first words. Plain as day, and *three* words, at that!"

"Wonderful!" enthused Sanford. "What did he say?"

"Mama, papa and gabardine!"

"Pop, when does old age start?" asked the youth as he viewed his image in the mirror and inspected a few imaginary lines at the corner of his eyes.

"It can start at any age, depending on the individual," said the father, smiling. "But actually, old age is the time when you find yourself giving good advice instead of setting a bad example."

Danny came home from school with some exciting news.

"Y'know somethin', pop," he began, "half of the kids in my class said their fathers have false teeth. Are yours false too?"

"No, Danny," said the father good-humoredly. "They're all mine."

"How come?"

"Well, for one thing I'm only thirty-five and my teeth are in good shape."

"Yeah," persisted Danny with all the determination of any six-year-old, "but how do you keep them in such good shape?"

"Very simple," said the young father, "I mind my own business."

Keenly aware of the old man's penchant for biting sarcasm, the young suitor was understandably nervous about asking him for his daughter's hand in marriage. Summoning up the necessary courage, he approached the girl's father and, in trembling tones, asked:

"May I have your daughter for my wife?"

"I don't know," came the reply. "Bring your wife around and let me have a look at her."

Edna's father was in a dither of outrage.

"I forbid you to marry this sailor!" he stormed. "Anyway, what respectable Jewish girl would marry a man, still in his twenties, who's been divorced three times?"

"Four!" Edna corrected.

"*What*?!" screamed her dad. "My God, that guy isn't a sailor, he's a *whole*saler!"

Walter had only been married two years but already his absentmindedness was causing friction at home. So he decided to seek the advice of his elderly father.

"Pop," he began, "is there anything I can do to help me remember my wife's birthday?"

"Sure," said the father promptly. "From my own long experience as a married man, my advice to you is that you should just try forgetting it once. Believe me, you'll never do it again!"

The young man looked up from the editorial page of the newspaper he had been reading.

"Dad, you're a man of the world," he said. "Tell me, what exactly is diplomacy?"

"Well, son," began the father, clearing his throat, "if you were to say to an ugly girl, 'Your face would stop a clock,' that would not only be undiplomatic but very unkind as well. However, if you said to that same ugly girl, 'When I look into your eyes, time stands still,' you'd be saying the same thing, but *that*, my boy, would be diplomacy!"

The ambitious daughter was growing increasingly irritated with her father's snorts of derision whenever she mentioned her favorite subject—the Women's Liberation movement.

"Daddy," she fumed, "do you really have any notion at all about the meaning of 'career woman'?"

"Sure," he replied cheerily. "A career woman is a gal who goes out and earns a man's salary—instead of staying home and *shlepping* it away from him!"

The boy's father was appalled at his son's liberal use of slang.

"Now see here," he demanded sternly, "there are three words I never want to hear you use again. One is *swell*, the other is *lousy* and the third is *screwy*."

"Okay, pop," the boy agreed. "What are they?"

"Whoever would have thought that our own son would turn out to be a hippie?" sighed the unhappy father.

"You mustn't judge Harold by his clothes," the mother protested. "Lots of boys are wearing toeless galoshes this year."

"Well, at least he could be a little neater. The last time that boy washed his face was when he cried."

"Harold explained it all to me," said the mother protectively. "He says a young person in today's world has to be a little crazy or he'll go nuts."

"That what I like about our son—a vast mind with half-vast notions," sighed the father. "His I.Q. finally caught up with his eyesight—20-20. Did I tell you what happened when he came home from the beach yesterday? He went right to the medicine cabinet. And when I asked him what he was looking for, he said he needed something for sunburn on top of poison ivy on top of acne."

"You shouldn't be so hard on our Harold," reproved the mother. "He's only trying to make a life for himself."

The father shook his head. "The only thing that boy makes around here are mistakes and cigarette ashes."

"You know, it could be a medical problem," suggested the mother after some thought. "The doctor advised that Harold should have a change."

"I already took his advice," said the father wearily. "I changed doctors!"

The kid looked up from the book on ancient history he was reading and asked his father, "Pop, what's a millennium?"

The father scratched his head and thought deeply.

"I think," he finally answered, "it's something like a centennial, only it has more legs!"

The father and his five-year-old son were in Wanamaker's Department Store. They were making the grand tour of the mezzanine when they were confronted by a formidable-looking woman—the type that would make Bella Abzug look like Miss Goodie-Goodie-Two-Shoes.

"Sir," she said in a steely voice, "don't you think you are walking too fast for that child?"

Without a word, the father slowed down.

On the second floor, whom should he meet again, but the old battle-axe.

"Sir," she grated once more, "isn't that boy a little thirsty?"

He bought the boy a Coke.

On the third floor: "Sir, don't you think the child might want to visit the bathroom?"

He took his son to the bathroom.

On the fourth floor, having seen all they cared to see for the day, they got on the "Down" elevator. It was quite crowded but they found a space.

"Sir," called a familiar voice in the back of the elevator, "don't you think he'll be crushed?"

"No, lady!" the father yelled at the top of his lungs. "The little stinker bites!"

"It says here," remarked ten-year-old David, his nose buried in a book, "Benjamin Franklin tied a key on his kite and discovered that lightning comes from 'lectricity."

"It's nice he found out," grunted the boy's father, engrossed in his newspaper.

"I don't get it," said the boy, puzzled. "Ain't lightning and 'lectricity the same thing?"

Annoyed with the interruptions, the father replied brusquely:

"No, Davey, they're not the same. Lightning we get free!"

The uneasy father confronted his daughter as she was leaving for the evening.

"Young lady, I'll expect you home by eleven, not a minute later," he said sternly.

"But, daddy," the daughter protested, "I'm not a child any

more."

"Exactly," he snapped. "That's why I want you home by eleven!"

Little Jesse had found a cheap paperback book and was now plying his father with some pointed questions.

"It says here in the book that a guy was fired for kissing the boss's daughter," said Jesse. "But, I wonder why he got fired for that."

"They're not supposed to kiss," explained the father vaguely.

"Why not? You and mama kiss all the time."

"That's different. We're married."

"What's the difference?" persisted Jesse.

"Well, son," the father began with a scarcely-concealed grin, "the difference between kissing your wife and kissing your sweetheart is about sixty seconds."

"I think," said the expectant mother, "we should name the baby Leonard."

"No, absolutely not!" shouted the father-to-be. "Every Tom, Dick and Harry is named Leonard!"

"Pop, can I ask you a very personal question?" queried teen-aged Bertram.

"Sure," came the obliging answer. "That's what fathers are for."

"Well, if I take a girl out for the evening and show her a good time at the movies and, on the way home, I buy her an ice-cream sundae, do you think it will be okay if I kiss her goodnight?"

"No, Bertram," he said at length, "don't kiss her. You did enough for her in just one evening."

In the waiting room of the maternity wing at Mt. Sinai Hospital, an expectant father paced the floor nervously while another calmly read his newspaper. Finally, a nurse appeared and greeted the calm one with a cheery smile. "Congratulations," she chirped.

"You have a beautiful new daughter."

"Hey, what's the big idea?" demanded the nervous pacer. "I was here first!"

The little boy's hands were none too clean.

"Georgie," demanded the father, "I want you to leave the table this instant and go wash your hands."

"Ya mean both of 'em?" asked the youngster.

"No," retorted the father, "I mean one of them. I'd be most interested to see how you do it!"

"When I first emigrated to America," reminisced Sam the radish exporter, "I was forced to settle in the Bronx instead of Schenectady. After all, who can spell a *meshuggeneh* name like that?"

Bill Isaacson and Andy Kuhn, the furniture moguls of Grand Rapids, were concerned about the future of their respective daughter.

"I just can't make up my mind about sending my daughter to college or not," said Bill. "It isn't the cost, though God knows it's high enough. But, it takes her out of the marriage market for four years. Who needs an educated old maid for a daughter?"

"It isn't all that much of a problem," replied Andy with an airy wave of hand. "I solved the situation, and now both of my older daughters are happily married."

"You solved it? How?"

"I spent $3,000 a year to send my oldest daughter, Edith, to college and it took her four years to capture a husband. But for my other daughter, Velma, it cost me only $300 to send her to the mountains for two weeks, and she came home married."

5

Foxy Grandmas and Feisty Grandpas

Introduction

Isaac Leibush Peretz was an illustrious Yiddish novelist who wrote beautifully and succinctly. But his view of old age, as a person gray and forlorn, did not represent the mainstream of Jewish thought then, nor does it now. True, there are a number of ancient sayings that seem to support his contention. The Talmud, for example, offers us the gratuitous diagnosis, "Old age is a bad sickness." But the Bible takes a more cheerful and traditional stand: "The hoary head is a crown of glory." Actually, the most practical approach is found in the old Jewish expression, "A man is as old as his wife looks." When you think about it, it makes sense.

Why is a grandparent's reaction to children different from that of a parent? Let us go back to beginnings. According to the rabbis, the unborn baby possesses the accumulated knowledge of all the past generations. But, when the infant is born, so goes the Talmudic legend, an angel touches its forehead, and it forgets everything. As a result, the child is much sweeter, friendlier and less inhibited because it has no memories. Dwelling in the past—living with old memories—represents a kind of regression, a going backward when we should be going forward.

Young parents have not yet reached the point where they can selectively blot out unhappy memories. They are still actively engaged in the busy process of living life's joys and sorrows: their memories have yet to be earned. But, lucky indeed are the grandparents—those fortunate ones who have attained the age where they can afford the gentle art of forgetting. In that context, they are closer to their grandchildren than they are to their own sons and daughters.

The small child, of course, has not lived long enough to store up a variety of experiences; the grandparent draws from his treasure-chest and dwells upon those memories which give him most pleasure. And if, in his nostalgia, he embellishes his recollections to the point of childlike naivete, and conveniently forgets the unpleasantries he has known, who shall blame him? It has taken him most of his lifetime to learn the difference between forgetting and forgetfulness. Awareness of that difference is a sign of wisdom.

The Jewish maxim, "Wine and wisdom improve with age," is no less valid today than it was centuries ago. Only the dates are changed. Men and women do not grow old because they have lived a certain number of years. They grow old only when they desert their ideals, when they no longer laugh at the foibles of humanity—and their own frailties as well. Are they living in a make-believe world? Perhaps, to a degree. But that is why they can enjoy such intimate rapport with their grandchildren. To grow old in years, but not in spirit; to attain a modicum of wisdom, but not vanity; to understand love, but not to use it as a lever; to accept mortality, but not to dread it; to understand that man is the only creature on earth to have knowledge of his grandchildren and grandparents, but to respect all other living things; and to savor one's anecdotage without becoming a bore or a burden—these make for the golden years and constitute the essence of a fruitful Jewish family life.

Some Jewish grandfathers in America would shock their shrouded ancestors if they could but hear some of the modern anecdotes. In 1974, at the Queen Esther Retirement Home in Chicago, a venerable old man in his early nineties was asked the customary question by a young reporter: "Sir, to what do you attribute your good health and longevity?" The oldtimer grinned and replied, "Drinking a fifth of *schnapps* every day and chasing girls." Like many another grandfather, he was not only adept at selective remembering, but he recalled things that probably never happened. Nevertheless, it is inconceivable that a grandfather in yesteryear's Europe would have made any such assertion. But these are "fun" rather than "wisdom" jokes. They have evolved quite naturally as a result of the freer climate in the United States.

Much of the same may be said of Israel, although there are subtle differences between Israeli humor and ours. As an example, who would have thought that the sedate Golda Meir, at age 75, would refer to herself as a militant grandmother who not only believed in women but in fighting for Lib as well? "I am no chicken libber," she said, chuckling over her use of the Jewish-Americanism. But why not? She spent her young years in the United States.

It has been said that one of the primary differences between the Jewish people of old Europe and those of the United States is that European Jews belonged to a patriarchal society, while modern America is matriarchal. Perhaps Portnoy did have something to complain about, at that. The American Jewish male is influenced by women from the time of his birth to the time of his death. As a child, he is ruled by his mother. During his school years, he is governed by a series of female teachers. When he marries, he is dominated by his wife. From the day his daughters learn to say Da-da, he comes under their jurisdiction. And, when they have little girls of their own, he is ruled by his granddaughters. Poor grandpa cannot remember a day when some female was not tugging at his heartstrings or purse-strings—or both. Needless to say, he does not want to remember! To him and to the doting grandmother, it is a constant source of amazement that their mediocre children managed to produce such geniuses of their own. Sam Levenson, probably the finest exponent of authentic Jewish humor in America, aptly defined a genius as ". . . a stupid kid with very happy grandparents."

To put it another way—and this is really what this chapter is intended to convey—we are truly grandparents when we realize that grandchildren are God's way of compensating us for old age.

H.D.S.

"Well, what did you learn today?" asked the grandfather as 12-year-old Izzy returned home from Hebrew school.

"All about the Exodus. Wow, what an adventure! The teacher told us how the Hebrews got chased all the way to the Red Sea, and how ten big boats in just two hours sailed them across to the other side. But when the Egyptian soldiers got to the Red Sea a big wave rolled up. It must've been a mile high—and it drowned all of them, and the Jews were saved!"

"What!" shouted the grandfather. "Your teacher told you that?"

"Well, not exactly, grandpapa," explained Izzy. "But if I told you the story he told us, you'd never believe it in a million years!"

The old couple was sitting at the kitchen table, sipping tea and listening to some vintage music on their ancient Victrola. The silver-haired lady grew misty-eyed.

"Hymie," she began nostalgically, "remember how romantical it was when we were young? Every minute you wanted to *shmoos.*"

"Yeah, I used to get pretty *schmaltzy,*" Hymie agreed with a chuckle.

"So why don't you ever nibble on my ears or bite me on my neck anymore? You're not too old for that."

He rose abruptly from his chair and started out of the room.

"Oh, Hymie, Hymie, I didn't mean to hurt your feelings," the old lady cried in dismay.

"What do you mean, hurt my feelings?" said Hymie cheerfully. "I'm going to get my teeth!"

Grumpy grandpa was his usual self this morning.

"Why is it," he growled as he struggled with a newly-washed shirt, "that a wife who can see right through her husband of forty years can't notice a missing button?"

A couple of old-timers were sunning themselves on a bench in Seward Park—when it was safe to do so.

"There's one thing I can say in defense of children and grandchildren," remarked the first graybeard. "They're such a comfort in our old age."

"True," agreed the other oldster, "and they also help us get there faster!"

"Grandma, how long have you and grandpa been married?" asked the romantic young granddaughter.

"Forty-nine years," replied the old lady.

"Oh, what a beautiful life you must have had," sighed the girl. "And I'll bet you never even thought of a divorce."

"Well," said grandma, "divorce, no—murder, yes!"

❖ ❖ ❖

Daniella was in a quandary. Her new boyfriend's birthday was approaching and she could not think of a suitable gift. Her grandmother noticed her worried expression.

"What's the matter?" she asked.

"You know how rich my new guy is, grandma. He drives a Rolls Royce from his town house to his country estate and uses a Lincoln Continental just for shopping. He already has diamond rings for each day of the week, platinum watches, mink-lined shoes, jeweled cigarette cases, eight electric shavers, 500 pairs of socks and 1,000 neckties. Tell me, what can a girl give to a man who has everything?"

"Encouragement" said the wise old grandma.

Plaintive voice from the fourth floor, rear:

"I wish you'd stay away from that electric fan, grandma; you're too old to be blowing your top!"

"My grandmother didn't understand English too well," explained the young fellow, "but what she heard she heard good.

"I recall the time I went to meet her at the bus stop. To my surprise I saw her get off the bus backwards. So I asked her the reason.

"'I get off backwards,' she explained, 'because your grandpa once told me that on New York buses everybody wants to grab your seat!'"

"I don't know what this world is coming to," sighed grandpa. "When grandma was a girl she didn't do the things girls do today. However," he added after a few reflective thoughts, "grandmas didn't do the things that grandmas do today, either."

"I knew my husband was getting old," averred the silver-haired lady, "when he started making excuses to stay home instead of to get out!"

Grandma was feeble of limb but still able to hobble around. She looked forward to Saturday nights when she could always count on an interesting speech at the community civic hall around the corner from where she lived.

Came this Saturday night and grandma reached the lecture hall.

"Mister," she said to a young fellow who was also about to enter, "would you be so kind to help me up the steps?"

"Sure," he agreed pleasantly.

"Tell me," she asked as they mounted the stairs, "who is speaking tonight?"

"Muhammad Ali. He'll be talking about the Black Muslims."

"Mister," said grandma, "would you be so kind to help me *down* the steps?"

"Grandpa, my new boyfriend will be twenty-one years old next week," confided the teenage girl. "I'd like to give him something nice for his birthday. What do you think he'd like?"

"Never mind what he'd like," snapped grandpa. "Give him a tie!"

"How's your arthritis today?" asked the sympathetic granddaughter.

"*Oy*, dollink, much worser!" groaned the old lady. She lifted her arm high above her head. "Yesterday I could get my hand way up there. But today," she said tearfully, lifting her hand only as high as her shoulder, "I can only lift it up to here!"

A little old lady decided to return to Europe for a short visit to see her sister before she died. So she went downtown to the Federal Building to apply for a passport.

"You'll have to take the oath first," said the passport clerk. "Raise your right hand."

The old lady raised her hand.

"Do you," he intoned, "swear to defend the Constitution of the United States against all its enemies, domestic or foreign?"

The old lady's face paled. "Who, me?" she asked in a quavering voice.

"Yes, lady, you. Just answer 'I do' if you want a passport."

"Mister, to tell you the truth, what with house cleaning, laundry, cooking and taking care on my grandchildren, who knows when I'd have time?"

"Look here," barked the exasperated clerk, "can't you do us both a favor and simply say 'I do?' That's all there is to it."

"B-b-but . . ."

"All right," he interrupted, "let me ask you this: Do you or don't you want a passport?"

"I do."

"Well," he smiled, handing her the document, "that wasn't so hard to say, was it?"

Sadie was engrossed in doing her homework when her grandfather's raucous voice, raised in song, shattered her trend of thought.

"Grandpa," she complained later, "you have a horrible voice. Why do you insist on singing in the shower?"

"Because," said grandpa with sweet reason, "there's no lock on the bathroom door."

Si and Dottie had never been to a fancy nightclub before. Now, on their 35th wedding anniversary, they were celebrating the occasion with a visit to a Las Vegas night spot.

The lights were dimmed and then the ageless Marlene Dietrich appeared on stage, her famous legs encased in sheer tights.

"Oh," gushed Dottie, "how marvelous for a grandmother!"

"You mean," corrected Si, enthralled, "how marvelous for a grandfather!"

The boy and his grandpa were discussing the youngster's future one evening, just after the Nixon expletive-deleted transcripts were made public. The grandson, it seemed, was interested in a political career.

"Watergate or no Watergate, I'd like to do something big—but clean," said the youth.

"The only political job left in that category," sighed the

grandfather, "is to get a position in the White House and then wash everybody's mouth out with soap."

Grandpa Kalman was grumbling through his beard as he read the evening paper.

"What's the matter? Why are you so mad?" asked grandma.

"It says here that a gang of loafers painted a swastika on a synagogue in Brooklyn and beat up the *shammes*," grandpa fumed, stabbing the paper with his forefinger. "And all the judge gave them was six months in jail."

Grandma clucked disapprovingly. "That wasn't enough," she agreed. "A year would have been better."

"*What?*" grandpa shouted. "A year they will spend in a nice warm jail with television and a radio? And with visitors yet, who will bring cakes with files in them like in the movies? Listen, if it was me, I'd give them 25 years in the electric chair!"

There was a loud knocking on the door and when grandpa opened it, there stood a distraught woman wringing her hands.

"Sir," she faltered in a choking voice, "do you own a calico cat with a red collar and a silver bell attached to it?"

"Yes, that's my cat," said grandpa.

"Well, I just ran over it," explained the woman, her face a picture of anguish. "I'm terribly, terribly sorry. Will you let me replace it?"

Grandpa shrugged. "It's all right with me if it's all right with you," he replied. "How are you at catching mice?"

The little girl asked her grandfather to mend her broken doll.

"Tomorrow," he promised.

"Grandpa," admonished the precocious youngster, "you must never put off until tomorrow what you can do today."

"You're right, little pigeon," he sighed. "Tomorrow there may be a law against it."

The venerable old man was celebrating his one-hundredth

birthday and was asked by a reporter: "To what do you attribute your advanced age and remarkable physical condition?"

"I'll tell you," replied the centenarian. "When my wife and I were first married, the rabbi who performed the ceremony suggested that whenever I saw an argument coming I should take a walk around the block. I took the rabbi's advice and I want you to know that for seventy years the constant exercise did wonders for my health."

Julius, the genius of CCNY, was giving his grandfather the benefit of his 18-year-old wisdom. Cliche after tired cliche flowed from the youth's mouth with all the effervescence of cold vaseline, and with each new banality the old man's irritation mounted.

"And another thing," pontificated Julius, "behind every successful man you'll find a woman."

"Yes, and usually one with a big mouth," observed the grandfather, oozing spite and malice.

Julius smiled. "Grandpa, you just don't believe in romance," he said indulgently. "You should go to the movies a little more."

"*Yingatsh!*" snapped the old man, "at my age, when a girl smiles at me in a movie she's probably after my popcorn!"

The old man's irate reaction startled the youth.

"I don't know what's gotten into you lately," he observed. "Maybe it's your diet. You should be like me, grandpa—a light eater."

"You're a dietitian all of a sudden?" demanded the oldster. "I know exactly what kind of a light eater you are. As soon as it gets light you start eating."

"B-b-but . . ."

"Don't but me no buts," rasped the grandfather, thoroughly aroused. "You are nothing but a long-distance talker. It's a wonder your tongue doesn't get sunburned. I get hoarse just listening to you. You are also disrespectful, arrogant ..." The old man abruptly halted his tirade, seeing the offended look on his grandson's face.

"However," he concluded in a kinder voice, "nobody's perfect!"

The social science major at Columbia University was on an "observation" tour of the lower East Side. She noticed a white-bearded, gnarled patriarch sitting on a bench.

"Sir," asked the student, "have you lived here in this neighborhood all your life?"

"No," he replied coldly, "not yet."

Old man Epstein had never strayed more than ten or fifteen blocks from his flat on Second Avenue since he emigrated to America fifty years earlier. So he was understandably taken aback when his little grandson broached a subject that was far beyond his area of knowledge.

"Today we learned in school that sailors can tell time by the sun," announced the boy. "Tell me, grandpa, how do they do that?"

Old Epstein, who hadn't even noticed the sun since the eclipse of 1925, pondered the question for several long moments before he answered.

"It's nothing new those sailors are doing," he declared. "Back in Minsk when I was a boy we used to do the same thing. First you shade your eyes so the sun shouldn't hurt them, then you look at your watch."

Pre-teenager Gertrude had been thumbing through a copy of *Mademoiselle.* An article caught her eye and, a few moments later, she turned to her grandfather.

"I was just reading about models," she began, "but I don't understand something. What's the difference between a model woman and a woman model?"

"There's really no difference," he finally explained after much thought. "I don't believe there ever was a woman who didn't think of herself as both."

6

Those Cockamamie Kids

Introduction

Scientists have for years attributed a sense of humor to porpoises, dogs and the great apes. Yet, for reasons never clearly defined, some psychologists will not concede a sense of humor to human children. Sigmund Freud, himself, not only denied that a child possesses wit and humor, but declared that it "lacks all feeling for the comic."

Freud, to be sure, adduced no facts to prove his stark assertion. It was an inference from his own theory that humor is all a matter of release from adult inhibition. If we may be forgiven an iconoclastic observation, the good doctor may have known his adult psychology, but he didn't know *beblach* about kids. Even an infant will squeal with laughter when his father playfully throws him into the air and safely catches him—fully aware that the smile on his father's face means it is all in fun. Or the mother will pretend to offer a tasty tidbit to her baby, and then, teasingly, pull back the spoon from the infant's waiting mouth. Again the baby joins in the merriment because the smile on his mother's face tells him it is only a joke. But, the very fact that the child participates in the little game indicates that he understands that he has only been teased. It is the ability to *take* a joke, not only to *make* one, that proves you have a sense of humor.

The comic sense in children is quicker and more active than in grown-ups, and less discriminating. They laugh at nothing, and that is precisely how we reprove them when we say, "Oh, stop laughing at nothing!" The older child will remain undaunted. "Mama, here a riddle," he will persist: "What's long and green, has warts, is shaped something like a banana, and flies through the

59

air like a bullet?" Mama gives up, and with whoops of delight, the child provides the answer: "Super pickle!" He has responded to his own question with the equivalent of nothing—but to him, a *funny* nothing!"

The pious and mature philosopher, Immanuel Kant, maintained that adults also laugh at nothing (". . . the sudden transformation of a strained expectation into nothing"). Small wonder, then, that grown-ups can enjoy the statement, "As to capital punishment, if it was good enough for my father, it's good enough for me!" Here we have a plausible movement of the mind that has come to nothing. It is childish, perhaps, but not childlike. The point is that while children are the greatest laughers, in later years their free and boisterous humor becomes refined and intellectualized. But until then, they laugh upon a less exquisite provocation that we do: they do not require that comic things mask a serious thought or tap the deeper reservoirs of feeling in order to give sanction to a hearty laugh.

Juvenile humor falls into two primary categories: Jokes told *by* children and those told by adults *about* children. A number of Yiddish proverbs illustrate the latter. "Small children disturb your sleep, big children your life" is one illustration. Another: "Small children, small joys; big children, big annoys." But those negative sayings are overwhelmed by the more tender expressions in Jewish literature which portray love and understanding. The compassionate Mendele, the Hebrew-Yiddish-Russian satirist (1837–1917), wrote: "Children without childhood are a frightful sight." This was written in a serious vein, of course, but Jewish humorists have used the tragedy of unhappy childhood to make the same statement. Consider the following from Jewish history of the last century.

In the 1880s and 1890s, Russian Jewish boys were often snatched off the streets and sent to the Czarist army. If they were unmarried, they would be conscripted at any age. As the story goes, "Jews being Jews, they found a way out." Children were married at age six and seven, and husbands could be seen playing marbles in short pants. One day, a Jew happened to see such a child and asked him why he wasn't in school. The little boy replied, "I don't go to school. I was married yesterday." So the Jew asked again: "If you got married yesterday, and are now the head of the family, why aren't you wearing long pants?" The child answered, "Yesterday I got married so I wore the long pants; today my little brother is getting married, so he's wearing the pants."

American humor, especially as it applies to jokes about children, is not nearly as grim as that of the past. Here, the *leitmotif* of the accumulated Jewish tragedy has given way to the carefree approach that more nearly coincides with the Jewish experience in the United States. This is not to say that the Jew has forgotten his heritage; nor is he any less concerned with his destiny. His humor is the barometer of the change from the past to the present.

We can laugh about that change. Historically, Jews have studied Torah in one form or another; the philosophy of Maimonides, Spinoza, Gabirol and other scholars of old. But today, Jewish adults acquire their wisdom from television: Kung Fu at one extreme and Archie Bunker at the other. Jewish youngsters in America derive most of their philosophical wisdom from Pogo the Opossum, Smokey the Bear, Snoopy the Dog and a seagull named Jonathan, all of whom appear to be *goyim*. Where else but in America would a nice Jewish boy name his four goldfish Matthew, Mark, Luke and John—and then feed them crumbled matzos for their evening *nosh*?

The Americanization of the Jewish joke has evolved so far that it is often difficult to distinguish it from its gentile counterpart. Even those jokes which originated in the first and second decades of this century in New York's teeming ghetto cannot always be labeled as uniquely Jewish, as the following anecdote suggests:

Miltie's mother had just bought him a new suit of clothes and sternly warned him to keep it clean. A half-hour later, he returned home from play, covered from head to foot with sticky, clinging mud. Grimly, the mother seized his arm and marched him into the basement, with Miltie screaming bloody murder all the way. "Oh, be quiet," snapped the mother, "you've been spanked before!" The boy stopped shrieking instantly. "Spanked?" he exclaimed with obvious relief. "Gosh, mom, I thought you wuz gonna *wash* me!"

A similar so-called "Yiddish joke" which knows no ethnic boundaries, but which was current in the 1930s on New York's East Side, is given here in translation: A father presented himself at the offices of the telephone company and requested a 50-foot extension cord for his phone. When asked the reason, he explained: "I want my teenage daughter to spend a little more time outdoors now that it's summer."

Obviously, the above jokes are not Jewish, even though originally told in the Yiddish tongue. Jewish humor, it is clear, has nothing to do with the employment of the Yiddish language, the use of Jewish names, or even the liberal use of ethnic words and phrases. It is the *circumstances* inherent in the joke that give it its sense of Jewishness—the flavor of *schmaltz* on pumpernickel.

So here's some humor about Jewish kids in America. America!—a *mazel auf Columbus!*—America where Jewish children run everything but the vacuum cleaner; where parents teach children who hit not to hit, and children who do not hit to hit back.

H.D.S.

Most of us are familiar with the reason given by mountain-climbers for their activities:—they climbed the highest peak because "it was there." One little boy recently brought the expression down to basics. The five-year-old kindergarten pupil was made to stand in the corner for putting mud in a girl's mouth during recess.

When the boy's mother heard of his misconduct she was aghast.

"Mud in a little girl's mouth? Why did you do such a thing?"

"Because," said the kid sullenly, "it was open."

Two small children were discussing the latest addition to their family.

I heard daddy say that a new baby costs almost a thousand dollars," said the little sister in a hushed voice.

"So what?" retorted her brother. "Look how long they last!"

It was a scene of tranquility as mama watched television, grandma knitted and little Johanan played on the floor. All at once there was a loud crash as the child knocked over the coffee table.

"Oh, Joey, what am I going to do with you?" wailed mama. "Every time you do something naughty I get another gray hair."

Johanan glanced at silver-thatched grandma and then turned to his mother.

"Wow," he cried, "you musta been horrible when you wuz my age!"

(If your IQ is over 75, do yourself a favor and skip this one.)

It was the Fourth of July and the Independence Day celebrations were being observed with the usual displays and noisemakers.

Little Shirley, the six-year-old patriot, rushed breathlessly into the house crying, "Mama, can you cut my hair real short on my forehead?"

"Why in the world should I do that?" asked the mother.

"It's for the holiday," explained Shirley excitedly. "My teacher said it would grow out in bangs!"

Danny's mother received a stern complaint that he had been throwing snowballs at the little girls in the neighborhood.

"Is this true?" she demanded.

"Yeah, but they threw 'em at me first," Danny protested, though not very convincingly.

"I don't care who started it," the boy's mother retorted. "The next time they throw snowballs at you, come and tell me."

"Aw, ma, what good would that do?" he asked plaintively. "You couldn't hit the side of a barn!"

The sweet old lady in tennis shoes stopped to chat with a new little boy in the neighborhood.

"What is your name, sonny?" she asked.

"Abe," he replied.

"Oh my, that's a famous name. Our greatest president was named Abe. Tell me, would you like to grow up to be like Lincoln?"

"What!" gasped the kid. "And be a tunnel?"

The lady who taught the "Small Fry" class on Fridays was on maternity leave, so a delegation from the synagogue called at Mrs. Abrams' home to ask if she would take over until the regular teacher returned to her duties. The rabbi, the *rebbetzn* and the *shammes* who comprised the delegation were greeted at the door by Mrs. Abrams' little daughter.

"Mommy is upstairs," said the child. "I'll go get her."

On the second floor, Mrs. Abrams was in the midst of spring cleaning. Boxes were strewn about, clothes were heaped on the bed, the draperies were down and she was busily engaged in washing the windows.

"Oh, my goodness," she groaned when her daughter told her

that "company" was waiting for her in the living room. "Honey, you go back downstairs and tell them to wait a few minutes. I'm loaded down with work."

Dutifully, the girl returned to the august delegation and conveyed the message:

"Mama can't come right now—she's loaded!"

Second-grade schoolperson (male) to third-grade schoolperson (female):
"Are you the opposite sex or am I?"

Irving and Marva, both in the same class in grade school, had little liking for each other. One day during recess, Marva came up to the teacher on the playground and tattled: "Irving said a four-letter word!"

The teacher called him over at once.

"Marva tells me you used a four-letter word," she said severely. "Is that true?"

"No, it ain't," said Irving, his face flushed with resentment. "I don't even know my three-letter words yet!"

A baby, according to Peeksville pediatrician Max Vogel, is an alimentary canal with a loud voice at one end and no responsibility at the other.

"Hello," came the voice at the other end of the line, "is this Sammy's mother?"

"Yes, it is."

"This is Miss Broyges, at the Hebrew School. I'm afraid you'll have to reprimand your son for upsetting class routine."

"What did he do that's so bad?"

"He made a tasteless joke, that's what he did. We were discussing the lesson for today—how Lot's wife, who looked back, turned into a pillar of salt. And your Sammy stood up and told the class that you once looked back while driving your car and turned into a telephone pole."

Little Ralphie came to visit his friend Arthur who happened to be in the tub.

"Wow," exclaimed Ralphie, "do you always take a bath in muddy water?"

"Aw, don't be such a wise guy," grumbled Arthur defensively. "It wasn't muddy when I got in!"

Joanie walked into the corner drugstore and, standing on tiptoe, just managed to peer over the counter. The pharmacist smiled down at her.

"Yes, little girl, what can I do for you?"

"My mama sent me for two rolls of toilet paper," said Joanie.

"All right, here y'are. That'll be sixty cents."

"Charge it, please."

"Okay," the pharmacist agreed pleasantly. "Who are they for?"

"They're for all of us," explained the blushing Joanie.

Voices in the night:
"Herbie, stop poking your baby sister!"
"I ain't pokin' her, ma. I'm countin' her measles."

Kenny the Kindergarten Komic has a riddle to present to the world:
What's the most popular gardening magazine?
Answer: Weeder's Digest.

The new little girl in the neighborhood had just made "best friends" with another little girl. They got around to discussing the new girl's poodle.

"Does your dog have fleas?" asked the best friend.

"Dogs don't have fleas, silly," giggled the other girl. "They have puppies."

Sylvia wondered whether her boyfriend was sophisticated enough to provide her with a corsage for the prom dance that night.

Her fears, however, were groundless. A messenger from the local florist delivered a lovely orchid, and with it was a note from her beau:

"With all my love and half of my allowance."

The late Irvin S. Cobb stands sponsor for this one, popular around 1918 or so.

Sounds betokening intense juvenile grief caused a passing lady to halt in front of a tenement. On the front stoop of the house sat a small boy. Tears coursed down his cheeks and from him issued a series of heartbroken laments.

"*Ai*, poor little boy," said the lady. "What's the matter you're crying like that?"

"Oh-h-h" the youngster howled. He brought his long-drawn wail to an abrupt end, sniffled deeply and checked his sobbing.

"Daddy and mommy won't take me to the movies tonight. And I wanna go to the movies with them. Oh-h-h! Wow-w-w!"

"But don't cry so," advised the sympathetic woman. "Are they ever taking you when you cry like that?"

"Sometimes they do and sometimes they don't," admitted the boy. "But what does it hurt to holler?"

"Bobby," exclaimed the shocked mother, "you mustn't pull the cat's tail!"

"I'm just holdin' it, ma," protested Bobby. "The cat's doin' all the pullin'!"

"And do you pray every night?" asked the new rabbi.

"No," answered the little boy. "Some nights I don't need nothin'!"

"Shirley, drink your milk like a good girl," ordered the child's mother. "It will make your teeth strong."

Shirley took an unwilling sip. "Mama, if it's so good for the teeth," she commented crossly, "why don't you give my share to grandma?"

Two little sisters were watching a British documentary about the royal family on television. Miriam, age seven, was perplexed by one of the scenes.

"I wonder how Queen Elizabeth knew she was gonna have a baby," she asked.

Her eight-year-old sister was disgusted with such a display of juvenile ignorance.

"Anybody knows that," said the child loftily. "She read it in the papers."

"Some people's voices," opined ten-year-old Thelma with unconscious wisdom, "are very hard to extinguish over the telephone."

Mother heaved a sigh of relief as she tucked the children into bed and went into the living room for a little peace and quiet. But in a moment there came the sounds of uproar in the bedroom. Wearily, she returned to the scene of battle where her two little boys were fighting.

"All right, enough is enough!" she snapped. "Who started this?"

"Harry did," yelled the younger of the two, pointing a finger at his brother. "He started it by hitting me back!"

If you have ever been the parent of an inquisitive child, this brief anecdote should help recall some nostalgic memories.

The young mother could not find a baby-sitter so she took her little boy with her on a shopping trip. But from the moment they left the house, the youngster began to ply her with questions. They came in a steady stream: questions about birds, questions about animals, questions about the stork, questions about God, questions about the sky, earth, the oceans—questions, questions,

questions. The mother's patience finally snapped.

"Now you listen to me," she hissed through clenched teeth. "If you ask me just one more question I'll give you a good spanking right here in the street!"

"But, mama," said the boy, "where would you sit?"

"Last year I caught the Hong Kong flu," bragged seven-year-old Raymond. "I couldn't even go to school. I had it so bad it almost kept me from building a snowman."

"Sylvia!" exclaimed the indignant mother. "Why did you kick your brother in the stomach?"

"It was an accident, mama," said the little girl defensively. "He turned around."

Kenny the Kindergarten Komic has another one for us:

Teacher: Stanley, will you please tell the class what happened on July 4th?

Stanley: Grandpa losted his glasses, an' now he hasta drink from the bottle.

It was the first time that little Benny of the East Side had ever been in the country. Now, thanks to the Hebrew Summer Camp Fund, he was spending two glorious weeks in this different world.

On the second day, Benny solemnly watched as one of the counselors buried a dead bird to demonstrate camp hygiene.

"Do you know what I am doing?" asked the counselor.

"Yeah," said the little East Sider, "but how much ya wanna bet it don't grow?"

It was necessary that dad work later than usual, and tonight he returned home after his wife and three children had had their dinner.

"Did you help mama today?" he asked the kids.

"Yes, papa," said Margaret. "I washed the dishes."

"I dried," announced Mannie.

The father smiled. "And what did *you* do?" he asked, giving his youngest child, Caria, an affectionate pat.

"I helped the betht," she cried, clapping her little hands. "I picked up all the pietheth!"

The late Rose Stein (no one ever knew whether she was Mrs. or Miss) went to her reward at the ripe old age of 87, after more than half a century of teaching in New York's public school system. Judge Leon Gwersky, at a testimonial dinner to the grand grammarian of the Grand Street school, recalled an incident which accurately portrayed her precise use of the English language.

"I was in the third grade," grinned Judge Gwersky, "and Miss Stein (we called her 'Miss' in the absence of 'Miz'—a title not yet coined), found good and sufficient reason to send me home with a note to my mother. Let me read it to you:

My Dear Mrs. Gwersky:

I am a strong advocate of the admonition, "Children should be seen and not heard."

But Leon I can smell!

Yours for more fragrance,
Rose Stein
Teacher, P.S. 40

"In my own defense," concluded his honor, "my mother had given me a good scrubbing before I set out for school, but en route to class I had gotten into a garbage-throwing contest with a school chum. However, my mother never forgave Miss Stein."

Mama: Get into your pajamas, Davey, and I'll tell you a nice story before you go to bed: The Three Bears.

Davey: Aw, ma, Idawanna hear about no bears. Tell me the one Daddy tells—about the Chicago hood. His name was Robin and he had a kid sister named Little Red Riding.

Father was scolding his teenage daughter for her slovenly appearance.

"You should be ashamed to be seen in public with those filthy blue jeans and torn sneakers," he carped. "And why can't you do something with your hair? It looks like a mop."

The girl's eyes widened. "Daddy," she asked, puzzled, "what's a mop?"

In Macy's, one afternoon, a woman was shopping for a suitable toy for her six-year-old son. The sales clerk brought her a large box, colorfully lettered "Today's World." At first she was delighted, but when she opened it and saw the assortment of cogs, cams and wheels inside she gasped in dismay.

"Don't you think this is far too complicated for a small boy?" she asked.

"Not at all," replied the clerk. "This is an educational toy, especially designed to help children adjust to the modern world. No matter how your little boy puts it together it'll be wrong!"

The family was just sitting down at the dinner table when their teenage son rambled into the dining room, tossed his baseball cap and glove aside, and slouched into a chair next to his father.

"Pass the potatoes, pop," he began.

"I'll pass you nothing!" retorted the father. "You go right into the bathroom and wash your hands."

"Aw, c'mon, pop," groaned the youth. "I'm just gonna eat, not do a heart transplant!"

"When I first came to Brandeis University as a raw freshman," observed the stately senior, "I was terribly conceited. But it didn't take long for that to get knocked out of me. Now I'm one of the nicest fellows in the whole school!"

A few years ago, the chancellor of Brandeis was accused of excessive permissiveness during the student protest movements that were sweeping the nation's campuses.

"It's not a question of being permissive at all," the chancellor retorted in his defense. "I just happen to be an ardent supporter of giving young people adult responsibilities."

When the student disorders finally abated, he decided to take a vacation deep in the north woods of Maine. One night, while resting in a clearing, a mile or two from a tiny village, he suffered a heart attack.

"And that was when I changed my mind about giving youngsters too many adult responsibilities," he said. "I found out that the local doctor was eighteen, and the pilot who was to fly me back to New York for an operation was only twelve!"

A young mother was about to light the Sabbath candles.

"Do you know what's happening?" she asked her six-year-old little girl, as she made ready to say the prayers.

"Yes," said the youngster. "Liberace's coming."

God's destruction of the wicked cities of Sodom and Gomorra is another story that makes a vivid impression. A teacher, relating the story to her class, explained: "Lot was warned to take his wife and flee out of the city which was about to be destroyed. They got away safely. Then Lot's wife looked back, and was turned into a pillar of salt.

"Now, children, do you have any questions to ask about this story?"

"Yeah, I have a question," announced one boy, raising his hand. "Could you please tell us what happened to the flea?"

Six-year-old Thelma rushed into the house and tearfully told her mother that her brother, Stanley, had hit her.

Stanley, two years older than his sister, was immediately summoned into the living room and asked to explain.

"We wuz playin' Adam 'n Eve," said Stanley defensively, "but instead of temptin' me with the apple—she ate it herself!"

7
Dialect Stories

Introduction

The use of dialect in the telling of a Jewish or Jewish-oriented joke has all but passed into history. Modern Americans consider it to be in poor taste—and sometimes it is. The gifted author, Nathan Ausubel, in *A Treasury of Jewish Folklore*, states: "A large body of Jewish dialect jokes are not Jewish at all, but the confections of anti-Semites who delight in ridiculing and slandering the Jews."

There is truth in Ausubel's assertion, of course. Accented jokes have, indeed, often been used as a cloak to obscure anti-Semitism. However, we must also remember that humorous anecdotes which are about Jews or about Jewish customs and mannerisms, and which are told by Jews to other Jews, are often told in dialect for a variety of valid reasons. One of them is simply that the denouement, or "punch line," might *require* an accent. Without it, the very point of the joke is lost.

Another point: Many of the stories are premised on a misunderstanding of the English language. For example, Mrs. Goldberg, who has been suffering from insomnia, is being questioned by a psychiatrist. "Tell me," he asks the grandmotherly woman, "what is your attitude toward sex?" And Mrs. Goldberg responds pertly, "I love it! It's the finest sturr on Fift' Evnoo."

But there is a more compelling reason for the proper use of dialect. The humorist, if he is true to himself and to his readers, understands that folk humor is not propaganda to be rewritten to accommodate the psychological and political views of each generation. As a social historian, he must record the experiences of each, maintaining intact those of previous generations. This is essential if there is to be a reliable history that embodies authenticity and

72

continuity. And there is no doubt that humor does reflect a people's history! Boiled down to its essence, the use of dialect, coupled with the authentic portrayal of a people, enables the humorist not only to "tell it like it is," but to "tell it like it was." He is a people's folklorist with a smile.

The properly accented anecdote should be recognized as a major component of Jewish-American lore because it accurately mimics (though often exaggerating) the Yiddish inflection and pronunciation of literally millions of immigrants for whom English always remained a second (and usually a third) language.

The telling of dialect stories in the United States began with the second generation of fun-loving American-born youngsters who delighted in exchanging among themselves the linguistic mistakes of their foreign-born parents and neighbors. From these inchoate beginnings, the dialect stories gained in popularity among the children, grandchildren and great-grandchildren of the immigrants who were discerning enough to acknowledge that their antecedents represented a slice of America.

Americanized Yiddish expressions have invaded every facet of life. Sometimes dialect is not used, but is implicit. One popular example, which probably never happened, is the delightfully warm invitation from an El Al Airlines stewardess at dinner time: "Ladies and gentlemen, please fasten your seat belts, you should eat a little something." And then there is the malediction: "All his teeth should fall out except one—and in that one he should have a toothache!" But these are Yiddish inflections and transpositions of words rather than actual dialect.

The exclamation, "*oy*" (the definition of which will be found in the glossary of this book), has a perfectly legitimate function and has been used for generations. When properly employed, it is marvelously expressive. Here is an example:

During the time of the French Revolution, when the guillotine was employed almost around the clock, a Jew who lived in a village outside of Paris met a friend who had just returned from the city.

"What's happening there in Paris?" asked the Jewish man nervously.

"Conditions are absolutely horrible," replied the friend. "They're cutting off heads by the thousands."

"*Oy*," moaned the villager, "and me in the hat business!"

But enough is enough! The author is reminded of the botanist who found a beautiful flower by the wayside. He sat down to analyze it. He pulled it apart and examined every part under a microscope. When he had finished he could tell the color of the flower, its classification, and the number of stamens and pistils and petals and bracts, but its beauty and fragrance and life were gone.

So let us be done with analyzing and enjoy a little reading. And, incidentally, should a Yiddish word appear here and there that you don't understand, don't be lazy, but turn to the Glossary in the back of the book.

H.D.S.

Three doting mothers met for the first time in the dining room of the "Founting Blue" hotel at Miami Beach. As good *Yiddishe* mamas will, they soon got around to discussing their sons.

"Tell me," said Mrs. Goldfarb, "vot is your son doing for a living?"

"Mine son Oiving, he should live *bis a hundert un tsvantsik*, he's treveling for a silk house," replied Mrs. Levy.

"Vere your Oiving is treveling?"

"In de Vest."

"Dot's nice," said Mrs. Goldfarb. "Mine son, Harry, he also is a salesman. He's treveling in de Vest too."

Mrs. Goldfarb and Mrs. Levy turned to the third lady. "And your son, Mrs. Silverstein—vot he does?"

"Mine Joey, he trevels also."

"Vere he trevels?"

"In de South, mine Joey trevels."

Mrs. Goldfarb and Mrs. Levy looked at each other in utter bewilderment, and then at Mrs. Silverstein.

"In *de South*? Vere is de South?"

"Vell, I'm not sure," said Mrs. Silverstein uncertainly, "but I tink it's also in de Vest."

Mrs. Rosenberg, whose features were as unmistakably Jewish as her accent, became stranded one evening in a very "exclusive" resort section of Cape Cod—"exclusive" meaning that Jews were excluded. She needed accommodations for the night so she entered the town's only good hotel, a posh establishment, and approached the desk.

"I vould like, please, a room for the night," said Mrs. Rosenberg.

The desk clerk made a quick appraisal of his visitor and shook his head.

"Sorry," he said curtly.

"Vy you're sorry?"

"The hotel is full, madam."

"So vy the sign says 'rooms available'?"

The desk clerk stammered, hesitated, made a few feeble attempts to dissuade her, and then confessed:

"We don't admit Jews. Now if you'll try the other side of town . . ."

Mrs. Rosenberg drew herself up to her full height of five feet and addressed him heatedly:

"Jewish? By you I'm Jewish all of a sudden? From vere you got such a crazy idea, from vere? It so heppens I'm a convoitable."

"You're a *what*?"

"A convoitable. For a long time I'm vatching on the television this Fulton Schine and finally he's making me a Kedillac."

"Ah, I see," the desk clerk said. "You're a Cadillac convertible."

"Execkly," Mrs. Rosenberg answered huffily.

"Well, I happen to be a Catholic myself," said the keeper of the hotel. "Do you mind if I test you with the catechism?"

"Test! Test!"

"How was Jesus born?"

"By a himmeculit contraption from Heaven. The mama's name vas Mary and the papa's name vas Yussel."

"Very good. Now tell me, where was Jesus born?"

"In a menager, he vas *gevayn ge-borned*."

"That's right. And why was he born in a manger?"

"Because," Mrs. Rosenberg snapped, "some *paskudnyak* like you wouldn't give to a Jewish lady a room for the night!"

"Hello, is this the Levy residence?"

"Ahah. Mit whom you vish to speak?"

"Is Mr. Levy there?"

"Dis time of day Mr. Levy he's voikink."

"Is Thelma at home?"

"In school is Thelma."

"Then how about Harry? Can I speak to him?"

"Harry? In colletch is Harry, he should be a doctor."

"I see. Is this Mrs. Levy?"

"Mrs. Levy she's shoppink in de supermokkit."

"Well, who is this?"

"Dis? Dis is Daisy, de *schvartze!*"

An immigrant, who is also an aspiring author, spills out his feelings:

Mine duble-spased tiping is svell,

Mine storys and pomes is strong,

Yet notting I'm riting don't sell—nu, tell me—what can be rong?

Old Mrs. Bender was called into court as a witness in a civil suit. It seems that her friend, Mrs. Gold, had been cheated by Mr. Gross, owner of a furniture store.

The judge entered the courtroom and took his seat at the bar of justice. The bailiff called Mrs. Bender as the opening witness.

"First," instructed the bailiff, "you'll have to swear in."

"Vell, if I must I must," agreed Mrs. Bender. "Dot Mr. Gross is a crook und a bestid!"

The following may be the only Martian joke to employ an accent:

A flying saucer landed in Miami Beach, and out stepped a Martian visitor to earth. He strode across the street to a filling station and tipped his hat to a gaudily painted gas pump.

"Hello, dollink, hoz by you this evenink? You'll take me please to your leader like a nize girl?"

There was no reply, so the Martian tried again.

"Swittie-pie, it's good you're not talkink with strange men, but all I'm eskink is you should take me to your leader. Yes?"

His polite request was again met with silence, and the Martian's patience came to an abrupt end.

"Lady," he snapped, "take your finger out from your ear when I'm spikkink, and pay a little attention!"

A Chassidic rabbi in Brooklyn, during World War II, received a telegram from his grandson who had been drafted into the Army and was now stationed at Camp Vernon, near Leesville, Louisiana. It seems that the young man had fallen in love with the only Jewish girl in Leesville—a Miss Rae Weill—and they had decided to marry before he was shipped overseas. Of course, nothing else would do but for the grandfather to perform the wedding ceremony.

What choice did the old man have? A grandson is a grandson and that's all there is to it! So he packed a few personal items in a cardboard box, fastened it securely with twine, boarded a train and rode for three days and nights until he arrived at the little town whose population at that time numbered about 3,000. An attendant at the depot pointed out the street where Miss Weill lived, and, with a slip of paper containing the address of his future grand-daughter-in-law clutched in one hand and his carton gripped in the other, he slowly set off in search of the girl's house.

As he trudged along, glancing down at the paper, children stared in astonishment at the weird figure. He was dressed in typical *Chassidic* garb: a long, black kaftan that reached almost down to his ankles; on his head was a black, broad-brimmed *shtreimel*; and to complete the picture, he displayed a pair of white woolen socks that were clearly visible over his black, highbutton shoes. Pepper-and-salt *peyess*, or side-curls, engulfed his ears and were lost in a bushy beard that hid his chest.

To the children of that little southern town he might have been a visitor from outer space. Soon a bevy of other youngsters joined their playmates and proceeded to follow the apparition down the street, but kept a sizable distance behind him.

From time to time the rabbi glanced around him, noting with growing irritation that the line of curious followers was becoming longer with every minute. When he stopped, they stopped. When he started, they started. And not a word did they dare utter.

The old man could stand it no longer. He halted, put his carton down on the sidewalk, turned around and glared at them. But the children, instead of fleeing before his fierce gaze, were frozen to the spot.

"Vot's de metter mit you kids?" the exasperated rabbi finally shouted. "You never before saw a Yenkeh?"

Teacher: And now, Isidor, can you name a delicious drink that begins with a G?

Isidor: G'malted.

This *klayneh tsimmes*, from Dr. Jerry Segal's delightful *God Bless Mine Patients*, was published by the dentist-writer in 1926, almost entirely in Yiddish. In order that it may also be enjoyed by those with a limited knowledge of that language we have taken the liberty of anglicizing part of the anecdote.

Faigele, a *griener*—or "greenhorn" in English—found it necessary to visit Dr. Seligman's dental office. From the moment she entered, it was evident that she was new at this sort of thing, and terribly nervous. She scrutinized the equipment with wide and apprehensive eyes. Reluctantly she seated herself in the chair, and it was only after much hesitation that she obeyed the dentist's request to open her mouth so that he might examine the tooth which had been misbehaving. Her nervousness perceptibly increased as he jabbed a sharp little instrument at the offending molar.

"I guess we can do something for it," he said in a tone meant to be soothing.

But Faigele was not to be thus soothed by mere words. Her rigid fingers gripped the arm-rests of the chair until her knuckles showed white through the skin.

The dentist filled an atomizer with an antiseptic fluid and treated the gum. As he withdrew the spray, she clamped her mouth shut tightly.

"You may expectorate now," said Dr. Seligman.

She turned her frightened eyes up to him, her face terror-stricken. Trembling, her voice strained with fear, her jaws still clenched, she gasped:

"I should expect *vot*?"

A muffled gong sounded as the little old lady opened the carved and gilded door and walked into the exotically furnished reception room. A silk-draped young woman appeared in a cloud of incense as if from nowhere and bowed.

"Do you wish to consult with the all-seeing, all-wise guru, Maharishi Mah-jongg?"

"Yes," said the visitor. "Tell mine Seymour his *mamaleh* is here."

❖ ❖ ❖

An *alteh bobeh*, in this country for half a century, never could get used to the American way of doing things, and had neither the intention nor the slightest desire to learn. But it was the last straw when she showed up at her granddaughter's wedding ceremony wearing curlers in her hair.

"Grandma, how could you!" stormed the humiliated bride.

"Dollink," explained *Bobeh*, "I only vanted I should look nice for the reception!"

Now that he had retired, old man Koenig was determined to spend the remainder of his life where he could enjoy peace and tranquillity in the warm sunshine.

"I tink maybe I'll settle in Pollim Beach, Kelifoornia," he announced.

"Oh, papa," cried his daughter, "how many times have I told you not to say Pollim Beach!"

"*Oy, shayneh*, I forgot!" he exclaimed, smacking his forehead with the heel of his hand. "It's my *goyishe kop*. Pollim Beach is in Florida. In Kelifoornia is Pollim *Springs*!"

An elderly couple, only a few weeks removed from Ellis Island, took their first tour of New York and wound up at Macy's Department Store. They had not taken a dozen steps inside the building when the wife stopped dead in her tracks, clutched her husband's arm and pointed wordlessly to the escalators laden with people riding up and down.

He was as thunderstruck as she, but as he watched the passengers moving and at the same time standing in one place, his amazement gave way to awe.

"*Ach, America goniff!*" he breathed admiringly. "*M'shtait, m'gait!*"*

It was graduation day at the Adult Citizenship Class, and Mrs.

---

*The Yiddish word *goniff*, used in this context, does not mean "thief," but rather "clever one" or "rascal." The translation, loosely, reads: "Ah, clever America! People stand, people go."

Pomerantz smiled with pleasure as the teacher announced that she was the winner of a prize for having the highest marks in the class.

"And here is your reward," said the teacher, handing her student a replica of the Liberty Bell.

"Denk you," said Mrs. Pomerantz. "Dis prize I'm graciously accpting, even if it *is* crecked!"

In days gone by, before the Catskills became a popular summer haven for Jewish vacationers, Grossinger's famous resort in the Borscht Belt was little more than a rural farmhouse. Inside plumbing had yet to be installed, so the newly-arrived Grossinger family constructed a three-hole privy at the rear of the place.

One day, the cry of "fire!" rang out. Family and guests rushed through the front door and gazed wildly about, but could see neither fire nor smoke.

Once again came the anguished yell: "Fire! Fire!"

Old man Grossinger ran to the back yard and this time the screaming seemed to emanate from the outhouse. He bolted inside, but the place was empty and not a sign of a blaze anywhere.

"Fire! Fire!" yelled the voice again.

Grossinger whirled about and suddenly realized that the screaming apparently came from below the seats. He peered down into the unpleasant depths and—behold!—there was a man at the bottom of the hole—up to his armpits.

"What are you hollering *fire* for?" demanded Grossinger. "I don't see any fire down there."

And the trapped man snarled back:

"*Shlemiel*! Mit all de ladies present, vot did you expect I should yell?"

Two young brothers, Maurice and Sammy, age eleven and twelve, were returning from a visit to their grandmother's house. As they sat on the crowded bus, a woman, laden with heavy packages, entered and clutched a straphanger in front of the two boys.

Maurice, always a perfect little gentleman, rose to give the lady his seat.

"Much obliged," said the grateful woman.

But Maurice promptly sat down again. Sammy, amazed at this impolite act, then arose and gave the woman his own seat.

When she finally got off the bus, Sammy confronted his brother.

"What's the big idea of getting up and then sitting down again, Maurice? Especially after she was nice enough to say 'much obliged'."

"*Much obliged!*" Maurice gasped in astonishment. "Holy mackerel—I thought she said '*Moishe, bleib!*'"*

"The British are coming! The British are coming!" screamed Paul Revere.

"*Nu*, let them come," said Mrs. Revere. "We got chicken soup, lox, bagel, chopped liver, schmaltz herring . . ."

Jascha Heifetz, the eminent concert violinist, had just finished a recital and was surrounded by a group of admirers. Among them was Mrs. Bloom, to whom he had just been introduced.

"Do you like Chopin?" asked Mr. Heifetz.

"Vell, frankleh," replied Mrs. Bloom, "it hoits mine feet, valking around from vun stur to de next. Better dey should deliver!"

"Mine American-born daughter she's telling me: 'Yeah, Popsi-wopsi, I gotcha, but you'll hafta lay some heavy bread on me so's I kin strut new threads at the establishment bust-out, ya dig?'

"So I'm digging for maybe a half-hour to learn she needs money she should have a new dress for the school dance —

"And she is criticizing *mine* dialect!"

Bleib: "Stay." As used here, it means "Maurice, remain seated."

8

Communication Capers

Introduction

The need for communication, both through the spoken and the written word is deeply rooted in the history, folklore, literature and religion of the Jewish people. Admittedly, communication got off to a bad start in the Garden of Eden, with serpents, streakers and Republicans getting the worst of it ever since. The Israelites learned at the outset that you not only can't fight City Hall, but you can't win an argument when the other party has access to all the miracles. Despite this, the Jews became proficient at arguing among themselves—and with everybody else, including the Arabs: *Especially* the Arabs! But the Arabs didn't succeed in outmaneuvering the Jews. The secret: superior communication among the rank and file of the Jewish masses.

In the dawn of Judaic history, the elders of Israel realized that the traditions and laws of their kinsmen could not be adequately transmitted from one generation to the next by work of mouth or through the use of hieroglyphics. The Hebrews needed a written language through which their spiritual philosophy and thought could be expressed. They needed a written language that would convey *ideas*. And so, they created the *Aleph-Bais*—the Hebrew alphabet based on phonetics rather than pictures; a system of writing that had occurred to no other people—one that employed consonants and (implicitly understood) vowel sounds to form root words, prefixes, suffixes and connecting phrases; in other terms, a disciplined structure of grammar. In more recent centuries, Yiddish, rather then Hebrew, became the common language of East European Jews in particular.

The written and spoken language of the ancients, with some

modifications, has survived to this day. In the United States, however, the number of Yiddish readers has declined in recent years, as
noted by the demise of the *Tag-Morgen Journal*, which passed
into history in January 1972, leaving the *Jewish Daily Forward* as
the only important Yiddish daily newspaper in the field. Regrettably, there is not much left of the once lively Yiddish press in
America. Jews have always liked newspapers. "When the *Mosheeach*
(Messiah) comes," it is said, "they will expect the papers to get
out an Extra." The late David Ben-Gurion added: "And why not?
When the Jews were in the wilderness, did they not have their
Daily Manna?"

The Yiddish press was a link that united the mass of Jews who
came to America during one of the great exoduses of history. The
Jews going out of Egypt had no need to learn a new language, but
those coming here from Europe did, and the Yiddish press served
as a vehicle of indoctrination to the ways of a new world. The
papers were held in very high esteem by a variety of Jews: immigrants from Bialystok and Grodno, Vilna and Cracow, Minsk,
Pinsk and Yekaterinoslav, representing many types and local cul-
tures—but brothers and sisters all, under the Star of David.

Among those who made the strongest journalistic impression
in the Yiddish press was Abraham Cahan, editor of the *Forward*,
or *Forvertz*, as it was and still is called by many of its readers. Cahan was a *Litvak* from a town near Vilna. When he liked a *Galitzianer*, he converted him into a *Litvak*. A case in point is the noted
humorist, B. Kovner, a *Galitzianer*. His real name was Adler, but
Cahan was so impressed with the man's humorous writings that
he persuaded him to change his name to that of a Lithuanian city,
Kovno. Thus, he became B. Kovner.

Cahan had worked for a time on several English-language
papers in America, and was no doubt influenced by them. Today,
editors are usually polite—or about as polite as an editor can be—
but in those days they were often somewhat rough. Abe Cahan
learned to be just as rough as his gentile counterparts—and often
tougher. To illustrate: A man came to the *Forvertz* office one day
and asked for a job. Cahan asked him what he could do.

"I can write poetry," explained the applicant.

"Poetry doesn't sell papers," snapped Cahan. "Can you make
pogroms? Pogroms sell papers!"

Bayarsky of the *Tag-Morgen Journal* was just as bellicose as
Cahan. He would hire some radicals for his religious-oriented
paper, and then mutter: "It gives me pleasure to see these atheists
praising Jewish religious institutions for a pittance."

But it wasn't all irony and sarcasm. There was the "Bintel

Brief" of the *Forvertz*, for example. English dailies have since appropriated the same idea with columns like "Dear Abby." In the *Morning Journal*, Abraham Shomer wrote novelettes which gave the Jewish mother a nice cry as she prepared *gefilte* fish. After the cry, she would use the paper to wrap herring in. And let us not forget Zevin, the interesting little hunchback who worked for the *Tageblatt*. We recall the likes of him with deep nostalgia. In order to reach his desk, he would sit on a big copy of *Webster's Unabridged Dictionary*, which inspired his colleagues to declare that he had the most educated *tuchus* on the staff.

Some people are less communicative than others, of course. Leo Aikman, in the *Atlanta Constitution*, told of seeing a Bell Telephone truck in New York which carried the message on its side panel: "Ask Me About Better Telephone Service." Underneath, in the dust, someone had scrawled, "I don't talk to no truck." In yet another sphere, that of television, communication can be anything but explicit. Consider the case of Herb Newman, the weather forecaster, who gloomily predicted, "There's a 100% chance of possible rain."

Many Jewish writers are engaged in the business of public relations. Somewhere in my earlier jottings, I mentioned the imaginative publicist who was handling the press notices for vocalist Eydie Gorme. He phones her one morning with a "terrific stupendous" idea for a photo that would "surely make page one in the dailies." It seems that the battleship *Missouri*—the famous "Mighty Mo"—had arrived in port and he wanted Eydie at the dock that very day so her picture could be taken alongside the ship. "Can't you just see the caption under that picture?" he rhapsodized: "Eydie Meetie Mighty Mo!"

I did not think that any other flack could top that one—at least not until I was informed otherwise by Dave Kellerman, the Hollywood press agent whose father, also a publicist, was responsible for the following press wizardry:

Down in Florida, papa Kellerman had been retained to publicize the Roney Plaza in Miami, one of a string of hotels owned by tycoon J. Myer Schine. Kellerman knew that Schine doted on personal publicity (and never mind the hotel), so he sat up all one night cudgeling his brain for an idea. Then, like the electric bulb in the old-time cartoons, the solution burst upon him with brilliant illumination. He drove out to the Gulfstream racetrack and, after some shopping around in the boneyard of the stables, found an old horse whose owner was happy to unload for only ten dollars. Kellerman promptly changed the horse's name from "Footloose Filly" to "Harvest Moon." Then he got J. Myer Schine to climb into the saddle while a photographer snapped his picture. A day or two later, press agent Kellerman released the photo to the newspapers with the inspired caption: "Schine on Harvest Moon."

Speech is actually the means by which the currency of mental wealth is passed from mind to mind. While this is basically true, it is also true that much of our speech is not all that rich in meaning—and the less said about some of the minds the better. Specifically, this applies to direct communication, or one-to-one speech with which individuals make their thoughts known to each other. When our thoughts are awry, so must be our speech. And, of all the transmitters of one-to-one speech, none can surpass the woman who worships at the feet of the Jewish goddess of communication, Yenteh Tellabendeh.

The *Yenteh* is purely mythical, of course, and is no more addicted to idle gossip than her gentile sisters—it's just that she does it better. But no other group of people has ever succeeded in individualizing and humanizing her as have the Jews. The most striking aspect of the *Yenteh's* proclivity for spreading rumors, or for minding everyone else's business but her own, is that her gossip and interference is seldom vicious. Usually she is quite perceptive. For example, a daughter reads a love letter aloud—one of many such tender missives from her beau. Mother says suspiciously: "If he loves you so much why doesn't he compromise himself a little?" Or take the neighbor who glances around furtively so no one else can overhear her, and then whispers: "About Mrs. Levy, you'll never in a million years believe this, but ...." And madame *yenteh* eagerly interrupts with: "I believe, I believe!" Small wonder, then, that a *yenteh's* idea of hell is a place where all are required to mind their own business.

And now, let's communicate.

H.D.S.

Who said that when a married woman begins misbehaving, her husband is the last person to hear the news? Whoever it was, he appears to have uttered a universal truism.

Take the case of Michael Helfman, recently of Hunters Point. It was a long time—so it seemed to the watchful and gossiping neighbors—before Mr. Helfman's jealous suspicions became aroused. However, once he was convinced that his wife's love of admiration had carried her beyond the bounds of discretion, he proceeded to act.

He sat down and wrote this note to the good-looking Mr. Dash, who lived just across the street, and sent it over by messenger:

Sir:
I shall expect you to appear at my office this afternoon at three o'clock to explain why you have been carrying on with my wife.

Yours truly,
Michael Helfman

Promptly the messenger returned with an answer, which read:

Dear Mr. Helfman:
Your circular letter of even date received and comments duly noted. Thanks for the invitation. I shall be very glad to attend the caucus.

Sincerely,
Morris H. Dash

A *palindrome* is a word, phrase or sentence which reads the same forwards or backwards. Considering the frequency with which these brain-twisters appear in the Jewish press, one might think that the Jews invented it. Perhaps they did, at that. According to this author's secret files, the first palindrome was created by that eminently respected Jewish boy, Adam. He introduced himself to Eve with the welcoming speech:
"Madam, I'm Adam."
"Eve," she responded with one of her own.
Here are a few others, some retaining the unmistakable flavor of *Yiddishkeit*:
Evade me, Dave.
No, Miss, it is Simon.
Able was I ere I saw Elba.
Lew, Otto has a hot towel.
Did Hannah see bees? Hannah did.
A man, a plan, a canal: Panama.
Semite Moses orders madam's red rose sometimes.

Nominated for the Bravest Letter of the Year Award:
Dear Teechr
Mannie Weil was lait for skool yestidy coze it wasint his folt.
My farver

Hubby: If there's anyone I can't stand, it's the person who interrupts a conversa. . . .

Wifey: And takes the words right out of your mouth.

"Dear Papa," wrote little Shirley to her father who was out of town on business, "we're having a speling b in school and I'm in the finnals."

Computers have a habit of going haywire, as thousands of hapless householders will attest—especially when bills are normally due at the first of the month. But no computer ever went so completely and vengefully mad as the one that singled out old Lou Lieberman as its legitimate prey.

Lieberman was minding his own business, tending his little dry cleaning agency, when the mailman came in one morning and dumped 143 letters on the counter—all of them identical requests that he renew his subscription to the *Catholic Digest.* It so happens that Lieberman had never heard of the magazine and would not have subscribed if he had. He threw the entire lot into the wastebasket.

But on the following day he received 153 more, on the next 278, and on the third day over 400. For the remainder of the week, he received the requests for renewal at the rate of a thousand or more a day.

Finally, he could stand it no longer. He closed the shop, went to the Western Union office and wired the *Catholic Digest* his payment, along with a cryptic telegram:

ALLRIGHT ALREADY, I GIVE UP. RENEW!

Motorists driving along Drexel Boulevard in Chicago were recently greeted with a bold new sign on Mendel's Modern Car Wash. It read:

— KEEP AMERICA CLEAN —
Run a Hippie Through Our Car Wash

Henrietta Szold (1860-1945), probably the most beloved and respected woman in American-Jewish history, was a founder of *Hadassah*. Born in Baltimore, she started her career as a teacher and, in 1893, she became an editor for the Jewish Publication Society. She is, however, best remembered for her long career in Zionist work and leadership. In 1916, she organized the American Zionist Medical Unit for Palestine and, in 1920, she became director of the School for Nursing in Jerusalem. She was chosen to be a member of the Zionist Executive in 1927 and served in many other high positions of Jewish interest in the United States and Palestine.

Of the several volumes written about this remarkable woman, only two humorous anecdotes about her have been found by this editor. Both are very brief; one from her early childhood, and the other, from the period before she left for the Holy Land, when she was still a young woman.

First, the anecdote told by her grade school teacher, Gladys Wickwire.*

"My third grade pupils were darlings. Especially Henrietta Szold, a serious little girl with an alert mind, but a child who smiled brightly enough when praised. I recall hugging her as a result of an incident that occurred just prior to George Washington's birthday, in 1867.

"During our history period I spent much time emphasizing the fine qualities of the Father of Our Country, telling the children of his bravery, his resourcefulness, his honesty, sincerity, kindness and faith in God. When the time for questions and answers arrived, I said to the class:

"And now, children, for what great position would such a man as this be most suited?

"Henrietta raised her hand and I gave her permission to speak.

"'Miss Wickwire,' said the girl, 'I think he would make a very nice husband.'"

Another remembrance: this time by one of America's great orators of yesteryear—William Jennings Bryan:**

"In 1892, as a freshman Congressman, I was introduced to a Miss Henrietta Szold, a lady whom I should not have wanted as an opponent in debate. That meeting is memorable for it was the first time in my life that I was left absolutely speechless—which, for me at any rate, was and is an event of cataclysmic proportions. That it was occasioned by a member of the gentler sex has, ever since, caused me to wonder if women are, in fact, as gentle as has

---

*From *All My Little Girls*, Gladys Wickwire, Baltimore Press, 1878.
**From *The Commoner*, William Jennings Bryan, ed., 1901.

been claimed.

"I had been declaiming at some length on the hardships endured by the Pilgrim Fathers when it gradually dawned on me that Miss Szold did not seem as impressed as the others of my audience. When I paused briefly for a glass of water, Miss Szold asked:

"'Mr. Bryan, have you nothing to say about the Pilgrim *Mothers?*'

"'Why, what about them?' I replied.

"'It would appear to me,' she said with an aplomb I admired on the instant, 'they endured all that the Pilgrim Fathers did, and the Pilgrim Fathers as well!'"

In the old days, before the invention of the air-brake simplified the dangerous job of coupling the steam cars that were then in use, and bringing to an end the many cases of accidental amputations that resulted from hand-coupling the cars, Arnold Bogen, the Chicago writer and lecturer, went to Peoria to make an address during a trainmen's convention.

Upon his return home, he wrote an account of his visit in his newspaper column:

"It was one of the most remarkable experiences in my entire career on the lecture platform. The guests of honor were all retired switchmen, and they attended in a body. They seemed to like my comments immensely but there were so many one-armed men down front that they had to do their applauding in pairs."

Bret Harte, the noted writer of short stories and humorous verse of Western local color, was a contemporary of Mark Twain. Both men detested each other. Harte was only part Jewish so we shall tell only part of the story—but the best part.

During a trip back East in 1871, Harte chanced to meet Twain while strolling on Fifth Avenue, adjacent to Central Park. It was a balmy day in early June, exactly suited for a pleasant walk in the sunshine. Both men would have preferred not to address the other at all, but some sort of comment at this face-to-face encounter could not be avoided.

"Nice day," said Twain, his voice cool.

"Yes," replied Harte dryly, "I've heard it very highly spoken of."

The late David Sarnoff, the radio and television pioneer who rose to the presidency of RCA, came to America from Russia in 1900 as a boy of nine. Securing a job with the Marconi Wireless Company, he won national recognition for his reporting of the news of the Titanic disaster. Marconi Wireless was later absorbed by Radio Corporation of America, and Sarnoff became a legend as well as an historical figure. We can thank the folklorists for the following tidbit.

As a telegrapher, young David received his share of complaints from subscribing newspapers to the wire service for which he worked. One telegraph editor of a Long Island paper complained because names were being omitted from the cabled stories. He wrote to the company that if it neglected this essential detail in the next wired yarn, he would cancel the paper's subscription. The telegraph company passed the ultimatum on to Sarnoff with the added postscript that if the offense were repeated, he would be discharged.

The young man was quickly converted to the idea of including names in his stories whenever possible. A few days later, the complaining editor received this dispatch:

VALLEY STREAM, L.I., N.Y. JUNE 6—A SEVERE STORM PASSED OVER THIS SECTION THIS AFTERNOON AND LIGHTNING STRUCK A BARBED-WIRE FENCE ON THE FARM OF HENRY WILSON, KILLING THREE COWS—THEIR NAMES BEING FLOSSIE, BOSSIE AND BUTTERCUP.

In Hebrew School, little Sarah was asked if she could repeat a verse from the Bible that they had studied last week. She replied, "Not only can I quote the verse, but I can also give you the zip code: Exodus 19:20."

For you English language buffs: The future of "courting" is "caught."

"In Russia," enthused a returned tourist, "the phones are really marvelous. In fact, the street-corner telephones are free. The only problem is that you can't hear anything."

"Kuhn, Kahn, Kohn and Gossmacher, good mo-o-orning."

"Is Mr. Grossmacher there?"

"Who's calling pleee-uz?"

"This is Shlessinger, Shlossinger and Shlepperman: Mr. Shlessinger calling."

"Just a mo-o-ment, I'll connect youuu."

"Mr. Grossmacher's office."

"Mr. Grossmacher, please. Mr. Shlessinger wishes to talk to him."

"Would you put Mr. Shlessinger on the line, please?"

"Mr. Shlessinger? Ready with Mr. Grossmacher."

"Hi, Jake? Mannie. OK for lunch? Atta boy—see ya!"

Stan and Sid, both on the road with non-competing merchandise, usually traveled together, sharing the same car and hotel rooms to save money. One evening, the two friends registered at a small hotel in Schenectady and Stan immediately sat down to write his wife a letter. Sid happened to notice his buddy's unusual salutation.

"Tell me something, Stan," he said curiously, "how come you always address your wife as 'Dear AT&T'? Is she a big investor?"

"No, nothing like that," answered Stan. "AT&T doesn't stand for American Telephone and Telegraph. It means 'Always Talking and Talking!'"

Sign in the window of Pechter's Bakery on Fairfax Avenue, Los Angeles:

UPSIDE DOWN CAKES 99¢

Paul Berger, owner of the LaSalle Furniture Store in Chicago, after a series of futile attempts to collect payment from a delinquent customer, sat down and wrote a personal letter. His command of English, however, was somewhat deficient, so he asked his college-educated son to read it and give his opinion.

"This isn't bad at all, dad," avowed the offspring. "You presented your case in a thoughtful, orderly and concise manner. In fact, you only made two little errors: *Momzer* is spelled with a *z*, not an *s*, and there is no *w* in 'louse'!"

Out of latter-day Jewish-American folk humor—the "Tin Lizzie" era of the mid-1920's—comes this Ferocious Ford Fable. In that period which marked the birth of assembly line production, Henry Ford was winning acclaim for his success in the mass production of cars, but he was also drawing scathing denunciation from Jews and informed gentiles for his support of the bogus *Protocols of the Learned Elders of Zion*.

The Protocols were purported to be the minutes of a secret international committee or congress of prominent Jewish leaders. According to this canard, these "Elders of Zion" devised a conspiracy whereby the Jewish people would dominate and control the world. Despite their indisputable falsity, the *Protocols* were taken seriously by millions of people throughout the world and, even today, Arab factions are still distributing copies of this literary garbage.

The most widespread dissemination in the United States occurred between 1920 and 1927, when the *Dearborn Independent*, which was controlled by Henry Ford, published excerpts periodically. Ford later apologized in order to "make amends for the wrong done to the Jews as fellow-men and brothers by asking their forgiveness."

It became well-known that Ford could shrug off the angry responses that resulted from his publishing of the *Protocols*, but he would go into a towering rage at the slightest criticism of his auto production techniques. Jewish wit rose to the occasion when this chink in his armor became apparent. If they could not needle him into anger with references to his gullibility, they could and did get to him with jokes about his cars—jokes that were created and gleefully repeated until Henry would turn purple with rage. A few of the humorous stories earned a niche in the annals of Jewish-American folk humor. Let us revive one of them.

The telephone rang in the inner sanctum of auto magnate Henry Ford. His secretary answered the ring:

"Mr. Ford's office. Who is calling?"

"This is Mr. Morris Luftmensch," said the voice at the other end of the line. "I would like to speak with Mr. Ford."

"Mr. Ford is very busy," explained the functionary. "May I take the message?"

"No, you can't," was the firm reply. "I must speak direct with your boss. I happen to be an important customer of your company, and what I have to say, only the head man should hear."

"Well, in that case, sir, kindly hold the wire," said the secretary in a respectful manner. Mr. Ford was quickly summoned to the phone.

"Well, what is it?" snapped the auto mogul.

"Mr. Ford," stated Luftmensch without preamble, "you advertised recently that your company is making a complete car in six minutes. Is that right? Yes or no!"

"Yes, in a test we did turn out a car in six minutes. What about it?"

"Well, I'm the guy who bought it!"

Announcement chalked on the blackboard in the San Francisco office of the Restaurant Employees Union:
MAN WANTED TO WASH DISHES AND TWO WAITRESSES

From the secret archives of the Government of Israel:
Dear Comrade Brezhnev:

You ask that I give you my reaction with reference to your publicly stated desire to permit all Jews who so desire to emigrate to Israel.

My secretary, being a gentleman, cannot type what I think of your promises; and I being a lady, won't dictate it. But you, being neither, will understand me fully.

Golda Meir

Conversation between two girls, overheard on the 7th Avenue Express at the Bronx Park Station:
". . . so I told him we were through, because all he cared about was my body. Then I heard this loud noise on the other end of the line."

"My goodness, you mean a pistol shot?"

"Well, n-no—it sounded more like a champagne cork."

The late Edward G. Robinson enjoyed telling the story of the hard-of-hearing man who was presented to a beautiful and charming young lady.

"Mr. Rubin," said the mutual friend, "I want you to meet Miss Heffelfinger."

Mr. Rubin's eyes widened in admiration of this gorgeous creature smiling at him. "I'm awfully glad to meet you, Miss—Miss—Miss . . ."

"Heffelfinger," prompted the mutual friend, raising his voice a decibel or two.

"I'm terribly sorry to be such a nuisance," said poor Rubin, "but, as the young lady can see for herself, I'm a little deaf." He cupped his hand behind his ear. "Now I think I can hear you. Would you mind repeating the name just once more?"

"HEFFELFINGER!" shouted the friend.

"It's no use," lamented Rubin. "I can't make it out at all. It still sounds to me like you're saying—please don't laugh—*Heffelfinger!*"

Back in the old days, language and citizenship classes were held during the afternoon and evening hours for the benefit of the many new immigrants seeking a better life in the *Goldeneh Medina*. These free classes were conducted at Cooper Union, the Henry Street Settlement, Workmen's Circle (*Arbeiter Ring*), and at a number of public schools in the various boroughs of New York, but mostly in downtown Manhattan. The Late Henry Eisenholtz, founder of the East Broadway Bon Ton Store, which later grew into the nationwide chain of retail outlets of today, told of a personal incident that occurred at Cooper Union which he himself attended as a new comer to the United States.

The instructor, a woman with the very soul of patience, was working mightily to help build a larger vocabulary among her adult pupils—teaching them how to pronounce the various parts of the human body in English. She would point to each place and then carefully enunciate, "Fingers—wrist—elbow—shoulder."

But it seemed that the more she labored, the more confused the students became. Not one could name the parts when called upon—that is, until she came to Henry Eisenholtz.

In a clear voice, and without the slightest hesitation, he pointed to each of the parts of his arm and correctly identified them: "Fingers—wrist—elbow—shoulder."

"Why, Mr. Eisenholtz, that was just fine!" gushed the happy teacher. "How in the world did you remember?"

"Easy," said Eisenholtz proudly, pointing to his head. "I used mine kidneys!"

9

Ask a Foolish Question

Introduction

"One fool can ask what
a thousand sages cannot answer."
—*Yiddish Proverb*

"Ask a foolish question and you get a foolish answer" is a Jewish maxim which has been repeated in one form or another for many centuries. The Talmud itself contains a full measure of peevish complaints about foolish questions, including the querulous utterance: "There are lions before you, and you ask about foxes?!"

Jews, it is said, would not be Jews if they did not contradict one another, so it should come as no surprise that the people's literature is replete with opposing viewpoints. An old Yiddish proverb states: "Each wherefore has its therefore." Mendele, however, in 1873, wrote his own cautious opinion: "Not all questions may be asked, nor is there an answer for every question." Perhaps he was right.

Someone once asked the late Rabbi Montague Isaacs, Los Angeles spiritual leader of Congregation Tifereth Jacob: "Rabbi, what would you do if the *Mosheeach* were to appear tomorrow?" The old rabbi, a witty man in and out of the pulpit, replied evenly, "I would first ask the Messiah what took him so long."

Clearly, then, the quality of the answer depends on the substance of the question. As Ibn Gabirol pointed out in the eleventh century: "A wise man's question is half the answer." In the modern context of humor, it is evident that the "foolish question" joke is incomplete without the so-called "foolish answer." But here we run into a paradox: the question may be foolish, but the reply can be (and usually is) astute, sardonic or downright insulting—anything but foolish. The answer may be stated in allegorical or hyperbolic terms so as to *sound* nonsensical at first hearing, but it might well be informative or convey a serious message or truth, despite its sarcasm.

Probably the best illustration of the withering reply is found in the classic story of the supposed meeting between King Faisal and David Ben-Gurion in Saudi Arabia. "Just look at all those gushing oil wells," boasted Faisal. "Isn't this a marvelous country?" Ben-Gurion regarded him with a cold eye. "Your Highness," he finally answered, "if it weren't for those wells, all you'd have is a million square miles of kitty-litter."

Allowing for the usual exceptions, the main difference between the old European "foolish question" joke and its American counterpart is that in the former both the questioner and the respondent are serious, while in the latter it is only the *questioner* who is serious. In old Europe, the *shnook* answered the question: in this country he *asks* it! Moreover, in the European version of yesteryear, it was the foolish respondent who enjoyed the "punch line," rather than the reverse, as is customary here today. One such old-time story tells about the son of a rich merchant of Bialystok who returns home from the university, proud that he has now acquired wisdom. His father tests him to determine if the youth is as wise as now claimed. He hides a small wooden disc in his fist and begins his interrogation: "The object I am holding in my hand is round and made of wood. Tell me, what is it?" Beaming, the son replies: "A wagon wheel." The moral, obviously, is that education can be equated with learning, but not necessarily with wisdom or even with common sense. In the United States, however, very few jokes in this category provide a moral; either implicit or explicit. Here, they are told "for the fun of it."

Many of these little anecdotes should properly be termed "foolish answer" rather than "foolish question" jokes. Often, they are based on misunderstanding. For example, a real estate broker asks: "Would you like to see our model home?" And the prospective customer eagerly responds: "I sure would! What time does she quit work?" But in the majority of such stories in the United States, the humor lies not so much in the foolish question but in the "squelch"—the "put-down"—the reply that satisfies. It serves notice that the question is as meaningless as a Russian election. Thus, we have the query: "Do you believe that the average Negro is really born with a banjo on his knee?" And the answer: "Yes, but when the child reaches the age of three his parents usually have it surgically removed."

"A fool says what he knows, a sage knows what he says," declares the Talmud. Having complied with the first half of the proverb, I ring down the curtain on this Introduction with an admonition of my own:

Beware of the man who asks you a question, answers it for you, and then says you're wrong. Verily, he is worse than the woman whose feminine questions at least give you a choice between two wrong answers.

H.D.S.

The Genealogy of Jack Waters is probably the longest of the "foolish question" anecdotes; it also ranks as one of the funniest *megillahs*, or complicated stories, in this genre. Now a classic, it has attained the venerable age of about half a century and will no doubt be around for decades to come, not only because of its humor and devastating "punch line" (in Yiddish) but also for its all-too-recognizable reality in this age of Anglicized names which have been adopted by many Jewish Americans. We might add that the denouement, or final word in this joke, would lose its verve, its hilarious connotation were it translated into English; therefore it has been left in the original. And now the story.

Two men happened to meet on a train and as they opened a discussion they soon learned that they were both Jewish.

"What is your name?" asked one.

"My name is Jack Waters."

"Jack Waters! How does it happen that a Jew should have the name Jack Waters? Are you an American-born Jew?"

"Well, no," replied the other. "As a matter of fact, before I came to this country I lived in England, and in England my name was Fountain."

"Oh, then you're an English Jew!"

"Not really. Before I lived in England I lived in France, and in France my name was LaFontaine. I came to England, so from La-Fontaine it became Fountain. When I came to the United States, from Fountain, Jack Waters."

"Aha, I see! You're a French Jew."

"Well, not exactly. Before I lived in France I lived in Germany. And there my name was Spritzwasser."

"Oh-h-h, now I got it!"

"Yes, and when I went to France, from Spritzwasser it became LaFontaine; from LaFontaine, Fountain; from Fountain, Jack

Waters."

"Actually, then, you're a German Jew?"

"Well," the man concluded, "I was really born in *Gubernja*, and there they used to call me Bevelterpisher."

For weeks he had been calling regularly on the young lady, spending the evenings at her house and discussing a variety of subjects, but not once did he ever get around to the subject she was waiting to hear—marriage. One evening she decided to put the question to him in a forthright manner.

"Look," she began rather tersely, "a man has honorable intentions or he doesn't, he's serious or he's not serious, and that's all there is to it. There's something wrong with me you're not popping the question?"

He knew, of course, that sooner or later she would bring up the subject, and he answered slowly but emphatically.

"*Shayneh*, I'm here in this country for five years now and I learned a little about American women. That's why I'm not talking on you about marriage. You ask me if something is wrong with you, and as long as you're asking, I got to confess I'm wondering. After all, what kind of a girl are you that every evening you're sitting down with a man like me who is forever sitting down to talk on a girl like you and we're doing nothing but sitting?"

Stewardesses employed by Israel's airline, *El Al*, are instructed in the technique for handling predatory males. Here are two of the standard questions and the girls' answer.

"What's your phone number, baby?"

"You'll find it in the directory, sir."

"Okay, what's your name?"

"You'll find that in the directory, too."

"Do you believe in love and marriage?"

"Yes, but not necessarily with the same person."

Steve and Stella were among the tourists in Washington, D.C., visiting the Lincoln Memorial on the occasion of the Great Emancipator's birthday.

"There will never be another like him," murmured Steve reverently as he gazed upon the noble statue. "Good old Honest Abe!"

A puzzled look crossed Stella's face. "Tell me something, Steve," she said hesitantly. "If Abraham Lincoln was so honest, why do they close all the banks on his birthday?"

Social Worker: Is the high cost of living a problem in your family?

Welfare Applicant: No, just the *taste* for high living!

"This airplane looks awfully old," said the nervous lady. "You're sure it's safe?"

"Of course it's safe," assured the pilot. "How else did the plane get so old?"

The rabbi was being considered for a position in a large synagogue.

"Do you have any difficulty making decisions?" asked a member of the congregation.

"Wel-l-ll," replied, the rabbi, "sometimes yes, sometimes no."

It is said that this story is true, but don't bet your month's rent on it. At any rate, back in the 1930's there used to be a permanent resident of "The Retreat," a private Jewish home for the mentally disturbed on the outskirts of Los Angeles. It seems that all at once he fancied himself a painter. Up until that time he had leaned to the theory that he was the biblical Isaiah, and before that he was of the opinion that he was Disraeli. But now, quite suddenly, he decided that he was intended to depict important historical episodes with pigment and brush.

In such privacy as the management afforded, he fitted himself up with a studio. The management also provided him with supplies. After some weeks he announced that he was prepared to hold a private unveiling of his first masterpiece. He invited the superintendent of the institution to be his chief guest on that occasion.

At the appointed moment, he brought forth a large frame shrouded in cloth. Having placed it where the light would bring out the best values of the composition, he removed the cover with a flourish. There was revealed a stretch of canvas untouched by so much as a single brush stroke. It was as free of paint as the day he purchased it.

"Now," said the artist with pride in his voice, "what do you think of that for a beginning?"

"Very fine," said the tactful superintendent. "But, pardon me for asking, what does it represent?"

"Why, don't you see? That represents the passage of the Children of Israel through the Red Sea."

"But where is the sea?"

"It has been driven back."

"And where are the Israelites?"

"They have crossed over."

"But the Egyptians—how about them?"

"What kind of a silly question is that? They've all drowned, naturally."

Flo: I hate to mention this, but did you know that your hair is thinning on top?

Moe: So let it get thin! Who needs fat hair?

It would seem that a regrettable occurrence—what is known in educational circles as a "hazing"—had taken place at Brandeis. A freshman was the victim and he complained to the faculty. The fact that he was the son of a wealthy donor to the university may have had something to do with the furor engendered by the complaint, but whatever the reason, the dean himself undertook an investigation.

One of the first to be summoned before him was a youth who owned up to the fact that he had participated in the festivities.

"Ah-*ha!*" erupted the dean. "You confess, then, that you, a supposedly decent Jewish boy, helped carry off this inoffensive young man by force, and took him to the campus fountain and there immersed him?"

"Yes, sir," said the culprit meekly.

"And what part did you take in this disgraceful affair?"

"The right leg, sir."

This one's for the birds.

Barbra Streisand, taking time off from her Hollywood chores, went shopping for a gift to present to her nephew. Visiting Farmer's Market in Los Angeles, she spied a handsome, talkative parrot and immediately took a fancy to it.

"Does he fly?" Barbra asked the pet shop owner.

"Usually," replied the owner. "But sometimes he takes the train."

A lonely traveling salesman struck up a conversation with another at a rural hotel.

"Does your wife miss you much?" asked one.

"No," said the other, "not with her aim!"

When her weight went over 200 pounds, the housewife thought it best to consult a doctor. In his office, he gave her a thorough examination.

"There is nothing wrong with your metabolism," said the physician. "In fact there is nothing organically wrong with you at all."

"That's nice," said the housewife. "But why am I so fat?"

"You are clearly eating too much. Tell me, what do you do all day?"

"Like you said, doctor. I eat, that's all."

"Don't you do any housework?"

"My three daughters do it for me," she said, becoming annoyed with the persistent questioning.

"Well, how about exercise?"

"Doctor," snapped the woman, now visibly irritated, "I'm over 200 pounds and I'm five feet tall. And you're asking me what exercise I do? Well, as long as you're asking I'll tell you: I read murder mysteries and let my flesh creep!"

Mendel: What's the difference between gossip and news?
Marvin: That depends on whether you're hearing or telling.

The visitor to New York rushed from the airport into a waiting taxi, trying to keep dry in the heavy downpour.

"Can you think of anything worse," grumbled the visitor, "than raining cats and dogs in New York?"

"Sure," said the cab driver cheerfully. "Hailing taxis!"

A man was found shot to death in his bedroom. The door had been locked from the inside and there were no windows in the room. No intruder could possibly have gotten inside. A note was found, in the man's handwriting, declaring that he had decided to take his own life.

"I still don't see why the coroner pronounced it suicide, do you?" asked the country cousin.

"He pronounced it suicide," said the dead man's brother acidly, "because that happens to be the way you pronounce it!"

The old lady in the black babushka was having difficulty selecting a suitable fish at the store. She'd pick one up, sniff, put it down again and then try another.

"Mister," she finally asked the annoyed proprietor in a voice loud enough for the other customers to hear, "don't you have any fish they're not smelling?"

The outraged merchant gritted his teeth.

"*Tanteh,*" he said when he had gained control of his temper, "you want a fish that don't smell? All right, just for you I'll cut off its nose!"

Seymour the Sheik: When we met on the street last night I had on my new suit. You didn't even know me, did you?
Sheila the Shikse: No, who were you?

10

Military Matters and Don't Matters

Introduction

The abhorrence of war and dedication to peace has always been emphasized in Judaic teachings. Over the many centuries, Jews have traditionally bestowed admiration and honors upon their scholars, poets and spiritual leaders, rather than upon their warriors. It is no accident that the biblical David, for instance, is more remembered for his psalms than for his valor in battle. This Hebraic yearning for peace was beautifully expressed by the English political economist, Leone Levi, in his rhetorical question: "Who can reflect on the sacredness of human life, in view of its eternal destinies, without coming to the conclusion that war, with its attendants of hatred, destruction and slaughter, is incompatible with the high dictates of religion?"

But, if Jews are dedicated to peace, they are not now, nor have they ever been pacifists. Had they been unwilling to fight for their existence, they would not have survived the onslaughts of their enemies and remained the unified people they are today. This is no apologia for war, of course. Only a fool would prefer military action to diplomacy. But some wars can be justified despite the idealists who confuse peacefulness with pacifism. "It is simply not true that war never settles anything," observed Felix Frankfurter. Justice Frankfurter might well have been referring to the American Revolution or the Civil War, or Hitler's try at world mastery, or one of a dozen other justified confrontations.

In the United States, Jewish fighting men have participated in every war this nation has ever had. Indeed, their *insistence* on serving in the armed forces began in the earliest colonial times when Jacob Barsimson and Asser Levy, among the first 23 Jews to settle in New Amsterdam in 1654, successfully challenged the anti-Semitic Governor Peter Stuyvesant who attempted to exclude Jews from guard duty (and then had the temerity to tax them as non-combatants). As a direct result of Levy's courageous persistence, the Jews of New Amsterdam (later New York) were finally granted full civil rights. Levy not only won the right to serve in the military establishment, but became the first American of the Jewish faith to be accorded complete citizenship in the New World. Barsimson, whose battles with Stuyvesant are legendary, earned the well-merited sobriquet, "America's first fighting Jew." And let it be remembered that this occurred more than 120 years *before* the signing of the Declaration of Independence.

This is not to say that Jewish humor connected with the military is devoid of the usual sarcasm, ridicule and natural reluctance to be shot full of holes—a type of humor which was prevalent among the millions of Jewish immigrants who brought their jokes with them from the early 1880's to about 1905. Their jests revolved around the absurdity of fighting in defense of their persecutors, and need no explanation here. These jokes were passed on to their American-born children and, in diminishing numbers, to their grandchildren.

The armed services are uniquely suited to ridicule. The unyielding, sometimes asinine orders; the pomposity of young officers; the necessary harshness during basic training; the very real possibility of death in combat—these and many other aspects of military life find expression in humor. The witticisms are as old as recorded history and as modern as nuclear warfare.

William Chernof, a New Yorker who enlisted in the Israeli army upon the advent of the Six Day War, commented in the *California Jewish Voice:* "I had heard much about the vast arsenal of weapons the Soviets had given to the Arabs, but I found it to be only half-vast."

Among the personalities frequently selected as a target for military as well as political jokes was Senator Barry Goldwater, the 1964 Republican candidate for President. As a conservative and an Army Reserve officer, he was something of a distinctive individual. According to the humorists, "he sent only half a jet plane to Israel because he happens to be only half Jewish." "We know he's only part Jewish," grinned one observer. "If he was a full Jew, Arizona would be irrigated by now." No one, however, enjoyed a joke about his Jewishness or conservatism more than Goldwater himself. Asked what he would do if the Soviet Union were to attack the

United States, he laughed and said, "I'd order the wagons to form a circle."

The military humor of Israel and the United States is often as alike as two *knaidlach* in a pot of soup. In fact, a number of jokes have evolved to the point where they are now interrelated. One of them, not too surprisingly, concerns Goldwater's son, Congressman Barry Goldwater, Jr., of California. *Azoi:*

Baruch Goldwasser, Jr., who, like his father, is licensed to fly a plane, heard about the Yom Kippur attack on Israel, and immediately flew to Tel Aviv to offer his services as a fighter pilot. He was closely examined by an Air Force colonel, but, although he easily passed the flying test, he was unable to pass the oral examination. Sadly, he returned home.

"Those questions must have been mighty tough," sympathized the elder Goldwasser.

"The stiffest test you can imagine," agreed young Baruch. "That Israeli colonel asked me what I would do if I was flying a Phantom jet at an altitude of 60,000 feet, at a speed of 1,200 miles an hour, and my oxygen tank was riddled by enemy bullets. Then he asked me what I'd do if one of my engines caught fire and the wing crumpled at the same time. After that, he wanted to know what I'd do if my ejection system failed and I was caught way up there without a parachute."

"What did you answer?" asked papa Goldwasser.

"Answer? Who answered?" demanded Baruch. "From the questions alone I blacked out!"

If the reader will permit a little *haimisheh* philosophy, arguing for peace with the Arabs is like running uphill with your pants down. It seems to me that all this *tsuris* between Jews and Mohammedans could have been avoided if they had tried to settle their differences in a Christianlike manner. But who knows? Maybe that's what started it in the first place!

H.D.S.

The infamous Yom Kippur attack on Israel by Egyptian and Syrian military forces had just begun. An Arab pilot and his co-pilot had flown over the Suez Canal and were crossing a desolate area of the Gaza Strip, many miles from the nearest habitation, where they thought they would be safe from detection. But they were quickly spotted by the crew of an Israeli Phantom Jet and a few seconds later the Egyptian invader was shot down from the skies.

As they parachuted to earth in that isolated wasteland, the Arab pilot snarled to his co-pilot:

"Now you can see for yourself how these Jews are. Their rescue trucks are probably miles away at the airbase."

A college student, home for the weekend, was reading the papers when a news item caught his eye.

"Say, pop, here's some pleasant news for a change!" exclaimed the youth. "It says here that Russia's intercontinental missiles are so primitive that only half of their rockets would ever hit their targets."

"That's nice," the father replied dryly. "Maybe now half of us will be only half dead."

Sol Silvers, the sage of Syracuse, was arguing that the Secretary of Defense had made a grievous error by cutting the Pentagon's budget for social studies.

"Now," moaned Sol, "we'll never find out why people don't like to be killed."

Like all other peoples, the Jews have their quota of eternal optimists and infernal pessimists.

Take the case of the two Israeli soldiers, Adir and Adiva, who became lost in the Negev Desert during the last hostilities. Fortunately, they had an ample supply of water in their canteens, but they were totally without food, and quite hungry.

"We'll never make it," wailed Adir, the pessimist. "We'll die of starvation before we reach a settlement."

"Cheer up," said Adiva encouragingly, "we're bound to find something to eat very soon. With all this sand there must be some spinach around here."

One of the most interesting families of the Revolutionary War period was the Franks clan of Philadelphia. This Jewish family was unique in being predominantly Tory but, as if to atone, it produced several outstanding patriots and rebel officers, among them

Colonel David Salisbury Franks, nephew of Tory David Franks. Well known to General Washington and Benjamin Franklin, he was closest to Thomas Jefferson and was a dinner guest at the home of the Sage of Monticello on a number of occasions.

The subject of this story, however, is yet another member of the famous family: Isaac Franks, who was only seventeen when he enlisted in the rebel army shortly after the Battle of Lexington. Young Ike served under Washington in the Battle of Long Island, was wounded several times in battle and at one time was taken prisoner by the British. He continued in active service in various posts until illness forced his retirement in 1782. It was at his home in Germantown that President Washington resided when the capital was located in Philadelphia. Isaac sat for Gilbert Stuart, renowned for his portraits of Washington and other colonial leaders. In 1794, he was appointed a lieutenant-colonel in the Pennsylvania militia.

If all this sounds rather austere, let it be said that Isaac Franks was all too human and committed his fair share of blunders. His most comical misadventure, in fact, earned him a special niche in the humorous folklore of the people. It occurred shortly after the Battle of Long Island, when teenaged Ike was ordered, by General Washington himself, to repair the roof of a building in which arms and ammunition were being stored. The episode, contained in a formal request for sick leave, must surely be the most uproariously funny document in the archives of the United States Government. But let young Ike's request speak for itself:

8 September, 1776

Gen. G. Washington
Respected Sir,

As per my orders to make repairs on the roof of Company Magazine B, I arrived at the building at seven o'clock in the morning, only to find that the storm of the previous night had torn loose some of the cross-beams from the eaves. I therefore rigged up a beam with a pulley at the top of the building and hoisted up six heavy iron brackets and a hundredweight kegge of nails.

Having effectuated the repairs I saw that I had brought up more brackets than I needed and I had used only a pound or two of the nails. So I hoisted up the empty kegge again and tied the rope at the bottom. Then I went up to the roof and filled the kegge with the iron brackets and nails. After that I returned to the ground to unfasten the rope.

Unhappily, the kegge of brackets and nails were heavier than my own weight, and ere I could say Jack Robinson, the kegge started down and jerked me into the atmosphere. I made a quick decision to hang onto the rope, but halfway up I met the kegge coming down and received a mightly blow on the head and shoulders. I then continued the rest of the way to the top, banging my head against the beam and getting my fingers caught in the pulley.

The kegge hit the ground with such force that the impact busted the bottom, allowing those heavy brackets and the near-hundred-weight of nails to spill out. I was now heavier then the broken kegge and so I started down again at an uncommonly fast rate of descent. Halfway down I met the kegge coming up and received several painful injuries to my legs.

When I hit ground I landed on the spilled brackets and sharp nails which resulted in my sustaining a number of grievous cuts from the sharp points. At that moment, I fear I lost presence of mind because I released my hold on the rope. The kegge then came down again, giving me another blow on the head and putting me in the infirmary.

I respectfully request sick leave.

Cpl. Isaac Franks*

At the height of the unfortunate American involvement in East Asia, an owlish-looking young fellow approached the recruiting officer's desk.

"What must I do to get to Vietnam as soon as possible?" asked the prospective soldier.

"Well, first you have to sign up," explained the officer with a grin.

"Do volunteers have to take a physical?"

"Certainly."

"Darn—that'll slow me up. I want to get to the front lines right away."

"In any case, you'd have to go to boot camp for training," explained the officer. "Nobody goes where the fighting is until he's properly trained."

---

*Adapted from *The Franks of Philadelphia*, Joseph Mendes, Baltimore, 1871. Also see, *Jews in American Wars*, J. George Friedman and Louis A. Falk, published by the Jewish War Veterans of the US, 1942.

"Then at least will the army fly me to Vietnam? I'd hate to go by slow boat."

"What are you so all-fired anxious about?" growled the army man. "Don't you realize you could get killed or wounded over there?"

"So I get killed or wounded: What's the difference, as long as I'm getting all the glory?"

"Listen, buddy," snapped the recruiter, "why don't you go home and forget the whole thing? You're crazy!"

The young fellow abruptly reached into his coat pocket, pulled out a paper and thrust it into the army officer's hands.

"Here," he said quickly. "Just sign!"

It isn't generally known (and remember, you saw the news here first), but after the Six Day War with Israel, Egypt's Nasser slept like a baby . . .

He woke up every four hours and cried.

A tough career sergeant of the old school was haranguing a squad of new recruits.

"Tell me," he barked, "why shouldn't a private smoke during drill?"

"I agree!" blurted a teenage rookie from the Bronx. "Why shouldn't he?"

It is stated in the *Encyclopedia of Jewish Humor* that Israel, with a population of two-and-a-half million Jewish citizens, has two-and-a-half million presidents. A military twist has been added to that quip which warns all soldiers to refrain from giving advice to their superior officers.

During the *Yom Kippur* War an Israeli division was about to drive the Syrians out of the Golan Heights, but there seemed to be some dissension as to the best way to accomplish it. The arguments about strategy and tactics grew so intense that General Moshe Dayan issued this stern directive:

"For the time being, all born generals will henceforth take their orders from all *commissioned* generals!"

Did you ever stop to think that the 1967 conflict between Israel and the Arab states was the only six-day war in history to last for seven years?

"Them Jews in Israel ain't so tough," sneered the redneck anti-Semite. "Back in 1967 it took 'em six whole days to defeat only five Arab states!"

D-Day had finally arrived, and with it the invasion of the European mainland by the American and British armed forces. Grandpa Isaacson was reading an account of the military invasion in the *New York Times*. His command of the English language was fairly good, but he came upon a word that perplexed him.

"Lena," he addressed his granddaughter, "it says here that General Eisenhower's strategy was excellent. *Vos maynt* strategy?"

Fifteen-year-old Lena's knowledge of military terms was somewhat less than that of a West Pointer's. She bit into an apple to help her think, munched for a while, and then gave her studied opinion.

"Strategy," she said carefully, "is when you don't let the other side know you are out of ammunition, but keep right on firing!"

"The reason we beat those Nazis," averred George the armchair general, "is that our sophisticated communications system was fifty years ahead of theirs. American scientists crossed a carrier pigeon with a woodpecker. It not only delivered messages . . . it even knocked on the door!"

The young recruit had just finished basic training and was home on leave for a few days.

"They made me take three physical examinations," he grumbled to his mother. "All those doctors thought I was deformed because my uniform was a perfect fit!"

World War II had just broken out and teenager Phil Feldman was drafted. For six whole weeks his anxious mother waited to learn if her darling little boy was to be shipped overseas. Finally, one day, her telephone rang. It was Phil.

"Mama, I got great news!" the son declared jubilantly. "I'm coming home on a furlough."

"Oh, Phil, I'm so happy!" cried Mrs. Feldman, her voice brimming with joy. "When you're coming..." She stopped abruptly in mid-sentence as her son's message registered in her mind.

"You're coming home on a *what*?"

"On a furlough."

She let this information sink in before expressing her maternal concern.

"Listen, Phil," she said nervously, "about furloughs I know from nothing, but what's the matter you can't take a bus like everybody else?"

"Squads right!" yelled the sergeant.

"So now he admits it!" muttered the weary recruit.

Jimmy Bortnik of the Bronx confesses that he might have gone farther in life had he not been so cautious.

"Even as a college student I was afraid to burn my draft card like the other fellows did," he admitted. "I boiled it!"

The new recruit had been in the United States for only a short time but he had already adopted all the pugnacity for which native-born Americans are so well noted.

On his first day at boot camp, the drill sergeant, a sarcastic if not too original man, barked, "You there, Private! You'll be interested to know that the whole Company is out of step but you."

"*Nu*, so tell 'em," shrugged the recruit. "You're the one in charge!"

A moment of silent prayer, please, for the submarine sailor who insisted on sleeping with the windows open.

Anecdotes about ferocious drill sergeants have been told by generations of hapless soldiers. But the toughest one who ever came to our attention was the World War I sergeant who became somewhat annoyed with one of his recruits who had overslept. He lined up his squad and, as they stood at rigid attention, he singled out the offender.

"Private Goldberg, step forward!" he bellowed.

Private Goldberg stepped forward.

"All right, Sleepin' Beauty," the sergeant snarled, "from now on you're gonna *rise* an' *shine* at five ayem if I hafta hand-feed ya a pound of *yeast* an' a bucket of *shoe polish* every night!"

It was 1967 and Egypt's President Nasser was making threatening gestures against Israel. Young Joe Skolnik, in New York, decided to fly to the Holy Land in defense of his ancestral homeland. He was immediately inducted into the Israeli army and sent to basic training camp.

Skolnik's heart was in the right place but he missed New York's social life—specifically, girls. He knew there would be no chance of socializing until he got out of boot camp. Three months later, just when his training period was over and young Joe was preparing to visit the nearest town for the evening, the Six Day War broke out and he was suddenly shipped to the front lines.

Throughout that first day he fought the Arabs, and when the sun went down he approached his commanding officer.

"Captain, how's chances of letting me go to town this evening?"

The captain looked at his in amazement.

"Private Skolnik," he barked, "it may not have occurred to you but there happens to be a war on. A visit to town is considered a reward in this army, and nobody gets a reward around here unless he earns it. You want a pass to get to town? Then do something heroic. Make a victory of some kind—win a battle—take a few prisoners—capture enemy equipment—be a *mentsch*! Then maybe I'll consider it."

Skolnik shrugged. "That's okay by me," he said.

The next day Private Skolnik showed up at the captain's tent with an Arab tank. "How's this for a start?" he asked.

The captain's eyes bulged. "Marvelous! Wonderful!" he exclaimed. "Do that just once more and I'll give you *two* days off!"

"Fine!" said Skolnik. On the following day he drove up to the captain's camp headquarters with another Arab tank, bigger than the first one.

The captain was ecstatic. "Listen, Skolnik," he enthused, "if you can capture just one more tank I'll give you a weekend pass to town. How would you like that? Three whole days!"

Sure enough, on the third day of the war, Joe Skolnik came rolling in with the biggest tank the Arabs had gotten from the Soviet Union, completely equipped with every modern device the Russians had secretly developed.

The overjoyed captain was as good as his word. He sat down to fill out the promised weekend pass.

"Tell me something, Private Skolnik," said the officer as he was writing, "how in the world did you ever manage to bring back those enemy tanks?"

"Nothing to it," explained Skolnik. "I simply drive up to the border and holler, 'Any of you guys want a pass to town?' Then we just exchange tanks!"

A number of these examples of Jewish-American military jokes indicate that they can be traced back to the earliest of colonial times. But it would be remiss to end this chapter without reference to the almost legendary hero of World War I, Sergeant Sam Dreben, whose exploits inspired Runyon's epic poem about this unassuming but truly heroic little immigrant:*

> There's a story in the paper
> I just tossed upon the floor,
> That speaks of prejudice against the Jews;
> There's a photo on the table,
> There's a memory of the war
> And a man who never figures in the news . . .
> He is short and fat and funny,
> And the nose upon his face
> Is about the size of bugler Dugan's horn;
> But the grin that plays behind
> Is wide and soft and sunny,
> And he wore it from the day that he was born.

---

*Excerpted from *The Fighting Jew,* Damon Runyon, The New York World Press, 1918.

> There's a cross upon his chest —
> That's the D.S.C.
> The Croix de Guerre, the Militaire,
> These, too.
> And I think, thank God, Almighty,
> We will always have a few,
> Like Dreben,
> A Jew.

Sergeant Sam Dreben was a fugitive from the Czarist *pogroms* in his native Russia. Failing to adjust to civilian life in America, bored with the humdrum jobs he was offered, he joined the army and found his career. He battled Pancho Villa's troops in Mexico under "Black Jack" Pershing, fought in the Spanish-American War and in the Philippine insurrection, and later in the Boxer rebellion in China. So, life amid the grim sights and sounds of World War I was hardly a novelty to him.

But the squad of new recruits to which he was assigned had not been informed that this helpless-looking little man was the famous "Fighting Jew" who had been awarded the French Government's highest honors, or that he had won the Distinguished Service Cross when he single-handedly rushed a German machine gun nest and killed 23 of the 40 Germans, capturing the survivors. To the new group of soldiers, toward the end of the war, Sergeant Dreben was just a quiet fellow who was "short and fat and funny."

As Dreben stood before the new men, many audible comments were made about his small size and apparent ineptness. From the rear of the ranks a voice called out:

"And a little child shall lead them."

Seemingly undisturbed, Sam Dreben finished the business of the day. On the following morning, there appeared a notice on the bulletin board:

> Company A will take a 25-mile hike today with full packs. And a little child shall lead them . . . on a damn big horse!

> Sgt. S. Dreben

11

Shnooks and Shnookesses

Introduction

The only thing some people ever learn from experience is that they've goofed again. Send a *shnook* to find a greenhorn and he'll look for a man with a pistachio nose. He's the *shmo* who can barely peel his own bananas. His left hand never knows what his left hand is doing. He's the *shlemiel* who goes through life *pushing* doors marked "pull." If he's in politics, as many of them seem to be, he proves that the tongue is mightier than the mind by telling his audience, "If elected, I promise to grab the bull by the tail and look the situation squarely in the face."

From whence came this anomaly that spring from the loins of a people renowned for their spiritual wisdom and earthy sagacity? Before we answer the question, let us first define the descriptive words themselves. "*Shnook*" is a slang expression usually meaning an unimportant or stupid person; a variant of the Yiddish word *shmok*, itself a slang term, denoting a fool or dope. From *shmok* we additionally derive the truncated word *shmo*, and also *shmuck*, meaning an oaf or jerk. The most popular of the expressions in the people's literature and folk humor is the Yiddish word, *shlemiel*, an awkward or unlucky person for whom things never turn out right because of his native stupidity—his lack of what is called *Yiddishe saichel*.

In 1813, Adalbert von Chamisso's Peter Schlemihl gave added currency to the word and it has been popularized by generations of Jewish humorists ever since.

There is one other word, *shlimazl*, which is often confused with *shlemiel*. One is merely a cousin to the latter. The *shlemiel*, as we have seen, is a failure because of his *own* stupidity, but the *shli-*

mazl fails because his lucklessness is due to conditions beyond himself. *Shlimazl* is a Yiddish word denoting a bungler who suffers from unremitting bad luck. The distinction between the two is expressed in the classic rule of thumb: a *shlemiel* spills the soup, but it falls into the lap of the *shlimazl*. The former's misfortune is his character; the latter's his position or situation.

Unlike the oral folk humor of the Jewish people—that is, the stories and witticisms handed down by word of mouth from one generation to the next—the written tradition, beginning with the Bible itself, has dealt harshly with the fool. But, that harshness, let it be understood, was born of necessity.

The early Israelites, as a numerically small, agrarian community of people, situated as they were at the strategic crossroads between the merchants and traders of the West and the spice and silk suppliers of the Far East, surrounded by stronger states who coveted their strategic bit of land, simply could not afford to tolerate the fool in their midst. His actions, quite understandably, elicited concern, not humor.

Later, beset on all sides by religious persecutors, confronted by inquisitions and pogroms, faced with genocide by Hitler who added a race rationale to the religious canards, and the specter of cultural and spiritual extermination in the Soviet Union, the Jew had, literally, as a matter of survival, been forced by circumstances to place a premium on intelligence. Lacking arms, and short on diplomatic muscle in the international halls of power, his strength was in the armory of his mind. It still is.

Nevertheless, frowned upon or not, the fool *did* exist, and while the earliest stories about him may have been told furtively, the decibels have increased with the march of the centuries, reaching full resonance only in the past 150 years or so. The fool, or *shlemiel* or *shnook*—call him what you will—has not only been around for a long time, but has been celebrated in such tales as the *Wise Men of Chelm* and the exploits of that lovable con-man of yesteryear, Hershel Ostropolier, among others. He has also been a subject of humor among the *Chassidim* who found virtue in simplicity over cleverness. The *schlimazl*, too, has been affectionately remembered in Yiddish literature in such stories as the mystically haunting *Bontshe the Silent*, by I. L. Peretz.

In the United States, the growth and popularity of the *shlemiel* joke may be attributed in large part to our democratic institutions. Here, in the freer atmosphere of a society devoid of religious and social repression, the very idea of somehow being "different" than others has waned to a degree where it is now almost non-existent.

The American Jew can laugh unselfconsciously at the *shlemiel* who hoped to reach Europe by stowing away on a ship and found himself on the Staten Island ferry. Our amusement is tolerant because we know we are all prone to errors of judgment, even though the *shnook* makes a career of it. Most importantly, the American of the Jewish faith can enjoy the humor objectively rather than subjectively, because he accepts the fact that some Jews are not *Bar Mitzvah* until they are sixty.

And now that you know what makes your brother-in-law tick, I present to you a collection of familiar characters. As my dear departed papa used to say, "May you find pleasure in shaking hands with so many old faces."

H.D.S.

Dov the dogcatcher was a typical *shlemiel.* He knew he was supposed to catch dogs but he didn't know what he was supposed to catch them at.

This one is probably as old as Aladdin and his lamp, and a whole lot sillier, but it's worth repeating.

Mordecai, an aged junk dealer, was rummaging through the pile of odds and ends he had accumulated that day when he came upon an old, dirt-encrusted bottle. It looked interesting, so he began to rub off some of the dirt to make the bottle shine.

Suddenly, the cork popped out and from the neck of the bottle there arose a spiral of thick smoke. And when the smoke cleared away, there before him towered a huge figure attired in Arab robes.

Mordecai stepped back. "What are you doing in my store?" he asked nervously.

"I'm a genie," replied the figure.

"What kind of a name is Jeannie for a respectable man?"

"It's a magic Arabic name."

"Arabs I don't need in my store. Out!"

"But you don't understand. I can make your every wish come true. I can do anything and make anything you desire."

"All right, if you're so smart," Mordecai retorted, "make me a malted."

The genie instantly complied:

"Abracadabra, zippity-zoom—you're a malted!"

The new baby was not expected for another week, but a sudden onslaught of labor pains, spaced five minutes apart, made it clear that the delivery was imminent. Hurriedly, Sadie threw a few necessities into a suitcase and waited at the front door while her husband, Morris, brought the car out of the garage, wheels screeching.

"Hurry, hurry!" she pleaded. "The pains are now coming two minutes apart!"

"All right already, I'm hurrying!" Morris assured her. And indeed he was. The car was soon speeding at an unholy clip, the engine wide open and roaring. An excitable fellow under normal circumstances, he was now so nervous that he lost control and the car careened off the highway, knocking them both unconscious.

When Morris finally awoke in the hospital, only dimly aware of what happened, he was aghast to learn that he had been unconscious for the past ten days. His first thoughts were of his wife.

"Sadie," he called anxiously. "How's my Sadie? Is she okay? Did she have the baby?"

"Take it easy—take it easy," advised the doctor. "Everything is under control. Your wife is fine. In fact, she not only had a baby—she gave birth to twins! A boy and a girl, no less."

"*Twins!*" Morris breathed ecstatically. "How marvelous!"

"But," added the doctor, "you were so sick that for a while we didn't think *you* would make it. We had to call your brother in to name the babies. We needed the names for the *bris* and the birth certificates."

"My brother! That *shlemiel*? He's a know-nothing—an empty-head! So what did he name my little girl?"

"He named your little girl Denise."

"Hey, that's not too bad. I like that. Denise is a pretty name. And what did he name my little boy?"

The doctor shrugged and said: "He named your little boy De Nephew!"

The story, *Bye-bye Feival*, was probably told by the ancient Israelites when the first travelers and explorers set off on camels across the uncharted deserts. Perhaps another variant was told by the first Jewish settlers to reach the Dutch colony of New Amsterdam in 1654. The following is the 20th century version.

Feival, the first Jewish astronaut, has passed beyond the outermost planet of the solar system, his rocket ship now hurtling into the farthest reaches of deep space. Back on Earth, the world's Jewish community waited breathlessly for his return. Now, at last, the Jews would be able to smile indulgently at the comparatively puny efforts of the *goyishe* astronauts who had not even reached Mars.

Feival, in his space ship, was now speeding high above the crescent of the Big Dipper and had long since lost radio contact with Earth. Far below, trillions of miles away, the outlines of the familiar Little Dipper faded from sight and disappeared. To his left, he could see what appeared to be a bright nova on some star he had never known existed. To his right, he observed whole new systems of strange constellations as he sped past the rim of the Milky Way and completely out of the galaxy. Now he was in a deep black void, his ship approaching the speed of light as all gravity was left far behind in the mysterious nothingness of outer space.

"Now let me think," muttered Feival. "In which direction was I headed?"

Herman, the famous private-eye, arrived at the scene of the crime. His steel-trap mind evaluated the clues with one sweeping glance.

"Gentlemen," he announced, "this was both an inside and an outside job. The window's broken on both sides."

For more than a week, Barney had been having difficulties with his vision, so he went to see his family physician.

"Doctor, something's wrong with my eyesight," complained the troubled patient. "For ten days I've been seeing blue and gold spots before my eyes."

"Have you seen an oculist yet?" asked the doctor.

"N-no," said Barney uncertainly. "Just blue and gold spots."

It was Sunday morning, but instead of sleeping an hour or so later as he usually did, Max sat upright in bed and groaned. The sound awakened his wife.

"Boy, did I have a nightmare," he muttered.

"Everybody gets bad dreams once in a while," said his wife soothingly. "Just forget it."

"I can't, Bertha."

"What was so bad about this nightmare?"

"It was like this: I'm driving along on the Parkway with you and your papa. All of a sudden I'm hearing a siren and when I stop the car a policeman comes up to me and he said 'Congratulations, Max, you just won $500 because you are the millionth driver on this new stretch of road.'"

Bertha stared at him, wide-eyes. "By you that's a bad dream?"

"Wait, I'm not finished. So I'm answering the policeman, 'With the $500 I'll take driving lessons and maybe get a driver's license.'"

"My goodness, what kind of an answer is that?" sympathized Bertha.

"That's nothing," said Max, his voice turning accusatory. "So you had to open your big mouth and say, 'Mr. Policeman, you shouldn't believe a word my Max is saying. He's all *shikkered* up!'"

"I did not!" retorted Bertha defensively.

"Yes, you did," was Max's bitter reply. "But your papa, in the back seat, really fixed me good. He hollers out to the policeman, 'I knew we wouldn't get far in this stolen car!'"

What happens when a man, raised in primitive surroundings, first comes to grips with the modern machine age? Hark to the tale of one such wandering soul, Ben-Ami Shlepper, newly arrived with his wife and son in the United States from a remote *shtetl* in the Pale of Settlement.

Ben-Ami was lucky enough to find a job in the shipping department of Bertram's Buttons & Bows, on lower Second Avenue. For a few days everything went swimmingly for good-natured Ben-Ami, but then a problem arose. He began to report late for work. After he had failed to arrive on time for several mornings inn a row, Bertram, the boss, suggested that Ben-Ami buy an alarm clock. But the poor immigrant had never heard of such a new-fangled contraption, let alone see or use one.

"Come along with me," said Bertram that afternoon at quitting time. He led the greenhorn to a department store, picked out an alarm clock and explained the general plan of its workings to his new employee.

For several days, the clock behaved perfectly. But a week or so later, Ben-Ami's little son, being of an inquiring turn of mind, opened the case to study the device during his father's absence. As small boys will, he removed some important parts which he forgot to put back. Next morning, the bell failed to ring and Ben-Ami overslept.

He couldn't understand why the clock had betrayed him. On his own account he undertook an investigation. He took the back off the clock, and there, mixed up with the machinery, he discovered the mortal remains of a large cockroach.

"Aha!" exclaimed Ben-Ami. "No wonder the clock wouldn't run. The engineer is dead!"

"*Aii,* my feet are killing me!" lamented unhappy grandpa. "I got up on the wrong side of the bed this morning, and all day I'm walking around in my wife's high-heeled slippers."

A man showed up at Dr. Kvetchmir's office. He stopped at the receptionist's desk and politely removed his hat, revealing a chrysanthemum growing from the top of his head.

"I would like to see Dr. Kvetchmir," he said.

"What about?" asked the receptionist.

They had met only two weeks earlier and their romance was beginning to blossom like a lovely flower. But the girl was troubled. She had a problem with her vision and was fearful of his reaction. Now the time had come for her to face the matter squarely.

"Darling," murmured the sweet young thing hesitantly, "could you love me in spite of myopia?"

"I don't know," he replied, anxiety showing in his face. "What's your opia look like?"

Olga Yosseloff, co-starring in the Los Angeles production, *My Fair Sadie,* started out for the theatre in plenty of time, but on the way her car developed engine trouble. It took a local garage mechanic a half hour to fix it, and now she was somewhat late. Afraid that she would not reach her destination by curtain time, she took a shortcut and found herself going the wrong way on a one-way street. A siren quickly sounded behind her and, in the rear-view mirror she caught sight of a patrol car. She pulled over to the curb and stopped.

"Lady," the policeman began sarcastically, "do you have any idea where you're going?"

"To the theatre," replied Olga, "but I'm sure it's too late. Everybody else seems to be going home!"

"I always have trouble remembering three things," commented the absent-minded professor: "Names, faces and—hmm—now what was that third thing again?"

Chauncey DePlotkin was suffering from the heartbreak of psoriasis. After vainly trying the usual patent medicines sold over the counter, he finally consulted a doctor and was given a prescription for medicine and told how and when to take it.

That evening, at home, Chauncey's wife was astonished to see her husband swallow a spoonful of the medicine, race out of the house and dash around the block. When he returned, he was so exhausted that he flopped down onto the bed and fought to catch his breath. On the second evening, he repeated the performance, gulping down the medicine, galloping around the block and returning home a few minutes later. On the third evening, he changed his tactics. This time he took his medicine as usual, but instead of racing he began to skip around the room with all the grace of a prancing pachyderm.

The wife could stand it no longer.

"Chauncey," she cried, "what in the world are you doing—racing around the block and jumping about like that? Have you lost your mind?"

"Of course not," replied the weary hubby. "I'm just following the doctor's orders. He told me to take my medicine two nights running and to skip the third night!"

The sign in the theatre's box-office window read: Service Men—90¢.

Anita Nahr went up to the window, laid down a five dollar bill and said, "I'll take two marines, two sailors and a paratrooper."

The judge looked down upon the quaking little man who stood at the bar of justice.

"Is this the first time you've been up before me?" he barked.

"I don't know, your honor," gulped the little guy, almost collapsing with fright. "What time do you get up?"

Senator Javits of New York was in England on one of those fact-finding junkets so early beloved by congressmen.

A constituent happened to be in Washington, D.C. and decided to stop in and see his senator. After wandering around the cavernous Senate Office Building for a while, he finally located the proper office and introduced himself.

"I'm sorry," said the secretary, "but Senator Javits has gone to the United Kingdom."

"Oh, my goodness!" exclaimed the visitor, clearly taken aback. "Is it too late to send flowers?"

A timid-looking young lady, the soul of honesty, was in the United Nations Building, applying for a job as U.S. translator. She was handed an application blank which she proceeded to fill out, thus and likewise:

Name: Nadine Berman
Age: 24
Present Position: Sitting down
Sex: Only once, at Lake Placid

Myron, a kibitzer, was strolling down Fairfax Avenue in Los Angeles when he came to the little diner owned by his friend Abe. Thinking to amuse himself, he stepped inside and went into the kitchen where Abe was making preparations for the dinner hour.

"Mind if I look at this?" asked Myron, picking up a slice of pastrami and, with seeming absent-mindedness, popping it into his mouth. His eyes fell on the pickle barrel. He fished around in the brine and picked one out. "Hmm, very nice. Mind if I look at this pickle?" he repeated, popping the pickle into his mouth.

Abe, watching his friend from a corner of his eye, retrieved a pan of baked potatoes from the oven, but said nothing.

Myron made a grab for one of the potatoes. "Mind if I have a look at this?" he asked innocently. But the potato was smoking hot and, with a yelp of pain, he dropped it.

"Burned you, didn't it?" asked Abe, grinning.

"No, it didn't," snapped Myron, ever unwilling to be on the losing end of a joke. "After all, how long does it take to look at a potato?"

The surly cop on the corner observed Vogel as he dashed across the street in the face of the oncoming traffic.

"What's the matter with you?" rasped the policeman, pointing to the *Don't Walk* sign. "Can't you read plain English?"

"I'm sorry, officer," replied Vogel, embarrassed. "But I thought it was just propaganda from the bus company."

Should you be one of those sensitive souls who cry at sad movies, consider yourself warned in advance: This one's a real hankie-wringer.

It was a bitter cold day in January. The streets were covered with hard-packed snow, and under the snow was a film of solid ice. Shivering, her lips blue with the cold, Lilith Eisenberg, the Jackson Heights librarian, was hurrying home to her husband and cozy apartment. On the way she passed a pet shop and, there in the window, she saw the sweetest little white rabbit she had ever seen in her life. She couldn't help but stop to look at it. The rabbit, looking out, stood up on its hind legs, pawing at the window as though begging her to take it home.

Lilith's resistance broke down completely. She went inside and bought the little bunny.

With her precious, quivering prize snuggled against her for warmth inside her coat, the young lady hurried on her way. Suddenly she slipped on the icy pavement. Her feet flew out from beneath her and she fell heavily to the sidewalk. Slightly stunned, she opened her coat and, to her horror, she found that she had crushed the poor little rabbit to death. Aghast at the accident, Lilith burst into tears.

At that moment, Herman the mortician rounded the corner and took in the scene with one sweeping glance. He noted the young woman lying on the sidewalk, sobbing her heart out, and the creature lying dead inside her open coat. He felt the need to comfort her somehow.

"Lady, please don't cry," he murmured, his voice full of sympathy. "It wouldn't have been normal anyway. Look at those ears!"

Here is a gem told by Bernard Baruch, sometime in 1918 or 1919.

In western New York, on the lower edge of the Adirondack region, there used to be a guide over in the mountains who, being reckless by nature, made a specialty of escorting city sportsmen into the wilderness during the hunting season. Any North Woods veteran will tell you this is a hazardous calling. Moreover, the mortality figures prove it. Green sportsmen invade the tall timber carrying high-power rifles and shoot at everything they see moving in the bushes. The result is that a few of them kill one another and the majority destroy their guides, even though the latter, for self-protection, wear red shirts and red hats and white neckerchiefs. It is a true state of affairs these days just as it was when this incident occurred.

This particular guide had several close calls. Finally, when a bullet had ripped his shoulder and another had blown his cap off, he had an inspiration. He made a suit of awning cloth of alternate white and blue stripes. But the first time he wore the costume they brought him home again—bored through and through. As he emerged from a thicket, a city gunner, one Arthur Blumenthal, stationed across a clearing had plugged him.

At the inquest, the remorseful Mr. Blumenthal was introduced as a witness.

"Now look here," said the coroner, "of course nobody accuses you of killing poor Jim intentionally. But it does seem curious to me—and I imagine it strikes everyone else in this room the same way—that when Jim was in striped clothes which could be seen a mile away, you, standing not a hundred yards distant, should mistake him for a deer."

"I didn't mistake him for a deer," said Blumenthal unhappily. "I thought he was a zebra."

12

Exaggerators, Distorters and Plain Liars

Introduction

Humor is truth in an intoxicated condition; a good reason why opera can lie, but seldom a comic opera. It may be attributed to the fact that humor is a gift of the heart, not the mind.

The bearer of false tales wears many hats. There is the teller of tall stories who spins his exuberant yarns for the pure enjoyment it affords. He's the one who will stoutly maintain that he caught a fish that was so big it took two men to carry the photograph.

Then there's the articulator of the white lie, often a compassionate person who adheres to the ancient Jewish maxim: "Better to tell a little lie that hurts no one, than a big truth that breaks someone's heart."

There is also the charming exaggerator or distorter who uses wild flights of allegory and imagery to convey his thoughts. This fellow isn't actually a liar—he's just gifted with a hyperactive imagination. If he happens to be an actor, he'll say, "I starred in a play titled *Oh, Sugar*, a musical spoof of diabetes." He loves the overstatement, and will unabashedly claim that he went to see an adult film where even the popcorn was over 18 years old. And he is often addicted to the understatement, as well. "I left my little home town in Montana," he will solemnly declare, "because it was a hotbed of tranquillity." This amusing raconteur gets his message across by means of hyperbole. Ask him if his wife is as pretty as ever, and he'll reply, "Yes, but it takes her a half-hour longer." The statement is not quite as false as it initially sounds.

And not to be ignored is the chronic liar, an individual who is usually a victim of his own sense of inferiority. In order to capture the admiration and applause of others, he embellishes his stories to attract attention to himself, consequently boosting his self-esteem. He often realizes his shortcoming, but he is like a rider on a runaway horse, desperately hanging on because he is afraid to get off. He epitomizes the difference between a liar and a damn liar.

Nevertheless, exaggeration has its supporters—especially in the realm of art. In his *Critic and the Drama*, George Jean Nathan wrote: "Art is a gross exaggeration of natural beauty: there never was a woman so beautiful as the Venus di Milo, or the song of a nightingale so beautiful as Ludwig von Beethoven's . . . or human speech so beautiful as Shakespeare's." However, Nathan himself exaggerates.

It would be nice to say that no hyperbole exists in Jewish literature—nice, but untrue. We find this statement in the Apocrypha, for example: "Each vine shall yield a thousand branches, each branch a thousand clusters, each cluster a thousand grapes, and each grape a barrel of wine." Gentlemen! Gentlemen!

On a somewhat grander scale, we find this enthusiastic description in the hallowed pages of the Talmud: "There were 365 thoroughfares in the great city of Rome, and each had 365 palaces; each palace had 365 stories, and each story had enough food for the whole world." All right already: *enough*!

But there are numerous references in the Bible and in Jewish traditional writings that take a dim view of the liar. "Lying lips are an abomination to the Lord," is one. Or, "The Messiah will come only when the world will realize that to speak an untruth is adultery," is a concept we are reminded of by the sages of old.

Yet, on the whole, the people's literature is surprisingly tolerant of the lie when there seems to be reasonable cause. Mendele, in 1878, for example, made the witty and unarguable assertion, "He who doesn't lie can't be a marriage broker." In the Talmud, we are politely informed: "You may tell an untruth in the interests of peace." And in the 12th century, anticipating Freud by some 700 years, Ibn Izra advanced his own unique theory for posterity: "People tend to lie because of impotence," he asserted. Well it takes all kinds . . .

The late author, Benjamin Di Casseres, valiantly sprang to the defense of the much-maligned fabricator. "The art of survival," he wrote in his *Fantasia Impromptu*, "is the art of lying to yourself, heroically, continuously, creatively. The senses lie to the mind; the mind lies to the senses. The truth-seeker is a liar; he is hunting for happiness, not truth." But before you accept Casseres' opinion at face value, hark to the admonition of Maimonides who wrote in his book, *Iggeret Teman,* "Do not consider it proof just because it is written in books, for a liar who will deceive with his tongue will not hesitate to do the same with his pen."

There are scores of American-Jewish "liar jokes" which follow the light-hearted banter of Old World Jewry, and which are still told as though the Jews did not have a care in the world. Among those anecdotes which have survived in somewhat altered form is this brief illustration: A Second Avenue dealer in antiques was using all his powers of persuasion to sell a pocket watch to a wealthy customer.

"This marvelous timepiece originally belonged to the great Maimonides himself," enthused the dealer. "He used this very watch to count the pulse-beats of his patients. A servant stole it and brought it to this country."

Obviously, that little story needed no alterations, except for the locale, because of its absurdity. Maimonides lived in the 12th century and there were no pocket watches in his day. The pulse was unknown: William Harvey discovered the circulation of the blood in the year 1628. And, of course, America was not discovered until some 300 years after Maimonides' death. But the tale of the dealer and the watch is only one of many that have remained virtually unchanged from its original European telling by the immigrants who flocked to these shores at the turn of the century.

The truly clever joke of universal appeal may be adapted and adopted, but seldom is forgotten. In any case, it is rather unseemly to criticize the dealer in a society where parents always demand that their children tell the truth, the whole truth, and nothing but the truth—except when there are visitors present.

And, lest we end this introduction on too frivolous a note, you are reminded of the stern injunction: Thou shalt not bear false witness against thy neighbor—without good reason.

H.D.S.

Little Alma, a pupil in the first grade, arrived home from school all out of breath.

"Daddy, daddy," she cried, her eyes sparkling with excitement, "we had our very first fire drill today!"

"That's good, *shayneh,*" he said, smiling. "I believe in fire drills. Why, I once almost died in a fire."

"Ooh, tell me."

"Well, it was like this: I fell into a great big vat of chicken soup. So I climbed on top of the *knaidlach* to keep from drowning and I hollered 'fire' at the top of my lungs."

"*Fire?*" exclaimed Alma. "Was there a fire, too?"

"No," grinned her father, patting her curls, "but who'd have helped me if I yelled 'chicken soup'!?"

The Wassermans were watching the six o'clock news on television. A fire had erupted in a downtown hotel and a number of guests had been injured.

"Those people shouldn't have panicked," observed Mr. Wasserman. "I remember the time I was once caught in a bad fire but I kept my head."

"You were in a bad fire?" echoed his wife. "For thirty years we're married but this I'm hearing for the first time. Where did it happen?"

"Back in Vilna, when I was a young fellow, just before I came to this country. I was working in a soap factory when all of a sudden the whole building went up in flames. I was the only one who escaped."

Mrs. Wasserman sighed. 'Trapped again, after all these years.' She should have known that her husband was off on one of his "stories." But she bravely played out the game.

"All right, I give up. So how did you escape from the soap factory?"

"Nothing to it," he grinned. "I climbed up on the roof and just waited for the firemen to come and shpritz water on the flames. When the soap bubbles reached up to where I was I just climbed down on the lather."

Kitzel, Karp and Kornblum were arguing as to who was the richest man in the world.

"It has to be Rothschild," said Kitzel. "I heard that he has a different dentist for each tooth. And cars—let me tell you: Rothschild has four Rolls Royces—one for each direction. And he has a station wagon that's bigger than the station. That guy doesn't even need to have his cars air conditioned. He just keeps a half-dozen cold ones in his freezer."

"Rothschild is a rich man—no question about it," agreed Karp, "but the Strausses are richer. Old man Strauss gave his six-year-old grandson a cowboy outfit for a birthday present—

110,000 acres, 2,000 head of cattle and 500 horses. I tell you, when this guy Strauss cashes a check, the bank bounces. Come to think of it, the finance companies owe *him* money!"

Kornblum dismissed his friends' arguments with an airy wave of his hand.

"Rothschild and Strauss are suffering from poverty compared to Solomon Guggenheim," he said lightly. "He doesn't count his money like those other two—he weighs it. The Chase National Bank has a branch office in his living room. Did you know that Guggenheim owns an unlisted telephone company? Believe me, he keeps Swiss money in an American bank. And you're talking about Rothschild's and Strauss's cars! I don't even know why you mentioned those welfare cases. Guggenheim buys only split-level Cadillacs, and he takes his change in Volkswagens. Even his bicycle is made by Lincoln Continental."

Kitzel and Karp surrendered before the onslaught.

"All right, Guggenheim is the richest," cried Karp, completely overwhelmed. "Just so he remembers that money isn't just for show. It should help others and also buy him some personal comforts, too."

"It does," replied Kornblum, enjoying his conquest. "The Guggenheim Foundation takes care of his philanthropies, and as to his personal comforts, the man has two armchairs—one for each arm. And you should see his bathroom! It has two tubs—one for rinsing. And each tub has three faucets," concluded Kornblum triumphantly, "hot, cold and luke!"

Karl Carlinsky, the same young gentleman from New England who won a Distinguished Service Cross in the Spanish-American War, had a peculiarity of character that remained with him until the day he died in 1929: Carlinsky could not stand to be bested in *anything!* No doubt there were psychological reasons for this quirk in his otherwise splendid nature, but that is not our concern. He was, in fact, a remarkably able man and, in his later years, he established the K-T Coal Mining Company and a K-T Railroad spur-line on the border of Kentucky and Tennessee.

There was one time, however, when he came perilously close to living in the shadow of someone else's greatness. It happened when he first migrated to the foothills of the Tennessee mountains from his native city of Newport, Rhode Island.

In a small town some fifty miles from Memphis, there resided a native whose claim to distinction lay in three things—his appetite, his capacity and his digestion. He played no favorites in the food line; he could and did eat anything that was edible, and in incredible quantities. But if he liked one thing a little better than anything else, that thing was the canned oyster—the kind that, 75 or so years ago, was packed in a circular can with a bull's head on the label, and which was customarily anointed with pepper sauce before being consumed.

Carlinsky, during a visit to the general store, was informed that the gluttonous one could do away with twenty cans of the bivalves. Immediately, he sensed a challenge to his sense of superiority. He knew he could not equal that kind of prodigious eating, but he also doubted the story. In the hope of testing the other man's storage facilities and, of course, reasserting his own status—at least to himself—he challenged the man to prove his claims. A group of hangers-on at the store formed a pool, each contributing half a dollar. The entire amount was invested in cove oysters and then the champion was invited to come to the general store on an appointed afternoon and show what he could do. He came before an awe-stricken audience and he showed. Oh, how he showed!

Disdaining all the tools prescribed by civilized etiquette, he swallowed down the provided oysters, juice and all, from the container. Almost before the storekeeper could open a fresh can, he had emptied the one opened a minute earlier. In half an hour the supply on the shelves had vanished and still the marvel showed no evidence of being satiated. He scooped up a few errant oysters which had lodged in his whiskers and in the opening of his waistcoat and sent them on their way to join their brethren. Then he remarked:

"Wal, sence thar don't 'pear to be no more eatin' goin' on I better be puttin' out fer home—it's gettin' on to'rd supper time."

Carlinsky and one of the other contributors to the purse drifted out on the porch to watch his slouching figure disappear in the dusk. For awhile they stood in silence. Then the local man said:

"Tain't no doubt about it—I reckon Gabe Coombs is shorely the champeen eater of all creation. He's the most important man hereabouts—that's fer shore."

Carlinsky, on the verge of impending ego-deflation, gave him a sour look but could think of nothing to say.

"I wonder how many cove oysters could he of et in one sittin'?" speculated the rural one. He mulled the idea in his mind for awhile and then added: "I'll bet he could eat all the oysters in the world."

It was an interesting theory and they were soon joined by the others who drifted out of the store to join the conversation.

At last! Here was Carl Carlinsky's opportunity to redeem himself in the eyes of his beholders.

"Do you have any idea how many oysters there are in the world?" he demanded.

The locals stared at each other blankly.

"More'n you and us could pay fer," opined one of the group.

"Not necessarily," countered Carlinsky. "If Gabe Coombs can eat all the oysters in the world, I am wealthy enough to pay for them. But if he is unable to finish them—and I mean each and every one—then you will pay me double the cost."

Startled, they shuffled their feet and whispered to each other, but could find little enthusiasm for so gigantic a bet. But to ease the uncertainty, one of them asked:

"How many oysters are there in the world?"

"There are in this world," began Carlinsky, his voice ringing with triumphant authority, "three billion, one hundred and eighteen million, seven hundred and ninety-four thousand, six hundred and eighty-two oysters alive at this very moment."

The hillbillies stared at him, open-mouthed.

"And what's more," added Carlinsky in his hour of glory, "I counted them twice—once last month and again this past Tuesday!"

The judge on the bench fixed a cold eye upon the defendant at the bar. "Why did you assault the plaintiff?" he asked sternly.

"Because he called me a liar, that's why!" stated the accused.

"Is that true?" inquired the judge, turning to the battered victim.

"Sure it's true," said the plaintiff. "I called him a liar because that's what he is, and I can prove it."

"What have you to say about that?" asked his honor of the defendant.

"That's got nothing to do with the case," came the heated retort. "All right, so I'm a liar, but what's the matter—I don't have a right to be sensitive about it?"

An auctioneer, opines Herman the hermit of Hester Street, is a man who can sell nothing for something to a buyer who is looking for something for nothing.

There's no use you should keep asking me for details," said the *yenta* with high moral purpose in her tones. "In fact, I already told you more than I heard myself!"

Fun from our Folklore Files:
Nearly everyone who went to Yellowstone National Park in the old days remembers—or should remember—Petrified Petrovsky. He was a picturesque man and his language was just as colorful. P.P. was born in New York but was taken to Arizona as a small child and was inordinately proud of the natural beauty of the state where he had grown to manhood . . . prouder even than he was of the beauties of Yellowstone, of which he was very proud indeed.

Petrified Petrovsky acquired his sobriquet because of a comment he made to a woman many long years ago. One day, so the folklorists tell us, he was decanting upon the marvels of Arizona's Petrified Forest.

"Is it really so very remarkable?" asked a lady visitor.

"Madam," said Petrovsky, "in the whole world there's nothing like it. It's the most petrified place there is. Believe me—why should I lie to a perfect stranger?—I once saw a petrified bird sitting on a petrified limb high up on top of a petrified tree. And what was that little petrified bird on that petrified limb in that petrified tree doing? It was singing a petrified song!"

Hollywood: The free-swinging city where some old-fashioned mothers who can remember their husband's first kiss, now have daughters who can't even remember their first husbands.

Anna's husband was scolded by a policeman for jaywalking, and the matter might have ended there without further incident, but he protested his innocence so vehemently that he was taken into custody. In court, he repeated his hot-tempered performance for the judge and wound up with a ten day jail sentence for contempt.

Anna, however, could not bring herself to tell anyone that she had married such a *shlemiel,* so she concocted a little white lie to explain his absence.

"My husband spent the last ten days in a revolving door," she said. "He was looking for the doorknob."

Al, Jake and Bill were discussing the merits—or rather the demerits—of their respective girlfriends.

"What can you do with a girl who can't even spell DDT?" groaned Al. "Her own father once told me she was ten before she learned to wave bye-bye."

"You're lucky to have such a genius," commented Jake. "My girl was flattered when the doctor told her she had acute appendicitis. Even as a kid, they had to keep her in summer school all winter. The poor girl needed a tutor just to pass recess."

"Listen, your girlfriends are Einsteins compared to mine," observed Bill. "How would you like to have a sweetheart who goes to the zoo to see Christmas seals? Only last week a fortune teller embarrassed us when he read my girl's mind for half price."

Bill paused reflectively. "I could forgive any of those things," he concluded with a sign. "But can you imagine being married to someone who runs after a street sprinkler for three blocks to tell the driver his truck is leaking?"

"Not that I'm making fun of her baby," declared the jealous *yenteh,* "but when she takes it out for an airing, people come up to her and say, "Oh, what a beautiful baby carriage!"

Old Moishe, an octogenarian who had long since retired from the silk factoring business, was hardly a man of mystery. Yet, there were a few things about his past, especially those events dating back to his youth, about which he would not speak. Rumor had it that he might not have been as scrupulously honest as he was in his later life. For example, in the corner of his living room was a huge grandfather's clock he had once brought home without a word of explanation. That was more than half-a-century ago, but no one, not even the closest members of his family, ever learned how he had come by the valuable antique, and old Moishe had vowed to take the secret with him to the grave. They suspected that he had not purchased it, but they did not even know that for a certainty.

One evening, during the *Chanukah* holidays, his old friend, Rabbi Jacobson, dropped in for a chat. As they were sipping a glass of festive wine, the rabbi happened to think about that big clock.

"Moishe, it has been many years since you were young and perhaps a little wild," he began. "Now that you are older, wise, and a citizen in good standing, why not satisfy my curiosity and tell me how you got that clock?"

"Very well," agreed Moishe, to the rabbi's great surprise. "It happened almost sixty years ago. I remember it well because it was the day before Passover and in my house there was nothing but poverty. There were no matzohs, no eggs, no meat—nothing! My bride was in tears and I was simply desperate. What to do?"

"Yes, yes! Go on!" urged the rabbi as Moishe paused to collect his thoughts.

"I went to the marketplace and wandered aimlessly about, praying for a miracle from heaven. Suddenly, a richly adorned carriage pulled up in front of me and a lady stepped out to enter one of the stores. She was dressed in beautiful satins and wore diamonds and jewels such as I had never seen before."

Again, Moishe lapsed into reverie and the rabbi, bursting with curiosity, begged him to continue.

"Well, as she passed me, the lady dropped her silk handkerchief, the four corners of which were tied together so as to make a tiny bundle. It fell right at my feet. 'Oh Lord,' I prayed, 'help me in this, my hour of need!' And the Almighty heard my prayers. I picked up that little bundle and opened it. There, in my very own hands, were ten gold coins, each worth a hundred dollars. I rushed home with an armload of food and from that very day my wife and I prospered."

"Is that all?" exclaimed the rabbi.

"That's all."

"But how about that enormous grandfather's clock?"

"Oh, the clock," added old Moishe innocently. "That was in the handkerchief also."

13

So Sue Me!

Introduction

Some 4,000 years ago, a Hebrew leader, not divine or perfect, but closer to God than other men, was commanded to promulgate the Law; not only the Ten Commandments, but the whole body of criminal and civil law as well. That man's name was Moses. It was he, the architect of the Hebrew people, who laid the foundation of a monotheistic religion based on the principles of love and justice. The great concern of this titan was to establish a social state in which perpetual poverty and degrading want would be unknown. Since that moment, when he descended from Mt. Sinai with his precious tablets, the influence of Moses has spread to all humanity.

Many Jews have been drawn toward the legal profession and who can doubt that Grandpa Moses is somewhat responsible. Yet, despite its noble roots, neither the profession nor the professors of the profession were held to be sacrosanct by their co-religionists. A people who can joke about their mothers, for instance, may almost be expected to aim barbs at mere lawyers—the Cardozas and the Frankfurters and the Brandeises and the Goldbergs and the Kissingers notwithstanding. Satire and irony tend to remind us that lawyers are also human and that ridicule serves the useful purpose of calling attention to correcting unjust or unnecessary legislation. Ludwig Bourne pointed this out in his jocular comment: "If nature had as many laws as the state, God Himself could not reign over it."

Hostility, whether conscious or subconscious, furnished yet another reason for the plethora of jokes about lawyers and the law in general. There are times when our fate, our fortune, occasionally even our personal freedom, depend upon the sagacity and knowledge of lawyers, as well as the decisions of judges and juries. The hostility which some of us feel is actually directed at the figure of stern, unbending authority. Should our experience in court be unpleasant, our animosity is intensified. It remains in our psyche long after the ordeal itself is but a faded memory, and is directed at the law in general rather than at a specific case or personality. And, like the beneficial result that comes from lancing a festering boil, we feel a sense of relief when our resentment is released in the form of derisive laughter.

"Lawyers are just like physicians," observed Sholom Aleichem in *Finf un Zibtzig Toisnt:* "what one says, the other contradicts." The reason, however, may not be due solely to contrariness, if we can believe Judith T. Younger, Dean of the Syracuse University Law School, who said, "Most law students don't even know how to use commas, sentences or paragraphs; they haven't the foggiest notion of how to spell ... Great men of the law speak brilliantly and beautifully, but most law students I've come in contact with— 75 percent of them—are illiterate. Nationwide, I'd say that 50 to 75 percent would be an accurate estimate." So the next time someone bitterly complains that he lost his case because of a stupid lawyer, just remember Dean Younger's value judgment, nod sympathetically and tell him you understand.

Fortunately, most lawyers have a keen sense of humor. They need it in their profession. *The California Law Review* once told of the lawyer who informed a siren, "My client wants you and himself to go your separate ways, and he's willing to pay you ten cents a mile." *The New York Law Review*, not especially noted for its comical articles, defined a jury as "the only thing that doesn't work right when it's fixed." In Chicago, the *Cook County Law Journal* related the story about the woman who told eleven exasperated male jurors, "If you men weren't so stubborn we could all go home." And the late Oscar Levant defined a lawyer as "a man who helps you get what's coming to him."

H.D.S.

Here is an unalloyed golden nugget of early Jewish Americana dealing with the high adventures of a "Jewish Indian" of bygone days—an anecdote that gives lusty voice to the expression popular in the 19th century: "The law is a ass." The subject of our present story is Edward Kantor, in later life a favorite of many Indians, who was accepted into their tribe and was known to them as "Bosh-bish-gay-bish-gon-sen," the Indian name for "firecracker," and a name he laughingly described as "more Jewish-sounding than my own."

Young Eddie was about 17 years old when he ran away from his home in Germany and came to America as a stowaway on a French vessel. After jumping ship in Charleston he took to peddling, then to clerking in a drug store. He was fired when he blew up the store during one of his "experiments." He then found a job as a stoker on a steamboat. Now it was the steamboat that blew up, but Kantor, who had to swim to shore to save his life, insisted that he was "only partly" responsible for the explosion. "The skipper wanted more speed and that's what he got," said Eddie.

He finally settled in Detroit where he opened a general store in 1849, trading mainly, at first, with the local Indian tribes. He soon won their friendship and they would often sit in a circle with their bearded, white-skinned comrade and smoke a peace pipe. Gradually he learned the languages of the Huron, the Chippewa and the Potawatami Indians, and they would listen, fascinated, as they heard of the adventures, told in their own tongues, of Edward Bosh-bish-gay-bish-gon-sen Kantor, the Jewish Indian.

Much of what befell Eddie can be verified. But there is much more that cannot. Among the legends attributed to him is the adventure which he is said to have experienced when he was 18 or 19 years old. The ancient classic has been heard in a dozen variants, with the proponent, as a rule, being Mexican, Irish or Indian. Most stem from the post-Civil War period. This one, however, a gem in the litany of Jewish-American folk humor, goes all the way back to 1817—about the time when another Jew, Abraham Mordecai, a veteran of the Revolutionary War, struck out from Pennsylvania and founded the city of Montgomery, Alabama.

It was a blustery day in March when the youthful horse-and-wagon peddler, Edward Kantor, pulled into Fort Deposit, Alabama, about four or five years after it was settled by Andrew Jackson. It was a crude, rough little town, inhabited by men and women who attended to their business with one hand while they kept the other on their rifles and power horns.

Eddie's horse had gone lame, but the traveling young merchant was able to trade some of his goods with an Indian for another horse. Before the day was over, however, he was arrested by the sheriff for horse-stealing, a capital offense in those days. The Indian, it seems, did not have clear title to the animal he had sold to the young stranger. In fact, he had no title at all and promptly disappeared as soon as the transaction was completed.

Northern peddlers were none too popular in the Deep South, and this one, with his accent and strange ways, became the object of an intense and general aversion by the sheriff, the judge and the jury—but especially the judge.

At the trial, the jury heard the evidence and the speeches, then closeted themselves in the saloon for their deliberations, and within an hour returned with a verdict of guilty. But, short as the time of their deliberation was, the judge had not wasted it. During the recess, he had retired to his private chambers where he had consumed a quart of prime rye whiskey. When he returned to the bench to hear the jurors' findings and to pass sentence, he was weaving gracefully. He slumped down in his chair and when the foreman had announced the result just arrived at in the jury room, he focused (with some difficulty) a wavering eye upon the convicted peddler and in a thick tone gave the order:

"Edward Kantor, stand up!"

The prisoner rose in his place.

"Edward Kantor," said His Honor, "in but a few short weeks it will be spring. The snows of winter will flee away, the ice will vanish and the air will become soft and balmy. In short, Edward Kantor, the annual miracle of the year's reawakening will come to pass.

"The rivulet will run its purling course to the sea. The first timid flowers of the season will put forth their tender shoots. The glorious valleys of this enchanted region will blossom as the rose. From every treetop some wildwood songster will carol his mating song. Butterflies will sport in the sunshine and the busy bee will hum happily as it pursues its accustomed avocation. And all of nature, Edward Kantor, will be glad.

"But you—you miserable, thieving, horse-stealing, foreign son of a bitch—you won't be here to see it, because you are going to be hanged four weeks from this coming Friday."*

For the next four weeks, Eddie languished in the town jail, visited only by the judge's young daughter, Geraldine, who brought him his scanty rations. Through a tiny, barred window he witnessed the construction of the scaffold that awaited him. Now, all was ready. Today was the day. The circuit hangman had arrived, the sheriff had polished his shiny new boots, and the townspeople were

---

*There is nothing more sinful in the telling of a story than an anti-climax. The sheer beauty of the Judge's opening remarks and the sudden switch to his cold-as-ice conclusion is funny enough. Indeed, it has always served as the ending of this folk tale. But in this, the Jewish variant, there is a continuation of the narrative which is far more than an anti-climax, for without it, Edward Kantor's life would have ended in his early youth.

dressed in their festive Sunday-go-to-meetin' clothes. The judge was prepared with a speech he had laboriously written for the gala occasion. Came the fateful hour in which the execution was to take place, and the sheriff entered the jailhouse to fetch the prisoner.

Lo and behold—the cell was empty! On the cot was a note addressed to His Honor:

> My dear Judge Murchison:
>
> Before the rising of the pale new moon in all its silv'ry glory, the Shenandoah Valley of Virginia will be fragrant with the scent of apple blossoms. The song of the meadow lark whistling in the grass will bring joy to the hearts of young lovers as they listen to nature's own music. Graceful swans will make silhouettes against the soft blue skies, and the setting sun will cast its amber glow upon that far-off area, bathing it in celestial beauty.
>
> And I shall be there to enjoy it, Your Honor, together with your daughter, Geraldine, whose permission was sweetly given to borrow your horse for my wagon.
>
> When Geraldine and I find pleasure in the fragrance of all the flowers, bask in the golden Virginia sun and bathe in the rippling stream as it runs its gentle course to the sea, we shall think of you, Your Honor, with affection and, most importantly, with happy forgetfulness.
>
> Edward Kantor
>
> N.B. You may call me Eddie.

Among the hardy souls who traversed the continent or sailed around the Horn to settle in California during the 1840s and early 1850s, was Samuel Ohrbach, an adventurous young attorney. In his later years, according to the California State Historical Society, Ohrbach devoted himself to the defense of the poor and downtrodden, and may well have been the first defender of civil rights for minority groups in the Golden State. This anecdote is especially rare because of its Oriental and Jewish cast.

On November 9, 1875, one of the first Tong wars broke out in San Francisco's Chinatown. A number of fatalities resulted in both factions. One morning, in the midst of the hostilities, a mild-appearing little Oriental came quietly into the office of the prominent criminal lawyer, Samuel Ohrbach. The caller opened negotiations without preamble:

"How much you charge, get Chinaman free for kill another Chinaman dead?"

"Two thousand dollars," answered the lawyer promptly.

"How much I pay down?"

"One thousand now—one thousand when I go to court for trial."

The visitor counted out a thousand dollars, placed it on the desk, and then started to leave.

"Just a moment, come back here," cried Ohrbach. "Where are you going?"

"I go kill him," said the Chinese client. "Be back bimeby."

Bloom, the button man, was charged with obtaining six boxes of buttonholes and two boxes of silk thread without notifying the owners thereof about the transaction. Having been indicted, he was arraigned before the court and the case against him was called. It then developed that he had no counsel.

"Why haven't you engaged an attorney to defend you?" inquired the judge on the bench.

"Who has money to waste on expensive lawyers?" demanded Bloom.

"Well, what do you propose to do, then, about the trial of your case?" asked His Honor. "The prosecutor tells me he is ready to go ahead and impanel a jury and present the evidence."

"Judge," answered the defendant, "as far as I am concerned, you can let the matter drop right here. I'll be better off, you'll be happy and the prosecutor won't have to work so hard."

But the court explained that this would hardly do. Glancing around the room, the judge noticed two fledgling lawyers just admitted to the practice, and the youngest and least experienced members of the bar.

"I shall appoint Mr. Newman and Mr. Levine to represent you," said the magistrate, indicating the striplings.

Bloom eyed the attorneys doubtfully.

"Your Honor," he said "I'd like to make a little proposition, if it's all right with you."

"What's your proposition?"

"If you don't mind, I'll trade you both of these lawyers for one good witness."

The defendant was accused of sullying the honor of a pure young maiden, according to the lady's testimony, and he was having a difficult time explaining the circumstances.

"I'm innocent, Your Honor," he declared. "All I did was offer her a scotch and sofa, and she reclined!"

The adage, "Truth is funnier than fiction," is borne out by the following actual cases, as reported by the National Shorthand Reporters Association, the organization to which most court reporters belong.

Q: Did you spend the night with Mr. Goldblatt at the Hotel Edison here in New York?

A: Such a question I'm refusing to answer.

Q: Well, did you ever stay all night with Mr. Goldblatt at the Chicago Hilton?:

A: That question I'm also refusing to answer.

Q: Did you spend the night with Mr. Goldblatt at the Americana Hotel in Miami?

A: No.

Mrs. Kahan, a widow, had been served with a subpoena to appear as a witness against Mr. Abeloff, a gentleman-friend of whom she was quite fond. With the defendant, Abeloff, sitting in the front row, it became clear from the outset that she would be a hostile witness. The little drama that ensued is taken from the actual transcript:

Q: How long have you known the defendant?

A: Five years—six years—who knows?

Q: What is his name?

A: Abeloff

Q: What is his first name?

A: This I don't remember.

Q: Madam, you've known your boyfriend for five or six years and you can't recall his first name?

A: No, I can't. Can't you see I'm excited? How can I remember when I'm excited? (*Rising from the witness chair and pointing to Abeloff*) Seymour, for God's sake tell them your first name.

"Hello—hello. That you, Moe? This is Mr. Schmaltz. Sorry to hear about your auto accident, but when are you coming back to work?"

"I don't really know, Mr. Schmaltz. My doctor said I can walk, but my lawyer says I can't."

A young lawyer, recently graduated from CCNY and newly admitted to the bar, was determined to specialize in civil rights cases. An idealistic fellow, he looked forward to aiding the poor and the downtrodden, hoping that his shoulder-length hair and hippie-style clothing would not be a detriment in his battle against the "establishment."

Setting up shop in Spanish Harlem, he quickly found out all about what he considered "justice" when he lost his first case. Frustrated, he appealed the verdict to a higher court, but this time his presentation was far more detailed. He cited precedent after precedent, case after case, pointing out many instances where the defendant had been acquitted in what he believed were similar circumstances.

"Please, counselor, desist!" interrupted the weary judge after listening to the droning voice for an hour. "You may rest assured that I understand the basics of equality under the law, and you can also take it for granted that this court is familiar with the elementary concepts of justice."

"Your Honor," sighed the crusading young lawyer, "that was the mistake I made in the lower court!"

Evelyn emerged from the courtroom waving the final decree of divorcement she had just been granted.

"Look," she exulted to her friend, Gloria, "I finally got it! Believe me, you'll never know the heartaches I went through with that man."

"What did you plead—mental cruelty?" asked Gloria.

"No, my lawyer suggested I should plead 'too much exercise,' and that's exactly what I did."

"Exercise?" echoed Gloria. "That's not grounds for divorce."

"You don't know my lawyer," retorted Evelyn. "He told the judge my husband got all his exercise by jumping to false conclusions, running me down in front of my friends, sidestepping his responsibilities, and pushing his luck too far!"

A customer bought some merchandise from Stanley on the installment plan, but refused to make the last payment. So Stanley went to see a lawyer.

"Before I take your case," said the counselor, "you'll have to give me a $50 retainer."

"All right, here's the fifty," agreed Stanley, handing over the money.

The lawyer raked in the bills. "Thank you," he murmured. "This entitled you to two questions."

"What! Fifty dollars for just two questions! Isn't that awfully high?"

"Yes, I suppose it is," said the lawyer, nodding. "Now, what's your second question?"

Sol the sliced-salami salesman from Scranton was doing his unsuccessful best to evade the responsibilities of a concerned citizen.

"I can't possibly serve on the jury, Your Honor," he protested. "Just one look at that horrible prisoner already convinced me that he's guilty!"

"Silence!" roared the judge. "That's the district attorney!"

Lawyer: Now let's get this straight. You say it was a very dark night, yet you maintain that you saw the auto accident 500 yards off. Sir, just how far do you think you can see on a dark night?

Witness: A million miles, maybe. How far is it to the moon?

The man had been hauled into court on a charge of reckless driving. But the story he told the judge was so sad, so poignant, so filled with the pathos of human heartbreak, that his honor had to brush the tears from his eyes before he could speak.

"I'm not blaming you," he finally said in a choked voice, "just fining you!"

Dep't. Of Lost Causes: "Your Honor, I have no defense except that she knew she had me on the spot so she took me to the cleaners."

Mr. Genzina and Mr. Gribben became involved in a controversy over who owed three thousand dollars to whom. So bitter was the dispute that they finally took the case to court. On the appointed day, they appeared before Judge Richard Watergate.

"Before proceeding with this case," announced His Honor, "I want to state right here and now that I received an envelope containing $500 from Mr. Genzina, the plaintiff, and another envelope containing $1,000 from Mr. Gribben, the defendant.

"The court wishes it known that it will return $500 to the defendant so that the case may be tried strictly on its own merit!"

Herewith and forthwith is the silliest courtroom drama in the annals of American jurisprudence:

Shulman the *shlepper* was summoned to court on the charge that he had ordered an expensive samovar from a mail-order import house and had thereafter responded negatively to the law of compensation. Rather than retain an attorney to represent him, he elected to plead his own case. Presiding was the eminent magistrate, Judge Farfelzup.

"First of all," began Shulman, "I never ordered that samovar. But even if I did, the plaintiff never sent it. And if he did send it, I never got it. And if I did get it, I paid for it. And if I didn't pay for it, then it arrived broken. Now, Your Honor, give me one logical reason why I should pay out good money for a broken samovar that the plaintiff never sent and I never got. That's normal by you?"

"No, I can't say it is," agreed the judge. "But the plaintiff states that you didn't even bother to reply to his several written requests for payment. You have to admit, Mr. Shulman, that isn't normal either."

"But, Your Honor, who cares what he says? Who are you gonna believe—me or that rotten liar?"

The judge turned to the court stenographer.

"Delete that word 'rotten,' he ordered sternly. "That determination will be made later, in due course."

His Honor now faced counsel for the plaintiff.

"All right, we will now hear your ridiculous side of the story, and let us bear in mind the serious consequences of perjury, shall we?"

"But, sir, we haven't said anything yet!"

"Proceed, before I find you in contempt."

"Your Honor, we wish to introduce as evidence this signed receipt in which the defendant certified that he not only received the goods but that it arrived in perfect condition."

Judge Farfelzup again addressed Shulman.

"*Nu?*"

"My client—that's me, Your Honor—and I, we both deny that such a receipt was ever signed by me. But even if I did sign it, I never mailed it. And if I did mail it, the plaintiff never received it. And if he did receive it, the signature was a forgery. And if it was a forgery, then I shouldn't be held accountable."

"That's what I say!" declared the judge.

The opposing attorney, who happened to be one-legged, jumped to his foot.

"But, Your Honor, it couldn't have been a forgery," he protested. "We not only have a handwriting analyst who will testify that it is the defendant's own signature, but we also have a fingerprint expert who will attest to the fact that the defendant's prints are all over the receipt."

"You don't say!" exclaimed the judge. "How about that, Shulman?"

"Your Honor," Shulman began bravely, "even if—even—er—hmm—fingerprints, the man said? With handwriting experts yet? *Ai-yi-yi!*"

"Well, say something!" snapped the judge. "In this court you have to plead one way or the other."

"I'm standing pat on executive privilege and *nolo contendere*."

Judge Farfelzup gave him a searching look.

"You know the meanings of those terms?"

"Sure! Executive privilege means I'm guilty but nobody can prove it. *Nolo contendere* means I'm innocent but how the hell do I prove it! So I'm asking you to show me mercy and I'm throwing myself on the ignorance of the court!"

14

Goniffs, Gamblers, Grabbers and Other No-Goodniks

Introduction

To be a practicing Jew is a career in itself—and a noble one. The trouble is that when some people finish practicing, they forget the nobility. Not that this makes them any different than gentiles—the lure of easy money tends to become an anesthetic that puts many a conscience to sleep, no matter what the race or religion. It also furnishes much of the grist for the American-Jewish humor mill.

A president can be pardoned for making tapes without the knowledge or consent of the tapee; but if *you* do it, you'll sit in the penitentiary for five years without benefit of connubial visitations: a respectable way of putting it, yes? The director of El Bandido Savings and Loan Association expropriates your deposits to buy his girlfriend mink-lined bras and panties with 24 carat gold filigree, and he gets off with a warning that henceforth he should mend his ways and be a good boy. The judge is not one of the depositors, of course—he's the bank president's golf partner. So they send him to Congress where he belongs. As to gamblers, has it ever occurred to you that the very kids who had too much *saichel* to believe in Santa Claus grow up and bet on horses? Go figure it out!

A current complaint is that prisons fail to do anything constructive toward the rehabilitation of inmates. Chief Justice Warren E. Burger, for one, believes that a man in prison without a trade should be taught one. Perhaps, he suggested, some incentive might be provided, such as a reduction of sentence for learning a useful occupation. In this, Chief Justice Burger seems to agree

147

with the Talmud. Rabbi Judah Ben Ilai said: "The parent who does not teach his child a trade teaches him thievery."

Ancient Israel apparently had little need of prisons. For some offenses, stripes (beatings) were administered. For stealing, double restitution was required. There were cities of refuge to which perpetrators of involuntary murder might flee, but there is little mention, if any, of imprisonment. Perhaps the heightened Jewish sense of social justice made for less of the kind of poverty which breeds crime. Conditions such as exist in Latin America and other areas where a few own most of the land are not tolerated under the Mosaic law which proclaims that the land cannot be owned by anyone forever.

The Bible tells us that Joseph was cast into prison, but that was in Egypt. Where else? Actually, he had a good case. Had Joseph retained a wide-awake lawyer to appeal the verdict on that trumped-up charge of assault, he might have been freed; but who knows about those Egyptian lawyers and judges? However, things didn't turn out too badly for Joseph. He parlayed his ability to interpret dreams, going from prisoner to prime minister, and all the inmates—Joseph's erstwhile companions—did revel and rejoice to the tune of Mairzy Doats, for they were given an increase in their halvah allowance. But their joy was short-lived: what the prime minister giveth, the pharaoh taketh away. It was all very un-Jewish. The point is that, according to Jewish teachings, prison inmates need a dream—a dream of future usefulness. The absence of such a dream is symbolic of all the other problems associated with the penal system. And here, too, is a further source of the biting wit and humor that often voices a need more forcefully than the direct approach of indignation and outrage.

For the Jewish people, it was not merely law which was responsible for the general avoidance of crime; religion was perhaps the supreme deterrent. It seems to have been forgotten that our parents and grandparents did not blame poverty for all the ills and misfortunes that beset them. Yesterday's Jews lived in the ghettos with very little crime among them. When disputes arose, the parties involved brought their problems before the rabbi for a *Din Torah*.

Of course, not every litigant was satisfied with the rabbi's verdict. We recall the saintly Rabbi Salanter who once decided against a man who threatened to break every window in the synagogue if the rabbi did not change his verdict.

"And if you break the windows, do you think I will just stand there and do nothing?" said the rabbi.

"What will you do?" demanded the belligerent defendant.

"I will immediately send for the glazier and have new windows installed," replied Rabbi Salanter.

The fellow shrugged resignedly and abided by the decision. "Who can fight with such a man?" he muttered.

Orthodox Judaism was never an especially convenient religion for the miscreant. In fact, it was difficult for a religious man to turn to crime. Imagine such a Jew who decides to become a robber. There is an ancient Jewish law which states that no one may enter a house without knocking. So the man, if he is serious about being a successful robber, and at the same time wishes to remain an observant Jew, is stumped at the outset. Even if he intended to enter through the window, he must first knock. That wasn't quite what Moses had in mind, but leave it to Jewish humorists (many of them rabbis) to create such zany analogies with the kernel of truth intact.

There is an old saying, "The Jews are like other people, only more so." That "more so" involved a heap o' tsuris, as they say down on the farm, when it comes to selecting judges. "A very old man, a eunuch or a childless person is not appointed to the Sanhedrin," averred Maimonides, "since they are apt to lack tenderness." Maimie—you should pardon the familiarity—must have been reading Mishna, which states, "The following are ineligible to serve as judges or witnesses: a gambler, a userer and a dealer in forbidden produce." By "forbidden produce," the sages probably meant such goodies as pickled pig's feet (or elbows, for that matter), and *escargots* which cannot be properly *kashered.* But it is the Talmud which lays down the toughest restrictions for aspirants to the bench: "Only those are appointed to the Sanhedrin who have stature, wisdom, good appearance, maturity, a knowledge of the tricks of sorcery, and familiarity with all the 70 languages of mankind." No wonder we have so few qualified judges.

Actually, and despite the unyielding injunction, "Thou shalt not steal," there are a number of Yiddish proverbs and expressions which take a compassionate view of the person who is compelled to steal because of dire stress. "He who would not steal to feed his starving child is an unworthy father," is one. The Bible itself tells us: "Men do not despise a thief if he steals to satisfy his soul when he is hungry." Also, we find, "Stolen waters are sweet."

Back in the third century, Rabbi Hiyya instructed: "Not the mouse, but the hole, is the thief." And another Jewish sage pointed out, "While forcing a lock, the burglar calls on divine aid." Nor can we forget Spinoza's challenge to hypocrisy, 300 years ago. In his monumental *Ethics,* the great philosopher declared: "Those who cry out the loudest against the misuse of honor and the vanity of the world, are those who most greedily covet it." A regular Jack Benny, that Spinoza.

As to gambling, the Talmud, surprisingly enough, seems to regard it with greater disfavor than stealing—probably because starvation may serve as an understandable reason for theft of food, but there is never an acceptable reason for heavy gambling. The Talmud speaks of two types of gambling: dice and pigeon racing. The Talmudic word for dice, *dubya,* seems to be of Greek origin, another example of the Hellenistic influence on the ancient Jews. Talmudic law held that a gambling debt was not legally collectable, and there was no Mafia in those days to force payment, either. What could the Greeks and Romans do about it? Cut your head off? Well, come to think about it, yes! But other than that, what?

The Mishna says, "A gambler is disqualified as a witness or judge," but doesn't say why. And Maimonides asserted, "A gambler always loses. He loses money, dignity and time. And if he wins, he weaves a spider's web around himself." In America, however, and with particular reference to New York's off-track betting, or the *meshuggeneh* antics around the crap tables in Las Vegas, Maimonides' spider would starve to death waiting for the big payoff.

One of the happy Jewish holidays has a gambling name: *Purim,* meaning "lots." Haman played bingo and cast lots on which day the Jews were to be annihilated. His game of bingo, however, didn't turn out too well for him, and he came down with a terminal case of *griener cholerya.* Nevertheless, when it comes to moderate card-playing as a pastime, the Jewish position, on the whole, has been tolerant.

There is an old story of the poor widow who was about to be evicted from her home because she had no money to pay the rent. So her rabbi went looking for the president of the synagogue to see if something could be done for the unfortunate woman. He finally located the officer and some of his cronies seated around a table, deeply engrossed in a pinochle game. Flustered at the unexpected visit, they tried to hide the cards, but the rabbi urged them to continue. "Keep playing," he insisted. The men went on with their game and, at the end, the rabbi scooped up all the winnings to pay the rent for the poor widow.

Every vice contains a spark of virtue, and so forth. That's what sentimentalists like about Jewish stories. They turn out so nice.

The most famous Jewish work against gambling was written in the 17th century by a rabbi who was himself a compulsive gambler. Leon of Modena was a scholar in rabbinics, and also in the secular field. His erudition and renown were such that even Christians came to hear him speak—not that it ever did them any good. The thesis of his anti-gambling sermons was that wagering was as dangerous as playing on the edge of a roof—a comment made long before the Fiddler got up there and had a Broadway play named after him.

Leon of Modena never lost his fascination for the roof's edge. Perhaps he was waiting for Maimonides' spider to tip him off on a sure thing at Hialeah. Had the good rabbi been born 300 years later, he might have learned a little something from David Ben-Gurion. A Hindu rajah wanted to take him to a horse race. Snapped Ben-Gurion: "I already know that one horse can run faster than another, and I am not interested in which one."

Once, long ago, to journey back in time for a moment, there lived a cobbler in the city of Chelm who committed a heinous crime and was sentenced to hang. But he was the only cobbler in town, so the Chelmites hanged one of the two tailors instead. "When the thief is needed," says the Talmud, "he is even taken off the gallows."

There are any number of contemporary folk tales which express the same general thought: The guilty person's social or economic position determines his degree of punishment—if, indeed, any. Old World traditional humor is not too different from its modern American counterpart. The crook, the gambler, the con man and others who depend upon cunning and stealth to turn a dishonest dollar have been with us ever since the Israelites took leave without asking permission of the Egyptians.

Some of the anecdotes in this chapter may appear to be new, but take heed, it is only the literary garments and change of time and locale which are different. The *goniffs*, gamblers and grabbers are the same.

H.D.S.

Not all descendants of Abraham earned their bread by the sweat of their brow. The connivers, *fenaiglers* and grabbers of Judaica Americana folklore have a worthy counterpart in the old-time *schnorrer* of European Jewish folklore—that crafty beggar who lived by his wits. There is, however, a sharp line of distinction between the *schnorrer* and his American successor, the con man. The former was a clever panhandler; the latter was, and is, a *goniff*—a swindler.

Such a man, it turned out, was Sam Fenster.* He burst upon the lower East Side like a Roman candle—and like that candle he was just as quickly extinguished. The story, according to those few who are still alive to remember it, was finally pieced together by Gordon Kramer who rented his store to Fenster, and by a sign-painter named Max Bender, both of whom had ample reason to recall him with regret and reluctant admiration for his magnificent *chutzpah.*

From the information available, it seems that on July 3, 1919, Kramer looked up from his desk when a little old man entered his real estate office—actually a store located at 157 Grand Street. The stranger was at least seventy years old, but clean-shaven and dapper. Standing not more than five feet tall, he sported an elaborately-carved swagger stick and was wearing one of those African-style safari helmets one sees in travel posters. The odd-looking but instantly likable oldster was one of those men who radiates self-confidence and good cheer—the kind of man you would choose to share a pleasant evening with, over a few glasses of *schnapps.*

The visitor smiled genially, extended his hand and introduced himself: "Sam Fenster, from the Belgiumeh Congo. Here, give a look on my expensive calling card." He handed it to Kramer:

FENSTER THE GREAT WHITE HUNTER
— English Spoken Here —
Also Yiddish, Congoleum & Belgium

"Lions and tigers I don't need this week," said Kramer, grinning broadly. "Come back better next Tuesday."

Fenster chuckled good-naturedly, retrieved his calling card which he carefully returned to his pocket, and then inquired about the sign in the window: Store for Rent—Reasonable.

"It's across the street," Kramer explained. The store had been vacant for several months and he was anxious to rent it.

"I want it only for a week, maybe two," Fenster said. "How much you're asking?"

Kramer rubbed his chin. He had hoped for a long-term tenant, but a week or two was better than nothing. "Well," he replied hesitantly, "I'm usually asking fifty a month—it's a good loca-

---

* There are a number of versions of *Fenster and His Ferocious Flugel* in the Jewish communities of New York, Chicago and Los Angeles—and probably elsewhere in the United States. An Irish variant, *The Flyin' Flooheel,* places this humorous folktale in San Francisco, circa 1889. A later version, entitled *The Sky Floogle,* was reported in *Chillicothe and Ross County,* compiled in 1938 by the Federal Writers Project of Ohio, Works Progress Administration. The Jewish version, above, has been handed down from one generation to the next in the oral tradition of folklore and is published here for the first time.

tion—but for such a short time ..."

"I'll pay for a whole month," Fenster promptly declared. He opened his wallet and handed Kramer a crisp five dollar bill. "By me, business is business," he said briskly. "Here's my deposit. I'll put up a few signs and move in on Monday. The rest of the rent I'll pay on Grand Opening Night."

The quick-talking little man was on his way out of the door when Kramer called to him: "Hey, Mr. Fenster, what line are you in?"

"Wild animals," answered the Great White Hunter. "What else?"

"My good man," said Kramer, suppressing a wild urge to roar with laughter, "if you're thinking maybe you could organize a safari it should go to Africa, you're in the wrong neighborhood."

Fenster smiled indulgently. "A show I'm putting on like you never saw before," he explained. "For the first time anywhere in the civilized world I'm presenting, in person, the most ferocious, man-eating monster what ever lived—the sky flugel!"

"*Wh-wwhaaat!*" Kramer gasped. "What's a sky flugel?"

"You know what an alligator is looking like? Well, a sky flugel is twice as long, and higher even than an elephant. It got claws like a Siberian tiger and six rows of big teeth like from a shark. It also got wings from forty feet across, like a wampire bat, so that it's not catching on the ground it's flying up in the air it should get a little something to eat. The sky flugel got a rotten temper like a rhino and it's eating mostly eagles, gorillas and human beans."

"Now hold on a minute!" snapped Kramer. "In my stores I don't allow such kinds of goings-on. Suppose that sky flugel gets loose and starts killing people?"

"It can't happen, believe me," Fenster replied soothingly. "Didn't it just pass through Ellis Island? And didn't the Customs agent say the sky flugel was safe so long as it was chained inside its cage? You got nothing to worry about."

Sam Fenster departed. Next on his list was Max Bender, the sign-painter at 169 Grand Street. In Bender's shop, Fenster ordered 100 signs, each four feet long by two feet high. Headlines, in red paint, were to read: SEE THE FEROCIOUS, MAN-EATING SKY FLUGEL. DEADLY MONSTER NEVER BEFORE SEEN IN CAPTIVITY. TICKETS ONLY ONE DOLLAR! He also ordered twenty streamers, sixty feet long and three feet high, measured to stretch across the street from building to building—these, too, with screaming headlines. He gave Bender a ten dollar deposit, promising to pay the entire balance on opening night.

The next several days were busy ones for Fenster. The signs were prominently displayed in a multitude of store windows on Houston, Rivington, Cherry, Grand, Orchard, Hester and Delancey Streets, with the blaring streamers strung overhead from one side of the street to the other. A reporter from the *Forvertz*, unable to collar Fenster for details about his remarkable animal, obtained his "inside story" from Kramer and Bender, and ran a feature article about the ferocious sky flugel.

On July 14th, Fenster ran out of tickets to sell. He had managed to scrounge sixty or seventy wooden boxes upon which the patrons were to sit. He would, he proclaimed, give a nightly performance for the next two weeks so that all ticket-holders could be accommodated. On opening night, the improvised "theatre" was packed with customers from wall to wall. The patrons were seated so that they were facing the back of the store, across which Fenster had hung a wide curtain, obviously to heighten the suspense and to separate the audience from the caged monster. They waited expectantly, and somewhat nervously, for their first glimpse of the huge and terrifying man-eater.

Suddenly, from behind the curtain, an ear-shattering, agonized scream caused the apprehensive customers to leap to their feet. There arose another scream—and then another—piercing outbursts of mortal agony. There was a loud rattling of chains, a series of sharp cracks as though heavy steel bars were being torn asunder, and then, like a *golem* in a bad dream, Fenster himself staggered out from behind the curtain. A wave of unholy fright rolled over the audience. Fenster's hair was wildly disheveled, his clothes torn, his face and shirt-front smeared with blood.

"The sky flugel is loose!" he yelled hoarsely. "Run for your lives!"

The customers made a frenzied dash for the door, men yelling, women fainting, children crying out in terror. Fortunately, no one was killed or seriously injured in the mad stampede to safety.

The police soon arrived and, with drawn guns, searched the premises, but no sign of the sky flugel could they find. Nor could they find Sam Fenster. Nor could they find the money he had charged for admissions. All that remained behind the curtain and next to the open back door was a length of rusty chain and a bottle of ketchup.

So whatever happened to the Great White Hunter? Who knows? He simply disappeared as though he had been swallowed up by the earth itself. On July 20, 1919, the editor of the *Forvertz* began an investigation of the case that lasted until Labor Day of that year, but without success. The plain truth is that nobody ever found out what became of Fenster, or, for that matter, of the sky flugel.

Pity poor Pineus, the one-fingered pickpocket. Arthritis caught up with him and he can't work.

Complaint has been made from time to time about some of the so-called model homes which are put up so fast in the suburbs. The tenor of such complaints revolves around the theory that these houses are built to be sold, not lived in. It is our personal opinion, however, that real estate brokers and builders are just as honest as people in other trades and professions, such as used car salesmen, television repairmen, White House lawyers, meat-market managers and politicians.

With that disclaimer out of the way, we shall now relate a little story currently in vogue about the real-estate operator whose activities in the commuting areas have been highly successful. The only problem he encounters in the course of earning his livelihood is that he can't work the same side of the street twice.

Not long ago, he snared a prospective buyer—one of those fifty-dollars-down-and-pay-as-long-as-you-live prospects. The promoter took him out in his car to the site on Long Island, to look at the house which, he thought, would suit the needs of the customer, to say nothing of invigorating his own exchequer.

The building was in the process of construction. It had been started on Monday—on Friday it would be ready for occupancy. But this was Wednesday, and while the foundation was finished and the sides were tacked up and the roof had been pasted on, the painting and the interior trim and other finishing touches were yet to be added. The dealer led the proposed victim inside the structure. The plasterers were just concluding their part of the contract.

"Here you are!" said the operator with a great show of pride. "What do you think of *this* for a house?"

"To tell you the truth," said the homeseeker, "it looks kind of flimsy."

"*Flimsy!*" screeched the indignant realtor. "You call this fortress flimsy? Wait, I'll show you."

"Hey, Jim," he called to a workman on the other side of the partition.

"What?" responded Jim.

"Just step up close to the dividing wall between us. Get as close as you can."

"All right," said Jim, "here I am, almost touching it."

"Good! Now, Jim, you can hear me speaking through the wall, can't you?"

"Sure."

"But you can't see me through this wall, can you, Jim?"

"Nope."

With a smile of triumph, the promoter turned to the customer:

"Now *that's* what I call a *wall!*"

Just as he was emerging from Hyman's Hoboken Haberdashery, Gedalia the *goniff* was caught red-handed with the loot he had just stolen.

"Before I read you your rights under the law," intoned the arresting officer, "I want you to know that I am charging you for possession of stolen property."

"Sorry," replied Gedalia, "I don't do business on credit!"

Shmuel, late for dinner, was confronted with the choice of facing an irate wife should he fail to arrive home on time, or taking a shortcut through Central Park. Choosing the lesser of two hazards, he took the shortcut, even though the sun had set and it was growing dark.

He hadn't gone a hundred feet into the park when a man rushed up to him.

"Listen, Mac, ya seen a cop aroun' anyplace?" he asked breathlessly.

"No, I'm sorry," said Shmuel. "There's never a policeman around when you need one."

"Yer right," snarled the man. "Hand over yer watch an' wallet!"

The shifty-eyed stranger glanced around the lavishly appointed office and furtively approached the lawyer's desk.

"Are you Mr. Ginsboig, da guy what sprung Lefty Louis las'

week?" asked the gnome-like little man nervously.

"Yes, I'm Ginsberg," affirmed the attorney.

"Lefty's a frennamine. He sent me here. Y'kinaskim."

"I don't have to ask him: I believe you. What's your name and what can I do for you?"

"Jus' call me Hubcap Hymie. I need a mout'piece, but I ain't got no bread. In fack, I'm dead broke."

"Mr.—ah—Hubcab—er—Hymie—didn't Lefty tell you I'm one of the most expensive lawyers in the city?"

"Yeah."

"Then how do you expect to pay my fee?"

"Wouldja take a 1974 blue an' gray Cadillac Fleetwood Limousine fer payment?"

"I certainly would! Tell me, what are you charged with?"

"I'm charged wit' stealin' a 1974 blue an' gray Cadillac Fleetwood Limousine!"

Two cronies were discussing the ever-popular subject of law and order.

"There's a lot of crime going on these days," observed the Manhattanite, "but they don't have tough neighborhoods like they used to when I was a boy. In those days, on the Lower East Side, when someone asked 'What time is it?' you first thanked him for asking, *then* you told him the time."

"That's nothing," retorted the Brooklynite. "Back when I was a kid in Greenpernt, *nobody* asked for the time. They just took your watch!"

The telephone rang at the 23rd Police Precinct and Sergeant Clancey picked up the receiver.

"Yeah?"

"Police?" came a frantic voice at the other end of the wire. "I wanna report a burglar trapped in an old maid's bedroom!"

"Who are you, a neighbor?" asked Sergeant Clancey.

"No," cried the distraught voice, "this is the burglar!"

George Birnbaum, known to all as comedian George Burns, was always able to fracture the friendly folk around the Fulton

Street Fish Market with this truncated description of his boyhood life.

"Our family was so poor," said George, "as children we used to help mother take in washing. We went around to other people's clotheslines!"

Davey and Sam were inveterate gamblers, and each weekend found them together at the local club where they played pinochle all night.

"Why the long face?" asked Davey as they sat down for their usual game.

"It's my wife," mourned Sam. "She gave me final warning that if I didn't give up cards she'd leave me."

"Hey, that's terrible," replied Davey. "I really sympathize with you."

"Yeah," muttered Sam disconsolately, "I'm sure gonna miss the old gal."

Felix, a professional crook, was taking his usual midnight constitutional down Broadway in search of business opportunities when he bumped into Simon, a fellow *goniff*.

"I hear you had some very good luck," observed Felix.

"Luck?" demanded Simon. "What kind of luck?"

"They tell me you were in Wanamaker's store when all the lights went out."

"That's right, I was. All of a sudden the whole place was in pitch black darkness. You couldn't see your hand in front of your face."

"Boy, what luck! Tell me, what did you get?"

"I got nothing—not a thing," moaned Simon. "When the lights went out I happened to be in the piano department!"

There is a delightful anecdote of ancient vintage concerning Diogenes who took up his lamp and went in search of an honest man. When he got to New York, somebody stole his lamp.

There's no use beating around the bush—Jay and Melvin were crooks and that's all there is to it. Everybody on the block knew it, too. But because of their ingenuity they had never been caught.

They had a *shtick*, these two. Jay posed as a deaf mute; Melvin as a cripple. They each carried a tin cup filled with pencils, and when suspicion pointed to them for some robbery or other, they would plead, in agonized tones, that they were only poor mendicants who just happened to be in the neighborhood at the time. How could a couple of impoverished beggars, one who could neither hear nor speak, and the other paralyzed so that he could hardly walk, be guilty of robbery?

Their assumed afflictions were wisely apportioned; they could not have done better had they taken aptitude tests. Jay was far from bright—a first-class *shlemiel,* according to his partner in crime. His vow of silence protected them both whenever they were questioned by the authorities. Melvin, on the other hand, was a consummate actor and would have won acclaim in the theatre had he chosen so rash an activity as honest toil.

But the inevitable day came when a dedicated police officer out-smarted them. A clothing store on Delancey Street had been burglarized and the weight of evidence overwhelmingly established Jay and Melvin as the culprits. Two policemen arrived at their humble flat, paid them an anti-social call and transported them, at city expense, to the local precinct headquarters. There they were grilled for nearly two hours by the most astute detective in all New York—a career enforcement officer named Brutus Nero. It fit, too.

But at the end of the two hours they were still just as adamant about their innocence as they had been at the beginning of the interrogation. Nero, his patience worn to shreds and shards, felt his anger surging as he viewed the impudent lawbreakers.

"Listen, you guys," he roared at last, "you're a couple of phonies. I don't believe that you can hardly walk, or that you can't speak or hear. I'm gonna get the truth out of you if it takes me all week."

Jay paled and his lower lip quivered.

'Aha!' thought Nero. 'This is the weak one. I'd better concentrate on him.' Aloud, he commanded Jay to empty his pockets.

"Put all your stuff on the table," he ordered.

With growing apprehension, Jay complied, laying out a few coins, a house key and some stray bits of paper and such.

"What's this key for?" demanded Nero.

Melvin interrupted. "He can't hear a thing you say, officer. I told you ten times, he's deaf. He can't talk, either. Anyway, the key is for our apartment."

But Nero was far from convinced. Again he addressed Jay.

"I know you're pretending," he rasped. "Why don't you confess and save us both a lot of time and trouble?"

"Like I said," Melvin interfered again, "he can't hear you."

The detective had been studying the debris Jay had placed on the table. Suddenly his eyes gleamed. Seizing one of the papers in the pile, he waved it underneath Jay's nose.

"Here is a receipt from Bouncing Benny's Music Store—a receipt for two long-playing records. So you can't hear, eh? But you buy records!"

Jay shrugged, a look of resignation darkening his face.

"All right, so I'm guilty," he confessed in a perfectly normal voice. "I can hear, I can speak, and I like music." He turned to his partner. "I'm sorry, Melvin. I forgot about that receipt."

"Idiot!" screamed Melvin. "Why didn't you tell him you bought those records for *me*?"

Fire insurance is a more delicate problem than life insurance for the dishonest fenaigler, as it is somewhat easier for him to set his store or house afire than to cut his own throat to collect for it. That brilliant observation leads us to Mottel, the owner of a large dry goods store. Mottel conceived the idea of turning a fast dollar and not too incidentally to get rid of an overstock of last season's merchandise. He would accomplish this by having a big, well-advertised fire sale. Now before one has a fire sale, it is customary to have a fire. And before one has a fire, it is prudent to be covered by a fire insurance policy. So Mottel, a perfect paragon of prudence, called an insurance agent and they sat down to work out the details.

"Tell me something," said Mottel when he had signed the policy, "just suppose—mind you, we're just supposing—that my store burned down to the ground tomorrow night. What would I get under the terms of this policy?"

"About ten years," said the agent.

A month after he had taken out his fire insurance policy, Mottel's store burned to the ground, and with it his entire inventory of last season's merchandise. Surprisingly, none of the new merchandise had been damaged. By a strange and fortuitous coincidence, he had removed all new shipments to another location. Naturally, he notified his agent at once. The agent, in turn, was ordered by his office manager to bring an insurance adjuster with him and, together, they sifted through the charred ruins for a full eight hours. At the end of the day, they returned to their office where the manager, understandably nervous, awaited them.

"Did you find out what caused the fire?" he asked.

"Yes, friction," said the adjuster tersely.

"You mean something rubbed against something else?"

"Yeah," the adjuster affirmed. "The fire was caused by rubbing a $25,000 insurance policy against a $10,000 dry goods store."

Honest Daniel, the used car dealer with the heart of pure, unalloyed two-carat gold, was forced into bankruptcy—for the fifth time. Glumly, he watched his accountant add up a column of figures, arrive at a sum total and then attempt to deduct a greater amount from the lesser figure.

"It's no use," said the accountant. "There's just no way you can pay more than four cents on a dollar."

"Now hold on there," retorted Honest Daniel. "I got a reputation to think about. In all my other bankruptcies I always paid eight cents on the dollar and I'm gonna do it this time, too, if I hafta take it out of my own pocket!"

At a formal dinner party one evening, a Californian, on business in New York, found himself sitting next to the banker, Otto Kahn, with whom he was only slightly familiar. He attempted to establish a friendly footing by mentioning a few mutual acquaintances.

"One of my dearest friends happens to work for you, Mr. Kahn," he began for openers.

"Who?" asked Kahn with his usual testiness.

"Bob Albertson. I understand he is one of your most tried and trusted employees."

The banker's aloof reserve froze into even colder hostility.

"Sir," he replied icily, "Mr. Albertson was trusted, yes; and if we're fortunate enough to find him he'll be tried."

15

Wine-Bibbers and Ad-Libbers

Introduction

The Jewish community in the United States seems to be plagued with an overabundance of savants who delight in intellectualizing humor on much the same level as a mortician explaining the technology of embalming. What's more, these wise men get paid for it! For them, a joke must have a psychological basis or they refuse to laugh. They apply psychology to humor in an attempt to endow it with neo-Freudian gibberish, always seeking to transform what is essentially an art form into a branch of medical science. The trouble with their reasoning, however, is that it stifles all jokes involving moral conduct which is in conflict with whatever standards happen to be in vogue. This, of course, includes their attitude towards the use of alcoholic beverages.

In 1892, Judah Leib (Leon) Gordon, the Hebrew poet, wrote: "Israel is ready to show the nations a phenomenon the like of which has never been seen: a peasantry not given to drink ... laborers not given to brawls." But the estimable Mr. Gordon should have added the qualifier, "much" drink. It is difficult to conceive of a long succession of sages inveighing against the evils of drink to a people who never drank anyway. And how does one explain that jolly Jewish proverb: "Who blows foam from his glass is not thirsty!" It is indeed true that most Jewish men imbibe only occasionally, and moderately; Jewish women hardly at all, although they are fond of the expression, "A little *schnapps* never hurt anyone."

Jewish drinkers seldom become aggressive; there are very few instances of a Jewish drunk declaiming that he can "lick any man in the house." Why, then do Jews drink?

Dr. Freud would utter a loud and thoroughly disgusted *"ach!"*

at this oversimplification: The average Jew drinks because it makes him happy. Brilliant, no. Happy, yes. Happiness, for him, is the agreeable sensation arising from contemplating the misery of the non-drinker, and reflecting on how miserable he would have been if he himself had not quaffed a few. As a rule, he prefers port or some other red wine—the fermented grape juice known to Temperance ladies as "liquor," and usually preceded by "the curse of." After a few samples, the male imbiber is quick to remind the opposing sex that wine is God's next best gift to women.

But there is a good reason why Jews, on the whole, avoid whiskey: It is bad for the liver. Mothers impart that information at the time they warn their little boys about naughty girls. The liver (for the benefit of those not well informed on the subject) is the large red organ thoughtfully provided by God. It is attractive and utilitarian, and it enjoys a long, highly-regarded history. The sentiments and emotions which are now ascribed to the heart, for example, were anciently believe to infest the liver; hence its name: liver—the thing we live with.

The liver is the heaviest organ, and that's why it is called *kaved* (heavy) in the Bible. Next to the brain, the liver is the closest organ Man and goose have in common. The liver is the Almighty's most beneficial endowment to the goose: without it he would be unable to supply us with Strasbourg *pâté*, to say nothing of *genzineh gribbenes*.

There is yet another reason why some of the more gregarious Jews, emotionalists that they are, tilt the bonnie bottle: It gives them that lovely feeling of being "wanted"—usually by the pretty shikse in the poopik-revealing bikini who serves the refreshments. This romantic glow, which transforms Sol's Saloon into the Taj Mahal, may be described as the offspring of a liaison between a bank account and a bald head. Most Jews, however, drink at home because they refuse to pay the outrageous prices required to get all *shikkered* up in today's expensive emporiums. But even when they do get sozzled in a public facility, they are seldom inclined to belligerence. When pandemonium reigns, the Jewish drinker quickly and unobtrusively zigzags toward the nearest exit.

The man who "can hold more than a camel," be he Jew, gentile or gentilishly Jewish, is decried in equal measure by abstainers and teetotalers alike. There is an important distinction between the latter two. The "abstainer" is a weak person who yields to the temptation of denying himself a pleasure, and it can be definitely stated that the bride who marries him has a fine prospect of happiness behind her. The "teetotaler," on the other hand, is one who also abstains from strong drink, sometimes totally, sometimes tolerably totally. He's the guy you usually get stuck with as a brother-in-law.

"Man comes from dust and ends in dust," says the liturgy of the Jew, "but in between, what does it hurt to have a drink?"

You just can't beat that sort of creative thinking.

Le'chayim!

H.D.S.

The War of 1812 was mainly a war of the sea and its outstanding battles were on the water. One of the most valorous men fighting for the United States was the French-Jewish privateersman, Commodore John Ordroneaux, who gained renown for his bravery and skill during the naval encounter between the British frigate *Endymion* and the tiny armed vessel *Prince de Neufchâtel*, a brief but bloody battle which Commodore Ordroneaux won through superior strategy and sheer courage.

But Ordroneaux was also something of a martinet, and while he may not have been another Captain Bligh, he was about as stern a disciplinarian as ever commanded an American ship. A tough man, yes—a comedian, no. This whimsical bit of folklore is the only known humorous anecdote which involves him, and even then shows him bested by a junior officer.

Shortly after his successful encounter with the British man o' war, Ordroneaux decided to allow a bit of shipboard revelry among the officers and crew for their gallantry under fire. But, immediately following the occasion, he entered a notation on the ship's log: "The first mate was drunk last night."

It so happened that the first mate, a new man on board and an able and conscientious individual, had never been drunk in his life until that night of celebration. He pleaded with the commodore for leniency, insisting that this was the first such offense he had ever committed and that it would never be repeated. He pointed to his record and reminded the commodore that he had been off duty anyway.

"This entry on the log will have a serious effect on my record, sir." He pleaded.

But the commodore was adamant. "You were drunk last night and I can't change the fact. The record will stand."

The first mate, deeply resentful, resumed his duties. That night, it fell to his lot to make the next entry on the log for the period of his watch. This he did, with what may be called a malicious scrupulousness of accuracy.

Next day, Ordroneaux found this innocently damning statement on the log:

"Commodore Ordroneaux was sober last night."

Here is a happy offering that was old—good and old—before Prohibition became the law of the land. It takes us back to an era when the newest dance vogue was the turkey trot; ragtime, the forerunner of modern jazz, was inching its way north from New Orleans and Memphis; the horse-car was the standard mode of urban transportation, and the neighborhood stable and blacksmith shop was a commonplace sight. It was a time when the huge wave of Jewish emigration from Eastern Europe had just begun to peak.

Ben, a baker, and Kalil, his friend, two gentlemen of ripened age, sat one evening by the wood stove in Ben's quarters when the shocking discovery was made that there wasn't a drop in the house to drink.

"Ronel! Ronel!" called Ben and, in prompt response, his young grandson appeared at the door.

"Listen, Ronel, I just found out that we ran out of—er—refreshments, and my friend Kalil and I are dying from thirst. So be a good boy and bring back for us a bottle of *schnapps*."

"But, grandpa," the youth protested, "the nearest place open at this late hour is ten blocks away. Besides, it's raining."

"Nobody's asking you should walk," said the oldster. "I already unhitched the horse from my bread-wagon. Just throw a saddle on him, get to the store as fast as you can and bring back the whiskey. If you'll hurry you should be back in fifteen minutes, and for that I'll give you a whole dollar. But don't lose any time—we can't wait a single minute longer than that. Remember—fifteen minutes!"

A dollar in those days was an unheard of gratuity for running an errand, and the grandson quickly agreed. "I'm on my way," he said, making a dash for the door.

"The streets are pretty slippery, Ben," observed old Kalil as the youth vanished. "I'm afraid the boy won't be able to get there and back in fifteen minutes. You didn't give him enough time."

"Don't worry, Kalil," said Ben comfortingly. "That grandson of mine is the most punctual boy on the whole East Side." He glanced at his pocket watch. "He's just galloping out of the stable now."

He sat down, his timepiece still in his hand. Kalil, drooling slightly, produced his own watch and mentally proceeded to follow the grandson on his errand.

"He's now on Cherry Street," said Ben, after a few minutes' wait.

"Yes, and he's now going past the car barn," agreed Kalil.

"He's just crossed over to Orchard Street."

"Seven minutes exactly—and he's hitching his horse at Zopp's Schnapps on East Broadway."

"Now he's out of the store with the whiskey in only half a minute."

"Yes, seven-and-a-half minutes exactly. If he returns with the same speed, he'll be back here in fifteen minutes on the dot."

"Nine minutes, and he's back on Orchard."

"Now his horse is galloping along real good. The streets are slippery from the rain but he's making good time."

"Fourteen minutes!" shouted Ben. "He must be downstairs, putting the horse away in the stable. Kalil, in just one minute from now that boy will be standing in the doorway—take my word!"

Scarcely breathing, the pair sat in silence, listening with all four of their ears. In the hallway there were the sounds of running feet.

"Kalil," whooped Ben jubilantly, "didn't I tell you I had the most punctual grandson on the whole East Side? Fifteen minutes to the second—and here he is!"

The door was thrust open. The two thirsty gentlemen, fairly frothing with anticipation, leaped to their feet.

"Grandpa," said the young man, "for the past fifteen minutes I've been looking high and low for that horse's saddle but I just can't find it anywhere."

Sign in Fein's Fine Tavern on lower Broadway:

NEVER DRINK WHILE DRIVING
— YOU MIGHT HIT A BUMP AND SPILL SOME —

Quoting from memory, here is another turn-of-the-century story told by the irrepressible Pitzy Katz during his vaudeville tours.

Jake the barber, passing by a tenement house in the predawn hours of the morning, saw a man leaning limply against the doorway.

"What's the matter?" he asked sympathetically. "Drunk?"

"Yeah, I'm 'fraid sho."

"Do you live in this house?"

"Yep."

"Want me to help you upstairs?"

"Yeah, shank you."

"What floor do you live on?"

"Shecon'."

With much difficulty, Jake half dragged, half carried the wilting figure up the dark stairway to the second floor.

"Is this your apartment?" he asked.

"Yep," affirmed the man, his eyes already closed in alcoholic slumber.

Jake opened the unlocked door and shoved the drunk inside. He then groped his way back downstairs. But as he was going through the vestibule, he made out the dim outline of another man, apparently in worse condition than the first, staggering in from out of the night.

"What's the trouble, mister?" he asked. "Are you drunk, too?"

"Yeah," came the feeble reply.

"Do you live in this house also?"

"Yeah."

"Don't tell me you live on the second floor, too."

"Yeah."

Again Jake half carried the stranger to the second floor. He pushed open the same door and shoved the man inside the darkened room.

As Jake was emerging from the building he discerned yet a third man, evidently worse off than either of the other two. This poor fellow was disheveled and bleeding from cuts and bruises on his head and face. He was about to approach him and offer his assistance when the object of his solicitude darted into the street and threw himself into the arms of a policeman.

"Offisher," he gasped, pointing a quivering finger at Jake, "perteck me from thish man. All night long he's done nothin' but drag me upstairsh an' throw me down th' elevator shaft!"

Horowitz of Dixie Fabrics, and Dormeir of Hudson Hi-Fashions, were unknown to each other until they happened to meet in a cocktail lounge one evening. Both had been imbibing freely of joy juice and they immediately experienced a bond of mutual congeniality. They fell into a somewhat hiccupy conversation.

"Seems to me like I've seen you somewhere before," said Horowitz as he vainly endeavored to light a sodden cigar stump with a dead match.

"I wouldn't be surprised," agreed Dormeir, always adept with a fancy phrase.

"Didn't I meet you at the Softwear Convention in Chicago, last year?"

"Not me. I never was in Chicago in my life."

"That's funny, neither was I."

"Well then," reflected Dormeir, pondering deeply, "the question now is, who the hell were those two guys who met in Chicago?"

Harry Baum, according to insiders who specialize in Los Angeles panhandlers, was usually called by his initials, which also stand for Hollywood Bum—an apt if inelegant nomenclature. H.B.'s place of business was on the sidewalk in front of the Brown Derby where he solicited alms from the passing gentry.

One Saturday evening, H.B.'s best customer, movie producer Darryl Zanuck, passed him by without extending the customary handful of coins. Indignantly, H.B. hailed the producer.

"Hey, Mr. Zanuck, you think I don't eat on Saturdays all of a sudden?"

Zanuck's mind had been elsewhere at the time and he hadn't even noticed the bum.

"I'm sorry," he said, "here's a dollar. Just don't give me that routine about starving. We both know what you really do with the money."

"All right," H.B. confessed. "I buy whiskey."

"Well, as long as you're so honest about it," said Zanuck, "come on inside with me and I'll buy you a drink."

They settled into a booth and producer Zanuck signaled the waiter.

"Two scotch and sodas," he ordered.

Said H.B. quickly: "Make mine the same."

Passing Beth Yisroel Synagogue in Staten Island, in the wee hours of the morning, a drunk noticed a sign that read: *Ring the Bell for the Shammes*. He did just that, and a sleepy-eyed old man came to the door.

"What do you want at this hour?" the *shammes* demanded crossly.

The drunk looked the old man over for a full 20 seconds and then retorted, "I want to know why you can't ring that silly bell yourself!"

Our next little tale dates back to long before the Prohibition era, when the Eighteenth Amendment finally gave Franklin D. Roosevelt a platform to run on. In those days there was a cozy, family-type saloon at 18 Chatham Square, in New York, called "The Schnapps Nook," but usually referred to by the local denizens as "The Shnookery." The specialty of the house was a mixed drink called "The Society Cocktail"—two of them and you wonder who's who.

Into "The Shnookery" one evening came two unsuspecting visitors to New York, eager to sample the "Society Cocktail," whose fame had spread even to their native hinterland. Obligingly, Harvey Roosevelt (born Henry Rosenfeld), poured a generous glassful for each of them. The concoction proved satisfactory in every respect.

When the two sojourners had finished their drinks, they immediately called for more of the same. The second service called for a third, but Harvey, the gentlemanly barkeep, raised a warning hand.

"No more, fellas," he said. "I'm sorry, but we never serve a customer more than two of these drinks. They're pretty strong."

"Just one more for the road," they pleaded.

"Can't be done. It's against the house rules. I'd advise you gents to go along now and take a little stroll in the fresh air. You'll feel better if you do."

After further fruitless argument the visitors departed into the night, arm in arm. Presently, as they progressed along a dark and quiet side street on legs which had suddenly grown somewhat unsteady, one of the pair remarked:

"Say, listen—don't you hear footsteps behind us?"

The other hearkened.

"B'lieve I do." he said. "What of it?"

"It—it might be s-somebody f-following us."

"So what? Let him follow."

"But he m-might be one of those m-muggers."

"Well, just let him try something! Little does he know there's four of us!"

"Happy *Chanukah*, everybody!" shouted the stranger as he staggered into a small, neighborhood tavern.

The bartender laughed aloud. "For your information, mister," he said, still chuckling, "today happens to be the Fourth of July."

"*Ai*, am I gonna catch it from my wife," he moaned. "Seems like only yesterday she sent me out for the candles!"

"Tell me, my good man," asked the kindly *rebbetzyn*, "why do you drink all that whiskey?"

"Madam," replied my good man, "what else should I do with it?"

Jerry Miller, who used to travel for the Hecker's Flour people, found himself in Indianapolis one summer when he happened to run into his old friend, George, who was now living in that city. It was the first meeting between the two in many long years.

"Well, George," said the flour salesman after their initial greetings were over, "how are you getting along?"

The question seemed superfluous, for George was shabby, down-at-the-heels, out-at-the-elbows, and generally of a woebegone aspect. He permitted himself a hollow laugh.

"I never had such a run of rotten luck in my whole life as I've had these past few years," he began. "My wife's been an invalid since her car accident last August and it cost me all my savings for doctor bills. I had a nice business going, but my partner—that dirty crook—cheated me so badly I went bankrupt. In fact, I've been flat broke ever since. My oldest son is a loafer who won't work or go to school, and my younger one isn't much better."

"That sure is tough," observed Jerry sympathetically. "Back in New York, your brother Joe is doing very well. Haven't you heard from him?"

"Yeah, about a year ago. There sure is a big difference between me and my brother. Last I heard, he was just loaded with money. Listen, Jerry, I certainly would appreciate it, should you see him when you return to New York, if you'd tell him his poor brother George could use a little financial help. Right now fifty dollars in cash would look as big as a house."

"Believe me, I'll make it a point to speak to him," said Jerry.

"After all, what are brothers—especially rich brothers—for? But, look, George I've got a couple of bottles of good Mount Carmel wine upstairs in my hotel room. Come on up with me and we'll sample it. You'll feel better."

George accompanied his friend upstairs to sample the potables. He sighed deeply as he gazed into his well-filled glass.

"Makes me think of happier times," he said, downing the contents of the tumbler while his Adam's apple danced a visible jig in his throat. He then accepted another offering of the same.

"Jerry," he continued after a minute or two, "maybe I was exaggerating awhile ago. The trouble with me is that I've been brooding so much I get positively melancholy sometimes. Now, of course, my wife is still laid up from that auto accident, but it's beginning to look like she'll be better soon."

He held out his glass for replenishment. The third sample put a sparkle in his theretofore dulled eyes. He continued:

"Y'know, when I come to think of it, I'm not so sorry about the business going into bankruptcy. I never did care much for the line I was in, and being out of it has sort of given me a chance to look around. Next time, when I get a fresh start, I won't make so many mistakes, and I won't have a crooked partner, either."

George imbibed another glass of Mount Carmel's delight.

"About my sons—well, you know how modern boys are," he went on. "They're intelligent, and before long, I'm sure, they'll be acting like responsible young men. And—oh yes—by the way, if you see my brother Joe when you get back to New York, tell him you saw George out here and that George is getting along as well as could be expected."

An hour passed and they were starting on the second bottle. With an effort, the expatriate New Yorker raised himself to his feet. His eyes gleamed, his face glowed, he expanded his chest and reared back on his heels, his hands clasped behind him under his coattails; a perfect, living portrait of Baron de Rothschild.

"Jerry," he said somewhat thickly, "when you see my brother Joe, you just tell him that if he needs money or anything, and never mind how much, all he has to do is just call on me!"

We tell this one exactly as it was told in 1905, the only change being the substitution of a bus for a horse-car.

An inebriated old-timer, swaying unsteadily and his arms gesticulating wildly, flagged down a bus on the corner.

"Driver," he cried when the door was opened for him, "do

you go to Forty-shecon' Shtreet?"

"Yes, I do," said the driver.

"An' Broadway?"

"That's right. Forty-second and Broadway."

"Well, g'bye," said the juiced-up old fellow, waving him on with a friendly gesture, "and have a good time!"

Freddie and Rae were out on the town, celebrating their tenth wedding anniversary. Freddie, it soon become apparent, had imbibed more than was compatible with sobriety.

"Shweetie-pie," declared Freddie, planting a husbandly kiss upon her cheek, "my whole worl' revolvsh aroun' you."

"I wouldn't be surprised," said Rae coldly. "Didn't I tell you not to take that last drink?"

A policeman appeared in court as a witness against Max Loeb, arrested for being drunk in public.

"How do you know the defendant was intoxicated?" inquired the magistrate.

"No doubt about it at all," said the officer. "When I saw him, he was dropping a penny in a parking meter. Then he looked up at the big clock on the City Hall building and moaned 'My God, I've gained eleven pounds!'"

The night clerk at the Hotel Algonquin was surprised to see a battered-looking man, wearing nothing but his undershorts, enter the lobby from the street. The stranger staggered to the desk and paused there, weaving groggily.

"What can I do for you?" inquired the clerk.

"I'd like to be 'scorted to the third floor—room 302," said the near naked man.

"Room 302?" repeated the clerk. He consulted the register. "I'm sorry, sir, but that room is occupied by Mr. Oscar J. Levine of Toledo. It's pretty late to be rousing a guest."

"I know what time it is, well as you do," retorted the inebriated one. "Jush show me to Room 302 without any further con—conver—any further talk."

"Well, what's your name?"

"My name is Oscar J. Levine, an' fer your information I jush fell outta the window!"

It was a slow evening at the Tenth Avenue Bar and Grille. Baruch the bartender was toying with the idea of closing early when in walked a man with his dog. The stranger, his face flushed and his nose a Manischevitz-red, lurched to the bar and addressed Baruch in a confident if somewhat blurry voice.

"Look, Mac, I got a proposition fer ya. See this here dog? Well, his name's Pooch, an' he *talks!* Yeah, s'help me, he kin answer any question ya wanna ast him. Is it woith a straight shotta boibon on the house if Pooch answers a question?"

Baruch shrugged. After all, it was a very slow night—what could a little diversion hurt?

"All right, let's see what he can do."

The man gulped his bourbon down in one practiced swallow and then turned to his dog.

"Okay, Pooch, let's go. We gotta perduce fer this here good Joe, right? Here's the question: A guy is buildin' a boid house, see? He gets the floor laid an' he puts up the walls. But the foist time it rains, the boid inside gits all wet. Now, Pooch, tell this here man, what did the guy fergit to put on top of the house?"

"R-r-ruff!" went the dog.

"See? What'd I tell ya?" exclaimed the drunk exultantly. "Ol' Pooch knows his stuff, don't he? A real genius! Say, how's about another boibon, pal? My dog'll be glad ta answer one more question."

"Mister, believe me, you're not fooling anybody," Baruch told him. "I know there's a trick to it. But for the entertainment on a slow night, all right."

Another shot of bourbon was poured for the man and when he had tossed it down, he again addressed his dog.

"Now listen good, Pooch—pay close attention. A carpenter has a board with lotsa splinters on the edge. So he planes it down until he thinks it smooth. Then he runs his finger over the board but it soitinly ain't smooth a'tall. Now, Pooch, if it ain't smooth, what is it?"

"R-r-ruff!" went the dog.

"Ya hear that?" shouted the stranger. "I told ya he's a genius! Tellya what, pal: One last boibon an' this here clever doggie will answer one final question."

"All right," agreed Baruch, "but this time let *me* ask the question."

"Sure! Anything ya say, pal. Whatsa difference who asts? This here dog is a intelleckshul. He got it up here—ya know what I mean? So gimme the boibon an' *you* ast the question."

Baruch brought the man his drink and then spoke directly to the dog.

"Tell me, Pooch, who is the greatest Jew who ever lived?"

The dog hesitated for a moment or two, perplexity clearly visible in its soft brown eyes, and then, in an uncertain voice, went —

"R-r-r—Tony Coitis?"

The gifted playwright, George S. Kaufman, once maintained that the following anecdote was his favorite drinking story. Having survived 100 years of circulation in one version or another, it seems well on the way toward achieving immortality.

As a young man, the distinguished critic, George Jean Nathan, enjoyed a bit of conviviality now and then. He attended a banquet given by some theatrical people one night and stayed late. It was three o'clock in the morning when he reached his home. In front of his house was a very small yard, hardly more than an ornamental grassplot; and in its exact center stood a maple sapling with a trunk about two inches in diameter.

Nathan made for the door, but he tacked off at an angle and bumped into the little tree. He made a fresh start, executed a wide detour, and came back—smack up against the maple. This time he put his back to its swaying trunk in order to be sure of getting the direction right, and off he went again, plowing up the grass. It was no use. He circled the lawn twice, but finished up holding on to the sapling.

Thereupon, Nathan sat himself down on the earth with great care, removed his hat, his shoes and his topcoat, and rolled up the coat for a pillow. As he sank to rest beneath the stars that shined down on Fourth Street and Ninth Avenue, he muttered in a voice of resignation:

"Lost, by heaven! Lost in the midsh of an impen'trable fore-sh!"

16

Cooking and Fressing

Introduction

The reader will notice a number of changes from the traditional humor of past generations as he reads this chapter. Some will be readily apparent; others more subtle. Unlike the "Yiddishe mama joke" which has, for the most part, retained its gentleness, the anecdotes in the following pages seem to have grown more sardonic. This does not necessarily mean that they are funnier or even more mature than yesteryear's jokes. They simply reflect the times in which we live. The flavor of *Yiddishkeit* is still here, albeit holding on with slippery fingertips.

The eating of *traif* (non-*kosher* food) by curious, careless or non-observing Jews, for example, has long been a staple of the people's humor. Following World War II, however, with memories of the Hitler obscenity still vividly alive, the emergence of the Arab threat to Israel's survival, and the Soviet Union's repression of its captive Jewish citizens, jokes concerning the religious injunctions about food all but disappeared—perhaps because the humorous stories seemed too inconsequential by contrast. Nevertheless, within more recent years there has been a mild reappearance of the quips and anecdotes, possibly due to the resurgence of interest in Judaism, especially among the younger men and women. But the dearth of such stories—at least of those comparable in excellence with the older jokes—is reflected in the collection presented in this chapter which contains only *one* funny story about the eating of forbidden food.

However, one facet of Jewish humor as it pertains to food and dining remains as popular as ever: the joke which revolved around that condescending, unflappable, arrogant, earthy and sullenly witty individual known, as "the Jewish waiter." He really did exist prior to the Great Depression of the early thirties, when, at last, hard times finally compelled him to adopt a more or less respectful manner toward his patrons. But the stories about him are still told and retold to this very day.

A few—*very* few—of these dour, sharp-tongued gentlemen continue their old and nefarious ways, mainly on New York's lower East Side, but regretfully, they too are becoming extinct. They shall be missed, those haughty remnants of an endangered species, for they not only exercised the right of veto over the customer's dinner selection, yielding with manifest reluctance to compromise, but they were usually right; the waiter was seemingly possessed of an unerring ability to match diner and dinner with the same analytical ingenuity as the old-time *shadchane* when it came to matching bride and groom.

The Jewish waiter, whatever else he may have been, was certainly no shrinking violet or cringing sycophant—and woe betide the patron who dared put on airs at *his* table! There is the delightful story about Sid Kramer, a waiter in Kaufman's East Side restaurant (a fabulous, turn-of-the-century eating place of which you will read more in the following pages). Back around 1920 or so, Edward, the Prince of Wales (who later became King of England only to abdicate his throne to marry Wally Simpson) entered the little East Side restaurant with his royal entourage. In those days, it was quite fashionable for upper strata socialites to go "slumming," so their appearance was not too great a surprise.

Kramer, who was not especially enthusiastic about slummers, straightened his apron, asked if anyone wanted water (he wasn't about to do unnecessary work for those who were not thirsty), and then listened carefully to their instructions. He was unable to write English, and simply memorized the orders. His power of recall must have been phenomenal, for he nodded after each of the party of 10 had stated their preference. He then sauntered off in the general direction of the kitchen, stopping meanwhile to pass the time of day with Kaufman, the proprietor, who saw nothing unusual, much less reprehensible, in such dalliance.

Returning to the visiting royalty with the first orders, which were perched precariously along the full length of his arm, Kramer leaned over Princess Elizabeth (to reign one day in the future as the queen), and murmured caressingly, "You're the cold salmon, Dollie?"

The astounded Prince of Wales looked up from his menu and was about to voice his displeasure, when Sid Kramer asked pleasantly, "Would you like, maybe, something superior for your interior, Eddie?" His face purple, the future monarch signaled for the proprietor, and Kaufman ambled over. He listed to the royal complaint, and then turned to his A-Number-One waiter.

"Listen, Sid, the man don't like you should call him Eddie," he explained reprovingly. "So call him Princie, or Harry."

Another interesting waiter episode involved the late Belle Baker, in those days a glittering star of show business. She went to Tomashevsky's, on Second Avenue, for an after-theater *nosh*. A young waiter took her order. He did not return for at least a half-hour, at which time Belle was fuming. "You mean to say you're the same waiter who took my order?" she asked incredulously. "Frankly, I expected a much older man."

Yes, there are countless jokes about the stereotypical Jewish waiter, but the joke is not on him—it is on society. The earliest of those impertinent waiters were the uneducated, unsophisticated immigrants whose insolence was really unintentional; they simply knew no better. There were also the educated newcomers who could find no work in their regular trades and professions, and were glad to obtain a paying job "waiting tables" in the new land. Unlike their illiterate colleagues, their impudence was intentional; they took out their personal frustrations on the customer. But, educated or not, those first waiters established a reputation for *chutzpah*—monumental gall—which has served as their image ever since. And the joke is on society because a succession of waiters, down through the years, perpetuated that image in one of the longest-running hoaxes in the people's folklore. As you read the jokes that unfold in this chapter, listen carefully and you may hear a mystic chuckle from somewhere in the room. It will be the ghost of that long since departed waiter having the last laugh!

Jewish humor, when it concerns the role of the sexes in the kitchen, is nearly always favorable to the male. Certainly, no female made the original observation that husbands usually miss their wives' cooking—every chance they get. Occasionally, of course, the missus emerges the winner: "You said you'd learn how to cook after we were married," growls hubby. And his bride of three months airily replies: "Oh, you know those campaign promises." It is one of those rare jokes about food in which the distaff side has the last word, but it is still an indirect put-down on the wife. And she doesn't exactly burst into gales of merriment, either, when the old man comes home from work and asks, "What's thawing?"

The mystery as to how our grandmothers and *their* grandmothers prepared all those bountiful, legendary meals without the aid of modern kitchen conveniences passeth all understanding. With that sort of family background in the culinary arts, one would think that today's husbands would be singing hallelujahs in praise of their wives' cooking. But if they are, it is not reflected in contemporary humor. Perhaps it is because the Jewish housewife—or houseperson if you please—is more liberated than her grandma who subscribed to the theory of male superiority. If so, the subscription has been canceled. Can you visualize ordering Bella Abzug to keep quiet already and fry the *latkes* or you'll give her *epis* she won't be able to sit down for a week? She'd holler for the fuzz. What's more, she'd tell you to go fry your own damn *latkes!*

Dietetics, the triumph of mind over platter, is yet another aspect of Jewish humor that was rarely evidenced in the older jokes. As might be expected, here, too, the quips and stories are slanted in favor of the male. Doctors tell us that more men than women are concerned about weight and dieting because of the higher incidence of heart attacks due to obesity among males. But you'd never know it by the jokes. It is no novelty to see a fat comedian unselfconsciously informing his amused audience that his wife has been on a diet for three weeks and all she has managed to take off is her hat. Actually, it is the woman who is the more careful weight-watcher. She knows that, while it may be true about a curved line being the loveliest distance between two points, when it gets too curvy it becomes a detour. She is now ready to diet—and let the hips fall where may.

Liberated or not, grandma would have beaned grandpa with a chicken had he continually joked about her cooking in the manner of so many younger husbands. However, what with the ladies becoming rabbis and plumbers nowadays, they will soon be getting the quaint notion into their heads that they merit equal treatment in the joke department also. Comedians in bloomers! It is to weep! Wisecracking wives in the kitchen nobody needs. Traditionalists prefer the kind of joke in which the father turns to his son at the dinner table and remarks icily: "If your mother can take the time to defrost this meal, then you can take the time to eat it!"

But, let us end this Introduction, and have some real nourishment.

H.D.S.

Part One
♦ ♦ ♦
DINING IN

The Pincus family fortunes had taken a turn for the better and nothing would do but that all the Pincii move to a nicer neighborhood. Grandpa Pincus, who never lived outside a Jewish *gegent* in his life, had some difficulty adjusting to his new gentile acquaintances.

"How does a Jew make these *narishkeit mentschen*—foolish people—understand why a Jew boils water to make hot tea, blows on it in a saucer to make it cool, adds sugar to make it sweet and then adds a little lemon to make it sour?" old man Pincus grumped. "The way they're looking on me you'd think I just came over on the boat."

"It's not the way you prepare the tea," explained his granddaughter, trying hard to suppress a grin, "it's the way you pour the tea into your saucer and cool it by blowing."

Grandpa Pincus stared at her as if she had lost her powers of reasoning.

"So how else should I cool my tea?" he demanded. "Fan it with my *yarmulke*?"

Little Danny finished his dinner and his mother set a bowl of quivering Jell-O on the table before him. "Here, eat your dessert like a good boy," she said.

"I can't eat that, mama," he protested. "It ain't dead yet."

It has been said of the late Oscar Levant that he was the champion misanthrope of his time. If this story is any criterion, he deserved the dubious distinction.

Levant, according to impeachable witnesses, was on his way home one evening after a rehearsal.

"By the time I get home my dinner should be about ready," he declared. "If it isn't ready and waiting, I'm going to raise unmitigated hell. And if it is ready. . . . I won't eat a damn bite!"

♦ ♦ ♦

In these days of the impersonal giant supermarkets, we tend to forget that only yesterday the "Mom and Pop" grocery store flourished on almost every corner. These family-run groceries (as the stores were called) delivered purchases to the customer's home as a matter of routine. Orders were often telephoned to the grocer. The old-fashioned service which the customer received is nicely illustrated in this story.

Mrs. Zimmerman phoned her neighborhood grocery and ordered a week's supply of food, including meat, vegetables and dairy products. The delivery boy soon brought the order to her house, but when she started to unpack she noticed that there were only ten eggs in the carton which was supposed to hold a dozen. She stalked to the telephone and angrily dialed the store.

"Hello, Mr. Gold, this is Mrs. Zimmerman. Listen, I got a complaint."

"*Nu*, unburden yourself," advised Mr. Gold soothingly. "You'll feel better."

"Well, I ordered a dozen eggs but you sent me only ten: That a dozen by you?"

"Is that what you're making such a big *tsimmes* about?" asked Mr. Gold in genuine surprise. "To tell you the truth, you should be thanking me instead of complaining."

"What have I got I should thank you for?"

"The service. Believe me, Mrs. Zimmerman, two of the eggs in that dozen were so bad I threw them out for you!"

A modern wife, according to Undernourished Untermyer, is one who can dish it out but can't cook it.

Cohen the Bensonhurst coin collector entered his brother's drugstore and asked for an Alka Seltzer.

"How come you got acid indigestion?" questioned the brother. "I thought your wife fixes three well-balanced square meals a day."

"She does," acknowledged Cohen wistfully, "but her square meals just don't balance in my round stomach."

"I'm not saying my family was poor," reminisced the late

heavy-weight boxing champion, Max Baer, "but when my mother sliced the corned beef it had only one side!"

Mrs. Umglik, a new arrival in America, was taking her first walk up Second Avenue, under escort of her older brother who had been living here for several years. In the window of a grocery store, she observed a great mound of cranberries.

"What are those?" she asked.

"Cranberries," explained her brother.

"They're good to eat?"

"Are they good to eat?" echoed the brother. "Listen, when those cranberries are stewed they make even better applesauce than prunes!"

Two-ton Tillie Sugarman answered a knock on the door, only to be greeted by the neighborhood *schnorrer.*

"Mrs. Sugarman" he whined, "for three days I haven't had a bite to eat."

"Oh goodness!" she exclaimed. "If only I had your will power!"

A new arrival at a mental institution joined a fellow patient at the dining table.

"Oh, wow, you really are *meshuggeh,*" he moaned, looking with unfeigned disgust at the other's laden plate. "Anybody who'd eat chocolate-covered meatballs *must* be nuts!"

"Oh, yeah?" snorted the other derisively. "You ain't so normal yourself. I noticed you eating your soup with a knife."

"Well, that's certainly not because I'm crazy," retorted the new arrival. "It's just that my fork leaks!"

If you have ever tried to feed a six or seven-month old baby and keep its face clean at the same time, this line of dialogue should bring back fond, if messy, memories.

The young mother was busy elsewhere in the house and the father had undertaken the task of feeding little Becky in her highchair. The sloppy procedure went about as expected, and after various and sundry starts, half-starts and accidents, he finally called out to his wife:

"Hey, honey, Becky finished the strained prunes but I think she wants more. Shall I give her a second coat?"

Part Two

◆ ◆ ◆

WHINING OUT

"We sold over 200 hamburgers last night," boasted Walter, the wily waiter, "and I want you to know we did it all with a half-pound of meat!"

Once again we turn back the leaves of the calendar to chuckle at the highly imaginative but almost believable incidents that amused our parents and grandparents. These colorful stories were usually told as "true facts" and any number of people could always be found who could and would vouch for the truthfulness of the event. Needless to say, these "eyewitnesses" invariably named different locales and even different years in which the incidents supposedly happened. Our version of the following tale places the scene in "Kaufman's Essen," sometime in the early 1930s.

Almost a half-century ago, a small restaurant on Grand Street, "Kaufman's Essen," achieved a sort of local fame on New York's lower East Side as a poor man's gourmet center. At prices for less than a dollar, Kaufman served such mouth-watering delicacies as stuffed *helzel*, roast goose with *genineh gribben*, *hockflaish* wrapped in sweet-and-sour cabbage, *tsimmis*, *kreplach*, *kishkeh*, and, for dessert, there was always *kugel* or some other pudding or pastry.

But running a restaurant is like running any other kind of business—there is always one customer you wish had stayed in the old country. Kaufman had such a patron—an old man named Sokolov. If he wasn't complaining about the service, he was griping about the prices. If the soup was too cold, the coffee was too hot. Always something with this Sokolov—there was no satisfying the man. As far as Kaufman was concerned, his customer started out as a pain in the neck and worked his way down.

Tonight it was the bread. Sokolov was unhappy because he

was served only two slices.

"Now just a minute!" Kaufman protested. "In here everybody gets treated equal. Two slices. You've been getting two slices ever since you started eating in this place, so why are you hollering now, all of a sudden?"

"Well, it ain't enough," Sokolov told him. "One slice I need with the soup, no? Another slice I need for the gravy, no? Another slice I need with the main course, no? Another slice I need with the coffee, no? Another slice. . ."

"All right, enough already!" Kaufman snapped. So he brought the man four slices of bread. After all, he was a steady customer, despite his complaining nature.

The next evening, Sokolov demanded still more slices. Kaufman sighed. "What can you do with a tightskate like this?" he muttered to himself. Teeth clenched, he put another four slices on the table.

On the following night, Sokolov looked at the ten slices of bread on his extra plate and then glanced up at Kaufman whose face was now grim.

"Kaufman, what's the matter—you're so poor you can't spare a few extra slices?"

In a rage, Kaufman sped back to the kitchen, grabbed a whole loaf of bread, cut it lengthwise in half, and rushed back into the dining area. He slammed the two halves down on the table, so infuriated he could not utter a single word.

Sokolov took one agonized look at the bread and cried:

"*Oy*, you're back to two slices!"

The diner ordered breaded veal cutlet, took a tentative first taste, frowned, took another bite, frowned some more and then called the waiter.

"I must say," he complained, "I've tasted better veal cutlet."

"Izzatso!" retorted the offended waiter. "Not in here!"

Josh, the talmudic student, was working his way through rabbinical college. On weekends, he served as a waiter at Sigmund's Seafood Stop-In. On this particular Sunday, the boss called Josh aside and informed him that the restaurant was stuck with over 50 pounds of flounder.

"I want you to recommend flounder to everyone who comes

in," Sigmund instructed the youthful waiter. "Tell the customers the flounders were caught just an hour ago—fresh from the ocean, and the tastiest fish on the menu."

"But, Sigmund, the flounder is a week old," protested the future rabbi. "You know I can't tell a lie like that. It would be against all my spiritual beliefs."

"All right, so don't lie. Just push the flounder," demanded Sigmund.

A few minutes later, a customer sat down at one of Josh's tables.

"What do you suggest?" asked the patron.

"The flounder," said Josh promptly, "but it stinks."

It was a cold and rainy evening in December, and the diner entered Dov's Hester Street Deli-Restaurant in a foul mood. He made his way to his customary table and sat down, muttering angrily to himself.

"You're a little late tonight," observed Dov as he approached the ill-humored customer. "The rain hold you up?"

"Yes," growled the patron. "I had to drive around for twenty minutes looking for a parking place. Why don't you build a parking lot for this restaurant?"

"Mister," replied Dov with sweet reason, "if I had a parking lot, would I need a restaurant?"

From the *American Israelite*, we learn of a delightful little episode in the life of Gustav Poznanski (1805-1897), a widely known *chazan* of his day. It illustrates what can happen to an observant Jew who flouts the dietary laws of his people. In all fairness to the cantor, however, let it be said that it happened before he embarked upon his life's calling.

Visiting a Louisiana town, and being so far from home, Poznanski gave way to a wild and sudden impulse to taste forbidden food—just this once, he assured himself. He entered a restaurant which, being near the Gulf, specialized in seafood.

For Poznanski, the two opening courses were in the nature of novelties. Nevertheless, he partook freely of the crawfish gumbo and jambalaya Creole. But when the waiter brought him an individual oyster patty containing one large swollen Bayou Creek oyster enveloped in fluffy pastry, the *chazan's* eyes widened. Gingerly, he touched the contents with his fork. Then, with an expression of mingled surprise and distress upon his face he summoned the waiter who chanced to be passing his table.

"Whut's de trouble, boss?" inquired that functionary, ranging up alongside.

"Really, I'm not sure," stated Poznanski, his voice wavering from apprehension to outright disgust, "but it would appear that something has crawled into my bun and expired."

Not that it's the most important statement in the lexicon of American literature, but on Fairfax Avenue in Los Angeles there used to be a small restaurant named Della's Delicate Essen. Della herself is the authority for this whimsical exchange of dialogue.

A gentleman was sitting alone, staring malignantly at his order of fried fish. His lips were moving as though arguing with someone.

Della, who also served as waitress on the girl's day off, observed the diner's angry expression and, figuring that his demeanor was bad for business, she approached him in a deferential manner—a manner, incidentally, which she rarely indulged.

"Something is wrong, sir?" she inquired.

"Wrong?" spat the customer. "Of course not! Why should there be something wrong? I'm complaining?"

"I thought you were saying something, sir."

"I was. Me and this fish here, we were having a nice little discussion."

"A *meshuggeneh*," Della thought. Aloud she said: "That's very good, sir. Ha-ha-ha—talking with the fish!" She turned away, wondering what institution he had escaped from, but determined not to offend him.

"Hold on, lady," cried the customer. "On me you don't have to smile to yourself. What's the matter—you never before heard a fish talk? No? Well, you wouldn't understand his dialect so I'll translate for you the discussion we just had.

"First, I said to the fish, 'Hello, my fried friend, how's by you this nice evening?'

"'I'm not feeling so good,' said the fish.

"'You don't look too good, either; you should pardon me for saying so,' I said. 'Tell me, how are things down in the river?'

"And the fish said, 'How should I know? I've been here for two weeks!'"

A stranger in town went into the Greps Cafe in Burpee, California, and imperiously summoned the waiter with a beckoning finger.

"How's the food and service in here?" he demanded.

"Mister," replied the short-tempered waiter, "I just serve the food in this place; I'm not a character witness!"

Pencil and order book in hand, the waitress hovered over the early morning customer.

"I'll have scrambled eggs, toast and coffee," he said.

"Try the breakfast special for today," the young lady suggested. "It's better."

"No, just the eggs, toast and coffee, please."

"But the special has bigger portions and its fifteen cents cheaper."

"Madam, will you kindly bring me my order?"

"B-b-but . . ."

"See here, young woman!" growled the exasperated patron, "if I wanted a fight before breakfast I'd have eaten at home!"

Rose Berson, the *femme fatale* of East 114th Street, was on a vegetarian kick.

"Please bring me some raw bean sprouts, some raw carrot sticks, some raw cauliflower and some raw fresh cabbage leaves," she instructed.

"Lady," barked the waiter, "this is a restaurant not a meadow!"

"Waiter," protested the diner, "I hate to say it, but the tapioca tastes like glue."

"Sorry," muttered the waiter as he removed the plate, "this must be the rice pudding. The tapioca tastes from plaster."

A visitor from a small town had heard that Chicago waiters were a tough breed. He didn't believe it, however—that is, not until he entered the Bagel Basket on Jefferson Street in the Windy City.

"I'll have mashed potatoes, peas and lamb chops," ordered the out-of-towner. "And be damn sure you tell the chef to make the chops lean."

"Okay," said the waiter agreeably. "Any particular direction?"

"I see that tips are forbidden in this restaurant," said the pleased customer.

"Yes," said the genial waiter, "but so were apples in the Garden of Eden!"

"What in heaven's name did your cook put into this meatloaf?" cried the customer, after one small taste.

"Nothing to worry about," replied the waiter. "Perfectly good leftovers from yesterday's leftovers."

The diner tried another bite and then slammed down his fork in disgust.

"Who can eat this stuff?" he demanded. "I don't mind eating leftovers and even leftovers from leftovers, but leftover leftovers from yesterday's leftover leftover leftovers is going too far!"

"Mister," complained the new patron, "these eggs smell bad."

"Well, don't blame me," retorted the waiter defensively. "I only laid the table!"

In his book, *Paul Muni: His Life and His Films*, Michael B. Druxman reminds us that Paul Muni believed that to be a good actor one had to prepare well, but the style and technique that each actor develops is the result of his own intuition and instinct. Muni was fond of comparing this approach, which he believe in strongly, to his wife's grandmother's method of making apple pie. She was an excellent baker, and when asked the secret of her delicious home-made pies, she would reply: "First I comb my hair. Then I wash my hands. Then I put on my apron. Then I make a pie."

17

Science and Scientists

Introduction

The number of Jewish scientists and inventors who have made lasting contributions to America's culture and prosperity are in the thousands. Charles P. Steinmetz, small in physical stature, but a giant in intellect, was the electrical wizard largely responsible for the early success of the General Electric Corporation. If it weren't for his contributions to science (to quote a new epigram), we would now be watching television by candlelight. And little need be said of the illustrious Albert Einstein whose wife didn't understand him. Whereas the noted physicist could produce nuclear fission by putting atomic particles under tremendous pressure, Mrs. Einstein claimed that she could produce flawless diamonds by subjecting her husband to the same pressure.

The *luftmentsch* of Jewish folklore remains with us in the scientific community. Dr. Isaac Ellenbogen, of Harvard, whose research into the cause and removal of pollutants in our atmosphere has won him plaudits and cash from private foundations and government agencies, has stated that no one has ever really understood air. Had Dr. Ellenbogen taken the trouble to inquire more deeply, he would have learned what the average person—not versed in science—knows intuitively, that although cold air is a product of refrigerators, hot air comes out of Washington.

The field of anthropology does not seem to have much appeal for Jewish students. Few, to my knowledge, have attained eminence in that sphere, preferring, instead, the security of working in their father's store. The cause may have its roots in their theological training. As the old-fashioned Yiddishe papa protested to his college son: "Maybe *your* father descended from monkeys, but not mine!"

Anthropologists these days are mostly concerned with the worldwide problem of excessive human reproduction. These are two types of people responsible for the population explosion, according to anthropologist Gertrude Segal: the male and the female. The male, says the lady scientist, is a member of the negligible sex, commonly known (to the female) as chauvinist *chozzerei*. His genes contain two varieties: good providers and bad providers, the latter usually dominant. It is noteworthy that most Jewish-American anthropologists are returning to the old Malthusian theory, which pertains to Malthus and his doctrines. Malthus believed in artificially limiting populations, but found that it could not be done by talking. However, neither Malthus nor any Jewish investigator into human behavior has ever matched Richard von Krafft-Ebing, who left these immortal words to posterity: "Say, if you think *that's* racy, listen to *this* one!"

It is only in the last 40 years or so that an appreciable number of Jews have become geologists—who are more important than anthropologists if only because the costs of their college tuitions are higher.

We now come to botany, a repugnant branch of learning that has had little appeal to the Jewish scientist—and he is undeniably right in ignoring it. Most aspects of this subject, especially those revolving around pollination, cannot be discussed in this respectable book without running afoul of the good people of Boston, but this much can now be revealed: Botany is the science of vegetables—those that are good to eat even when they taste rotten. It deals largely with the flowers and roots which are usually badly designed, inartistic in color, and ill-smelling. Better to stick to dairy and chopped meat—vegetarians to the contrary notwithstanding. A little gout never killed anybody.

In retrospect, the "mad scientist" of legend, myth and movies may yet prove to be mankind's (you should pardon the expression) savior. It is he who seems to create the most practical consumer goods, such as the new aspirin tablet that beats the *schnapps* through your bloodstream. A mad scientist is one who does not conform to standards of thought, speech, dress and action which are derived by the conformants from study of themselves. He is at odds with the majority; in short, unusual. It is noteworthy that persons are adjudged mad by officials who are destitute of evidence that they themselves are sane.

In this brief Introduction, I have, by indirection, tried to establish a frame of reference. The point is this: NO area of science is immune to burlesque; no scientist too lofty and important to escape the barbs of the satirist.

Only one question remains to be answered: "Why is it that American Jews, comprising a tiny percentage of the population of the United States, and considered a race of mere dreamers, have been able to attain pre-eminence in so many scientific areas?" The key word, I think, is "dreamers." Rabbi Maurice Davis provides the answer:

> Every act of progress the world had ever known first began with a dreamer. After him came the scientist or the statesman, the expert or the technician. But first came the dreamer.

And we laugh, because we are proud—and well pleased!

H.D.S.

"One beautiful thing about the photos of earth from outer space," declared physics professor Murray Klugman of M.I.T., "is that you can't see a single protest demonstration.

"The astronauts said the moon looks like a 'dirty beach,'" Klugman recalled. "Perhaps so, but to me it still looks cleaner than Coney Island after the Fourth of July.

"We have had many tangible benefits from space technology," concluded the professor, "although not all are adaptable to everyday needs. Take those new astronaut watches, for example. You can't tell time unless you're standing on your head."

Mrs. Frieda Rothafel, wife of nuclear scientist Dr. Emanuel Rothafel, once on the NASA staff at Cape Kennedy, is justifiably proud of her famous husband. But a woman cannot live with a man for thirty years without realizing that these upper strata wizards may know very little else outside of their esoteric professions. Mrs. Rothafel explained it this way:

"My husband has one of the finest minds in the whole country. It starts working the minute he wakes up and doesn't stop until I ask him something!"

"Milton," the sixth grade science teacher called out, "can you tell me the difference between ohms and watts and volts?"

"No ma'am," replied Milton, "but I don't blame ya fer askin'."

Pincus the Pitkin Avenue presser is also a part-time scientist. He just figured out why summer days are longer than winter days. . . . The heat expands them.

Professor Gregor Muzhik of the Soviet Union and Professor George Kaplan of the United States met during one of the ongoing SALT international conferences in 1974. They soon were embroiled in an argument about genetics.

"I can tell you definitely," said Dr. Muzhik, "that in our classless society we have proved beyond the shadow of a doubt that it is environment, not heredity, that accounts for a person's appearance."

Dr. Kaplan frowned. "You Russian scientists have committed the sin of allowing your political ideology to run away with your common sense," he remarked dryly. "Any college student can prove that heredity and environment each have their own characteristics and produce their own unique results."

"Prove it," demanded the Soviet professor.

"Very well," agreed Dr. Kaplan. "If a person looks like his father, his appearance will be the result of heredity. But if he looks like the milkman it will be the result of environment."

Dr. Klugmentsch, the scientist of advanced sonics, had made the remarkable discovery that turtles cannot hear the highest notes of a soprano, a flute or a violin.

"This explains," said Dr. Klugmentsch, "why turtles are seldom invited to concerts."

Shed a furtive tear for the poor professor who spent thirty years in intensive research, trying to find out why his colleagues were so absentminded—then forgot the answer!

Dr. Albert Einstein, the most eminent physicist and mathematician the world has ever known, was on the podium explaining the rudiments of time-space calculations to an audience of graduating students and their guests. In the back row, sitting next to their son who had just received his diploma, were Mr. And Mrs. Meyers, ten years removed from their tiny *shtetl* in Russia. They watched with rapt if uncomprehending attention as Dr. Einstein illustrated his comments on a huge blackboard.

"The theory has been advanced," said the great scientist, "that the nearest habitable star is four light years from Earth."

"So what's four years?" whispered Mr. Meyers, *sotto voce.*

His embarrassed son silenced him with a fierce "shhh!"

Dr. Einstein continued: "There are 60 seconds in a minute and 60 minutes in an hour."

"This guy Einstein gets paid for such information?" demanded Mr. Meyers.

His wife gave him a wifely elbow to his ribs. "Sharrop already, you're disturbing the people."

"In a 24-hour day there are 86,400 second," Einstein went on, chalkmarking the blackboard with figures. "Multiply that by 365, the number of days in 12 months, and we arrive at a total of 31,536,000 seconds in a year."

"Big deal!" muttered Mr. Meyers.

"Now then, we enter the realm of astronomics," the scientist further explained. "Light travels at a speed of 186,000 miles per second. If we multiply that figure by 31,536,000—the number of seconds in a year—we find that the resultant number of seconds, 5,865,676,000, represents one light year. And as the nearest habitable is four light years away, we know that it would take us 23,462,704,000 seconds to get there—provided we are traveling at a speed of 186,000 miles a second."

"Who has gas for such a trip?" asked Mrs. Meyers.

Mr. Meyers nodded. "The fare alone would set me back maybe a whole year's wages."

Dr. Einstein now concluded his address:

"In other words, ladies and gentlemen, relating those four light years to our own measurement of time, it would take us 744 years to reach another planet on which human beings could survive."

"I should live so long," commented Mr. Meyers.

"Maybe this Einstein doesn't like it in this country," surmised Mrs. Meyers, "so he's thinking *efsher* he'll emigrate."

Their son, who had been shushing them throughout the scientist's discourse, could no longer contain his irritation.

"What's the matter with you two? Have you got something

against the great Einstein?"

His mother stared at him in surprise.

"Why should I have anything against him? He did me something? Personally, I think he writes very good on blackboards."

"Well, *I* have something against him!" snapped Mr. Meyers. "Here he's standing up on the stage and he's directing us like he's a traffic cop to a place that's a billion-shmillion miles away. But only an hour ago your great Einstein stopped me in the hall and asked me directions to the men's room!"

"Gee, grandpa, I sure wish I could be an astronaut," sighed little Mikey, his voice wistful.

"Then study astronomy."

"But, grandpa," argued Mikey, "I'm only seven."

"So what?" demanded the old-timer. "When I was your age, I was already self-taught. Like it was only yesterday I remember wondering where the sun went after dark, so I stayed up all night studying the sky."

"Did you find out?"

"I sure did!" affirmed grandpa with a broad grin. "It finally dawned on me."

Doctor Fahni Halavah, distinguished president of the Egyptian Academy of Science, upon hearing of the electric sundial, was heard to comment learnedly, in Latin:

"*Vos maynt electric?*"

American Jewish folklore is replete with humorous incidents which illustrate the human side of heroic figures in our nation's history. The story of the devilish disappearance of Professor Einstein's check is an example. This true anecdote was reported by Dr. William Hess, Archivist, *RF Illustrated* (publication of the Rockefeller Institute), from letters dated 1923:*

Dr. Albert Einstein wrote from Berlin to Dr. Jacques Loeb of the Rockefeller Institute in New York, that he had an idea "which

*From *RF Illustrated*, publication of the Rockefeller Institute, Vol. 1, No. 4, Nov. 1973.

arouses the hope of solving the riddle of the quantum theory." To make the calculations to test this idea, he'd need a theoretical assistant; but he couldn't afford one. He thought $360 a year would suffice.

Dr. Loeb sent the request to Dr. Abraham Flexner of the General Education Board, adding his belief that "Einstein in his excessive modesty has reduced it to an almost impossible minimum." Dr. Loeb considered $500 more realistic. And so, Dr. Einstein was informed in a letter that the International Education Board had granted him $500 annually; the first check was enclosed in the letter.

Word next reached Dr. Flexner, from Dr. Heinrich Poll of Berlin, that Dr. Einstein had received the check but was not sure who had caused it to be sent; that he had mislaid or lost the check or someone had stolen it from him; and that "he is now in the greatest anxiety about what to do next."

Dr. Flexner wrote, while enclosing a replacement for the check:

"The last doubt should be removed. Einstein is a great genius. Nobody but a great genius would be so careless in the handling of a check."

The above Einstein tale, occurring as it did in 1923, may be the first of the humorous anecdotes about the pre-eminent physicist to enjoy wide dissemination in Europe and the United States. But the following story is uniquely American, although it is not, of course, presented as fact. The imaginative incident gained currency shortly after the scientist, stripped of his citizenship and deprived of his possessions, fled Nazi Germany and arrived in the United States in 1934, where he accepted a post at the Institute for Advanced Study, Princeton. The story goes as follows:

Yoel the tailor was busily engaged at his pressing iron when who should walk into his humble shop but the great Albert Einstein, in person. Yoel, himself a refugee from Hitler's insane Third Reich and still unfamiliar with the English language, recognized the famous scientist immediately from pictures he had seen in the *Forverts*. When the visitor had concluded his business and was turning to leave, the tailor laid a hand on the physicist's arm.

"Before you go, Dr. Einstein, would you do me a big favor?" he asked, his voice brimming with respect and eager curiosity.

"If I can," Einstein agreed, smiling genially.

"Then tell me, what is this relativity business all about?"

"Well, to begin with," the great man responded, "relativity is a theory in physics which I happened to introduce. It discards the concept of time and space as absolute entities and views them as relative to moving systems or frames of reference. However, full comprehension of the mathematical formulation of my theory can be attained only through a study of certain branches of mathematics as, for example, tensor calculus."

Yoel nodded wisely and thanked the scientist for his explanation. When he was gone, the little tailor turned to his assistant.

"You know something?" he declared. "This Einstein thinks just like me!"

Zimmerman, the zoologist, recently informed a waiting world that he had successfully crossed a tiger with a parakeet. He doesn't know what to call the offspring, but when it talks you listen!

At least it's an improvement on his previous experiment when he crossed a mink with an octopus and got a coat with eight sleeves.

The second grade teacher had just finished explaining, in very elementary terms, how Sir Isaac Newton had formulated his theory about gravity. Now she was ready to test her little students with a few simple questions.

"Edith," she began, "what did Isaac Newton say when the apple fell on his head?"

"I know," replied Edith, smiling brightly: "The sky is falling; I must go and tell the king!"

Mr. Abraams was comfortably seated on the living room couch, reading the evening paper after a hard day's work. In the next room, his son was at the dining table studying for his college exams.

"Hey, dad, here's something interesting," the student called out, shattering the peaceful silence. "In my textbook it says that atomic scientists will soon have a way to heat a whole house on a single lump of coal."

"What's new about that?" snorted Mr. Abraams. "Our landlord has been doing it for years!"

18

Doctors, Nurses
and Hospitals

Introduction

It is no secret that most Jews hold the medical profession in high esteem. If we are to believe the *bobeh mysehs* of folklore, Jewish mothers produce doctors; gentile mothers, patients. Yet, despite the favorable publicity engendered by the Yiddishe mama jokes, doctors have received a rather bad press in the people's oral and written literature. It is a situation I intend to encourage, for no other reason than the approval of my peer group—the happychondriacs of life.

The most illustrious Jewish doctor in history was Maimonides, whose "Physicians' Prayer" is not only a beautiful tribute to the practice of medicine, but provides a remarkable insight into the humane and spiritual qualities of that great and good man. But the veneration which has rightfully been accorded him for so many generations has not generally been proffered to other medical practitioners—allowing for the usual exceptions. A passage from the Mishna, for example, declares flatly: "The best of doctors are destined for Gehenna." Another ancient Jewish proverb warns: "Ask the patient, not the doctor" (especially if you want to know where it hurts). Even when a physician is moved by compassion for the poor and offers his ministrations without charge, he's "damned if he does and damned if he doesn't." The Talmud puts it this way: "A physician who heals for nothing is worth nothing"—a sentiment doubtless written by a scholar who practiced medicine on the side.

The humorous coupling of the *Malach-Hamoves* with the

medical fraternity has long been employed in Jewish witticisms. In 1809, the *Chassidic* rabbi, Nahman Bratzlav, wrote: "It was difficult for the Angel of Death to kill everybody in the whole world, so he appointed doctors to assist him." But Rabbi Bratzlav was by no means the first to associate the two. Joseph Zabara, the 13th century Hebrew satirist of Barcelona, made the observation, "Both the doctor and the Angel of Death kill, but the doctor charges a fee." Nevertheless, we can all take heart and breathe a little easier. An American physician, Dr. Meyer Perlstein, in his book, *Amusing Quotations*, has given us these words of reassurance: "If your time hasn't come, not even a doctor can kill you!"

Most of the characters of bygone days are still represented in American-Jewish humor through their modern counterparts. Occasionally, one can still find a religious Jew who, like his ancestors, is convinced that prayer alone will cure all sickness. He, too, is a legitimate target for humor. He believes that the laws of the universe can be annulled on behalf of a single petitioner. This devout person looks upon the Deity as a neurologist, proctologist, opthalmologist, chiropodist and celestial eye, ear, nose and throat specialist. Of the latter four parts of the body, the nose is given the least consideration, it being the farthest outpost of the face. As will be seen in this chapter, jokes about divine healing are limited, due, no doubt, to a large number of states in which the American Medical Association does not allow God to practice without a license.

Very few Jews are impressed by cultish health exercises. It is not easy to imagine Golda Meir, for example, sitting cross-legged in the approved Yoga position, and meditating with a guru who intones *hare krishna* with a Bronx accent, and whose costume matches her draperies. A similar disdain is felt for such occult beliefs as phrenology: the science of picking the pocket through the scalp.

Voodoo medicine is yet another area that has been shunned ever since a 19th century researcher, Dr. Emmanuel Isaacson, went to Africa to study the influence of insect venom on tribal health. He left this mortal coil involuntarily, but proved to medical science that the bite of the African tsetse fly is most efficacious as a remedy for insomnia. Isaacson's colleagues have since warned that it is easy enough to make jokes about witch doctors as long as you are far enough away so that when you look in the mirror you won't notice your head shrinking. There is no known antidote for this phenomenon, but there are plenty of jokes about it.

Nobody is neutral about dentists: you either dislike them or you hate them. The dentist is a latter-day prestidigitator who has mastered the art of putting forceps into your mouth while extract-

ing currency from your wallet. He is adept at causing pain—a dis-
agreeable feeling that may have a physical basis in something he is
doing to your mouth; or it may be mental, caused by the good
fortune of another patient whose appointment was canceled.
There are not many jokes about dentists. Getting them to say
something funny is like pulling teeth.

Psychiatry, for the Jewish masses, is just coming into its own as
a more or less respectable branch of medicine. For many years,
psychiatry was thought to be a rather shady technique used by
Jewish doctors to find out what the *goyim* were up to that they
should be ashamed of. Nowadays, if you wish to talk therapy, you
are required to lie down on an analyst's couch at the going rate of
$25 an hour—and up. But the old-timers can recall when talk on
the East Side was free; and, because they were able to talk out
their hostilities, it never even occurred to them to take such drastic steps as, for example, busing *Litvak* and *Galitzianer* children to
each other's school.

Another source of humor is the psychiatrist's penchant for
cloaking simple answers with the jargon of his profession. Tell him
that you are depressed because of an unrequited love, and instead
of telling you to find someone else, he will gravely inform you that
"love is a temporary insanity curable by marriage or by removal of
the patient from the influence under which he incurred the disor-
der. This disease," you'll be told, "is like cavities or diabetes, and
is prevalent only among civilized races living under artificial conditions. Primitive people in backward nations, breathing pure air
and eating simple foods, enjoy immunity from the ravages of
love," he will conclude. He will then charge you fifty dollars, and
all you will have learned is that love is sometimes fatal—and more
frequently to the psychiatrist than the patient. And you will still
feel lousy.

It should come as no surprise, in light of the foregoing, that
Jewish humor is abundantly rich in those anecdotes which show
the psychiatrist getting his comeuppance from the patient. One of
them concerns the 86-year-old great-grandma, Mrs. Feldman,
who sternly admonishes a young psychiatrist: "Look, mister, don't
tell me I really got nothing to worry about. I was feeling rotten
long before you were born!"

The average Jewish-American may pay lip service to the psychiatrist, but he secretly believes that most problems can be solved
by an application of old-fashioned *Yiddishe saichel.* And, if he is
unable to analyze his problem, he is more likely to consult his
rabbi than a doctor. There is a well-known statement, attributed
to the late film producer, Sam Goldwyn, which sums up this feel-

ing of disbelief: "Anyone who goes to a psychiatrist ought to have his head examined." That, in essence, is the basis for many of the Jewish jokes associated with psychiatry.

Should you feel a slight attack of neurosis coming on as you read these pages, it is always helpful to realize that anybody who is not neurotic these days is probably underprivileged. In any case, this chapter is guaranteed to satisfy—or your mania will be cheerfully refunded.

H.D.S.

Part One
♦ ♦ ♦
OY, DOCTOR!

Mr. and Mrs. Roger Cohen announce the birth
of their son Bertram the doctor.

The new father-to-be paced the waiting room floor at the maternity hospital, wringing his hands and wailing, "Oh, my wife is so delicate! I just *know* she's too delicate for this!"

Finally, a nurse appeared. He rushed over to her, his face pale with worry.

"My delicate wife—she's all right?"

"Yes," she said, smiling reassuringly. "You're delicate wife is just fine."

"So tell me, quick," he cried, "is it a boy?"

She took a good look at the distraught husband's face.

"Well," she tactfully replied, "the middle one is!"

It is reported on absolutely unreliable authority that the following incident actually occurred to movie mogul Louis Selznick when he was a youth, newly arrived in this country.

It seems that Selznick suffered from a serious internal complaint, but his fear of surgeons and hospitals kept him from having the necessary work done to alleviate his condition. As might be expected, he became exceedingly low in spirits when a local practitioner told him it was now imperative that he undergo an operation. Tersely, the doctor ordered him to Mt. Sinai Hospital. There, after further diagnosis and X-rays, he was sent to the operating room.

Hours later, he recovered from the effects of the ether to find himself in a ward with other surgical cases in various stages of post-operative convalescence.

"Ohh," groaned Selznick, realizing he was still among the living, "am I glad that's over! I wouldn't go through that again for a million dollars—and thank God I don't have to!"

"Is that so?" inquired the patient in the bed on his right. "How do you know you won't have to go through it again—and soon?"

"Because my appendix is out," Selznick explained. "The whole thing's done. After all, how many times can you take out a man's appendix?"

"That's what I thought, too," stated Job's comforter. "But what happened? Fifteen minutes after I came to, they were rushing me back upstairs and opening me up again. One of those careless doctors left a sponge and a towel inside of me."

"Huh, you got off lucky," spoke up another patient from his cot nearby. "They had to hustle me back to the operating table and rip out all the stitches to get a pair of forceps and three scalpels they'd lost. Say, the way those doctors mislay things is..."

At that moment the surgeon who had officiated at Selznick's coming-out party opened the door to the ward and glanced at the sweating patient.

"I can't find that damned hat of mine anywhere..." he began, but got no further.

With a loud and anguished cry, Louis Selznick swooned.

"How's the missus?" asked the doctor in his usual jovial manner.

"She's better," replied the husband, "but if you want my opinion, the way she carries on when she's better I think she's better when she's worse!"

With the possible exception of Oscar Levant, Al Jolson was probably the most dedicated hypochondriac who ever gladdened a doctor's heart.

At a party one evening, one of the guests, a Hollywood medic, was telling Jolson about a new virus that had apparently been brought to this country by some Asian seaman.

"It's difficult to detect the virus," explained the doctor, "because the patient is outwardly unaffected. In fact, the man who gets the disease usually as a good, healthy complexion; his muscular and nervous systems are in perfect working condition; his digestion is good."

"Ohmygod!" cried Jolson, clutching his chest. "*My* symptoms exactly!"

The young student nurse was on duty in the maternity ward at Montefiore Hospital one day when she happened to see a new mother reading the book *Doctor Zhivago*.

"Look," said the trainee, "about this doctor I don't know very much, but you can't beat Doctor Spock!"

Once again we enter that handy vehicle, the time capsule, and journey back through the sexy sixties, the nifty fifties, the fightin' forties, the dirty thirties, and on into the roaring twenties where we stop, hat askew and shirttails flying from that fast and breezy trip. We are at that "point in time," as our Washington friends used to say, when the transplanting of monkey glands and other such operations for the restoration of male vigor were in vogue.

Surgery for the restoration of youth had just been performed on a 70-year-old man who had hoped that, as a result, his chromosomes would henceforth be bouncing off the ceiling. As he came out from under the influence of the ether, he began to weep bitterly.

Mrs. Bernstein, the attending nurse, bent over him.

"Mister, it isn't necessary for you to feel worried," she said kindly. "The operation was a big success. Take my word, when you leave here you'll feel 20 years younger. Maybe more, who knows?"

But the poor old man only continued to wail, the tears coursing down his cheeks and losing themselves in his long white whiskers.

"Please, don't cry," pleaded Mrs. Bernstein. "The pain will soon go away."

"Who's crying from pain?" sobbed the patient. "I'm afraid I'll be late for school."

Back during Prohibition days—that era when some of the people decided what was best for all of the people—Jack "Legs" Diamond, the black sheep of an Orthodox Jewish family, was feuding with Dutch Schultz, Al Capone and sundry other gentlemen over the division of their respective territories.

One day, Jack ran into a crossfire from both the Schultz and Capone gangs and was taken to Bellevue Hospital for the removal of miscellaneous bullets which had found lodgment in his innards. After the operation, he was wheeled into the intensive care unit where he slowly came out of the anesthesia. He looked about, puzzled.

"Nurse," he finally murmured in a weak voice, "why are the blinds drawn in this room?"

"Because there's a fire across the street," she replied coldly. "We didn't want you to think the operation failed."

Mr. Gross showed up at the Cedars of Lebanon clinic with a very rare skin disease. The intern, just two weeks out of medical school, gave him the usual once-over.

"Let me see your tongue," requested the young doctor.

Mr. Gross self-consciously complied. The medic took a good look, nodded wisely, and offered his studied advice:

"What you need is to get outdoors more—let the warm sun shine on that skin of yours. Do a little exercise in the open air."

"But, doctor," protested Mr. Gross, "I'm a mailman!"

"Hmmm," mumbled the doctor. "Let's see that tongue again!"

There's a vignette that is told about the late Bugs Baer. It seems that he woke up one morning and discovered that he had no sight in his left eye. So he telephones a friend to tell him the bad news. The friend offered his deep regrets and went on at great length to express his sympathy for the misfortune.

After several minutes of the tearful monologue, Bugs had had just about all he could stand.

"Look, do me a favor, willya?" he pleaded. "It's not all that terrible. I already saw all I wanted on that side!"

"Papa," asked the inquisitive daughter, "does a doctor ever doctor another doctor?"

The father laughed and gave the little girl an affectionate pat on the head.

"Why do you ask such a funny question?" he chuckled.

"Because Dr. Zucker gave me that nasty-tasting medicine even though I told him I hated it. So I was just wondering—does a doctor doctor a doctor the way a doctored doctor wants to be doctored, or does the doctor doing the doctoring doctor the other doctor the way he wants to?"

"Honey, take it from your papa," smiled the father. "By the time the doctor first gets his doctorate, he already knows too much about doctors to trust another doctor to doctor him!"

"My little brother, Baruch, went to the hospital yesterday," Rachel solemnly informed her second grade teacher. "They took his utensils out."

The physician finished examining his patient, an impoverished denizen of the lower East Side.

"I recommend that you take a long rest," he advised. "Go to the mountains for a few months."

"The mountains!" exclaimed the penniless man. "I can't even afford to go to Central Park. Why is it that you doctors always advise such expensive vacations? Don't you know what it means to be poor?"

"Now see here," said the doctor sternly, "I know exactly what it feels like. When I first started out to practice medicine I was so poor my stethoscope was on a party line."

"I want you to drink a cup of hot water every morning," prescribed the doctor.

"You gotta be kiddin', doc," said the patient crossly. "I've been doin' that for years, but my wife calls it coffee!"

Dr. Vaytig: No, Mr. Blum, your ulcers are not caused by business worries or family troubles. It's caused by eye-strain. That's what's causing your insomnia and loss of appetite, too.

Mr. Blum: Eyestrain? But, Doctor Vaytig, all I watch is the news on television.

Dr. Vaytig: Exactly! When you watch the six o'clock news you can't eat, and when you watch the eleven o'clock news you can't sleep. And when you worry about not eating and sleeping you get ulcers. See? *Eyestrain!*"

Dr. Randolph Salinger of Beverly Hills was once summoned to the home of Chico Marx, one of the famous Marx brothers comedy team. The piano-playing entertainer with the Italian accent and funny hat was suffering severe stomach pains. According to Chico, the doctor gave him some pills and prescribed plenty of milk.

"I'll drop by again this evening to give you another once-over," said Dr. Salinger as he made ready to leave. "In the meantime, be sure to drink at least four glasses of milk. The more milk the better."

That evening the doctor returned as he had promised and examined the comedian once again.

"You're doing just fine," said the physician encouragingly. "Just be sure to stay away from milk."

"But, Dr. Salinger, only this morning you told me to drink plenty of milk," Chico protested.

"Oh, did I?" replied Salinger smoothly. "Well, that certainly shows the progress we've made in medicine since I last saw you!"

Nurse: That's a pretty bad cold you have, sir. What are you taking for it?

Patient: Make me an offer!

The boy had been playing baseball and, while sliding into home plate, broke his leg. His mother, who was watching the game, frantically rushed him to the hospital.

"Madam," said the staff doctor gravely, "I'm afraid your son has a compound fracture."

"Please, doctor," wailed the mother, "tell me in plain English. Who knows from arithmetic?"

Young Arthur Waxman, a first-year student at the Columbia School of Medicine, wanted to do something that was socially significant, so he got a summer job with Ralph Nader's task force.

Arthur's job was to investigate phony medical claims made by national advertisers. He was an instant success. At the end of his very first day with Nader's Raiders, he returned home brimming with enthusiasm and a true reformer's zeal.

"Boy, am I gonna fix those giant cigarette corporations!" he shouted happily. "Today I wrote a letter to every one of the big tobacco companies demanding that they prove their claim, 'Cigarette smoking is harmful to your health!'"

Mrs. Cohen met her neighbor, Mrs. Levy, at the Laundromat. Mrs. Cohen had the sniffles.

"I'b id awful shape," moaned Mrs. C. "I thig I'b cobig dowd with the flu."

"I know just how you're feeling," sympathized Mrs. L. "But you got nothing to worry about. Just go see my doctor. He has a brand new drug it cures the flu in one day."

"This brad dew drug is so strog?"

"Strong? Listen, this drug is so strong," Mrs. L. said cheerfully, "you have to be in perfect health to take it!"

Coughing and wheezing, the skinny, stoop-shouldered old guy was on the examination table, getting a check-up for an insurance policy.

"I'm afraid the company will have to turn you down," said the doctor when he concluded his examination. "I don't think you are a good insurance risk."

"Why not?" demanded the man belligerently. "What's wrong with me?"

"Let's put it this way," said the unfeeling doctor: "If you were a building you'd be condemned!"

"If you ever expect to cure your insomnia," advised the doctor, "you'll have to quite taking your trouble to bed with you."

"But I can't" protested the unhappy patient. "My wife refuses to sleep alone."

Part Two
◆ ◆ ◆

THE MESHUGGENEH WORLD OF PSYCHIATRY

Maxwell Shapiro, he of the nimble fingers who serves as *croupier* at the Gold Dust Casino's crap tables in Las Vegas, told this mournful story of his visit to a psychiatrist.

"Doc, I have a very serious problem," Max began. "I'm losing my memory—maybe I've already lost it completely. I can't seem to remember anything."

The psychiatrist smiled indulgently.

"I'm sure it isn't quite that drastic. You must remember *something*."

"No, nothing at all. I tell you, I can't remember a single thing."

"You mean, of course, such things as names and faces and dates? We all tend to forget them now and then."

"Doc, you don't understand. I mean *everything*!"

"Oh, that's pure nonsense!" snapped the doctor. "No one just forgets everything he has ever known. Even a person suffering from amnesia remembers *some*thing—such as whether he drinks coffee or tea or whether he smokes cigarettes or not."

"Listen, doc," Maxwell said despairingly, "I'm telling you for the last time; I can't remember anything at all. Everything I see, everything I hear, everything I read—it just makes a temporary impression and then goes out of my head forever. That's it, doc, I swear to you. I simply can't remember one—single—god—damn—thing!"

The psychiatrist frowned, leaned back in his chair and pondered this unique malady for several moments. Then he asked:

"How long as this been going on?"

"How long has *what* been going on?"

✧ ✧ ✧

Psychiatrist: Tell me, Mrs. Stein, do you usually wake up grumpy in the morning?

Mrs. Stein: No, I'm usually letting him sleep late.

The intelligentsia along Pelham Parkway swear and avow that this story is true—but please, you shouldn't bet on it.

Two aged male patients at the *Goldeneh Medina* Sanitarium were sitting on a bench, sunning themselves on the front lawn of the institution. They were chatting amiably with Mrs. Berkowitz, their nurse, when a seagull flew over them and in passing dropped its calling card right on the bald head of one of the patients.

Mrs. Berkowitz, a most dedicated nurse indeed, rose to the occasion.

"Now Mendel, don't get emotionally upset. Don't move! You just sit right here on the bench and in two minutes I'm coming back with some toilet paper."

Mendel watched her as she scurried back to the main building and disappeared inside the door. He turned to the other patient and, in a voice tinged with sad disbelief, he gave voice to his suspicions.

"It hurts me I should say this, but for a nurse, Mrs. Berkowitz is setting us a poor example. By the time she gets back here with the toilet paper that bird will be fifty miles away!"

The late Senator Jacob Javits was inspecting the various hospital facilities in New York State. Toward the end of his tour, the Senator visited the *Sholem Aleichem Sanitarium* in Great Neck, Long Island. After inspecting the place and interviewing a few of the disturbed patients, he thanked the staff of administrators and started for the exit.

"Just a minute," snapped a guard as Javits was going through the gate, "you can't leave here."

The Senator smiled, realizing that he had been mistaken for one of the patients.

"Do you know who I happen to be?" he asked.

"No," said the guard, "but I happen to know where you are!"

Everyone thought that Harvey was just plain lazy, until a high-priced specialist finally diagnosed his case:

Voluntary inertia.

At the Brighton Beach Home for Meshuggeneh Mentschen, a new patient was observed swaying from side to side like a pendulum.

"Are you *davening* sideways?" asked the institution's rabbi.

"No, I'm keeping time," replied the patient.

"Hmm. So what time is it?"

"Eight-thirty."

"You're wrong," said the rabbi, looking at his watch. "It's nine o'clock."

"Oh, my goodness!" exclaimed the patient, speeding up his motion. "I'll have to go a little faster!"

From the Presidium of Psoviet Psience and Psychiatry:

"All right, doctor, I'll lie down on the couch. Like this? Fine. Now, what questions do you want me to answer? My dreams? Well, as a matter of fact I do have this recurrent dream—at least two or three times a week. I keep dreaming I'm in this big city, see? And I'm surrounded by thousands and thousands of Poles, Czechs, East Germans, Rumanians, Hungarians and Lithuanians. And—get this doctor—they're all eating motzoh balls with chopsticks. Tell me, do you think there's a Freudian significance hidden away in that dream?"

"Well, that's hard to say, Comrade Kosygin . . ."

Feingold the blouse manufacturer had just experienced the worst season of his business life. So severe was the catastrophe that, as a consequence, he suffered a nervous breakdown. There remained nothing else for him to do but consult a psychiatrist.

"I'm feeling so low I'm even thinking of suicide," wept poor Mr. Feingold. "Doctor, can you tell me what to do?"

"Yes," said the headshrinker. "Pay in advance!"

"I've got a problem, doc," the new patient began.

"We all have problems," replied the doctor, smiling his assurance.

"My problem's this, doc: I get migraine headaches every time

I think of my wife. I break out in a rash every time I think of my job. I get cold sweats every time I think of my bank account. Talk about problems! Boy, I got 'em!"

"Every problem has it's answer, of course, and I understand this one perfectly," said the psychiatrist, nodding. "You will need 100 sessions on the couch, at $25 per session."

The patient gulped. "Well, doc," he said after a painful pause, "that solves your problem. Now, how about mine?"

Rabbi Israel Walters told of the time he served as an Army chaplain during World War II. Among his responsibilities was the spiritual ministering to the needs of the soldiers in Ward Eight—the "psycho ward" as it was called by the patients themselves.

"I was leaving the hospital one day when I noticed that my car, which was parked just outside the front gate, had a flat tire," recalled Rabbi Walters. "I jacked up the car and got the tire off, putting the nuts in the hubcap as most people usually do. However, while putting on the spare tire I accidentally tipped over the hubcap and the nuts rolled through the iron grille of a drain. I was standing there, no doubt looking as perplexed as I felt, and wondering how I was going to secure the wheel, when one of the boys to whom I had just spoken called to me through the chain link fence:

'Chaplain, sir, why don't you just take one nut off each of the other three wheels and use them on the fourth? They'll hold until you can get to a filling station.'

"'Say, that's a perfectly marvelous idea,' I exclaimed, full of admiration. 'How did you ever think of it?'

'Why not?' he answered with a cheerful smile. 'I may be crazy but I'm not stupid!'"

19

Dollars and Scents

Introduction

Jokes are sometimes a gauge by which the attitudes and beliefs of a nation, group or individual may be measured. Probably nowhere else is this more manifest than in the many misnamed "Jewish" jokes which make an unsavory association between Jews and money. Many of them originated in the minds of 19th century bigots, and were crude caricatures whose primary function, it seemed, was to denigrate the ambitious German-Jewish immigrants and the Eastern European Jews who followed them in the 1880s and onward. The same scorn was seldom heaped upon the thrifty Scotsman. The canny New England trader who could "skin you out of a fly's eye" was likewise considered to be an altogether admirable character. Clearly, the abusive "Jewish money" joke was a veiled expression of anti-Semitism.

American-Jewish humor recognizes the simple fact that the good Lord created too many people for the available cash that's around, and that money and credit are curious articles: money is needed most when you haven't got it, and credit is something you have plenty of when you need it least. Contrary to the abusive nature of the old-time joke, Jewish humor advocated the wise use of money—never greed. "Look for cake and lose your break," declares a Yiddish proverb, cautioning against acquisitiveness. And the Talmud states: "Money legitimates a bastard"—which explains why there are so many oil-producing states sitting as legitimate members of the United Nations.

A cursory analysis of true American-Jewish humor provides a revelation: those anecdotes and witticisms revolving around the subject of money itself—that is, for its own sake—rank very low in the esteem of the Jewish people.

There are, of course, other subjects involving money which enjoy continuing popularity in the people's humor, but in those instances it is not the money itself that provides the *motif* or driving force behind the anecdote. Instead, money is considered for what it is: merely the accepted medium of exchange—the manner in which the energy expended in our labor is transposed into the things we use in our daily lives. Thus, in the following three chapters, "Commerce and Trade," "Yiddishe Blarney in the Workaday World," and "Keeping Up With the Kohnses," we find ordinary (and some extraordinary) people meeting the challenges of the business world, others coping with the ever-present problems of earning a living, and the fortunate ones enjoying the good life to which they hope to become accustomed.

In all these instances, the characters pursue their objectives with varying degrees of success and failure, courage and timidity, cleverness and foolishness. They are *people*, not just faceless names in a book, and many of the stories can be traced back to incidents that actually occurred. Some of the jokes, of course, depend for their humor on sheer absurdity. But they have this in common: money is only peripheral to the point of the story. Allow me, if you will, to illustrate with an anecdote in which the subject of money is understood but in which the word is never used—the main focus being on the legal complications of settling an estate:

"Your Honor," said attorney Klein as he rose from his chair, "what is the status, so far, of this case?"

"It's all over," explained the judge. "I have given a judgment for the residuary legatee under the will, put the costs upon the contestants, decided all questions relating to fees and other charges, and, in short, the estate in litigation has been settled, with all controversies, disputes, misunderstandings and differences of opinion thereunto appertaining."

"Good—very good!" exclaimed the attorney. "We're really making progress!"

"Progress?" echoed the judge. "Didn't you hear what I said, Mr. Klein? I just told you the case is closed; the matter is concluded."

"Yes, of course, Your Honor. In fact, it *had* to be concluded in order to give relevancy to the motion I'm about to make. Sir, I move that the judgment of the court be set aside and the case reopened."

"Upon what ground?" asked the judge in surprise.

"Upon the ground," replied the attorney, "that after paying all fees and expenses of litigation and all charges against the estate there will still be something left."

"Hmm, there must have been an error somewhere," said His Honor thoughtfully. "The court may have underestimated the value of the estate. The motion is taken under advisement."

Another example in which money is peripheral to a larger theme is found in this observation: "Many people complain that the mail service is slow, but let me ask you a civil question: When was the last time your gas, electric or phone bills were late?"

In the following little exchange of dialogue from the 1960s, we have a specific reference to dollars and cents, but here we are really concerned with the issue of inflation:

"That will be $3.50, sir," said the young lady in the box office as she handed the moviegoer his ticket.

The customer glanced up at the sign reading "Popular Prices" and demanded: "You call $3.50 a popular price?"

"Well," she replied sweetly, "we like it!"

It is clear, then, that the lively imagination with which so many Jews are endowed finds marvelous expression in jocular references to money matters—some of them oblique, others more direct. The characters in these jokes range from bank absconders to beggars. In that context, "abscond" means to "move in a mysterious way," commonly with other people's property. A "beggar" is one who asks for something with an earnestness that is proportioned to his belief that it will not be given. He is a descendant of the *schnorrer*, that grand anti-hero of Jewish folklore who was an *artiste* in the art of wheedling and fenaigling as compared with the crude American panhandler. Having passed through Ellis Island, the *schnorrer* surveyed his new territory and adapted his techniques to meet the challenge of New York's "tightskates and cheapwads," perceiving that his European tactics stamped him as a greenhorn—a designation that was something less than flattering.

For those not old enough to recall the meaning of the word, a "greenhorn" was an immigrant who arrived in this country two months after you did. The *schnorrer*, let it be said, quickly realized that the impoverished *griener* of the East Side, contrary to what he had heard in his home town, was no cornucopia and had little or nothing to give. Before long, after much soul searching and searing doubts, there came his moment of truth and he, too, joined the labor force. But he had one unexpected compensation: now that he had a job he could look down upon the next boatload of alms-seekers and coin his own hyphenated, scornful epithet—"Those *griener-schnorrers!*"

Jewish humor in America contains many allusions to overpricing and to the outrage of bamboozled customers. For some retailers, the price of an article is generally its value plus a reasonable sum for the wear and tear on their conscience in demanding it. Some of the jokes overlap into other categories. As an example, here is an illustration in which we not only have a confusion of price, but of accent as well:

Joseph, a comparatively new immigrant to the United States, purchased a suit of clothes which had been advertising at $58. But when he was presented with a bill for $89.50 he was horrified. There was an alterations charge, a city sales tax, a state tax, a federal tax, and a surplus tax—sort of a tax on taxes, or a tax-tax. Indignantly, he refused to pay anything above the advertised price. Flinging the original $58 down on the counter, he stalked out of the store with the new suit. The proprietor, seeing his 400% profit watered down to a measly 100%, called the police, and Joseph was hauled into court.

This was Joseph's first such experience in his adopted homeland and he shook with fear as he faced the bar of justice.

"Jotch," he said, after explaining his case in his broken English, "you should pliz haxcuse mine Hinglishe spitch, what mine heccent it shouldn't give me trouble I should losink this case."

"Sir," replied the judge, leaning forward, his manner brimming with kindness and understanding, "joosta because you talka-like dat, you no gonna have-a no trouble long-a as I'm-a judge!"

Note, please, that while the theme of the above story concerns the subject of money, the surprise ending offers a resolution which has nothing whatsoever to do with money itself. It should also be noted that no racial or national bias is inherent in the tale, nor is it even implied that the defendant will receive anything other than a fair hearing. Jokes such as this bear little resemblance to some of the thinly-veiled canards which masquerade as "Jewish" humor, and whose characters exist only in the thoughts of their shadowy creators.

As I suggested earlier, money jokes are often linked with political sallies. At any moment, for example, we can expect an Israeli poet to compose an elegy to the United Nations: *They are Loyal to the Ones with Oyal*. But political situations change with the years, as does its humor. Those that endure are the witticisms and stories to which we can personally relate—those closest to home. Many express the wistful yearnings of a bygone generation of European Jews, now restructured to express similar longings in America. Others still retain their Old World simplicity, revived every half-century or so to delight a young generation for whom the stories are new. Such a joke is the one about the thrifty wife who cut off her cat's tail so that it would not take so long to leave or enter the house, thus saving heat. American-Jewish humor, however, when it involves money, is mostly native to this country. One of its many products is this witty observation: "Early settlers may have started this country, but it's those who settle on the first of the month that keep it going."

What is this business of money all about? Never mind the economists. Gertrude Stein figured it out for us when she wrote:

"Money is always there, but the pockets change. It is not in the same pockets after a change, and that is all there is to say about money."

H.D.S.

"Pop, any chance of you lending me ten bucks til payday?" asked the always-broke son.

"Why should I lend you money when you're wearing $200 suits?" demanded the father indignantly. "Look at me. All I have to my name is this old fifty-dollar rag—I'm even ashamed to call it a suit."

"Listen, pop, it's true my suit sells for $200, but I just put a few bucks down, that's all. I haven't made a payment in over a year."

For a moment or two the father was too surprised to answer.

"All right, I'll be glad to lend you the ten dollars," he finally said, "provided you get *me* a $200 suit on the same installment plan!"

During a fund-raising tour of the United States, after a State visit with President Richard Nixon in 1968, Golda Meir was asked, "How was it possible for Israel to defeat all those Arabs in 1967 in just seven short days?"

"It was our army," she replied. "It was the way we were organized. Our reserves saved the day."

"How so?"

"First," she explained, "we called up all the doctors and trained them well. Then we called up all the dentists and trained them well. Then we called up all the lawyers and trained them well. Then we called in our Minister of Defense, Moshe Dayan, and he gave the order: CHARGE!—and boy, *did they know how to charge!*"

Jack and Judy had saved their money for years and, despite Jack's limited income, they finally accumulated enough to buy a house in the suburbs.

"I hate to bring this up, Judy," said Jack hesitantly, "but in this high-class neighborhood it isn't nice for people to talk about their personal business. My salary, for instance. You'll have to stop talking about it to our new neighbors."

"Who's mentioning your salary?" yelled Judy. "I'm just as ashamed of it as you are!"

The husband had just taken out a new life insurance policy and was explaining the various clauses to his wife. Her eyes widened as she beheld the figures.

"Thirty-thousand dollars is a lot of money," she murmured.

"No, honey, the face amount is for $15,000," he explained patiently. "It pays $30,000 under the double-indemnity clause—but that's only in case something should happen to me through an accident."

The wife pondered this bit of financial manipulation which, to her, sounded as though it had been concocted by a Watergate lawyer.

"This double-indemnity business—it isn't fair," she complained when its full significance dawned on her. "Do you mean to say that just because you should die a natural death I only get half?"

There is a certain type of fellow who is automatically conditioned to raise unmitigated hell about the injustices he sees or hears about—or even imagines. He is a radical only when the conservatives are in power. When the radical or liberal element is at the helm he is just as apt to be a conservative—as long as he has something to rave about. His bloodthirsty curses are hyperbolic, not what he really feels; as for example, when he expresses that magnificent Yiddish malediction: "It should grow inside your stomach a trolley car!" Such a man was Peretz Weintraub who graced the lower East Side some forty or more years ago.

In 1929, after the Wall Street crash, banks everywhere were failing by the dozens. On Grand Street, Peretz strode up and down in front of the Bank of the United States (a misnomer that fooled thousands of hapless depositors), shaking his fist at the closed doors and literally snarling:

"In the electric chair they should put such people! A fire on their heads it should burn for ninety years and six months! By the neck they should hang, those crooks, until they're dead—dead—*dead*! The president from the bank, the vice-president, the board of directors—everybody—should be put on a guillotine and chopped off from them the heads—those bums, those *goniffs*, those gangsters!"

Officer Muldooney, the cop on the beat, walked up to him.

"Hello there, Mr. Weintraub. What're you so worked up about? Did you have your money in this bank?"

"No, I didn't," confessed the overwrought Peretz. "But if I *did*!—*ach*, would I give a *geshrei*!"

Two garment workers were bewailing the high cost of everything from lox to socks.

"This inflation business is sending me to the poorhouse," groaned one. "I don't know how, but we got to have more money."

"Making more money is no problem these days," sighed the other. "What's so hard is making a living!"

On June 16, 1969, Joe and Edith decided to celebrate their fifth wedding anniversary by going to a movie—their first in as many years. When they got to the box office, the price of admission almost bowled them over.

"I wonder where the fifty-cent movie ticket went," murmured Edith.

"Ya wanna know?" rasped Joe, his face livid with outrage. "I'll tell ya where the fifty-cent ticket went! It went to three dollars!"

The late George Kaufman, playwright and critic, was visiting the country home of Moss Hart, another eminent writer.

Hart, inordinately proud of his estate, insisted on taking Kaufman on a personally conducted tour of the grounds. He pointed out where he had diverted a brook, created a waterfall and pond, transplanted several shade and fruit trees to provide a better view, and landscaped the terrain with various exotic plants—all at tremendous expense.

Kaufman was greatly impressed.

"Just think, Mosseleh," he enthused, "what God could have done with this place if He'd had your money!"

The late Sophie Tucker recalled the poverty into which she was born.

"We were so poor," claimed Sophie, "my parents couldn't afford children. The lady next door had me."

Meyer Lansky, a somewhat questionable character in Las Vegas, was being interrogated by the district attorney.

"Now that Howard Hughes has bought the Sahara, would you say that the mobster element is no longer involved in the hotel business here?"

Meyer looked the DA right in the eye—his good one.

"Hell, Mac, you got it all wrong," he explained in his own delicate way. "Howard Hughes did buy the Sahara all right, but not the hotel—the *desert!*"

There are tens of thousands of poor Jews in America. And they too have their stories. Here's a sample.

Mrs. Goldberg was in her Orchard Street flat, sipping a glass of tea and conversing with her next-door neighbor.

"This business of government assistance is all right, but it's taking away from us our dignity," she grumbled. "If it wasn't for the food stamps, the free day nursery for the children, free medical care, rent allowances, supplemental payments and the regular monthly check, I'd get off welfare tomorrow!"

"Talk about extravagant wives," complained Max. "Her idea of holding down the bills is to put a paperweight on them."

"You should teach her the virtues of thrift," counseled a friend. "Persuade her to start saving."

"I tried that," explained Max wearily. "So she invented a new way to save money. . . . She uses mine!"

It was a tender, poignant scene at the airport. The wife tearfully kissed her husband good-bye.

"Don't forget to write, darling," she said between sobs, "even if it's only a check!"

Here's a golden oldie that still retains its humorous charm. It goes way back to those days when a five-and-dime store meant just that, and not a place where a customer is offered a bedroom suite or a barrel of British chutney. The tale is about a mild-mannered, timid little man who had recently emigrated to this country. Without loss of time, he began to familiarize himself with American mores and institutions.

The newcomer to our shores was taking his first walk down Lexington Avenue when he was halted by a sign over a large red storefront. Laboriously, with his scant understanding of the English language, he made it out: *Five and Ten Cent Store.*

He considered the sign at some length. Next, he studied the contents of the wide show windows where domestic utensils, toys and a wide variety of other goods were displayed. Then he entered. Inside the wide double door, he encountered one of those impressive and dignified beings who seem to have been ordained by the Almighty to serve mankind as assistant store managers. To the little immigrant's vast relief, the store's major domo was Jewish.

"Is it true, sir," inquired the new arrival in Yiddish, "that nothing in this establishment costs more than five or ten cents?"

"That is correct," replied the store official.

"Good, good!" smiled the new American. "You'll be so kind, please, to direct me to the shoe department?"

One thing you have to admire about the present administration—its efficient Bureau of Statistics.

The Bureau just figured out that the best time to buy anything is about 30 years ago.

"Of course my wife and I are compatible," the husband told his analyst. "In fact we both like the same thing. It's just that I like to save it and she likes to spend it!"

The sweet-faced, white-haired old lady cashed her check at the supermarket and then profusely thanked the cashier.

"It's very nice you're helping me out," she said warmly. "You wouldn't believe it, but even the banks they're refusing to cash my checks!"

The frugal housewife was looking over the ads in the evening paper when she came to a full-page display.

"Ooh, Myron," she called to her husband who was watching a baseball game on television, "they're having a monster sale at Klein's!"

He looked up, irritated by the distraction.

"Listen, I ask you like a normal person," he growled: "Who needs a monster around the house?"

It was National Book Week, and for the past half-hour the English prof had been discoursing on the importance of literature in general. Now he addressed his first question to Miriam, the prettiest coed in the class.

"Young lady, if you could have only one book in your entire life, which book would you choose?"

"I think," replied Miriam after due and deliberate consideration, "I'd choose a checkbook!"

Mrs. Fein received a sternly worded notice from her bank that her checking account was overdrawn.

Embarrassed, Mrs. Fein sat right down, wrote a note of apology and sent them a check.

Willy Wexler, of West Weehawken Waterproofing, Window-

Washing, Wood-Waxing & Wall-Wiping While-U-Wait, Inc., came home with furrows of care on his brow.

"Marianne," he said, "the way bills keep piling up is scandalous. I'm spending more than I can make. We've just got to cut down on expenses—both of us!"

"How?" asked Marianne.

"Well, we can start with a few personal sacrifices and then go on toward higher cost things. Now, what would you suggest to begin with?"

Marianne pondered a moment.

"I'll tell you how we'll begin," she said brightly. "Hereafter you can shine your own shoes. And I'll do my part too—I'll cut your hair!"

"Papa, can I have a quarter?" begged the moppet for the fifth time.

"Stop making such a pest of yourself!' growled the father. "Why, when I was your age I asked for pennies."

"Okay, papa," said the little boy, his eyes lighting up, "can I have 25 pennies?"

Joey was only five years old but was very sharp indeed. The neighbors loved to play a game with him; one in which Joey was always glad to participate. They would offer him a nickel and a dime in their open palms and ask which one he would rather have. To the unending delight of the grown-ups, Joey always chose the larger coin.

One day, an older boy asked him the inevitable question:

"What's the matter with you, dummy? Don't you know that a dime is twice as good as a nickel?"

"Sure," answered Joey, "but business is business. Why should I spoil a paying proposition?"

A young college dropout had been searching for a job for a whole hour. He could find nothing suitable; the companies seemed to have no need for new vice-presidents, board chairmen, marketing consultants, efficiency experts or other positions paying $30,000 a year or more.

"I'm a victim of current inflationary tendencies," he sighed from the depths of his 18-year-old heart.

"Listen, if you think these are hard times," scolded the youth's father, "you should have been around during the Depression. I remember once I dropped a nickel in the telephone slot and the operator said 'God bless you, sir!"

Abe and Dave, somewhat in their cups, were enjoying a convivial evening together at the local tavern. Their conversation drifted around to the subject of wealth, and who was the richest man in the world.

"It's gotta be Howard Hughes," said Abe. "His bank once returned one of his checks with a memo: 'Insufficient Funds. Us, Not You!"

"That's nothing," retorted Dave. "I heard that old man Rothschild once sent a check to his bank and it bounced... Not the check, the bank!"

"Live it up while you can," advised the spendthrift. "Money is for the good life. Who needs money lying around in a bank?"

"But don't you believe in putting something aside for a rainy day?" asked his frugal companion.

"Of course not! Name me one person who ever really benefited by saving for a rainy day."

The friend considered the challenge for a moment or two and then answered tersely: "Noah!"

"I'm saving up for a new bike, dad," ventured the small boy hopefully. "Do you have any odd jobs around the house I can do?"

"I'm afraid not, son," replied the father.

"Well then," suggested the boy, "how about putting me on welfare?"

The two old codgers, brothers in their seventies, were as identical in appearance as twins could possibly be. But emotionally and intellectually they might as well have been strangers. One was a generous, outgoing type; the other was a taciturn miser.

It so happened that one day the generous brother called on his twin for a donation to the synagogue where they both attended.

"No," declared the surly miser. "I'm not giving my hard-earned money for any such purpose. I'll keep it where it belongs—in the bank."

"Listen, I know you are too old to change your ways," argued the generous one with a sigh. "But let me remind you of a Jewish proverb. It says in the Talmud—I don't remember exactly where—'Money is like fertilizer. It does no good unless it is spread around.'"

His full name was Marie Joseph Paul Yves Roch Gilbert du Motier, Marquis de Lafayette, but let us not hold that against him. The distinguished French general served with rare honor and courage in the American Revolution.

Among Lafayette's friends was Jacob Harte, a Baltimore merchant who loaned the General the sum of $7,256 with no more security than a handshake. Harte, who came to this country from Germany in 1775, was the father-in-law of Haym M. Salomon, son of the patriot Haym Salomon. But let us return to Jacob Harte.

"Jacob, my dear friend," said General Lafayette, "you need have no fears about the money I owe you. It will be repaid in full."

"I know that," replied Harte. "I have no fears whatsoever."

"You can be sure that every penny will be returned."

"Please, General, let us discuss it no further," said Harte with a wave of his hand. "I am not concerned about the repayment."

"My people have a very long history of honest dealing."

"All right already, you're an honest man," retorted Harte with some irritation.

"In fact," Lafayette persisted, "the records prove that my family goes back to Charlemagne, and I assure . . ."

"*Himmel*, enough is enough!" Harte interrupted. "My family lost its records in the Great Flood, but does that cast suspicion on me?"

Among the more interesting characters in American history was Mordecai Manuel Noah (1785-1851), writer, statesman and visionary; known to many as "Major Noah." Born in Philadelphia, he studied law but became a journalist and playwright. As a result of his worldwide travels and his diplomatic post in Tunis, North Africa, where he served as American consul (1813-1816), he became an advocate of Zionism. However, he realized that the creation of a Jewish state in Palestine was impractical at that time, so he conceived the idea of establishing a Jewish settlement at Grand Island, New York, near Buffalo. He named the proposed Jewish colony "Ararat," and on September 15, 1825, the foundation stone for the "City of Refuge for the Jews" was laid. But the plan was deemed fantastic and his appeal for followers and supporters was largely unanswered. The only remaining trace of this project is the foundation stone which is kept by the Buffalo Historical Society.

But Major Noah, it appears, was able to retain his sense of humor in the face of the almost universal hostility to his scheme for a Jewish State within the United States. In 1824, in an attempt to raise funds for the establishment of "Ararat," he traveled to Georgia where he made several vain efforts to meet with members of the influential Sheftall family who were not only wealthy but whose roots were established in the United States long before the Revolutionary War. The prestige of the Sheftall name would be almost as important as their money.

After a number of vain attempts to meet with the leading member of the famous family, and growing increasingly angry at the obvious snubs, Major Noah finally walked up to the Sheftall mansion without an invitation and sounded the knocker on the door. When a servant responded, Noah wasted no time on preliminaries.

"Tell Mr. Sheftall I am here," he said, giving his name.

A few minutes later the servant reappeared. "I'm sorry," he apologized, "but Mr. Sheftall says he can't see you today. He has a sprained back."

"What kind of an excuse is that?" roared Noah in a voice that could be heard to the topmost rafters. "You go back and tell Sheftall that I just want to talk to him—I didn't come here to wrestle!"

20

Commerce and Trade

Introduction

American-Jewish business humor is characterized mainly by four rather unflattering elements: foolishness, cleverness, greed and resignation. I have excluded the designation of honesty because that attribute itself forms the general thrust of the jokes. One can be honest or dishonest at the same time that he is foolish, clever, greedy or resigned. Very few Jewish jokes laud dishonesty, but even in those rare instances where it does occur the emphasis lies elsewhere.

An old story tells of the man whose family was close to starvation and, in desperation, he stole an egg from a rich landowner who had 100 dozen eggs in his larder. But, goes the joke, the impoverished culprit did not feel he should have to bear the expense of cooking the egg on his own stove and was caught while frying it on the stove of the rich man.

In that illustration, of course, the thrust is upon the inequity of one man having nothing while another has more than he needs. This category of joke often goes to extremes, however, as in the following folk tale, obviously mythical, wherein the moral is *caveat emptor*—let the buyer beware.

In the year of 1879, shortly after he was appointed a justice of the State Supreme Court, Judge Robert Weiss purchased a lakefront summer home. One day, he and his wife, Faye, were sitting on the bank, in front of their residence when a stranger approached.

"I wish to cross over to the other side," explained the visitor. "Would you be kind enough to rent your boat to me? I will return with it before the day is over."

"Yes, of course," replied the judge.

The stranger paid the rental in advance and also left a substantial deposit to be returned when the boat was brought back. He then got into the boat, pushed off, and rowed away. A hundred yards off shore, the boat suddenly sank and the man drowned.

"Oh, Robert," cried Faye, "that was a terrible thing to do to that poor stranger—and after taking all that money, too! Why didn't you tell him that the boat had a hole in it?"

"Because," said Judge Weiss patiently, "the matter of the boat's condition was not brought before me."

The above bit of piracy, according to time-honored custom, is excusable on the ground that piracy is simply another name for business without its frills and customer relations departments—just as God made it.

The cries of anguish emanating from American manufacturers, usually accompanied by the shedding of copious tears acquired from the nearest crocodile farm, have for many decades served as a legitimate target for Jewish humor. This is especially true of such centers of commerce and trade as New York, Chicago and Los Angeles, where they have been most successful in the fine art of separating the fleece from the sheep in sheep's clothing. The producer's problem arises from the low tariff or scale of taxes placed on foreign-made goods. His complaint is that these import duties should be much higher in order to protect him from his greedy consumers.

It should be noted that the hostility which is evident in Jewish jokes involving commerce and trade is commonly directed toward "big business"—the larger corporations, cartels, national chain stores, and the like. But these very same jokes preserve a spirit akin to paternal affection and amused understanding for the small merchant who, in his never-ending struggle to remain afloat in the changing financial tides, displays an aptitude for competitive ingenuity and resourcefulness so dear to the Jewish heart. The effort need not even bring success: a man can be tripped by his own cleverness in this type of humor, just as long as the effort, *on the surface*, appears to be intelligent. An example is found in the shoe-biz caper that occurred in the Windy City not long ago.

Sid Michaelson, proprietor of the shoe store at the intersection of LaSalle and Washington in Chicago's loop, prided himself on his self-taught scholarship; that condition in which a person knows a little about a lot of subjects. It was his belief, for instance, that the word "mind" derived from the Latin *mens*. So, seized with an inspirational idea one morning, he proudly displayed a sign over the door of his shop with the motto, *Mens conscia recti.*

Across the street, Irv Gold, Sid's equally learned competitor, not to be outdone, emblazoned his window with his own sign: "Men's, Women's and Children's conscia recti."

Another illustration of the lighthearted touch is apparent in a story that was popular during the depths of the Great Depression. A young man who suffered a nervous breakdown was sent by his parents to see a psychiatrist. After a lengthy and involved examination and series of tests, the doctor recommended that the youth be put someplace where he would not be disturbed...so they put him in business.

Now, having said all I know and don't know about the subject of commerce and trade, I refer you to the following anecdotes about those stalwarts who valiantly keep their shops and factories open during war and peace—peace being that period of fenaigling between two periods of fighting.

H.D.S.

The owner of a big textile plant hired one of those so-called efficiency experts to cut down on waste, speed up production and nail down loose ends.

Filled with self-importance and determined to exercise his authority, the expert made a tour of the factory on his very first day of employment. He had made his way through only one department, doing whatever it is that such people do for a living, when he came upon a spectacle that shocked his efficient being to its very core.

On a bench before him was a languid-looking young woman in a rumpled smock, busily engaged in sitting. That's all—just sitting. Only the jaws of this girl showed any signs of activity: she was masticating Juicy Fruit with a vigor that would have brought delight to Mr. Wrigley. Presently she stopped chewing, drew in her breath and blew an orange-sized bubble. Then she resumed her former posture of *rigor mortis.*

With mounting indignation the expert watched her. Then, approaching her, he fixed a stern, accusing eye upon the delinquent.

"See here, young lady," he snapped. "What do you think you're doing?"

"Who, me?" inquired the girl in a brilliant bit of repartee. "I ain't doin' nothin'."

"If you don't mind telling me, what do you expect to do

when you get through doing nothing?"

"Nothin'."

"Well, what have you been doing?"

"Nothin'."

"And how long have you been sitting here doing nothing?"

The girl opened a cavernous mouth and yawned.

"I been sittin' here 'bout an hour—maybe an hour-an'-a-half."

"Is that so. How much do you earn a week?"

"Sixty-fi' dollars."

"Well," said the expert, "we'll stop that right now. When is your week up?"

"T'morrer."

"You needn't wait until tomorrow. You can go right now."

The efficiency man reached into his pocket, hauled out his own personal bankroll, peeled off six tens and a five and pressed the total into the sitting gum-chewer's outstretched hand.

"Here!" he rasped. "Take your money and get out of here. I don't ever want to see you inside this plant again."

"Yes sir," promised the young lady meekly. She rose from the bench, smiled a weak farewell and slouched out.

"I guess that's inaugurating a little rough-and-ready reform right at the outset," said the expert to himself. He beckoned to the foreman of the department and the latter came forward.

"Who is that girl I just chased out of here?" he asked.

"Her first name's Becky—that's all we ever called her. I don't know her last name," replied the foreman. "She works for Knickerbocker Fabrics downtown. She was waiting here for a receipt!"

"These long-haired hippies will ruin me," moaned Sam the barber. "Just today one kid came into the shop and told me to take just a little off around the hips."

The American Jewish Committee decided to cut its budget, so the well-known efficiency expert, Dr. Felix Kaplan, was appointed to carry out the task.

Determined to reduce costs wherever possible, he snooped around the AJC offices, pencil and pad in hand, to see what he could learn.

On the first floor he found a clerk with his feet propped up on the desk, sipping a cup of coffee and reading a copy of *Commentary* magazine.

"Just what do you do here for a living?" asked the visibly irritated Dr. Kaplan.

"Just what it looks like—nothing!" came the answer.

Kaplan wrote it down on his pad and went to the second floor. There he found another clerk, also with his feet propped up on the desk. And he, too, was drinking coffee and reading *Commentary.*

"What are *you* doing to earn your keep?" demanded Kaplan.

"Nothing," replied the clerk.

"Ah-*hah!*" cried Dr. Kaplan triumphantly. "So that's what's wrong with AJC's labor force—duplication!"

Newsboy: Swindle! Big swindle! Read all about it! Thirty-nine victims!

Tightwad: Here's your money, boy. Gimme a paper...Hey, wait a minute—I don't see anything about a swindle!

Newsboy: Swindle! Big swindle! Forty victims!

Secretary of State Henry Kissinger had just returned from Beijing where he had successfully concluded arrangements for a rapprochement between the People's Republic of China and the United States. In America, the business community hummed with anticipation as visions of immense trade with China appeared on the horizon.

At his curbside pushcart on Hester Street, Yankel perused the news account of Kissinger's trip, one eye on the *Forvertz* he was reading and the other on his display of merchandise.

A woman with slanted eyes, high cheekbones and yellow-tinted skin—clearly Oriental—stopped in front of his cart and speculatively fingered some of his goods.

"How much for this?" she asked.

"Missus, believe me, that goods is 60 cents a yard," he answered eagerly. "But for you I'll make it 40 cents—I want the China trade!"

Two cloak-and-suiters were complaining about the demands

of the labor unions.

"It's gotten to the point where my own secretary is now on a four-day week," moaned one.

"So's mine," agreed the other sadly, "but it takes her six days to do the work."

"Well, at least they always hurry back to the office after their last coffee break," said the first boss. "They don't want to be late for quitting time."

Al Uhlman, sales manager for Aunt Bertha's Undies, Unlimited, was called into the big boss' office.

"Al, you're the smartest man we ever had in this company," the chief began. "You've demonstrated your ability by working your way up from rookie salesman to manager of the whole sales department in just two years. You've outsold all the other men combined. You know all these is to know about our whole line of undergarments and your suggestions for next year's line are really brilliant."

Al smiled, wondering how big his raise was going to be.

"Thank you, sir," he murmured with false humility.

"And so," concluded the boss, "you're fired!"

"*Fired!*" the sales manager gasped. "In heaven's name, what for?"

"I'll tell you what for!" exclaimed the boss, his voice rising. "It's guys like you who always start their own companies and give me all that *tsuris* with the buyers!"

Stanley, traveling for Fabulous Frocks of Flatbush, expected to be on the road for several weeks, so he had his mail forwarded to his Nashville customer, Leo Levy, of Lee's Ladieswear.

But no sooner did Stanley arrive at the store when Leo handed him a special delivery letter. He read the terse message and a pallor spread across his face.

"What's the matter?" asked Leo. "You look worried."

"It's my wife," explained Stanley. "She just had triplets. Holy mackerel—we never expected anything like this! And take a look at the size of this hospital bill!"

"Congratulations," said Leo, grinning. "Now you know how it feels to be billed for more merchandise than you ordered."

The season had been one of the worst in the garment manufacturer's memory. He was on the verge of bankruptcy.

"Miss Tellabenda," he called to his secretary, "get my broker on the phone."

"Which one?" she asked sprightly. "Stock or pawn?"

An ambitious young man once asked philosopher-statesman-financier Bernard Baruch if there was a formula that would absolutely guarantee success in business.

"Yes," replied Baruch. "Think up something that costs ten cents or less to make, sells for a dollar or more, and is habit-forming."

Berel the butcher from Williamsburg had been in this country for less than a year and was experiencing some difficulty with the English language. His friend, old Guri the grocer, had arrived in the United States 15 years earlier and often helped Berel with his linguistic problems.

One afternoon, when they met for lunch, Berel brought up a subject that had perplexed him for days.

"Guri," he asked, "what means 'recession' and 'depression'? There's a difference?"

"Of course," said Guri patiently. "To tell the truth, they both mean *gehakhta tsuris*, but people interpret it differently. For instance, if you lost your job, that would be a recession. But if I lost mine, *that*, my friend, would be a depression!"

"Grandpa, listen to what it says here in the morning paper," cried Herbert. The price of postage is going up again!"

Grandpa shook his head. "I just don't understand those people in Washington," he said dolefully. "If I was running the Post Office Department, instead of increasing the cost of postage I'd just decrease the size of the stamps."

Paul Muni took great delight in narrating this minor adventure story. It happened in his earlier years when he was playing an engagement in Chicago. One day he went for a stroll along South Clark Street and came to a district of second-hand clothing shops. A sight that greeted him there sent him back with great haste to find three of his friends and take them with him to help him enjoy his discovery.

They halted in front of a store window filled with garments bearing seductively worded legends purporting to represent that these offerings had been cast back upon the makers' hands through no fault of their own but rather because of the captiousness of the original purchaser.

The words "Misfit," "Not Claimed," "Tailor's Sample" and so on, recurred time and again. But in the central display, originality in the gentle art of advertising phraseology had scored a triumph. Behind the glass dangled a pair of trousers of a most startling cut and an even more startling pattern. The colors fairly leaped through the window to smite the passerby in the eye. To the garment was affixed a card bearing the statement:

THESE PANTS WERE UNCALLED FOR

Now that his oldest boy was of age, the father changed the sign over the store from "Kaplan's" to "Kaplan & Son."

"Well, well," commented the neighboring storekeeper, "you and your son are now carrying on the business together?"

"Fifty-fifty," Kaplan grunted. "I run the business and my son does the carrying-on."

Mr. Birnbaum, sales manager for Modern Men's Clothes of New York, was returning to America after a business trip to Israel. On the way back, he decided to stop off in Rome and take in the sights. Two weeks later, he finally arrived home.

"How was the trip?" asked the big boss.

"Fantastic!" enthused Birnbaum. "In Israel I sold a thousand more suits than any of us expected. Then I stopped off in Rome and saw all the historical sights. I got in with a sight-seeing group and we had an audience with the Pope."

"The Pope himself? You don't say!" marveled the boss. "What does he look like?"

"Oh," ventured Birnbaum, "I'd say about a 38-short."

"Hello, Ralph. How's by you?"
"Don't talk to me!"
"Hey, what's the matter?"
"Did you or didn't you sell me the shop as a going business?"
"I did."
"Well, it's gone!"

Mr. Zabarsky was the sole owner of My Cups Runneth Over Manufacturing Company, the giant producer of high fashion brassieres. So it was no wonder that the foreman of the shipping department was somewhat nervous when he was handed a note from Zabarsky—Mr. Z himself.

With trembling hands he opened the envelope. Then he gulped as he read the message:

> I'm sending my son to your department so he can learn the business from the ground up. But don't show him any favoritism. I want you to treat him like any other son of mine.

When Morris, the insurance broker, heard there were no agents within 200 miles of Broken Bottle, Wyoming, he was overjoyed. "At last!" he exulted. "No competition and a wide-open field!" Within a week he left New York and opened his new insurance office over the Broken Bottle Saloon.

On his first day of business, a cowboy applied for a policy.

"Have you had any recent accidents?" asked Morris as he busily filled in the insurance form.

"Nope."

"Well, have you had any accidents at all in your life?"

"Nary a one, unless you count the time a steer once busted most of my ribs and a sidewinder set his durn fangs in me."

"For heaven's sake!" Morris exclaimed. "Wouldn't you call those accidents?"

"No, I shore wouldn't," drawled the cowpoke. "Them varmints done it apurpose!"

21

Yiddishe Blarney in the Workaday World

Introduction

The dignity of honest toil has long been rooted in Jewish history. Indeed, the work ethic has been associated with Judaism ever since the Pharaoh commanded the Israelites to make bricks from straw. The edict did not meet with their enthusiastic approval. "You gotta be kiddin'!" they protested to the Strawboss of the Nile. The controversy led to the first organized labor dispute of record. They walked off the job and kept on walking for forty years.

Having reached their own homeland (and never mind what the Arabs claim), the Decalogue served as a handy labor-management device with which to shaft the bosses of the day. The ancients formed two unions, each consisting of six locals, or tribes. In Israel, there was the COI (Chosen Ones, Industrialwise), later changed to the CIO to accommodate the Unchosen Ones. There was also the AF of L (Ashkenazic Federation of Litvaks), whose hiring hall was in Judea. Additionally, there was a 13th local, or tribe, comprised of Galitzianers, but they signed a sweetheart contract with the indigenous management, and were not heard from again until they surfaced in New York to establish the costume jewelry business. The lost local's motto was: *Ver Fahrblunjhet!*

Then came King Solomon with big ideas for the construction of hanging gardens and a splendid palace with a thousand master bedrooms, each with a golden sink so his pampered wives could do the dishes in bed. Now, Sol wasn't a bad sort of fellow if you didn't get to know him, but the unauthorized demands for fringe benefits and other aggravations he suffered from the hired help soon gave him a royal pain in the assets. So he decided to have it out with the architect—once and for all.

"Now see here, Archie," Sol began, "I don't want you to think I forgot my campaign promises or that I'm anti-union, but the place you selected for my garden is so hot, it even killed my artificial flowers. Then, there's the problem with the plumbing. I know I ordered running water in every room, but who needs it should run down from the ceiling? Another thing, I didn't complain when the goldfish pond caught fire and burned to the ground, but whoever heard of going downstairs to get to the attic? This is efficiency by you?"

It pains us to report that Sol's trouble didn't end there. When he moved into the palace and carried his thousandth bride over the threshold, the poor man got a hernia.

In America, the organized labor tradition not only continued, but reached new heights. It also reached new lows, depending on which side of the bargaining table you happened to occupy. It even invaded the hallowed temples of worship. The following vignette is an illustration:

Cantor Rosenblatt, accompanied by two burly workmen in overalls, entered the synagogue a few minutes before services were to begin. He introduced the strangers to the rabbi: "This is Pat Murphy, and this man is Mike O'Sullivan."

Puzzled, the rabbi drew Rosenblatt aside. "Why did you bring them here, of all places?" he asked.

"Who had a choice?" the cantor replied dolefully. "Last week I bought a new hearing aid, and the union ordered I should hire two electricians!"

But, to give the labor organizers their due, they themselves realize that their demands can sometimes jeopardize management's financial stability. Consider the case of Mannie Manischevitz, mogul of the baking empire. After a month of negotiations in which neither side would yield, Mannie finally caved in to the union's demands.

"Okay, you win," he told the bargaining agent. "The employees get the ten-dollar-an-hour minimum wage with an escalator clause, 60 days a year paid sick-leave, with three-months paid maternity leave for men as well as women, retirement at full salary at age 38, a 20-hour work week, and 20-minute coffee break every hour—all clauses guaranteed by the management."

"I'm sorry, but our membership will need one more guarantee," said the union agent brusquely. "With all those corporate expenses, we'll require a guarantee that you won't go broke!"

Jewish workaday humor does not exclude the onerous household chore. Unlike the man of wealth, the ordinary citizen can always find work that needs doing at home. The rich man, for example, may boast of a fine, dry wine cellar, but the average workingman's basement is so damp he can't even set a mousetrap down there for fear of catching a herring. Then there's the electric appliance that always needs fixing. Usually it's the toaster that works on AC or DC, but not on bread. It goes without saying that disaster enters the picture when terrified little Rosie rushes into the house yelling, "Mommy, Mommy! Daddy just fell off the roof!" And Mommy answers pleasantly, "I know, Rosie dear. I just saw him pass the window."

Jewish humor also allows the hapless victim to complain about the complaint department. It permits him to confess, "I like my job; it's just the work I hate." What he cannot smite he bites—with a sharp-toothed quip.

Even his annual two-week vacation is not immune. The hotel's condescending desk clerk who asks, "Do you have a reservation?" is slapped down with the retort, "What do I look like, an Indian?"

The bellboy, with his ever-present palm extended, is another target. "Carry your bag, sir?" The hotel guest glares and squelches him with, "No, let her walk!"

Back home again, the weary, unrested vacationer indulges in some rueful recollections. "The hotel was so big," he muses, "that by the time I got from the lobby to my room, I owed for another day. I even had to dial long distance to call the desk. And the arrogant waiters in the hotel's dining room! I had a tip-top waiter. If I didn't tip, he blew his top. I remember asking him how to get to the washroom, and he snarled, 'Mister, this is no place to do your laundry!' Even the water he served was positively cloudy, and I told him so. But he just brushed aside my complaint. 'The water's okay, go ahead and drink it,' he assured me. 'It's just the glass that's dirty!'"

Another guy we can't fight, but whom we can smite with a derisive joke is the frozen-faced boss with a heart to match. It's the familiar old story: he is free to joke and ridicule at your expense, but you dare not reply in kind. Jewish humor, particularly the audacious *American*-Jewish humor, provides the outlet for marvelous escapist fantasies. The boss calls you into his office in the morning when business is so quiet you can hear the overhead piling up. You are dying to say, "Don't worry, boss, business is always slow at this hour, but it's sure to drop off in the afternoon." Instead, you maintain a discreet silence. With his usual rasp, the boss launches into the subject at hand—*you*:

"This is just a suggestion and you don't have to follow it, unless, of course, you don't want to keep your job."

Then comes your moment of triumph. You've had all you can take from this pompous ass, you should pardon the expression, and so you give it to him straight from the clavicle:

"Sir—and I use the title advisedly—my aptitude test shows that I'm best suited for prolonged vacations. I quit!"

For the first time since you've known him, he actually smiles.

"Are you really quitting?" he croons, "or are you just trying to brighten my day?"

The incorrigible old reprobate! He simply *must* have the last word! You feel like telling him your only regret about quitting is that now you'll be drinking coffee on your own time, but you have an uneasy feeling he'll top that one, too. He's had more practice with the put-down than you. So, on your way out, you slam the door and yell, "Good-bye, Fido! Don't forget to give your mother a bone!"

No, it isn't like that in the real workaday world, but that's the way it is in Jewish humor—bless it!

H.D.S.

The owner of a closed union shop was on an inspection tour of his fabricating plant when a large scaffold accidentally toppled over and landed on him, pinioning him beneath the wooden structure.

"Help!" he yelled to an electrician who was working nearby. "Get this thing off me!"

"Sorry, but you'll have to ask a carpenter," apologized the electrician. "My union doesn't allow me."

Melvin and a co-worker were at lunch in *Lottie's Latke and Leber Luau*, on Fairfax Avenue in Los Angeles. As usual, Melvin was complaining about his boss.

"That man is so dumb he can't spell DDT," he grumbled. "He thinks a blood vessel is some kind of Red Cross ship."

"You oughtta be glad he's so dumb," said his co-worker, shrugging. "If he was any smarter he'd fire you!"

✧ ✧ ✧

Pauline had been hired as the new secretary only two weeks earlier, but already she was having notions about her handsome boss. What worried her, though, was that he was engaged. Oh well, a girl can dream, can't she?

One morning, Mr. Right called her into his office to take some dictation. His fiancée was visiting her mother in another city and he had promised to write regularly. Dutifully, he dictated a warm and affectionate letter.

Pauline expertly took it all down in her flawless shorthand, went back to her desk to type the letter and then brought it to her boss for his signature.

"What's this?" he snapped as he was about to sign it. "You left out 'I love you.'"

"Oh," she whispered in her best sultry voice, "I thought you had stopped dictating."

It was the salesman's first day out pounding the pavements. He returned to the office that evening and was greeted by the sales manager:

"Get any orders?"

"Two," moaned the unhappy huckster: "'Get out!' and 'Stay out!'"

Bang the cymbals, twang the lyre! Hackensack is checking in with one.

Hal Bruck, sales manager for the New Jersey Jobbing Company, distributors of tobacco products, candy and other vital necessities, assembled all the salesmen on his staff for a meeting.

"Gentlemen," Hal began, "I've called you together to announce a big sales contest—the most important one our company has ever conducted. It will run for eight weeks and each of you has an equal chance to hit the jackpot."

The salesmen, naturally, were excited at this rare opportunity. From the rear of the room an eager voice rang out:

"What does the winner get?"

"The winner," declared Hal, "gets to keep his job!"

Eighteen-year-old Walter—that stalwart member of the Great

Unwashed—sauntered into the State Employment Office and informed the placement clerk that he would consider a position in keeping with his sense of values and philosophy.

The employment counselor stared at the long-haired youth, noted the holes and patches in his faded, unfragrant jeans, and regarded his four-inch unkempt whiskers.

"I'm not sure we have anything in your line," she finally said. "Tell me what have you done?"

"Who, me?" exclaimed the puzzled young man. "About what?"

Sammy the labor leader, age fifty-one, had been a widower for five years and now he wanted to marry again. So he went to one of those Jewish introduction firms with fancy computers that are advertised to match personalities "and make your dream come true with a scientifically selected mate."

Sammy took one look at the computers and demanded: "Is this a union shop?"

"Certainly," said the manager. "*Shadchans* Local 102."

"All right, then, let's see some pictures."

The manager brought out a large album and Sammy glanced through the pages until he came upon the photograph of a curvaceous young lady of about twenty-four.

"Here's the one for me," he announced. "Wrap 'er up."

"Sorry, but you'll have to take Mrs. Umglik instead," declared the manager, pointing to the photo of a wrinkled, toothless old crone, clearly a widowed great-grandmother of Napoleonic vintage.

"*A klug tsu Columbus!*" howled the outraged labor leader. "What the hell for?"

"Because this is a union shop," explained the manager, "and this one has seniority!"

It really doesn't pay to hire relatives," moaned Bernie the furrier. "Only last week I hired my niece as a bookkeeper and the first thing she did was to bring me a column of figures with a wrong answer. So I told her to go back and add it up again five times. After about an hour she came into my office and gave me the results—five different answers!"

Finkel, employed by Amalgamated Clothing Company, timidly knocked on the boss's office door.

"Come in, it ain't locked!" hollered Mr. Amalgamated.

Finkel shuffled over to the boss's desk and, in his usual diffident manner, asked for a raise in pay.

"After all," he added, summoning up what little boldness he possessed, "I'm entitled. I have twenty years experience."

"Finkel, you ain't had twenty years experience," barked the brains of Amalgamated. "You've had one year's experience twenty times!"

The shop foreman, irritation showing plainly in his face, strode over to Sheldon, a hippie.

"Listen," he grated, "do me and everyone else in the shop a big favor and quit whistling while you work."

"Hey, man," retorted Sheldon defensively, "who's working?"

In September, 1974, William Roth, President of Queensborough Woollens, Inc., put up a sign on the bulletin board which the International Ladies Garment Workers Union found offensive. The union jumped all over him and made him take it down, but the announcement was salvaged for posterity:

ATTENTION, ALL EMPLOYEES!

It would be appreciated by the management if, somewhere between starting and quitting time—without infringing on lunch time, coffee breaks, rest periods, ticket-selling and vacation planning—each employee finds some time that can be devoted to what we, in our old-fashioned way, like to call the Work Break.

It is our earnest opinion that this will be an aid to steady employment and regular pay checks, and it is our hope that each employee will give it a fair trial.

Bella the bookkeeper was due at the office at eight-thirty sharp, but this morning she sauntered in at nine. There was an indefinable something in her manner that seemed to indicate that her tardiness was deliberate.

"Good afternoon, your highness," greeted the boss, his voice oozing sarcasm. "This is the earliest you've ever been late."

"My dear Mr. Bergdorf," replied Bella coolly, "I'm giving it to you straight from the elbow. When a person does not like another person she does not have to work for such a person. To be employed here is no longer my glass of tea."

"You mean you're quitting because there's somebody here you don't like?" he asked, genuinely surprised.

"Precisely, Mr. Bergdorf."

"Who?"

"You, Mr. Bergdorf!"

The young man had just graduated from the New York College of Optometry and was lucky enough to find an immediate position at "Cheap Charlie's—the Eyeglass King of Mosholu Parkway."

"The rules around here are very simple," instructed Charlie. "When a customer comes in for a pair of glasses, you must first get the examination part over with as soon as possible. Then show him a few samples, always starting off with the most expensive frames we have."

"Okay," agreed the neophyte, "but I don't see any price tags. How much do I charge?"

"We don't have a set price," explained Charlie. "When the customer asks you the cost, just tell him 'forty dollars.' If he accepts without saying anything, you add, 'That's for the frames—the lenses are ten dollars more.' And if he still doesn't complain, you say, 'each!'"

Izzy, the top salesman for a large publishing house, returned to the New York office after a book-selling journey to the West Coast where he had called on the distributors and retailers in the trade. Pleased with the results of his trip, he triumphantly laid a batch of orders on the desk of his boss and then presented him with his expense account.

The boss scanned the expense sheet for a few long moments and then glanced up at the salesman who was hovering over him.

"Look, Izzy," he said, "I'll okay this expense account on one condition—that you give me the fiction rights!"

The recent college grad found a job and, after working for a whole week without a raise in pay, went to the boss to find out why he had been so sorely neglected.

"Now just a herring-pickin' minute!" protested the boss. "You can't just waltz into my office like this and ask for a raise. You have to be like everyone else around here and work yourself up."

"Work myself up!" echoed the young fellow indignantly. "Waddya think I been doing for the past hour? Look, I'm trembling all over!"

The distinguished Guggenheim family, prominent in metal smelting and refining, as well as in philanthropy, was founded by Meyer Guggenheim who came to the United States from Switzerland in 1847, when he was 19 years old. He started out as a peddler, eventually entered the embroidery importing business and then bought a mine in Colorado. From that point on his industrial empire grew.

But we are concerned here with Meyer Guggenheim's first venture into business in America, when he trudged through the mining towns of Pennsylvania with a pack on his back, selling stove polish, ribbons, thread and a few other items, such as spices and lace.

It was a cool autumn day in the year 1848 when young Guggenheim, his peddler's knapsack secured to his aching back, turned into the short road leading to a farmhouse. At once he noticed that the roof of the house was ablaze. He gesticulated wildly to an elderly woman who was standing in the doorway.

"Lady, lady!" he yelled. "Your houze iss alreatty on vire!"

"What?"

"Your houze is burning."

"Wha'ja say? I'm a leedle deef."

"I said your houze iss ge-full mit vire."

"Oh, is that all?"

"Vell," said Guggenheim, taken aback, "dot's all I can t'ink of right now."

22

Keeping Up With the Kohnses

Introduction

The average American of the Jewish faith has prospered since those days when he lived in an East Side flat overlooking the rent. A few have even attained wealth, and therein lies a paradox: the rich man is often someone you like better the more you see him less. He worships bigness. Even his bank is so huge it has a special window for robbers. That enormous house he owns is another example: if you happen to be in the living room and you gotta go, you'll just make it. And have you ever seen those 18-inch *mezuzahs* on his front portal? He keeps his checkbooks in them.

It is a fact to be regretted, but too many of our wealthy *landsleit* have forgotten when they were so poor they could afford to buy only one shoe at a time, or had to walk to the opera to save carfare. And they have the *chutzpah* to laugh and invest little jokes about the poor, yet! It makes you wonder how some people can look so clean and laugh so dirty. The rich man will grin and tell you that in these hard times you should be happy about your poverty because it's so inexpensive. "Poverty," he will announce like *Moishe Rebbenu* with the tablets, "is the one thing money can't buy."

So you ask him for a little financial help: "Can you lend me a fiver for a week, old boy?" And he makes with another flippant retort: "What does a week-old boy need with a fiver?" Witticisms like that you don't need, so you tell him he should only live to be so old as his jokes. What that Wall Streeter neglects to tell you is that he was fooling around with the birds and the bees instead of the bulls and the bears. He put half of his money in revolving doors and half in Ex Lax, and was cleaned out before he could turn around. It's different with small investors like us. We buy a little stock in a company that pays quarterly dividends, and every three months they send us a quarter. *Nu*, go fight the Stock Exchange!

A few of the *nouveaux* Rolls Roycers now have unlisted wives. But Jewish humor has long espoused equal rights for women—it clobbers the female as well as the male—especially the affluent lady who pays her Diner's Club card with her American Express card. She's the woman who goes to the corner store and buys two corners. The less well-heeled observer, particularly if his credit is so bad the stores won't even accept his cash, views her as a pampered pet who would fall down and *plotz* from sheer fright if her fortune cookie contradicted her horoscope. Yet, he's fascinated with her because she never opens her mouth—she's had so many face lifts she talks through her eyes. As for her pompous, rich hubby, the poor man sees him as an arrogant braggart, a selfish *chozzer*, a snob and a first-class exploiter—and those are his *good* points!

The difference between the Jewish woman of means and her poor working sister is even apparent in (how shall I phrase it?) their climactic heights of intimacy. Velma van Papilary moans, "Oh, Myron, we just can't go on like this, as if we were strangers. All you want is my body." Sophie the sewing machine girl groans: "*Oy*, Jake, stop this very instant—I forgot the Pill! Jake, *stop*. You're deaf all of a sudden? Jake, I'm ordering you, at. . . . *Oyyy*, Jaaake!"

The opposing attitudes between the haves and wish-they-hads include such esoteric preferences as, of all things, birds! For example, the wealthy American Jew likes the Tarrytown titwillow; the poor one settles for little Rubin redbreast. The rich man is smitten with the fortnightly nightingale; the working man is happy with the Israeli six-day warbler. The man of means adores the Bar Harbor bluebird; the poor man is contented with the Bronx blueberg, to say nothing of the Golan Heights goldberg. And the rich man loves the California condor; while the poor man, in his patriotic zeal, is happy with America's national symbol, the bald-headed siegel.

These jokes, of course, do not pretend to mirror the lifestyle of the privileged classes, but rather how we think they live—or ought to live. And underlying all this satirical humor is its theme of equality. We can almost hear a biblical Israelite protesting: "So enlighten me, mister *balaboosteh*! Who gave you permission you should eat *challeh* while I get stuck with all the manna? And where does it say I must *walk* to Jericho in this desert for 40 years while you ride around on a camel, *noch*? You, too, were born in the bulrushes you should be maybe more chosen than the rest of us?"

The monetary disparity between the rich and the poor has long been a staple of European-Jewish humor. In the United States, it gets downright hilarious. When Mr. ShapEYEro, for instance, loses on the stock market, it means his 7-Up dropped 2-down—but if *you* drop anything in the market it's because your shopping bag broke. What makes it such a coincidence is that ITT and your shopping bag split on the same day. Rich people, of course, don't shop at supermarkets or buy from Pincus the pushcart peddler. Instead, they patronize those fancy shoppes where they sell gifts you wouldn't have as a gift, including barometers made in Japan so you should always know when it's raining in Yokahama. Those Park Avenue shoppes even have a specialty grocery department where Mrs. LevEYEne buys steak, caviar and truffles—for Fifi, her French poodle!

Should you make the mistake of entering one of those exclusive shoppes in search of a wash-and-wear mink coat for your wife, don't even bother asking. Better to go see Pincus who'll sell you an Indian washing machine—a rock. You don't think your wife would be too impressed with such a gift, so you settle for a ring with a stone that's so tiny you need a magnifying glass to see it. Your wife complains, "Why did you buy me such a small diamond?" And that quick Jewish mind of yours is ready with a plausible answer: "Because, honey, I didn't want the glare to hurt your eyes."

If you are like most of us, you have enough money to last you a lifetime—unless you buy something. That "something" is usually an automobile. Actually, for those who are intent on keeping up with the Kohnses, it isn't a cheaper car that's wanted, but an expensive car that costs less. But rich folks have their problems, too. Every time Mr. Kohn's auto is in the middle of a car wash, his dashboard phone starts ringing. With you, it's different. Your wife wants a mink stole and you want a car. So you compromise—you get the mink stole and keep it in the garage. I know just how you feel, friend. When she demands a foreign convertible, you'd secretly like to buy her a rickshaw.

A very brief parable, please. Two goldfish in a bowl were having an argument about religion. Finally, one said in disgust: "But if there's no God, who changes the water every day?" My point is this: In Jewish humor, the differences between the Jews, like those goldfish, are outweighed by their similarities. Rich or poor, their responses are much the same. Wealthy or not, a Jewish boy becomes a man on his 13th birthday when he stops asking his father for money and requests a loan. *Yiddishe* mamas are also the same. In Texas, mama tells her kids, "Be careful when you go to school today, children. We had another well come in last night and it's slippery out." And in New York, mama is finding out that English is a funny language. A fat chance and a slim chance mean the same thing. When you're tight, your tongue's loose. Her educated daughter tells her, "Mama, your main trouble is with your vowels." And mama replies anxiously, "Maybe I should see a doctor."

But, whether you bought your wife that lovely fur coat or whether you killed it yourself, this chapter is for you!

H.D.S.

The fancy-shmancy Fagins of Mamaroneck have a perfect marriage, according to that authoritative and distinguished journal, the *Yonkers Daily Yenta*. He's got what it takes and she takes what he's got.

Two brothers-in-law, Sol and Myer, were intensely jealous of each other's business successes and, as a result, the competition between them always raged at fever pitch. Even their wives, sisters though they were, joined in the rivalry.

One evening, when Sol returned home from the office, his wife greeted him with some disconcerting news.

"That sister of mine told me today that Myer just bought the latest model Cadillac," she cried, almost tearfully.

"Oh, he did, did he?" growled Sol, heretofore the proud owner of a Chevy. "Well, the first thing tomorrow morning we'll buy a Lincoln Continental. That'll show him who's who and what's what!"

Myer's wife soon learned from her sister that their social status was again quo, with Sol now a little quoer, alas. Upon hearing of this act of one-upmanship, Myer waxed wroth indeed, and proceeded to grow wrother by the hour. The very next day, he had a telephone installed in his Cadillac.

"Now," exulted Myer, "let that cheap chiseler beat this!"

Myer's wife, of course, could scarcely wait to tell her sister about the engineering coup.

As might be expected, Sol immediately had a phone installed in *his* car. This time, however, he decided to do a little gloating. So he made a call to his brother-in-law.

"Hello, Myer," he crowed, "this is Sol. I'm calling your

Cadillac from my Lincoln Continental. Just thought I'd let you know I have a phone in my car, too."

"Glad to hear from you, Sol," answered Myer briskly, "but, say, would you mind holding the wire for a minute? I'm on another line!"

From our Entrancing Trivia Department: The Internal Revenue Service knows just what to give the man who has everything—an audit!

Now that her papa had made it big in the kosher-leather shoe business, teenaged Lisa decided to break into "society." The best way to demonstrate her new breeding, she felt, was to inject a few well-chosen French words into her everyday conversation. So she bought a French-English dictionary.

A few evenings later, as she and her family were watching television, President Ford was shown speaking a few words to the Ambassador of France, and conversing in the Ambassador's own tongue. When Ford finished his brief comments, the girl's father turned to her.

"*Nu,* Lisa, you're the expert around here since last week. Tell me, does the President speak good French?"

"Papa, believe me, I'm really too-too shocked," murmured Lisa in her newly-acquired ladylike manner. "He made not one, not two, not three, but *faux pas!*"

Sol Lapidus never did change his miserly ways after he became rich. When he was poor he knew where his wife hid her nickels and dimes. Now that he's wealthy he knows where the maid's quarters are.

Becky, a five-year-old little girl, lived with her parents on the East Side of New York. Her rich cousin, Frieda (now Frederika), who was six, lived in a mansion near Halfshell-on-the-Hudson. One day, the wealthy part of the family invited their poor relations to spend the day at their estate. Becky and Frederika met for the first time.

"Tan oo say 'Dere was a 'ittle dirl an' she had a 'ittle turl inner forrid?'" asked Becky.

"Perhaps not in the prescribed phraseology," replied Frederika. "If memory serves me correctly, it runs about as follows: 'At a recent period in the annals of organized society, there existed a diminutive feminine specimen of the human family whose conspicuous decoration was a capillary spiral appendage of minute dimensions descending perpendicularly from the forefront of her head. When she was amiably disposed, she produced the impression of being excessively agreeable, but when she abandoned herself to the natural inclinations of an unregenerate spirit, her deportment became unacceptable.'"

"Oh, wow!" exclaimed Becky, wide-eyed with admiration and curiosity. "How tum oo know Jewish so good?"

Another Mrs. Yifnif story:

Now that she was rich, Yetta Yifnif bought a French poodle, dyed it pink like the other fancy poodles in the new neighborhood, and joined the Larchmont Kennel Club. She then entered her poodle in the forthcoming show for purebreds.

As the handlers prepared the pampered canines for the showing, the Ladies Poodle Society members got together in the clubhouse for cocktails. Proudly they discussed their entries: Henri, Andre, Babette, Lamour and Suzette.

"Mine poodle's name is Fido," said Mrs. Yifnif.

"Fido!" they exclaimed. "What kind of French name is that?"

"By me it's very French," replied Mrs. Yifnif huffily. "On the registration papers I'm spelling it P-h-i-d-e-a-u-x."

"Chrysanthemum, look at this!" chided Mrs. Klaynekeit. "I can write your name on the piano with my finger, it's so dusty."

"Yes'm," replied the cheeky maid, "an' you done spelt it wrong."

There was great excitement in the Prinzmetal family. A real English lord was coming to pay them a visit! Mr. and Mrs. Prinzmetal had met His Lordship while returning from their latest

European trip, and the important man had graciously accepted their invitation to spend his first weekend in the United States as a guest under their roof.

Now he had arrived and, after an effusive welcome, he was sitting at the Prinzmetal's table. Mrs. Prinzmetal, flustered and flattered, urged My Lord to eat heartily. Her husband, beginning or ending every sentence with the noble-sounding "M'lord," was swollen with a sense of the honor which had descended upon his household. The dinner hour was being invested with a reverential, not to say worshipful, air.

As a special privilege—something he might talk about in his later years—little Charlie, age five, had been permitted to attend the function, on condition that he refrain from speaking unless first spoken to. Mindful of his pledge, the youngster remained quiet, his large round eyes fixed in a state upon the face and form of the British lord.

But an innate sense of Jewish hospitality moved him to break his vow of silence when he noticed His Lordship's eyes roaming hither and yon across the table as though in search of something.

"Mama," said Charlie. "Oh, mama!"

"What is it, Charles dear?"

"God wants a pickle!"

It was one of the most fashionable weddings of the year, if not the decade. Everyone, but *everyone*, my dear, was there: the Loebs, the Guggenheims, the Rothschilds, the Kahns, the Strausses, the Cardozas, the Lehmans and the Morganthaus. The exclusive Park Avenue temple glittered with jeweled matrons and their suave and handsome escorts.

Rabbi Schwab finished his ceremonial functions, stepped back and smiled. A hush fell over the synagogue as the groom slipped the wedding ring on the bride's finger. At that moment, the reverent silence was shattered by the excited voice of a little girl in the rear of the temple:

"Mommy, is this where he sprinkles the pollen on her?"

Now that Jake and Irma were rich, they decided to add a little culture to their hitherto shallow lives. At their first opportunity, they went to the Metropolitan Museum of Art and took a guided tour of the exhibits.

"Say, this is a fine bust of Michelangelo," said Jake admiringly.

"That's not Michelangelo," explained the guide. "That's Leonardo da Vinci."

Irma, acutely embarrassed by her husband's ignorance, tugged at his sleeve.

"Jake," she hissed, "why do you have to open your big mouth when you don't know a single thing about the New Testament?"

The affluent have just as many problems with their offspring as do the rest of us. They differ only in degree. Take the case of the pretty sophomore at Radcliffe, Gloria de Sable, formerly Gertrude Fox. For weeks on end she had badgered her father for a fast and flashy new car, but the old man, aware of his daughter's wild nature, had stubbornly refused. At last, however, her persistence wore him down and he gave in—with a brand new Mercedes Benz. But he also warned her that the car would be taken away if she received so much as one traffic ticket. He meant it—and she knew it.

Gloria promptly took the Mercedes to one of those outfits that specialize in "customizing" stock cars. The chassis was widened, the body lowered and the engine souped up so that it would do 130 with ease. Now Gloria was ready to drive.

She was tooling down the highway at a mere 110 when, in her rear-view mirror, she spied a motorcycle cop in hot pursuit. With her father's warning still fresh in her mind, she pushed down on the gas pedal and the car leaped forward like Secretariat at the Kentucky Derby. But the police officer somehow managed to tail her. She grew increasingly worried. One way or another, she thought, she must evade that policeman. A citation for speeding and perhaps reckless driving was a certainty should she be caught.

But Gloria was a resourceful as well as a pretty girl. Seeing a filling station about a half-mile ahead, she slowed down just enough to turn into the driveway without overturning the car, and then, with the cop not far behind, she jerked open the door and raced into the ladies room. When she came out a few minutes later, there was the motorcycle officer, one foot on the bumper of her car, his citation book in hand.

Without a word she got back into her new Mercedes Benz, looked at him with a knowing smile on her face, and cooed:

"Bet you thought I wouldn't make it!"

Mrs. Vanderkatz reminded her housekeeper that her husband had invited a number of his business associates and their wives to spend the weekend with them.

"You done tol' me," said the housekeeper, "Wunst wuz enough."

"You're all prepared?"

"No ma'am," snapped the housekeeper. "I'm all *packed!*"

Big executives have their problems, too. Julius Rosenwald, head of Sears, Roebuck and Company, put in such long hours and hard work that he finally suffered a physical collapse. He was rushed to a fancy private hospital where he was given a sedative. He awoke the next morning to find a crisply starched young nurse in his room.

"Good morning," she greeted him cheerfully. "You're due for surgery in an hour."

"Surgery? What for?"

"Ulcers."

"Oh," he responded nervously, "I hope I'll have a strong anesthetic. What about this twilight sleep I've heard so much about?"

The nurse smiled. "That's for labor."

"I see," replied the big executive thoughtfully. "So what do you have for management?"

Let it be said that members of the Jewish aristocracy are just as attentive to *Chanukah* as the gentile elite are of Christmas. Witness:

Back in the 1900s B.T. (Before Taxes), old Lazarus Strauss called his son, Nathan, into his study and asked: "What would you like for *Chanukah?*"

"A chemical outfit," said Nathan promptly.

So Lazarus shopped around for the best chemical outfit on the market and finally bought one —

DuPont!

All her life, Flo Malkes had lived on the shadowy edge of poverty, but such was her nature that she saw not the dilapidated tenements, the pushcarts and the shabbily dressed people among whom she lived on Henry Street. In her mind's eye she saw only the midtown mansions, stunning gowns and all the other habiliments of the very rich. Perhaps it was better that way: It saved her much suffering.

But miracle of miracles—she was notified one day that she had been bequeathed a substantial fortune by a distant relative whom she only vaguely remembered from her childhood.

Flo Malkes became Fifi Midas. She moved uptown, into a plush condominium on Fifth Avenue, acquired a Rolls Royce and a chauffeur, and generally lived it up in high style.

Naturally, she dined only in the best establishments and, as befits a lady of her refinements, the day came when she entered *Pierre's*, the most exclusive French restaurant in all of New York. The menu was printed in French, of course, but Mrs. Malkes, or Midas, had no intention of admitting that she lacked acquaintance with that language. She took the bill of fare from the hovering *maitre d'* and studied it with an air of great intentness. Then she aimed a pudgy finger at an item near the top of the card.

"To start off with," she said, "please bring me that."

"But, *Madame*," the headwaiter protested, "ze orchestra ees playing zat!"

There is an old, thrice-told tale about the society woman who looks down her nose, raises her lorgnette and says to her housekeeper, "We usually spend our summers in Europe." And the housekeeper replies matter-of-factly, "So what? I was born there." The affectations assumed by the few have long provided mirth for the many. Stella Adler, the truly great actress, was especially adept in the art of lancing inflated egos and laughing at false pretensions. Here is a story that illustrates the point.

One autumn day during World War II, shortly after the Nazis had launched their all-out buzz-bomb attack on London, Stella was preparing to go to the theatre for a rehearsal when she noticed that one of the jewels in her favorite ring had fallen out. She promptly went to Cartier's to have the stone reset.

The deferential clerk, impressed by her grand manner, her precise articulation, her obvious *savoir-vivre*, said:

"Please accept my sympathy, *Madame*, for the difficulties you British people are experiencing in England these days."

Always the consummate actress, Stella drew herself up in that awe-inspiring, regal manner of hers.

"My deah man," she replied haughtily, "Ay'm not Br-r-itish, Ay'm just affected!"

Mrs. Shayneh Balabatish was guiding the new maid, Amanda, around her Park Avenue mansion, explaining the maid's duties and acquainting her with the various furnishings and the individual care they required. She pointed out the Chippendales, the French Provincial and Italian Renaissance pieces, the Louis IV bedroom suite and the Victorian dining room ensemble.

As they entered the library, they were confronted by the Balabatish grandchildren, all five of whom were cavorting, laughing and shouting with glee as they pounded nails into the valuable furniture. The maid gasped in horror.

"Oh, it's perfectly all right," smiled Mrs. Balabatish.

"But," protested Amanda, "how can you afford to let them?"

"Nothing to worry about," said Mrs. Balabatish reassuringly. "Nails we can always get wholesale."

Now that I. J. Fox had made his second (or maybe it was his third) million dollars, he decided that the time had arrived when he could afford to emulate his fellow millionaires and do a little relaxing. But sitting around a fashionable country club or playing golf with a bunch of old duffers was not to his liking. I. J. Fox was an adventurous soul. He craved excitement. Then came an inspired thought: He would go on an African safari to hunt big game.

The next morning found him at the offices of Congo Safe, Sane & Sanitary Safaris, Inc., an organization that promoted such expeditions. After listening to the sales pitch and studying the colorful brochures, the prospective Great White Hunter nervously cleared his throat.

"Tell me something," he began. "It's true that a berserk elephant or a rhino will sometimes charge a safari truck?"

"Well, yes, it's true to a certain extent," replied the office manager haughtily, "but I assure you, sir, we frown on the practice!"

Oscar and Beatrice of Orchard Street were overwhelmed to learn that a distant relative had died and left them a million dollars. Nothing would do but that they leave the lower East Side immediately and rent an apartment on Central Park West. Now they were busily engaged in planning the artistic decor in keeping with their new station in life.

"I think," suggested Oscar, "that on the dining room wall we should have something in oil."

"You mean," asked Beatrice hesitantly, "a sardine?"

As a United Jewish Appeal rally, speaker after speaker exhorted the vast audience to contribute to its utmost ability. Finally the moment came when the speeches were finished and the donors were expected to make their pledges. Suddenly, from the rear of the auditorium, a booming voice rang out:

"My name is Howard Mishkin, of Mishkin Furs, Inc., 128 East 37th Street, New York City, New York, and I pledge $1,000 anonymously!"

Jack Benny, speaking of a heritage-happy, ancestor-worshipping, self-important snob:

"He wasn't brought by the stork. He was brought by a man from the Audubon Society personally!"

Abe Kantor had struggled all his life to make a success of the little manufacturing concern of which he and his wife were the sole owners as well as workers. They made wallpaper paste from a secret formula their janitor had sold to them for a dollar many years before. Then, one day, by the sheerest of accidents, they found out that their wallpaper paste was not only edible but very low in cholesterol. Overnight, they became wealthy.

Abe and his wife bought a co-op apartment on Fifth Avenue and furnished it sumptuously. Then they hired a butler—right out of Buckingham Palace.

On their first day of residence in the fashionable new quarters, they celebrated with a dinner by candlelight. The butler served them beautifully, as though they were born to royalty. When they finished dining, the impeccable butler bowed over them and asked, "Will the marster and moddum have their arfter-dinnah brandy in the library?"

"How do you like that?" he asked. "Here's a guy who buttled for the king of England and he don't even know the library closes at six!"

23

Sports

Introduction

Jewish intellectuals, adhering to long tradition, continue to view excessive interest in athletics as an unhealthy phenomenon, but you know how those intellectuals are: let anyone get a little pleasure out of life and they can give you more reasons to abstain than can the Lubavitcher rebbe. Nevertheless, some of their observations are very well taken.

"Exaggerated respect for athletics," said Albert Einstein in 1934, "is hostile to the ripening of the character and the desire for real culture. It stamps our age as barbarous, materialist and superficial."

Dr. Sigmund Freud was equally vehement in his denunciation: "The preference which the Jews have given to spiritual endeavor for 2,000 years has had its effect; it has helped against brutality and the inclination to violence which are usually found where athletic development becomes the ideal of the people."

Needless to say (but I'll say it anyway), neither Al nor Siggie ever yelled themselves hoarse at a baseball game and consumed indigestible hot dogs and warm beer that tasted like it had been bottled in a barn. But, as grandpa used to say, what's right is right: Einstein and Freud were opposed to the *idealization* of athletics, rather than to the sports themselves, especially when they tended to overshadow education or supersede the spiritual and cultural values of a supposedly civilized people.

When we speak of Jewish prize fighters, we must go back in time a bit—quite a bit—about 2,000 years. Had I been alive at that time, and my typewriter already invented, I would have written a biography titled, *Resh Lakish: The Gladiator Who Became a Famous*

Rabbi. Who could resist such a title? It would have become an immediate best-seller. Resh Lakish, who became one of the foremost Talmudic sages, fought in the Roman gladiatorial arenas. He must have been a mighty fighter, for there is no record of his having ever suffered a defeat. Of course, when a man was defeated in the arena he was dead, and Lakish lived to a respectable old age. He believed in beating his sword into a plowshare and then attacking with the plowshare.

How does a fighting champion become a spiritual leader? It all started when he went for a swim at a Mediterranean beach. There, he was seen by a great rabbi and his youngest and prettiest daughter who marveled at the gladiator's handsome features and beautifully muscled body—at least the daughter marveled. Her father was just interested. At her gentle, indirect, ladylike hint ("Papa, I want that guy!"), the old man arranged a match—but only on the condition that Resh Lakish catch up on his Torah lessons. Resh studied, married the girl, and became one of the shining lights of the Talmud. He is quoted in the Talmud as saying that in every crime there is a bit of insanity, an observation frequently used by psychiatrists these days, particularly when paid to say so in court.

Having thus covered the last 2,000 years of Jewish sports figures, let's turn our attention to more recent times.

In America, the once lively Yiddish press had no sports section, nor did it need one. Few of its readers were interested in who made a home run. The immigrants from Kovno or Bialystok were sufficiently happy that they were not required to run home from work, but could take the trolley car. Billiards and pool hustling failed to answer their cultural needs (like pinochle, for instance), and a game between Minnesota Fats and Wisconsin Skinny was, for them, a *goyishe* curiosity. ("So you hit a cue ball with a stick it should hit another ball it should roll into a corner pocket! *Nu*, this makes you a *shammes* in the Swiss Navy?")

Football and basketball were even less interesting to the turn-of-the century immigrants. There were no wails of anguish on the East Side when CCNY lost to Bryn Mawr in the *Lokshen* Bowl.

As for prize fights, anyone who fought with his fists was a bum, a loafer, a no-goodnik. Those early immigrants would not pay a nickel to see two men beating each other up in Madison Square Garden. They thought they should be arrested.

But that attitude was not entirely shared by the second generation of American Jews. Prior to World War II, boxing was one of the most popular sports among the Jewish masses, though we must admit that the intellectuals still preferred violin lessons. The greatest interest in prize fighting was evident during its heyday when Irish, Italian and Jewish boxers vied for the purses that could provide escape from the slums in which many of them lived. And it was during that period when nearly all of the classic boxing jokes arose.

Returning to the nostalgia theme, the boxing ring produced a number of outstanding fighters in the various weight divisions. Among them were Max Baer, Al Singer, Benny Leonard, Maxie Rosenbloom, Barney Ross, Lou Tendler and King Levinsky. Many humorous anecdotes about them have survived, some of which are presented in this collection.

I have coupled the words "intellectual" and "sports" more than once in this Introduction, and may the *Mosheeach* show compassion for my indiscretion when and if he gets here to tally up the Divine score. However, although it pains me to admit it, the intellectuals are quite right, for a change, in their denunciation of excessive college sports as being detrimental to education.

Several stories in this chapter deal with the supposed ignorance of women when the subject involves sports. One such joke tells of the annoyed husband who snaps at his wife: "Why do you always cry and sniff at a movie over people you never met?" And the wife retorts: "For the same reason you scream and holler when a man you never met hits a home run." However, let us be fair to the ladies. In all honesty we must agree that today's generation of young women knows all about the national pastime. They understand baseball, too.

Also represented in this chapter are a few humorous anecdotes aimed at the more technically-minded baseball fan. To illustrate: A rookie had just walked six batters in a row, then hit two, then balked, then threw wildly in three pick-off attempts. The manager strode out on the field to take him out of the game. "What!" cried the indignant kid—"When I've got a no-hitter going!"

And now, let's hear it for good ol' Yeshivah . . .

Gimme a G; gimme an E; gimme a V; gimme an A; gimme an L; gimme a T. *Oyyy Gevaaalllt!*

H.D.S.

Now that Berman was retired and finally had the time, he yielded to his lifelong ambition—golfing. He went to the best golf pro in the city and they made an appointment to meet on the links for his very first game.

On the following Friday, the instructor showed Berman how

to tee up the ball and then said, "Hit the ball as near to that flag as you can."

Berman took a mighty swing and the ball soared to within four inches of the flag.

"Not bad," complimented the instructor. "In fact, that's pretty good."

"So what do I do next?" asked Berman.

"Now you have to knock the ball into the hole."

"What?" roared Berman, outraged. "Why the hell didn't you tell me that in the first place!"

Several decades ago, when the world of pugilism ranked such champions as Al Singer, Benny Leonard, Barney Ross and "Slapsie" Maxie Rosenbloom, among many others, there was a little boxing club on East Broadway owned by one Murray Adelson, a tough, shrewd little man. Murray's gym was not merely undercapitalized, it was shaky to the point of collapse, and one night the attendance was woefully slim.

This situation prompted some deep thought. Having done his heavy thinking, Murray entered the ring before the first scheduled bout and, his accented voice ringing with sincerity, he made an announcement:

"Gennelmun, I received today a letter from the Markweezy from Queensberg, and he's telling me, straight out with no baloney, I got to pay him $25 for using his rules here tonight.

"The hat will now be passed!"

Nathan had been going over his old scrapbook, rereading the college newspaper accounts of his former exploits on the gridiron. He had even saved his old football. Full of nostalgic self-admiration, he turned to his mother.

"Just think, mom, I've been out of college for five years now, and I still have my pigskin."

"*Oy*, Natie!" she gasped. "Maybe you should quick see a doimatologist!"

The late L. Wolfe Gilbert, affectionately known as "Wolfie," was scarcely over five feet tall but was as active physically as he was mentally. He was a sharp but lovable character. Long before he attained fame as the composer of such popular songs as *Waiting for the Robert E. Lee, Ramona, Down Yonder, The Peanut Vendor* and *Jeannine, I Dream of Lilac Time*, among a score of other hits of the day, Wolfie had a vaudeville act with Pitzy Katz, the comedian. They were billed as Gilbert and Katen—a song, dance and patter team. Wolfie was later to become board chairman of ASCAP, but he always delighted in reminiscing about his early days on the theatrical circuit. This little gem occurred in 1912 or thereabouts.

Wolfie and his vaudeville partner, Pitzy, found themselves in London one summer. The balmy days made the pair homesick for baseball. They combed the Savoy Hotel and the theatre where they were appearing and found just enough Americans who loved the sport to form two scratch teams. Then they borrowed the use of a cricket field for an afternoon and marked out a rough sort of diamond. After taking care of these preliminaries, plans were concluded for the All-American Baseball Championship of the British Empire, the game to be held on the following Sunday, Wolfie serving as captain of one team and Pitzy the other.

When they arrived at the scene of conflict, a difficulty arose. There were exactly 18 Americans present and all of them expected to play. Where would they get an umpire? Choice fell upon a Britisher among the spectators. He was selected because he had served as a referee at cricket games. He had no knowledge of the rules of baseball but he thought he could learn. His name was Walberg.

So Walberg was given a drilling. He grasped the fine distinctions between a strike and a ball and a foul; the matter of what happened when a fielder caught a fly was easily explained to him, but at the end of a half-hour he was still unsure of the more subtle aspects of the game. Still, the rival teams were anxious to start and the commanders decided to get on with it.

After some extra coaching, umpire Walberg stationed himself behind the catcher and the battle began. The lead-off man on Wolfie's team whanged the first offering of the rival pitcher squarely on the nose and sent the ball high in the air. The centerfielder caught it.

"You are through, sir; quite through," called the umpire, leaping forward.

There was loud applause from both sides. Pleased at having so quickly mastered the intricate phraseology of the Americans' pastime, Walberg strutted back to position.

The next man slammed a wicked grounder toward Pitzy's

shortstop. The latter scooped it up and threw it to first base. But the play at the bag was close.

The catcher swung on the umpire.

"How was that?" he barked.

With unfeigned admiration in his voice, Walberg gave his decision:

"Ma-a-h-velous, sir! Absolutely ma-a-h-velous!"

"Just remember," consoled the trainer as his bruised and battered fighter staggered back to his corner of the ring, "if the other guy was any good he wouldn't be fighting you!"

Benny Leonard was thrashing the daylights out of Lefty Louie, his opponent in the ring. The bell sounded, signaling the end of the third round and the opponent returned unsteadily to his corner.

"Did I land any good shots?" Lefty asked his manager.

"Not yet," said the manager, "but keep on swinging. Leonard might catch a cold from the draft!"

"Pop," asked the sports-minded youngster, "what's the main difference between an amateur and a professional?"

"As far as I can see," replied the father, "the *only* difference is that the pro gets paid by check!"

Hubby took the missus to see her first game of baseball. It was the last half of the ninth inning, with the bases loaded, two out and three balls called. The pitcher threw a red-hot sizzler and the batter for the visiting team lifted a fly ball to left center. The center fielder for the home team, leaping high into the air, made an "impossible" catch, fell backwards and then rolled over on the ground—but he held on to that ball!

Thirty thousand fans lost their minds and went wild in the stands, roaring their approval. Hubby yelled and jumped about in a frenzy of delight. And through it all, his wife looked at him with mouth agape.

"Why were you hollering and jumping like that?" she asked when he had quieted down somewhat.

"Are you blind?" he demanded. "Didn't you see him catch that ball?"

"So?" replied the missus, shrugging. "That's not what he's getting paid for?"

Two middle-aged men were walking off the tennis court after only a few minutes of play. The older, somewhat corpulent fellow was puffing heavily.

"I guess I'm in pretty poor share," he confessed ruefully.

"How long have you been playing, Herbie?" asked the younger man.

"About two weeks."

"Then let me give you a little practical advice. Try the Christian Science way—mind over matter."

"I already have," admitted the fat one. "When my opponent serves the ball to me, my Christian Science mind says, 'Now, Herbie, you just race right up to that net, slam a blistering drive to the far corner of the court and then jump back into position.' That's exactly what my Christian Science mind tells me . . .

"But my Jewish body says, 'Herbie, to make a *shlemiel* out of yourself you don't need!"

There are still a few oldsters wandering about this mortal coil who will recall with fond nostalgia the vaudeville team of Potash and Perlmutter. The two comedy stars regaled their audiences with Jewish-accented jokes, as was the style at the turn of the century, but they were equally adept with "straight" stories which they often told off-stage. One of their favorite exchanges concerned an athletic event in which a young American lad had just broken the world pole-vaulting record. As the applause died away, Potash remarked:

"He did real good, that boy, and I'm proud he's an American. But in the old country I saw a young man who jumped a foot higher than this new champion . . . I said a foot? *Two* feet, maybe!"

"What kind of foolish talk is that?" demanded Perlmutter. "Don't you understand this boy set a new world's record? Don't you understand that nobody in the whole world ever jumped so high before? Don't you understand that it may be years and years

before anyone jumps so high again? Two feet higher, you say?
How can you make such a stupid remark?"

"I don't care," said Potash stubbornly. "Back in Minsk I saw
the boy jump so high with my own eyes. In fact, I knew him personally. He was a neighbor."

"What?" blared Perlmutter incredulously. "You knew him, you
say? What was he?"

"It was your own kid brother, Morris," stated Potash gently.

"Oh-h-h, you mean my kid brother, Morris!" exclaimed Perlmutter in an altered voice. "Well, it stands to reason . . ."

The battle-scarred prize fighter strode into the manager's
office.

"When ya gonna sign me up fer a fight?" he demanded, weaving about and shadowboxing with an opponent who did not happen to be present at the moment. "I'm really ready! Looka 'at
footwoik! Watch 'at lef' jab! Obsoive 'at ol' reflex. I'm inna bes'
shape of m'life. So when're ya gonna get me a match?"

"Well, if you're as ready as you say," the manager replied somewhat dubiously, "I'll get you a match. Anybody in particular you'd
like to fight?"

"Yeah, one guy in pertickla. I wanna fight King Kohen."

"Now look here," said the manager sternly. "If I told you
once I told you a hundred times—*you're* King Kohen!"

Reuben, billed as "The Roaring Rassler from Rochester," arrived home in a dark mood. His wife, Ida, met him at the door.

"I saw the match on TV," she said, her voice full of sympathy.
"I'm sorry you lost."

"I just can't understand why they gave the decision to the
other guy," answered Reuben disconsolately. "How could I lose
the bout when I won the two rehearsals?"

Due and proper credit must be given to Al Brancato, former
Toronto infielder, for the most fascinating alibi in all the history of
baseball.

One night Al went out on the town and had a great time, living it up until three in the morning. As he weaved up the steps in

front of his house, he slipped and gave his backbone a whack. The next day, he came to practice limping, and slightly stooped over.

"What happened to you?" demanded the worried manager.

Al was not about to confess his previous night's misconduct and run the risk of a heavy fine.

"Wrenched my back," he said evasively.

"Yeah, I can see that. But how?"

"You won't believe this," declared Al, a devout Catholic, "but on my way home from practice yesterday I just happened to step inside a synagogue and before I knew it my spine went out of joint while I was *davening!*"

There is no record of this event in any of the official sports annuals. But the story has been so persistent it would be a shame to ignore it. It goes like this:

Hank Greenberg, when he was a top Yankee star, was having a running feud with Iz Goodman, the umpire. Hank was an articulate guy and a fast-thinker, but poor Iz could never win an argument—except on the field, of course, where his word was final. Oh, how Iz longed to put Hank "in his place"—just once—to show the world that he could defeat his nemesis with his intellect and not just with the authority of his office.

The Great Umpire in the Sky must have heard his prayers. The day came when Iz was presented with his shining hour; when, before 50,000 wildly cheering fans, he not only vanquished the pride of the Yankees but absolutely demolished him. It happened thisawise:

Greenberg drove a high, deep fly to center. He raced to first base, the ump running right alongside him, making absolutely certain that he touched the bag; then on to second, third and home, and Iz accompanying him all the way, calling "touch that base!" Hank, understandably, was burned up—to a crisp. "Oh, well," he thought, "what the hell, it's a homer."

But as Hank slid into home base, umpire Goodman yelled — "You're out! Fly ball to center!"

At the ball park, the husband's wife began to pester him with a running barrage of questions about the game until his disposition went from sour to bad to horrible. Yet, he somehow managed to restrain his temper and politely answer all her innocent questions.

"Now tell me this," she said, pointing to the catcher: "Why is that man wearing a mask?"

But this time the dam broke and hubby's soigné reserve evaporated in a red mist.

"That, my dear wife," he said in a voice that hovered at thirty below zero, "is to prevent him from biting the batter!"

Bobby: Riddle me this, Grandpa: What has 18 legs and catches flies?

Grandpa: Nine birds?

Bobby: No.

Grandpa: All right, so what has 18 legs and it's catching flies?

Bobby: The New York Mets.

Grandpa: Impossible! The Mets is popping, not catching!

Mr. Finkel, the haberdasher, was known on his block as something of a baseball expert. One Saturday afternoon, a couple of stern-faced, hulking young men came into his store and demanded that he umpire their Sunday game. Their regular umpire, it seems, had been stabbed, shot, beaten and poisoned after having rendered a decision which did not meet with the popular approval of the home team. Mr. Finkel, who stood an even five feet in his socks, took one analytical look at their glowering faces and decided that discretion was definitely the better part of valor. He agreed to be at the local ballpark early the next day, Sunday.

The game was between the Black Panthers and the Hell's Angels. The man at bat weighed about 240 pounds, was at least six-foot-three and had the arms and shoulders of a gorilla. The catcher was built like Grant's Tomb, only stronger. The pitcher could have passed for the Abominable Snowman. Tiny Mr. Finkel looked like a grasshopper beside them.

The first ball came over the plate. "Strike one!" called the nervous umpire, as the batter glared at him menacingly.

The next offering whizzed over, just outside the plate.

"Ball one!" called Mr. Finkel. This time the pitcher, Joe Behemoth, gave him an icy stage.

Now the third pitched ball whipped over a corner of the plate. The catcher tore the mask from his snarling face and waiting for the umpire's decision.

"Two!" called Mr. Finkel.

"Two *what*!" yelled the batter, the pitcher and the catcher in ugly unison.

Shrinking back into his padding, Mr. Finkel stammered—

"Too close to call!"

There's a fanatical doggedness about a fight fan that will not be swayed. Nothing can divert his attention once he starts to expound on his favorite sport. A case in point was the man with the asbestos stomach lining. The late heavyweight boxing champion, Max Baer, claimed that it really happened. Here is the story in Max's own words:

"After I won the crown, my face became familiar to the general public. Wherever I went, people who knew me only by my picture would stop me, introduce themselves and want to talk with me. At first, so much fame was agreeable—I was flattered. But after a while, when the novelty had worn thin, I began to cherish my privacy. I found out what many other men had learned before me: being in the public eye had its drawbacks.

"One summer night, being alone for a change, I slipped into a quiet tavern for a cool glass of beer. Besides the bartender there was only one other person in the place—a middle-aged Jewish man in his shirtsleeves. The bartender recognized me and, when he spoke my name, the little stranger gave a happy yell and threw himself at me and grabbed my hand and pumped it up and down and wouldn't let go of it and began talking excitedly, sometimes in pure Yiddish which, thankfully, I had a working knowledge of, but mostly in his heavily accented English.

"I understand how these boxing fans are and I didn't want to hurt his feelings. But he almost talked my ear off. He asked a thousand questions. How did I beat Carnera? What was my opinion of Max Schmeling, the darling of the Nazis? Did I think I could take Joe Louis? Was it true that Jack Sharkey wanted to make a comeback? And so on and so forth. Language poured out of that guy in a steady stream. I broke in just long enough to invite him to join me in a drink, hoping that would silence him for a few minutes, but, without missing a beat, he downed his beer with two swallows and kept right on talking.

"I was getting desperate. I tried to dodge him by edging away but he followed me down the bar, hanging on to my elbow and firing more questions at me like bullets out of a rapid-fire machine gun.

"All of a sudden, I spied a bottle of Tabasco sauce on a table behind me. I reached out with my free arm and grabbed the bottle, unscrewed the cap and winked at the bartender. He caught my meaning—after all, it's an old custom in New York bars—and he quickly drew two more beers and placed them in front of us. Then, on another signal from me, he distracted the man's attention for a few moments and I emptied the whole bottle of that red-hot hell-fire into the guy's beer.

"It wasn't a nice thing to do, I admit, but like I said, I was desperate. I figured the Tabasco would heat up that non-stop mouth of his, and while the bartender was extinguishing the fire I'd make my escape.

"The man swung around—the bartender and I watching him intently—and he lifted his schooner.

"'Vell, Max, mine boy,' he said, '*le' chayim!*'

"With one gulp he swallowed that fiery brew and, as we waited for him to give a howl of agony and for the flames to burst out of his mouth, nose and ears, he set the emptied mug down, wiped his lips with the back of his hand, and said:

"'Tell me, Maxeleh, you t'ink maybe did Gene Tooney beat Dempseh mit a long count?'"

Feibush was flabby-fat and sixty. His doctor suggested that he take up golf for his health. So he joined the Gotham Golf Club, and though he had never played a game before in his life, his scores were amazingly low. On his first day, he played the course at par. On his second day, he shot a seven below par, and on the third day he made it at ten below par.

"Look here," said a fellow golfer who had been keeping a sharp eye on this astounding golfer from the beginning, "you know perfectly well that you didn't make this course with those low scores. I've been watching you. What's the idea of cheating like that?"

"Mister," replied Feibush calmly, "my doctor said I should play golf for my health, and low scores make me feel much better."

Sandy Koufax, the unparalleled pitching star of the Los Angeles Dodgers, was in Japan with his team where they were playing a couple of exhibition games.

On behalf of one of the host villages near Tokyo, a little girl brought a bouquet of lovely flowers and presented the gift to

Sandy. Struggling with her limited English, the child said:

"These flowers will die, Sandy Koufax *san*, but you will smell forever!"

For years, Sidney had been a rabid baseball fan. When he wasn't at a ballgame, he was watching one on TV. He read nothing but the sports pages of his newspaper and, even then, only the baseball articles. He subscribed to all the baseball magazines and had lately taken to claiming that he, himself, was one of the greatest pitchers and hitters who ever lived—a startling statement considering the fact that he had not played a single game since his first year in high school. Things got so bad that, at last, his family sent him to the almond and pecan orchard for treatment.

The resident psychiatrist, who hadn't deviated from Freud's teachings for the past thirty years, began with the customary question: "Tell me about your dreams."

"I dream every single night," declared the new patient.

"What about?"

"About baseball, of course!"

"But surely you dream about girls."

"What!" demanded the outraged Sidney, "and miss my turn at bat?"

Harry Shreiber, sports columnist for the Los Angeles *Herald*, was covering the Olympic games for his paper. Everywhere he looked he could see athletes representing almost every country on earth. All were busily engaged in setting up their equipment, practicing, huddling with their teammates or talking with their coaches. They included swimmers, divers, gymnasts, runners, basketball and volleyball players, boxers, wrestlers and many other athletes.

Usually, Shreiber could tell at a glance which sport the contestants represented, but there was one fellow who did not seem to fit in any category. Try as he might, he couldn't match the man with his particular field of athletics.

Suddenly, the fellow picked up a long pole. The newspaperman's eyes lit up. 'Aha,' he thought, 'now I know!' But to make sure, he decided to ask. So he walked over to the stranger.

"Pardon me," he began, after introducing himself, "but are you a pole vaulter?"

The guy looked at him in complete amazement.

"*Nyet*," he replied, shaking his head, "I vas being Russki. But how did you know my name vas Valter?"

Arnold was taking an unusually long time to finish his homework.

"What's the matter?" asked his father. "Stuck for the answers?"

"Yeah," said Arnold. "I'm supposed to pick the nine greatest Americans, but I can't decide who to put on first base."

During his presidential years, Dwight D. Eisenhower spent much of his leisure time at the Burning Tree golf links on the outskirts of the nation's capital. An Arnold Palmer he was not, but sometimes he made the course at par, and once in a while below par. His favorite caddy was Danny Marcus, formerly of New York but at the time living in nearby Arlington, Virginia, with his parents.

Despite President Eisenhower's liking for his caddy, however, he was growing increasingly irritated with the young man's habit of denigrating his best shots.

"My pop could do better than that," he would comment, no matter how far or how accurately the ball had been hit. The day finally came when Ike reached the end of his patience.

"This father of yours; how old is he?" demanded the President

"Seventy-six," replied Danny promptly.

"And how long has he been playing golf?"

"Well, to tell you the truth, sir, he only played three times in his life. Still, if you'll pardon me for saying so, Mr. President, he could beat you easily."

"He's seventy-six years old!" exclaimed Ike, understandably incredulous. "And he's only played three games in his life? You have some nerve comparing him to me! I'll bet you fifty dollars he can't beat me."

So it was arranged. The next day the elder Mr. Marcus, a short man with shoulders about three feet wide, appeared on the links where his son introduced him to the Chief Executive. Ike reaffirmed that he would play the old man 18 holes for a $50 bet. Ground rules were established and it was agreed that the visitor should drive first.

Old Mr. Marcus stepped up to the tee, squared his huge

shoulders, and then, using an extremely unorthodox stance, he gave the ball such a mighty slam that it was flattened on one side. The ball rose to the upper reaches of the atmosphere—God knows how high—and sailed four hundred and fifty yards right to the rim of the green.

Eisenhower's eyes grew as big as saucers.

"Good heavens," he cried, "this man can't be beaten!" He threw up his hands in defeat. "I'm calling it quits. I give up! Here's your fifty dollars. There's no use going any further!"

Grinning, Danny accepted the money and started to walk towards the car where his father was waiting for a ride back home, when Ike commented:

"I must admit, Danny, that your father hit that ball farther and straighter than anyone else in all the history of the sport. But tell me something, how does he putt?"

"Same as he drives," said the proud son. "Wham! Zoom! Four hundred and fifty yards!"

It is a well-known fact that a man looks larger with his clothes off than he does when fully dressed. The point was driven home one day when Max Baer, a huge, powerfully-muscled hulk of a man, stretched out on a couch in the cooling room of a Turkish bath. A stranger, coming in from the steam room and blinking as the sweat ran down his face, spied the giant of a man and halted. He wiped his eyes clear and approached the reclining figure.

"I beg your pardon for addressing a perfect stranger," he said in a deferential voice, "but would you mind telling me who you are?"

"Not at all," said the other affably. "My name is Max Baer. I'm a jockey."

24

Interfaith Ecumania

Introduction

Throughout history, a nation's moral health and cultural maturity could usually be determined by its treatment of the Jews. But the word "treatment" has little significance in America where, as a policy of state, the Jewish citizen is not "treated" as a separate entity but "accepted" as an integral part of society. Freed from the mailed fist of arbitrary power in Europe, enjoying the same rights accorded any other American, he is at liberty to express himself as prophet, sage or fool, dependent only upon his individual talents and proclivities.

The uninhibited exchange of interreligious banter with members of the various Christian faiths represents a departure for the Jew. In the Old World, it was unusual in some countries and unthinkable in others. Derision was acceptable when applied to Jewish religious beliefs, but blasphemous when the same joke was deflected back to the teller. What was sauce for the goose was vitriol for the gander.

To the credit of the American Jew, his interfaith jokes bear no resemblance to the barbs which passed for humor on the continent—particularly in Eastern Europe. The difference is that the American joke in this category is a concord of good will, good nature, good humor and good taste—told with playful intent; sometimes to make a point, but more often because the anecdote or quip is simply funny. These inoffensive jokes, some of which are represented in this chapter, revolve around the similarities as well as differences between synagogue and church practices, theological and philosophical viewpoints, rabbis and priests, and the tongue-in-cheek "misunderstandings" that arise from these similarities and differences. If there is any undercurrent of hostility in the jokes, they are well hidden beneath layers of absurdities and ludicrous characters.

According to the late Ralph Weingart, the waggish, turn-of-the-century rabbi of Baltimore, "it sometimes appears that the only true Christians are found among the Jews." But what is a Jew? That thorny question has been plaguing Jewry for eons; but, as a sort of extra bonus to the reader, I shall answer it and settle the argument once and for all. And, like a lion in a den of Daniels, I shall not only emerge unscathed, but earn the undying gratitude of a noble people.

First, to be a Christian is a fate; to be a Jew is a destiny. I am not quite sure what that means, but we have to start somewhere, and it does sound intelligent.

Isaac Bashevis Singer wrote that Jews are "a people who can't sleep themselves, and let nobody else sleep." Singer sang a sad song with that observation, but we note a suggestion of frivolity in it which may be a little out of place in this serious quest for eternal truth.

Let us consider a few other sources of enlightenment. Isaac Peretz, the famed Yiddish novelist, stated, "We are more than a people. . . . We are of pure blood." But no less an authority than Rabbi Stephen S. Wise declared, "We are a race by religion, *not* of blood!" And that about sums that up.

Now that you know what a Jew is, let us discuss our Christian brethren. It seems to me that every Jewish humor book should also have something nice to say about gentile humor, if for nothing else than to show there are no hard feelings. After all, look how good they've been to the Jewish people all these years.

Gentiles claim there are only seven basic jokes. Here they are, in the order of their unimportance:

1. On West 53rd Street and 10th Avenue, there's a sports-minded fellow who spent all evening trying to get the English Channel on his TV set.

2. A pretty girl is like a melody—after you marry her you have to face the music.

3. There once was an ambitious band leader who hired more musicians than he could shake a stick at.

4. The Madison Avenue bus was so crowded last week that even the driver had to move to the rear.

5. A banker called his stockbroker for some quick cash, only to learn that the broker was broker than he.

6. A cannibal finally left the Congo for the big city to visit a psychiatrist because he was fed up with people.

7. Pat McNulty was ordered to get an immediate flu shot, but his bartender didn't know how to mix one.

Those are the funniest of the elemental gentile jokes—now you know why there is such a crying need for *Jewish* humor!

The cement that bonds Christian and Jewish humor is "understanding"—a cerebral secretion that enables one having it to know a house from a horse by the roof on the house. It's nature and laws have been intensively expounded by Locke, who rode a house, and by Kant, who lived in a horse.

Another ingredient of interfaith amity is common sense. One simply does not call up the Pope and tell him he can resign because he's in good hands with AllState. Nor is it necessary to remind priest or rabbi that purgatory is hell.

Having exhausted all the similarities in the Judeo-Christian relationship, we now turn our objective attention to its differences. The modern American Jew, it has been pointed out by the philosopher, Boris Bluebelly, believes in the religion of Jesus; he just cannot bring himself to accept the religion *about* Jesus. One area of disagreement which is frequently mentioned—at least in this book—is the idea of a soul, a spiritual entity concerning which there hath been brave disputation. Bluebelly held that the soul has its seat in the liver and he has often been quoted as saying, "He who destroyeth his liver through strong drink loses his soul and shall suffer eternal damnation," a viewpoint which gave rise to the phrase, "That damned drunk!" The Jewish view, especially among the Reform and Reconstructionists, is that the soul resides in the upper duodenum where ulcers attack the less pious. The thoughtful reader would be well advised to accept a little of both theories and thus assure himself a front-row seat in heaven.

A majority of the interfaith jokes in this section can be traced back to the latter part of the 19th century and the first two decades of the 20th. A few are obviously new, such as the quip about the banning of Xerox machines by the Catholic Church because they interfere with natural reproduction. One quip, dated at about 1890, describes a saint as a dead sinner, revised and edited. Another of that era announces that New York's priests were planning to organize a union because they wanted Sundays off.

The closeness of Catholic and Jewish humor in the United States probably had its start in the 1870s, at a time when Jewish immigrants began to inherit the East Side tenements from the Irish who preceded them to this country. Both lived together amicably for as long as the dwindling Irish cave dwellers inhabited the East Side, and until their improved financial circumstances permitted them to leave for better neighborhoods—with the empty caves being quickly occupied by tens of thousands of new Jewish residents. These immigrants, let it be noted, were not the first cave men and women in Jewish history. A famous community of troglodytes dwelt with David in the Cave of Adullam. The colony consisted of "every one that was in distress, and every one that was in debt, and every one that was discontented"—in brief, all the socialists of Judah.

The caustic humor that emanated from the lower East Side of New York may best be explained by David Ben Gurion's witty statement: "The outlook of the ghetto divided the universe into two: this world for the gentiles, the hereafter for the Jews." The Scriptures, for another example, were described as the sacred books of the Old Testament, as distinguished from the false writings on which all other faiths are based. The Sabbath was known as a weekly festival having its origin in the fact that God made the world in six days and was arrested on the seventh. Observance of this day, according to humorists of the 1890s, is enforced by the commandment: "Remember the seventh day to make thy neighbor keep it wholly." In that connection, a point of controversy still exists between Jew and Christian as to whether the week begins or ends with the Sabbath. To the Creator, it seemed fit and expedient that the Sabbath should be the last day of the week, but the Early Fathers of the Church held other views.

Nevertheless, despite all this pseudo-intellectual badinage, the most enduring of the interfaith jokes will still be found among those that depend for their humor on naiveté, inoffensive impertinence and the stereotypes (gleefully promoted by the Jewish people themselves) that have long been associated with this genre. They should be. Despite their simple-mindedness, these jokes are often the funniest. We are reminded of the time Mrs. Lefkowitz was granted an audience with the Pope. "Mr. Holiness," she said boldly, "how come a man so successful like you never got married?"

H.D.S.

Ask anyone you happen to meet along Tremont Avenue in the Bronx if he ever heard the one about the local Jewish kid who once enacted the role of the infant Jesus in a school play, and he'll slap his thigh, roar with laughter at the very mention of the tale, and then say, "No, tell me about it." That reaction notwithstanding, let us now spread the cheerful story beyond the confines of the East Bronx and far from the madding I.R.T.

On the momentous day of November 10, 1943, Wally Wexler, a kindergarten pupil at PS 67, was about to be touched by the hand of destiny. Mrs. Murphy, the assistant principal, was directing that year's Christmas pageant and, since few babies are normally registered in grade schools, the lady was feverishly casting about for a handsome little boy to portray the infant Jesus. The moment she laid eyes on Wally Wexler's angelic face she knew in her heart that he would be perfect for the part. Because he was Jewish, she experienced a few hours of anxiety until she secured his parents' permission, and then she joyfully went ahead with the rehearsals.

As for Wally, he was about as ccstatic as a six-year-old budding actor could possibly be. His role called for him to lie on a nice, soft cushion inside a laundry basket and remain "as quiet as a mouse" while the older boys and girls performed. Everyone was in costume, and Wally himself was wrapped in a sheet which served as swaddling clothes.

Came the great night. The curtain went up and there, stage center, was Wally, but hidden, of course, in his "manger." A trumpet sounded and Herod gave a soprano cry of rage. Other actors in their costumes representing sheep, goats and cows, milled about, baaing, bleating and mooing. Mary and Joseph, looking a little young for their age, gave forth with the glad news of the first Yuletide, and at the door of the impromptu stable the Three Wise Men prepared to enter on-stage.

Wally's performance, thus far, had been exemplary—in fact, just marvelous—as he lay in the "manger" without sound or motion. He could not see over the rim of the basket and he wondered how the other actors were faring. The sounds of the "farm animals" and the dialogue and murmurings of the players increased his curiosity. But it was the reaction of the audience that intrigued him most. He could hear their whispers, the rustle of their clothing, the creaking of their chairs and an occasional cough. Then came a round of applause beyond isolated Wally's understanding.

Whatever Biblical teachings, traditions and history had been imparted to him in his six years of life, they were sadly deficient in the details surrounding the birth of the Galilean. Nor had his limited knowledge of Mosaic law prepared him for receiving such gifts as precious stones and frankincense, to say nothing of myrrh. Vaguely, he comprehended that somebody was about to offer him a bunch of presents, and that he was somehow important in the general scheme of things, but a laundry basket tends to shut off the view.

Wally could stand it no longer. The unseen activity proved too much for an inquisitive little boy. He raised one experimental eye over the side of the manger. A rolling chuckle spread through the audience at the unexpected debut. This appreciation of his acting ability encouraged him to sit up in full view of the spectators. Now Mrs. Murphy groaned in anguish, the other participants in the Nativity play joined the audience as interested observers, and the pageant ground to an inglorious halt.

Wally smiled happily. All eyes were fastened on him! He was the *star!*

Surrounded by King Herod, Mary and Joseph, the Three Wise Men and all the players representing the farm animals, Wally aimed both index fingers at the audience like two spraying machine guns and went —

"Ack-ack-ack-ack-ack-ack-ack-ack-ack!"

Six-year-old Rachel persuaded her friend Constance, a little Methodist girl, to attend synagogue with her. All went well. On the following Sunday, Rachel's parents agreed that their daughter could go to the Methodist Sunday School with Constance as a return courtesy.

The Sunday School teacher spoke at length of the Good Samaritan, adding a few gory details of her own that made Rachel's stomach a little queasy. When the teacher finished, she decided to put the moral of the parable to practical use.

"Now, children," she began, "if you saw a man lying in the street after being hit by a speeding car, and he was bleeding all over from ugly wounds, what would you do?"

Volunteered Rachel: "I'd frow up!"

A wealthy black executive hired a butler who was Jewish. On the first New Year's Eve after his employment, as the family sat down to dinner, the butler was summoned by the man of the house:

"Sam, would you please bring a bottle of '59 Beaujolais?"

The butler, fingers snapping, danced out of the room singing:

> Bring out de cream cheese,
> Slice dat bagel,
> Spread on de schmaltz, please,

Taste dat knaidel —
Ya dig, man?

The black employer smiled indulgently.

"You have to give those Jews credit," he commented to his family at the table. "They sure got rhythm!"

Patricia, a Catholic girl, and David, a Jewish boy, were very much in love. However, because of her religious convictions, she refused to marry him unless he converted to Catholicism. After much soul-searching, he finally gave in to her tearful pleading and agreed to undertake the Church's required course of study. And now that he had made up his mind, he threw himself into his labors with a vengeance, poring over his books night and day, speaking with Church officials and asking profound questions of his instructors.

One evening, three months after her sweetheart had begun his studies, Patricia came home sobbing.

"What's the matter, dear?" asked her mother. "Why are you crying?"

"It's David," she wept. "He's decided to become a priest!"

Let us go back to the second decade of this century.

Father Ducey, a famous New York clergyman, was the resident priest at St. Leo's, one of the most widely-known Catholic churches in the downtown area.

One weekend, in the spring of 1919, Father Ducey became ill, as did many others during the flu epidemic that claimed so many victims that year. His assistants had also fallen before the rampaging virus, so, out of desperation, he sent an emissary to the equally famous Rabbi Stephen S. Wise, pleading that he conduct the Sunday confessional hearings in his stead. The good rabbi, possessor of a sharp and cultivated wit, saw the humor as well as the urgency of the situation, and he consented to sit in his friend's place.

Early the next Sunday morning, a woman entered and coughed nervously. From the other side of the partition she heard a voice—a voice that was kindly and inviting:

"Well, my daughter, what have you to tell me?"

"F-f-father Ducey," sputtered the lady, "I-I-I'm embarrassed to say this—I've always b-b-been a good Catholic . . ."

"I absolve you of that," interrupted Rabbi Wise. "Go on with your confession."

But the horror-stricken penitent had fled.

Inside a little country church near Landover Hills, Maryland, the rector was in the midst of a Sunday morning sermon. Mrs. Anderson sat in a front pew with her daughter, Catherine, and the little girl's friend, Mildred Cohen, age nine.

Mildred had never been to church before and the activities held her interest for a while, but soon she began to fidget. To make matters worse, the three candy bars she had eaten without her parents' knowledge had upset her stomach. Presently, she glanced up with a distressed look on her face.

"Mrs. Anderson," she whispered.

"Shh!" hissed the lady.

"But, Mrs. Anderson, I feel sick," persisted Mildred.

"Sit still and think of something else," suggested Mrs. Anderson, regretting that she had allowed herself to be talked into bringing the child.

"But, Mrs. Anderson, I'm gonna be awful sick in just a minute!"

"Oh, all right!" snapped the irritated woman. "Just slip out very quietly and go behind that big tree in the churchyard. When you feel better you can come back."

Her eyes now glassy, her skin tinted yellow and her jaws tightly locked, Mildred trotted down the aisle. In what seemed to be an amazingly short time, everything considered, the little girl returned to her seat.

"Feel better?" inquired the lady rather testily.

"Uh-huh, I feel okay now."

"You weren't gone very long. You must have found the big tree very quickly."

"No, ma'am. I didn't hafta go way out in the yard. Right outside the church door, in the lobby, I saw a box and it had a little sign on it. And the sign said —

"*For the Sick!*"

When a Jew converts to Christianity all he gets is a new religious title. But when a Christian converts to Judaism—ahh!—he at once becomes retroactively eligible for 2,000 years of persecution!

It has been said that Judaism is not only a religion; it is a state of mind. For some, it approaches religious chauvinism, which isn't necessarily bad. Witness:

Pincus and his family of little Pincii were returning home from *shul* one day when his youngest son stopped to talk with another boy. In the course of their brief discussion, the youngster asked the other boy his religion. After some hesitation, he replied that he was a Catholic.

"Son," asked papa Pincus a little while later, "did I hear you ask that boy his religion?"

"Yes, I did."

"Let me give you a word of advice, young man," counseled the father. "Never ask a person his religion. If he's Jewish he'll tell you soon enough. If he's not, there's no point in embarrassing him!"

Four separate shipwrecks occurred and four survivors were cast up on a lonely island far off the regular shipping routes. Two of the men were Americans, the other two were Englishmen. After several months, a passing steamer hove to and took the four aboard. The Americans, Sidney and Stanley, were escorted to the skipper's cabin, there to relate their experiences.

"Captain," said Stanley, "it would really grieve you to see the way those two Englishmen ignored each other. In the whole time we were on that island neither of them said a single word to the other. You ask why? Simply because they weren't properly introduced."

"And how did you two fellows make out?" asked the skipper.

"We didn't need introductions," said Sidney. "On the very same day I found Stanley on the beach, we organized a reform and conservative temple, a debating society, a golf club, a Bonds for Israel chapter and an Impeach Nixon protest!"

Orthodox rabbis do not, as a general rule, attend Catholic Church services—at least not in Milwaukee where this story has been making the rounds since the last Iroquois uprising.

A gentile friend cajoled Rabbi Berkowitz into attending St. Joseph's in the city that made Schlitz famous. The old rabbi, long since retired, finally agreed when it was explained that a visiting dignitary would speak about the Jewish influence on the formation of the Church.

In the front row, Rabbi Berkowitz's eyes widened as the visiting lecturer announced his topic: *My name is Joseph, father of Jesus.*

At the conclusion of the talk, when they had been introduced, the rabbi said dryly:

"My friend, you have had a most unusual experience!"

Two youngsters were arguing the relative merits of their respective faiths.

"Bet you don't even know the difference between a Methodist, a Baptist and a Jew," taunted the Protestant boy.

"Oh, yeah? I do so!" retorted the Jewish boy. "A Baptist gets dunked in water over his head, but a Methodist only get sprinkled."

"What happens to the Jew?"

"A Jew—well—hmm—a Jew, I think, gets dry-cleaned!"

The members of St. Thomas Aquinas Church in the Bronx were so fond of their priest that they presented him with a brand new Cadillac.

Across the street, at Temple Yisroel, the congregants watched as the priest came out, inspected the car appreciatively and blessed it by making the sign of the cross.

Not to be outdone, the Jewish worshipers immediately bought their rabbi a new Cadillac also. Then he came out, inspected the car, and snipped off the tip of the radiator hose.

Groucho Marx, who once said of a woman, "She speaks 120 words a minute with gusts up to 160," was well known for his jaggedly serrated tongue. Years ago, he was approached by a certain highly-respected priest.

"I want to thank you for all the joy you've brought into the world," said the good father.

Snapped Groucho: "I want to thank you for all the joy you've taken out of it!"

A spiritualist séance was in progress. The medium, Mrs. Hannah Goldberg, specialized in summoning the spirits of great historical figures from the Other Shore. Tonight was especially rewarding for the assembled True Believers. The Czarina rapped on a table and made a chair waltz on two legs. Albert Einstein strummed a guitar and sang excerpts from *Fiddler on the Roof.* King Solomon recited his famous passages with a pronounced Flatbush accent.

At this juncture, Louis Goldberg, the medium's husband, made a special announcement. If anyone present wished to communicate with the shade of some illustrious one who had not already taken part in the evening's program, the medium—for a slight fee—would endeavor to materialize the individual desired.

A visiting True Believer, Mrs. Sullivan, spoke up. She would give anything, she stated, if she could just have a direct blessing from her Lord and Savior.

"Oh," she cried, "if only I could have His personal benediction!"

"A benediction!" called out someone else in the audience.

"A benediction! A benediction! A benediction!" chanted the others in unison.

Madame Goldberg agreed to try. As her husband hastily retreated, she went off in a trance, uttering muffled, moaning sounds. Presently, the black draperies at the entrance to the room were agitated and then, in the pale bluish light that shone dimly upon the curtains and left the rest of the room in darkness, there appeared a ghostly figure swathed in white.

In the midst of the ensuing silence that was as still and quiet as death itself, the apparition took one step forward, raised two fingers of its right hand in the gesture of apostolic blessing and, in impressively deep tones, uttered the word they had all been waiting to hear:

"Benedictine!"

The Rev. Billy Graham was putting on his biggest revival meeting in the history of Los Angeles and Shirley Rapoport decided to attend. So persuasive, so powerful a speaker was the popular evangelist that before his sermon was over, Shirley was "saved."

"Oh, Dr. Graham," she gushed, completely overwhelmed in her new-found faith for the evening, "before you came, I didn't know what sin was!"

Mr. Kramer was not too happy with the news that his daughter was keeping company with a gentile fellow. "A million fine Jewish boys in America," he would scold, "and you have to pick a *shaigetz!*"

One evening the daughter brought her boyfriend home to dinner. The young fellow, not a bad sort of chap, thought it might be prudent to ingratiate himself with old man Kramer. What better way than to claim a small bit of Jewish ancestry? In any case, it was rather stylish to be Jewish these days.

"You'll be surprised to know, sir," the boyfriend began, "that I am part Jewish."

"You're right," snapped the father. "With a name like Patrick Clancey, I *am* surprised. So enlighten me."

"It happens that I have one-sixteenth Jewish blood in my veins."

"In that case I'd be very careful if I were you," said Kramer, his voice grim. "One nosebleed and you're out of the tribe!"

Did you ever wonder why the Jewish people have for so long been termed "stiff-necked"—even by their own prophets? Perhaps a clue is provided in the following exchange.

A rabbi and a priest were discussing the differences between the Old Testament and the New. It was the priest's contention that the New Testament gave more proof of Divine cooperation because of all its purported miracles.

"Remember," argued the priest, "our Lord walked on water, he raised the dead, he fed hundreds of people with a few loaves of bread and some little fishes, he changed water into wine, and he ascended bodily into Heaven."

"So what does that prove?" insisted the rabbi. "The Old Testament includes such miracles as parting the Red Sea, making the sun stand still, Moses ascending bodily to Mt. Sinai to talk personally with God and to receive the Decalogue from the very hands of the Almighty."

The priest nodded. "I believe in those miracles, too," he acknowledged. "But be honest about it—do you really think your miracles have as much substance as ours?"

The rabbi glared at him.

"What's the matter with you?" he snapped crossly. "Can't you distinguish between fact and fiction?"

To be orthodox in everything in which a policeman figures, the said policeman should be of Irish extraction. Any departure from this is a violation of all folklore tradition. Nevertheless, convention notwithstanding, the hero of this story is a policeman who was not an Irishman. He was a Scot. But, before introducing him, it is necessary to present the other principal character involved in this little tragedy, circa 1890.

That other character was Jewish, but he was not a police officer. He was, in fact, an elderly civilian who had stopped during a stroll to watch a job of street repairing.

Three stories up above his head, a housewife placed a large platter of cheese *blintzes* to cool on the front window ledge of her tenement. The ledge had a slant to it. The platter slid off and, descending, struck the elderly gentleman squarely on the head, bruising his scalp and covering him with the contents of the dish.

He gave a loud cry of pain and astonishment and sank to the sidewalk. He was not badly hurt but he had suffered a rather severe shock. As sympathetic onlookers pulled him up to a sitting position, the Scot policeman ranged up alongside and took in the sight.

"Well," he said, "I kenned you Jews were fond of *blintzes*, but, laddie, you're the first one I ever knew to decorate himself with 'em."

Theodore Roosevelt's dislike of bigotry can be traced back to his early days in politics when he served as Police Commissioner of New York City from 1895 to 1897.

"While I was in that post," he reminisced, "an anti-Semitic preacher from Berlin, Rector Ahlwardt, came to New York to preach a crusade against the Jews.

"Many Jews were quite excited and asked me to prevent him from speaking and not to give him police protection. But this, I told them, was impossible, and even if it were possible it would have been undesirable because it would make a martyr of him. The proper thing to do was to make him appear ridiculous.

"Accordingly, I sent a detail of police under a Jewish sergeant, and the Jew-baiter made his harangue under the active protection of some 40 police officers, every one of them Jewish.

25

Rabbis

Introduction

Since pre-Colonial times, the American rabbinate has distinguished itself as a source of inspiration and leadership for the nation's Jews. It has also produced a vanguard of leaders who contributed greatly to the ethical and physical well-being of the United States itself—promoting the human rights of all citizens, Jew and gentile alike, in their struggle for a better society. America's rabbis participated in the War of Independence, the Abolitionist crusade, the struggle to organize and maintain a viable labor movement, the establishment of the public school system, non-sectarian hospitals for the poor, and many other affairs of state and community.

But it is not the purpose of this book to recount the honorable achievements of the rabbinate. We are concerned here only with Jewish humor as it applied to rabbis. The jokes by and about them are not confined to their role as teachers and scholars. The anecdotes concern their attitudes and personalities. They tell of every kind of rabbi: the serious-minded and the jocular, the simple and the profound, the tolerant and the intolerant, the placid and the combative.

True rabbinical humor, some of which is incorporated in this Introduction, is almost invariably on a higher intellectual plane than are the "rabbi jokes" told by the laity. The former are best enjoyed by those with at least a working knowledge of the Bible, a history of the Jewish people, and some familiarity with world events. The latter is not nearly as cerebral, but is usually more "human" and relies for its laughter on the outrageously comic, rather than on clever wit. Both have equal stature in American-

Jewish humor, and can be equally funny.

According to the Talmud, "A rabbinic decree must not assume the character of a jest." A few of the ultra-Orthodox rabbis have interpreted this to mean that they themselves must be excluded from all humorous references. "To that opinion," snorted one Reform rabbi, "I must reluctantly bow-wow!" Since rabbis do not or are not supposed to argue among themselves, they *discuss* matters, their discussions being a method of calling attention to the errors made by those who disagree with them. The Orthodox rabbi is a strong believer in strict allegiance to traditional beliefs and ritual—more so than are the Conservative and Reform, but the *tzaddik*—the *Chassidic* leader—takes a dim view of strict Orthodoxy. Nephtali Zevi Horowitz, an articulate *tzaddik* with a broad sense of humor, made this cynical (but funny) observation about what he believed to be unfounded loyalty to any of the other Judaic sects:

> This thing "allegiance," I suppose,
> Is a ring fitted in the Jewish nose,
> Whereby that organ is kept righteously pointed,
> To smell the sweetness of the Lord's anointed.

Unlike most other rabbis, Horowitz made no grand claims of a Heavenly call when he decided to enter the rabbinate. He said:

"At first I did not want to be a rabbi, for a rabbi has to flatter his flock, and so I thought of being a tailor. Then I saw that a tailor has to flatter his customers, and so does a shoemaker, and a bath-attendant; and I asked myself, 'Where, then, is a rabbi worse off?' And so," he concluded, "I became a rabbi."

Intra-Judaic squabbles have produced numerous gems of wit. The *Chassid*, Reb Yitzhok Levi, once took it upon himself to defend the Jewish people against God: "Lord, if ever Thou shouldst issue a hard decree against the Jews, we *tzaddikim* will not fulfill Thy commands!" The statement apparently did not coincide with the views held by the Yiddish writer, Shmuel Jaffe, who retorted, "One more rabbi like Yitzhok Levi and God will cancel our contract!"

In all fairness to Levi, let it be said that he was a kind and good man, deeply involved in community affairs. Indeed, his philosophy of communal involvement was supported by none other than Dr. Kaufmann Kohler when he delivered his inaugural address in 1903, upon becoming president of Hebrew Union College. "All the knowledge the future rabbi acquires," he told the assembled rabbinical students, "must be subordinate to the higher tasks of practical communal service which he is expected to assume."

That comment elicited a blast from the Hebrew scholar, Abraham Kahana, who made a brief icy reference to Rabbi Kohler, but saved his heavier ammunition for Reb Levi:

"For community affairs, we have politicians, not political rabbis. Dr. Kohler should go back to *cheder* and study all over again for his *Bar Mitzvah*, and never mind presiding over a college. As for that *person*, Yitzhok Levi, when he was about to be born, Satan complained that if Levi's soul were to descend on earth it would reform the world, and his own power would come to an end. Then the Holy One comforted Satan and said: 'But he will be a rabbi and he will be too occupied with communal affairs!'"

Solomon Schechter, the rabbinical scholar and author, once discussed the intra-Judaic controversy with Rabbi Louis Finkelstein, the noted leader of American Conservative Judaism and his successor (once removed) as head of the Jewish Theological Seminary. "Whatever the faults of the rabbis, consistency is not one of them," grinned Schechter, refusing to take the matter seriously. "As I see it, the only problem these days is that unless you can play baseball, you'll never get to be a rabbi in America."

Another writer, Israel Lipkin, dismissed the whole argument of creed and deed with a few brief words: "The *Chassidim* think they have a rabbi; their opponents think they need no rabbi. Both are mistaken." To which Herschel Mishkin, an Orthodox rabbi, added: "I pay no attention to the silly chatter of the *Chassidim*. Of course, I pay no attention to the prattle of the Reform and Conservative, either. I only hope and pray they will all return some day to the Jewish faith!"

American-Jewish humor takes a tolerant view of the disputes among the Judaic sects, kept alive, in the main, by the rabbis themselves. The only real difference among them is that a Reform rabbi speaks *about* God, a Conservative rabbi *to* God, and an Orthodox rabbi answers them according to the holy dictates of his conscience.

They all believe in the Decalogue: a series of commandments, ten in number, which are just enough to permit an intelligent person to make a selection for his own degree of observance, and not so many as to embarrass him by those he overlooks. A good Jew, therefore, in the modern tradition, is one who believes that the Decalogue is Divinely inspired, and is admirably suited to the spiritual needs of his neighbors. He follows the Mosaic Laws insofar as they are not in conflict with the little pleasantries of life.

The Ten Commandments are highly respected in the North Temperate Zone. We are assured that if we obey the Divine injunctions, our prayers will be answered. Most people, the rabbis tell us, pray for good health, happy marriages and riches. The trouble arises from our interpretation of all these celestial favors. For example, riches is considered as a gift from Heaven signifying "the reward of toil, virtue and piety," said Rabbi Stephen S. Wise. It is "the savings of many in the hands of one," said Golda Meir.

All rabbis, regardless of the branch of Judaism they may represent, are in accord in their reactions to the Neanderthal who mouths anti-Semitic jokes. Prejudice, to the rabbi, is a vagrant opinion with no visible means of support. The bigot who repeats the hoary canards under the guise of humor is looked upon as a prevaricator—a liar in the caterpillar stage who, at molting time, blossoms forth as an adult cretin upon whom a scathing retort would be wasted. Another point of agreement among modern-minded rabbis is their doubt as to the physical existence of a place called Hades, the nether world where the dead live. Among the ancient Greeks, Hades was not synonymous with our Hell. Many of the most respected citizens of antiquity resided there in a very comfortable manner. Indeed, the Elysian Fields themselves were a part of Hades, though they have since been removed to 42nd Street and Eighth Avenue.

The greatest area of agreement among orthodox rabbis is found in their unyielding conviction that all observances must be in strict accordance with the ancient religious laws, particularly those concerning ritualism, that Garden of God where He walks in rectilinear freedom, keeping off the grass. But if there is any one rallying point around which all rabbis can gather in unanimous certitude, it is in their hostility to the agnostic posing as an iconoclast—the self-appointed breaker of idols. It makes no difference that the Jewish people have not fraternized with idols since the Golden Calf episode: when a Jew sets his mind to it, he can argue about anything. So, as a substitute for idols, he inveighs against ritual and even the basic beliefs in God and Torah to advance his notions. The rabbis most strenuously protest that the Jewish iconoclast pulleth down but pileth not up. For, should he have his way, the poor worshipers would soon have other idols or beliefs in place of those he wacketh upon the noggin. The iconoclast saith: "Ye shall have none at all, for ye heed them not." And the rabbi respondeth: "If the rebuilder fooleth around hereabouts, behold, we shall depress his head and sit thereon till he squawketh."

The foregoing clearly demonstrates—or should have by now—that American-Jewish humor as it pertains to the rabbinate is pretty hairy stuff, profound and intellectually stimulating. It bears no resemblance to the frivolous jokes one usually hears about the old-fashioned *rebbe* preparing a class of fresh kids for their *bar mitzvahs*.

By-the-bye, as they like to say in the more elegant circles, have you heard the one about the old-fashioned *rebbe* who was preparing a class of fresh kids for their *bar mitzvahs?* Read on, but just smile, smirk or grin a little—it isn't nice to laugh at old people.

H.D.S.

Rebbe Saul Isaacson, who for 45 years conducted the store front *cheder* at 157 Grand Street on the lower East Side, was a very old man when he finally went to his reward in 1927. How old he was, God only knows—and He won't tell. In that last year of his teaching, Rebbe Isaacson had 18 pupils. The smarter boys—those with retentive memories—could sail through the hour-long sessions with little more than a cuff on the ear and a few glowering looks—just to let them know who was who and what was what. The fumblers got their smacks along with pertinent and unflattering commentaries on their mental processes. The slow learners received the royal treatment, with whacks to whatever portion of their anatomies was most convenient, or whose backsides were in perihelion, so to speak, with his ruler. It was with these latter that Rebbe Isaacson, bristling through his salt-and-pepper whiskers, would demonstrate his more unrabbinical talent for sarcasm, disparagement, contumely, affront and derision.

In his defense, however, let it be said that the fathers of the youngsters had themselves, in many cases, been prepared for their own Bar Mitzvahs by the irascible old man and they were aware that his scowling demeanor hid a deep anxiety that his *boychiks* might not be ready for their communion. He was, in short, a born teacher—an East Side Hebrew Mr. Chips straight out of Jewish-American folklore. His boys were carbon copies of the fathers and, in some families, the grandfathers he had dragged, kicking and squirming, to the thresholds of their Bar Mitzvahs. For him, the tricks they loved to play on their aged teacher were all part of the burden a Talmudic scholar in his position was destined to endure. His departed wife once remarked that he would arrive home in a ferocious mood because of some prank played on him by one of his pupils. "But after supper, and over a glass of tea and lemon," the *rebbetzyn* smiled, "he would recount the episode and chuckle. 'A wild one, that stinker, but not as bad as his father was at his age, nor even his grandfather: Now *there* was an incorrigible one! So today he's a rabbi in a big, fancy temple with a rich congregation. And how does he repay me? He sends his son's offspring to torture me in my old age!'"

One such "offspring" was twelve-year-old Ira Shmulowitz (later a judge of the Circuit Court in New York). On this particular afternoon in 1927 of which we speak, Rebbe Isaacson's disposition had deteriorated from vile to unspeakable. Unfortunately for young Ira, it was his turn for reading and answering questions. The rebbe glared at his victim, his ever-present ruler gripped firmly in his bony hand. Ira was one of the slow learners, and to compound the teacher's aggravation, the boy also fancied himself as something of a kibitzer. On that day, however, Isaacson's foul mood intimidated the class in general and, at least for now, even Ira. He listened carefully as the rabbi spoke:

"Mister Intellectual, you remember yesterday I spoke of Moses?"

"Yeah, sort of," mumbled Ira, slouching alongside the teacher's table.

Splat! Went the ruler across Ira's behind.

"Sort of?" fumed the rabbi. "You will be *sort of* Bar Mitzvah when you reach thirteen? You will be *sort of* Jewish?" He made a valiant effort to compose himself. "Now, without 'sort-ofs', and if it isn't putting you out too much, what can you tell me about Moses?"

"He led the Israelites outta Egypt an' acrosst the Suez Can . . ."

Splat!

"Oww!" Ira howled. "You said so yerself! Ask the other kids!"

"I have to ask those idiots what I said? They're your character witnesses all of a sudden?" *Splat!* "Now, do me a big, personal favor and answer the question."

"I fergot what it was."

"I asked about Moses. Maybe you heard of him somewhere in your world-wide travels."

A gleam came into your Ira's eyes. So the *rebbe* wanted to make jokes, eh? Okay, he asked for it.

"I know about Moses," he said, nodding. "I saw him in the movies. He got them tablets, see, an' he came down offa Mount Sinai, an' there was this girl, see, an' . . ."

Splat!

"Dumkopf!" Isaacson exploded in wrath. "May the waters of Jordan back up into your *lokshen* soup! What has Hollywood to do with the noblest rabbi of all time?"

Ira dared not show the slightest of smiles. He had really provoked the old man this time, and the other students, vastly entertained, burst into joyful laughter, a reaction which did little to improve the old man's disposition. They were silenced only upon his snarling command that they cease their hilarity forthwith or suffer a physical confrontation of their own.

But Ira was enjoying his co-starring role and he was in no hurry to relinquish the spotlight. He waited for the rabbi to resume his questioning.

"We will try another subject," Rebbe Isaacson said darkly. "I assume you can at least *daven*."

"No," replied Ira, unable to suppress a grin, "but I can somersault."

Splat! Whap! Splat!

"Comedians in *cheder* we need, hah, *yingatsh*?" In a red fury, Rebbe Isaacson rose from his chair to deliver a *coup de' état* with his upraised ruler. Ira, in an effort to dodge the descending blow, lurched to one side and inadvertently bumped the table with his body. The table slammed into old Isaacson and knocked him off his feet.

"Well, don't just stand there!" the rabbi barked as he struggled to get up. "Give me a hand!"

And the students, for the first time in his memory, complied with waves of enthusiastic applause, giving him the biggest hand he had ever received in his life.

You heard maybe about the unemployed cantor who is now making a fortune? He learned the Wedding March backwards, and now he sings it at divorces!

A rabbinical student returned to his room at the seminary, his sullen face clearly indicating distress.

"What's with you?" asked his roommate.

"I just asked permission to smoke while praying but I got turned down—and in no uncertain terms, too," moaned the unhappy future rabbi.

"You should have used a little psychology and done what I did," suggested the other prospective spiritual leader. "I just reversed the question and asked if it would be okay if I prayed while smoking!"

This author once referred to his dear friend, the late rabbi Montagu Katz of Los Angeles as "Holy Katz," at which he did wroth exceedingly wax, or whatever. But he was, nevertheless, possessed of a delightful sense of humor, as witness this tale—one of his favorites.

Rabbi Katz had an old friend, another rabbi named Solow. It seems that Rabbi Solow was afflicted with a galloping tongue—a man who from time to time during the course of his sermons, would begin a new phrase with the line, "Just one more word, my dear friends," and then never keep his promise.

On this particular Sabbath, Rabbi Solow droned on and on and on, interminably. The congregation grew impatient and fretful. A hum of conversation could be heard, at first an almost indiscernible whisper until, growing in volume, it threatened to drown him out entirely.

Now Rabbi Solow, if it has not yet been established, was a unique character. As an accoutrement of his calling, and with good reason, he kept a gavel on the lectern beside the *Torah* so that he could rap for silence when necessary—and he would indeed find it necessary at least once during each of his long-winded sermons. The irreverent buzzing in the audience was now so audible that he felt it his duty to God and his own honor to bang for order. As he brought his gavel down with emphasis, the handle snapped. The hardwood head hurtled through the air and struck with a resounding thud squarely on the forehead of a congregant in the front row. The victim sank back in his seat, glassy-eyed.

A horrified hush followed the accident. Rabbi Solow took advantage of the quiet to go on with his sermon.

At this, the injured gentleman revived slightly. With his eyes still closed, he murmured in a voice that could be heard by all:

"Hit me again. I can still hear him!"

"Rabbi," said the worried father, "I wish you'd speak to my son. Here he is, *Bar Mitzvah* age, and all he ever thinks about is baseball."

The rabbi sighed to himself. 'With so many delinquent children getting into trouble,' he thought, 'this is indeed a minor problem.'

"I'm sorry to disappoint you," he said, suppressing a desire to show his annoyance, "but I cannot scold your boy for something we Jews have been practicing for thousands of years. In fact, there are several references to baseball in the Bible."

"Are you serious?" demanded the father incredulously. "What are they?"

"Well, for example, you will recall that Eve stole first and Adam stole second; Gideon rattled the pitchers; Goliath was put out by David; and the prodigal son made a home run!"

The *shammes* of the Utica Avenue Synagogue and the *shammes* of Temple Beth Israel, both in Brooklyn, were bewailing the unkind fates that had brought them into association with their respective rabbis.

"Our rabbi is an educated man," grumbled the first, "but he just doesn't think before he speaks. Only last Friday he organized a Young Mothers Group—and did he embarrass me! He gets up in the pulpit and announces, 'All ladies of this congregation who wish to become Young Mothers should see the *shammes* this evening and he'll give you the best dates for the recreation room.'"

The other *shammes* nodded sympathetically.

"And that's what everybody calls executive ability," he sighed. "Believe me, my friend, when they say a rabbi is a good administrator it means he's taking credit for all the hard work done by the *shammes*. Sometimes it shakes my religious faith."

"Well, I wouldn't go so far as to say that," replied the first *shammes*. "I've seen nine rabbis come and go at the Utica Avenue Synagogue, and I still believe in God!"

To make a brief story briefer, when a Canadian railroad journal published an advertisement seeking 200 sleepers for a new cross-country line, Rabbi Albert R. Coleman of Detroit offered them his entire congregation.

The rabbi was expounding on the various interpretations of Biblical lore when sounds of a heated debate in the rear of the class brought his lecture to a halt.

"All right," he snapped, "what's so important back there that you're interrupting the class?"

"We were just arguing about Reform and Orthodox Judaism," explained one of the students.

"What's to argue?"

"He says there is no difference of real importance," said the student, pointing to the young man sitting next to him. "But I say there is."

"Then I'll settle the argument for you," said the rabbi, impatient to get on with his discourse. "The difference is actually very small. Orthodox Jews believe that the Pharaoh's daughter found Moses in the bulrushes. But Reform Jews believe the Pharaoh's daughter only *said* she found Moses in the bulrushes!"

Bill Bennett, the barber, was a good Christian and widely known for his religious fervor. His deep respect for the clergy was the talk of the neighborhood.

One day a Protestant minister came into his barbershop and got a haircut. When Bennett was finished, the minister reached for his wallet but the barber shook his head and smiled.

"Put your wallet away, Reverend," he said. "I never charge a man of the cloth."

The minister thanked him and left, but he soon returned and presented the pious barber with a Bible.

A few hours later, a priest entered Bennett's shop and he, too got a haircut. Once again the barber refused to accept any payment.

"Forget it, Father," he said. "I never accept money from a priest."

The priest left and shortly thereafter returned with a crucifix which he presented to the barber as a token of his appreciation.

Toward evening a rabbi entered the shop. He also got a haircut. When the rabbi reached into his pocket, the barber waved the money aside.

"That's all right, Rabbi," he said. "You don't owe me a thing. I never accept payment from men who do the Lord's work."

So the rabbi left, and soon returned—with another rabbi!

Three rabbis, representing the three main sects of Judaism, were having a mild argument about religious matters.

"It seems to me," said the Reform rabbi, "that the best way to approach Jewish theology is from the standpoint of an umpire at a ballgame. For example, as a Reform rabbi, I call 'em as I see 'em."

"Well," said the Conservative rabbi, "I call 'em as they are."

"As far as I am concerned," countered the Orthodox rabbi, "you can call it a ball or you can call it a strike—but it's neither until *I* call it!"

The old rabbi listened patiently while the youthful agnostic expounded his views.

"According to Nietzsche," observed the non-believer, "God is dead."

"According to God," said the rabbi calmly, "Nietzsche is dead!"

Cincinnati's Rabbi Roger Kahn, to his congregation: "I have always publicly stated that the poor are welcome in this synagogue at all times, and I see by last month's receipts that they have indeed come!"

Forget what your rabbi told you! What does he know about romance? Here's the way it *really* happened.

"Adam, baby," said Eve as she presented him with a bouquet of forget-me-nots she had picked in the Garden of Eden, "do you absolutely and truly love me?"

"Sure," said Adam. "Who else?"

Rabbi Langbleibt of Far Rockaway had a well-deserved reputation for being long-winded. On this Sabbath, he was in especially good form. His topic for the day was "Prophets of the Bible."

"Now then," he added after speaking for a half hour, "we have disposed of the major prophets. Next we come to the minor prophets. To what place, my dear friends, shall we assign them?"

From a seat in the rear of the temple, a bored-looking stranger arose. He waved an explanatory hand at the seat he had just vacated and said:

"One of them can have my place!"

The 1920s produced a large number of humorous stories in which the "fresh little kid" is pitted against the short-tempered Hebrew teacher. Here is another from that period.

Mortie, the sporty shortie, did not exactly endear himself to the *rebbe* at the Delancey Street *cheder* when he asserted, "David just couldn'ta been a psalmist!"

"*Nu*, supply me please with information to the contrary," demanded the *rebbe*.

"Because a psalmist tells fortunes by reading palms," replied Mortie, grinning.

"Ah-*hah*! A regular Eddie Cantor in our midst, *noch*!" growled the *rebbe*. "All right, *ingel*, as long as you are such a *galernter*, such a *dinchazzan*, I have a question for you."

"I din't unnastan' all them Joosh words," Mortie mumbled.

"I'll be happy to articulate my query in lucid English."

"I din't unnastan' that, either."

"*Klayneh nahr*, my question shall be asked in plain English, but first I want to know something," the *rebbe* went on, his voice ominously low. "Did it ever occur to you that you might study for your *Bar Mitzvah* on Broadway where Charlie Chaplins are more appreciated? No? Then perhaps you might enjoy receiving your instructions on the vaudeville stage where you could make jokes and be confirmed at the same time. This too did not occur to you?"

Mortie made the mistake of laughing and the good *rebbe's* eyes blazed. "You see, young man, I can also make with the jokes. But there is a time and a place for everything—and *cheder* is definitely not the place for anything except study."

"But I *was* studyin'," argued the irrepressible Mortie. "I was studyin' how long it would take before I could go home."

The *rebbe* groaned and rolled his eyes toward heaven as though beseeching aid from above.

"I'm giving you one more chance—only one question to answer—and then you may go home," he said wearily. "And" he added, consulting his watch, "you'd better hurry—the zoo closes in an hour."

"Okay, what's the question?"

"In the year 165 B.C.E., the Maccabees celebrated a great victory. We will commemorate that occasion by lighting candles for eight days, children play *dreidel* games, and we have lately taken to exchanging cards and gifts during this festive week. Now, to what holiday do I refer?"

"Christmas?" responded Mortie tentatively.

"*Gottenyu!*" the teacher exploded, his beloved *Chanukah* thus desecrated. He managed to compose himself and, with a resigned wave of his hand he dismissed his student.

"To my deep regret, Mortie, I shall see you again tomorrow," he sighed. "But, for me, the intervening 24 hours without your presence will seem like a month in the Catskills!"

Rabbi Simon Mendes, who settled near the headwaters of the Susquehanna in 1840 or thereabouts, was a good man—pious but full of humor and adept at quick repartee.

One Sunday morning, he was presented with a fine string of pickerel, caught by one Heinrich Herrman, a member of his tiny congregation.

"Rabbi, I want you to have the fish," said the man somewhat nervously, "but it's only fair to tell you that they were caught on *Shabbes*."

"Heinrich," replied Rabbi Mendes as he reached for the string, "the Lord and I both know that the pickerel were not to blame."

Although Rabbi Isaac Mayer Wise (1818-1900) is remembered as one of the outstanding pioneers of Reform Judaism in America, it seems to have been forgotten that he possessed a keen wit and could, when the mood was upon him, be quite amusing. And when he chose to turn a joke upon himself, he could be savagely satirical. This tale, dripping with irony, presents the articulate rabbi at his humorous and intellectual best.

It was a lovely day in May, 1899, and Rabbi Wise, age 81, was slowly and feebly walking down a street in Cincinnati. As he faltered along, he met the young and vigorous Rabbi Yosef Alman, professor of languages at the Hebrew Union College, the institution which Wise himself founded in 1875.

The young rabbi shook his older colleague's trembling hand and respectfully murmured, "Good morning, sir. And how is Isaac Mayer Wise today?"

"Isaac Mayer Wise is well, quite well, thank you," said the aged rabbi. "But the house in which he lives at present is becoming quite dilapidated. It is tottering upon its foundations. Time and the seasons have nearly destroyed it. Its roof is pretty well worn out. It's walls are much shattered and it trembles with every wind. The old tenement is becoming almost uninhabitable, and I think Isaac Mayer Wise will have to move out of it soon. But he himself is quite well, thank you."

26

Magen David over Follywood

Introduction

The movies—a medium of entertainment designed to hold an audience open-mouthed, especially when everybody is yawning—began as a peep show at the turn of the century. For the trifling sum of one cent, the patron of the arts was privileged to peer into a machine, turn a crank, and watch a rather corpulent female, several buds past the first bloom of youth, in the act of disrobing. Printed dialogue was added later to give the presentations a little class, although the *artiste* continued to divest herself of her pantaloons.

Picture it in your mind. The movie is a strip-comedy "burley-cue" titled, *The Shenandoah Shlepper*, starring Harlowe Anderson, born Hymie Aarons. Co-starring is the Indian maiden, Evening Blackwing, a former bubble-dancer, named Eva Schwartzfliegel, whose career blew up in her face. Hymie tenderly murmurs, "Darling, your boyish bob makes you look like a new man." So Eva coyly replies (in those days the actresses were always coy, even *sans* bloomers), "I hope I don't lose my looks when I get old." And Hymie gives it to her good: "You should be so lucky!" Well, back in those days, producers wrote their own material.

Then came the founding fathers of the motion picture industry, looking for something to found. At that time, the hub of the film business was in New York where immigrants from Dnepropetrovsk used to laugh at the funny names of such American towns as Poughkeepsie and Hackensack. Among those first entrepreneurs was Jesse Lasky, who remembered that the sun shone 365 days a year in California, if not more. Sun was all-important to filming. A cloudy day meant a day wasted; a bright one was cause for rejoicing—and work! Upon Lasky's arrival in Hollywood, the major declared a holiday, and the key to the city was sent out to be cleaned and pressed. At the railroad station, all the studio employees were on hand to greet him. Someone, in hopes of getting special screen credit, hollered, "Speech!" Lasky cleared his throat, cast his eyes in the customary direction of heaven, and began: "In mine heart the sun is shining." He looked up again and yelled, "*Oy vay,* the sun *is* shining! Why the hell ain't you woiking?"

Next came Samuel Goldfish, who launched a film company with a producer named Selwyn. But the name Sel-Fish Productions sounded as though it belonged on Fulton Street. What to do? Sam kept the "Gold"—natch!—and gave the "fish" to charity. It is not generally known, but he kept Charity hidden in a Westwood apartment. Anyway, as Sam Goldwyn, he is best remembered for his defiant statement: "Don't give up the ship—sell it!"

Then there was Adolph Zukor, the smartest of all the movie pioneers. He was rumored to be secretly in love with actress Zasu Pitts, but she wouldn't marry him: "Who needs a name like Zasu Zukor?" The lady first caught Adolph's attention when she came to him with an idea for a new film in which she wanted to star. "Say," he enthused, "you got the mucus of a great story!"

Carl Laemmle, the ex-clothing salesman with the imported accent, decided to do things in a big way. This was the Era of the Bathroom. They were no longer Cans, they were *Objets d'Art*—palatial affairs wherein milady bathed in a marble pool that could double for the Red Sea—and did, in several pictures.

Laemmle may not have made films better, but he made them bigger. There was the time, for instance, when he was filming *The Last Supper.* He viewed the day's rushes and storm clouds gathered on his Noble Brow. He summoned the director. "What?" he thundered. "In a gigantic, super-special extravaganza like this you want I should make a supper scene with only twelve apostles? Get me fifty!"

Another of the early producers was Louis J. Selznick, who shared Laemmle's affection for big extravaganzas. There was the time he interviewed Cecil B. DeMille, when Mr. C was still plain Cecil the *shreiber.* "You got any original ideas for a comedy?" asked Louie.

"Sure," replied Cecil, "the funniest comedy routine I ever wrote goes like this: One day I shower her with apostrophes. The next day, night-blooming asterisks. The next I carpet her path with sweet-scented parentheses, and then Gorgonzolas . . ."

Louie interrupted, his voice suspicious: "Gorgonzola! That's a cheese!" His tone brooked no argument. "Stick to the flowers!"

DeMille was undaunted—although he got plenty daunted

later on. "Look, why don't we film a classic drama instead of a comedy?" he persisted. "How about *The Hunchback of Notre Dame* or *The Four Horsemen of the Apocalypse?*"

"My answer to that I'll give you in two words: Im-possible!" declared Louis, his voice grim. "There ain't a dime in those Notary Dame football stories; and, as for horsemen, the public is sick of westerns!"

There were other founding fathers, of course. Men like Marcus Loew, originally a ventriloquist who was so bad his lips moved even when he wasn't saying anything. And there was Darryl Zanuck, who once asked Selznick, "What do you think of my last picture?" Selznick moaned, "Please, not while I'm eating!" There is also the memory of Harry Cohn, the man who single-handedly brought Columbia Pictures to eminence. No one seems to have had a good word for the late lamented Harry, except his former secretary, Virginia Smith, but she forgot what it was.

Other areas of show business are also represented in American Jewish humor. Eddie Cantor, for example, made the big time with his song, "Anything is Finer than to See my Carolina in the Morning." And who can forget the night Belle Baker squelched a heckler with: "If you think my act is monotonous, you should see my home life!" Yes, and Ethel Merman, who not only had a beautiful voice but a gorgeous profile—all the way down. "If I were a girl and had a profile as lovely as Ethel's," said Cantor, "I'd always walk sideways."

"But not everyone makes it to Broadway," Pitzy Katz, the vaudeville comic of yesteryear, mourned. "How can I get famous or make any money with such a peculiar agency contract? The first clause forbids me to read any of the other clauses!"

H.D.S.

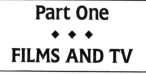

Simson Carlebach, former film critic for *The Jerusalem Post*, tells the story about film-maker David Lean's *Bridge on the River Kwai*. A *rebbetzyn* once told Carlebach that it was her husband's favorite picture. She then revealed that the ultra-orthodox rabbi had seen exactly two movies in his life: *The Bridge* and *Exodus*.

METRO-GOLDA-MEIR
Proudly Presents
Spartacush

Kirk Douglas...Spartacush
Tony Curtis ....Demonstratov
Leo the Lion ....Himself

Scene One
Kirk Douglas, Tony Curtis, Leo the Lion
Scene Two
Tony Curtis and Leo the Lion
Scene Three
Leo the Lion

Greta Garbo went to extreme lengths to preserve her isolation from the public's prying eye. She would do anything to protect her privacy. So the storekeeper was rather surprised when she came in personally and ordered a pound of grass seed.

"Miss Garbo, pardon my curiosity," he said, "but you don't even have a garden. What are you going to do with all this seed?"

"I vill sprinkle it on my hair," she told him.

"But why?"

"Because," she answered, "I vant to be a lawn!"

A columnist on the staff of *Variety*, the show business trade journal, was bemoaning the lack of lively news.

"If only Tuesday Weld would marry Hal March and then have a daughter," he signed. "What a line I could write! Just imagine it in your mind: 'Tuesday March the Second!'"

In the pre-television 1930s, Phil Baker conducted a show called *The $64 Question*. A person who was selected from the studio audience would start out with two dollars and if he or she answered the question correctly, another try was made for four dollars, then eight and so forth, until the $64 jackpot was reached.

One of the more popular figures who regularly attended these programs was Mary Malkin of the Bronx. Mary, a widow with little else to occupy her mind, spent much of her time going to quiz shows in the various studios of the networks. She was always welcome and was usually called upon to answer questions because her responses were often quite amusing, and sometimes exceedingly clever.

One evening, Baker, the host, asked her what was meant by Shakespeare's line: "Good night, good night! Parting is such sweet sorrow, That I shall say good night till it be morrow."

"Now, Mary," said Baker, "tell me exactly what Juliet meant when she uttered that line to Romeo."

"Hmm, that's a hard one," replied Mary, furrowing her brow in deep thought. "Maybe you better say it again."

He repeated it. "Now, for the $64 question, what was she saying to Romeo?"

"G'night," said Mary with a certitude that brooked no denial, "seeyuh t'marruh!"

William Friedkind is known in cinema circles as a martinet who always demands the very best from his actors. Once, while directing the film *The Exorcist*, he called out to the cast:

"Perfect, ladies and gentlemen! That scene was absolutely perfect! Now let's do it one more time—only better!"

The crew and cast of a film company specializing in TV commercials were warned by the director, a strict disciplinarian named von Eichmann, to be on location on time. They were to assemble that evening on Columbus Circle at precisely five o'clock. Von Eichmann made it clear to all concerned that he did not mean one minute before five or one minute after five; when he said five he meant *five!*

Came the appointed hour and everybody was on hand—everybody, that is, but Dave Tolar, the star. As the minutes flew by, the director was tearing his hair out in bunches, and as the clock neared six and it grew too dark for the cameras to get the required shots, von Eichmann was frothing at the mouth.

Suddenly there was a commotion at the fringe of the group of actors and technicians, and Dave burst into view. His hair was disheveled, his clothes torn and his face battered and bloody.

"Where the hell have you been?" screamed the director.

"Sorry," said Dave, out of breath, "but I started out early enough. I thought I'd take a shortcut through Central Park and on the way I got mugged."

"That's no excuse!" roared von Eichmann. "It takes a whole hour to get mugged?"

"I'm going back to Broadway," said the disgruntled actor. "Hollywood never contributed anything to either the arts or to history."

"Don't sell Hollywood short," cautioned another actor who happened to be working. "Remember, the Red Sea has only been parted three times in all history—twice by Cecil B. DeMille."

The Hollywood actor Yancey Summers, known informally to his parents as Yaacov Zimmer, was standing in line for his unemployment check. Another actor in front of him was bemoaning the Watergate scandals. Yancey nodded in agreement.

"It really scares me," he affirmed. "Just think, this administration with all its irresponsibilities and dirty tricks is my sole means of support!"

Among the founding fathers of the motion picture industry were the fun-loving Louis J. Selznick and the irascible but brilliant Adolph Zukor.

Zukor was not only a dynamic theatrical producer but also a unique character. His own generation knew him as a shrewd and canny individual who was always ready to take a chance—and his business gambles usually paid off handsomely. He was self-educated, but in some respects, according to Selznick, his knowledge was woefully lacking.

Their continuing feud was notorious. Zukor, always the more powerful and practical, froze Selznick out of lucrative business deals whenever possible. Selznick, on the other hand, seized every opportunity to relate stories about his arch-nemesis—stories that were carefully designed to present his rival in something short of a flattering light. The following yarn about Mr. Zukor was told with great glee by the irrepressible Mr. Selznick—and you needn't believe the tale to enjoy it.

One day, at his New York office, Zukor was visited by an aspiring playwright who brought along the script of a melodrama he had written. The young man may have been gifted in other regards but, so far as his speech was concerned, he suffered a severe handicap—he stammered terribly. Being sensitive, he rarely mentioned his affliction. Indeed, he had no need to do so—as soon as he opened his mouth it advertised itself.

He came now by appointment to see the great producer. As he entered the room where Zukor sat at his desk, he was greeted with a blast from the Great One:

"Okay, skip the introductions—you know who I am and I know who you are. You say you have a play? All right, I'm a busy man. Sit right down there and open it up and read it to me."

The young dramatist shakily obeyed. He made heavy going of it but eventually he finished.

"I'll take your play and film it," said Zukor. He pressed a button and his assistant entered.

"Fix up a contract for this young man," commanded the chief. "I'm going to take his story. It's not much of a play—in fact, I think it stinks—but it's got one terrific novelty in it that ought to make an audience laugh their heads off:

"All the characters stutter!"

The late Edward G. Robinson once remarked:

"I've been in the film business so long, I can remember when actresses would bare only their souls!"

It could only happen in Hollywood. The television star's little boy came home from school in a jubilant mood.

"Aha!" exclaimed the kid's father. "You've been promoted after all!"

"Better'n that, pop," exulted the boy. "I been held over fer another twenny-six weeks!"

Academy Awards Presentations, 1974:
"Will you hand me the envelope, please?"
"Thank you,"
"For best editing of a tape not specifically intended for theatri-

cal distribution, the Oscar winner is . . .
"Richard M. Nixon!"

Several years ago, when Dorothy H. Rochmis was drama editor for the *California Jewish Voice*, she wrote a well-researched column which clearly indicated much burning of the midnight schmaltz. It's a game the talented lady still enjoys playing: a sort of Revelations you won't find in the New Testament, in which she offers some unfamiliar names and then reveals their true identities.* See if you can beat her to the punch.

> Suppose I were writing my usual bits of news about the big and little stars in our town and I told you that while I lunched at the Brown Derby (does anyone who is anyone eat lunch any place else?), I saw *Benjamin Kubelsky* kibitzing with *Nathan Birnbaum, Emanual Goldenberg* and *Melvin Allen Israel*. The talk was about *David Green*, with a little bit of *Mavis Fluck* thrown in, because, after all, the big stars aren't going to spend their lunchtime talking only politics. Actually, what they were doing was comparing *Mavis* with *Helen Gould Beck* (about whom everyone insists there is not and never was anything but friendship for *Arthur Teichman*).

> "It was a friendly, quiet lunch when suddenly the three noticed a flock of autograph hounds around *Isaiah Edwin Leopold*.

> "Well," scoffed *Kubelsky*, "just look at that old codger. You sure have to give him credit, not only for longevity and versatility, but for being one of the busiest stars in Hollywood. Not only that, but his son is busy—and now his grandson is a comer."

> "Not that I want to change the subject," grumbled *Birnbaum*, "but you remember when Mrs. Poetry-Reciter who claims she's Shakespeare's third cousin eleven times removed, used to be just plain *Mrs. Aaron Goldbogen*, may he rest in peace?"

> Just at that moment who should walk in but *David Kominski* with *Issur Danielovitch, Julius Mark,* and *Aaron Chwatt*. And right behind them, none other than *Simone Kaminker*—unescorted.

> They all called out to each other and for a while the Brown Derby was buzzing with hellos and darlings and kissing and hugging.

*From "Film Folk & Fare," by Dorothy H. Rochmis published in *The California Jewish Voice*, September 1970.

But when they resumed talking, the conversation was not unified.

One group talked about that "golden boy" *Julius Garfinkle*. Another talked about their friend *Jacob Pinkus Perelmuth's* son who had just produced his first film about one potato, two potatoes; maybe he'd make a bushelful. Another group talked about that movie, *To Russia, With Love*, and the part that *Karoline Blamauer* had in it. And what is a luncheon without talk about *Frances Gumm?*

Now, how many luminaries in my little game have you been able to identify?

Kubelsky, Birnbaum, Goldenberg and *Israel* are Jack Benny, George Burns, Edward G. Robinson and Mel Allen. *David Green* is, of course, David Ben Gurion. *Mavis Fluck* is Diana Dors. *Helen Gould Beck*, none other than Sally Rand. And *Arthur Teichman* is that master-teacher of the dance, Arthur Murray.

Isaiah Edwin Leopold is Ed Wynn. *Aaron Goldbogen*, the Todd (so of course, the wife they referred to as "Mrs. Poety-Reciter" is Elizabeth Taylor). *David Kominsky* and *Issur Danielovitch* are, as you probably know, Danny Kaye and Kirk Douglas. *Julius Mark* and *Aaron Chwatt* are Groucho Marx and Red Buttons. The lady behind them, *Miss Kaminker*, Simone Signoret.

Julius Garfinkle is John Garfield, and *Jacob Pinkus Perelmuth* is Jan Peerce, whose son, Larry, made the movie "One Potato, Two Potato," *Karoline Blamauer* is Lotte Lenya; and *Frances Gumm?*—surely you know she's Judy Garland.

The Brown Derby hasn't changed its spots and it's fun playing this game. Just remember, it was Mr. Berman who, when he finally agreed to let his son go into show business, admonished him not to change his name. And *Sheldon Berman* didn't though he's know professionally as Shelley Berman.

Part Two
◆ ◆ ◆
MUSIC AND MUSICKERS

For this offering, we journey back in time to the days when both Ziegfeld and the New York Metropolitan Opera Company were doing a big business . . . separately, to be sure.

The American Jewish Committee was holding the biggest benefit in its history. Among the top stars of the entertainment world who were scheduled to perform were Fannie Brice, of beloved memory, and Madam Ernestine Schumann-Heink, greatest contralto of her time.

As the opera star was waiting in the wings, preparing to enter on-stage, Fannie tapped her on the shoulder.

"Listen, Stena," she murmured, "do me a favor, will ya? Don't sing *My Heart Belongs to Daddy*—I use it for my finale!"

Jascha Heifetz, the distinguished violinist, was in London where he was scheduled to give a concert. A few hours before curtain time, he noticed that a violin string had broken, so he hurried to a music supply shop for a replacement. He was waited on by a girl who was new to the business.

"I'd like to have an *E* string for my violin," said Heifetz.

"A *what*?" asked the uncomprehending girl.

"An *E* string."

"Sorry, luv," she replied apologetically, "but ye'll 'ave ter pick it out yerself. I can't tell the 'e's from the she's!"

Fractured Follies from the Flaming Forties:

Sam and Bella, by way of celebrating their 20th wedding anniversary, were taking in a movie. Bella's eyes brimmed with romantic tears as Nelson Eddy sang the beautiful "Indian Love Call" to Jeannette MacDonald:

"When I'm calling you-hoo-hoo-hoo, ha-ha-hoo . . ."

Bella squeezed her husband's hand with a tender feeling of affection. "Oh, Sam darling, that's what happens when a man really has love in his heart," she crooned.

"No it ain't," snorted unromantic Sam. "That's what happens when a man runs out of words before he runs out of music!"

Albert Spalding, the famous violinist and an uncle five or six times removed from the present author, passed this one along for posterity.

He was doing a recital in the hinterlands of the Bronx and had in his program the Bach *Chaconne*. Standing in the wings, Spalding peeked through the curtain and gave the audience a quick appraisal. They were mostly housewives and workingmen—ordinary folks one might expect to find strolling along Intervale Avenue. So he decided that the *Chaconne* would be wasted on them and that he would be better received if he played something lighter.

When the concert was over, a native of the region came to his dressing room with a complaint.

"Mr. Spalding," he said, "I work hard for a living, and when I'm spending my few pennies I like to get my money's worth."

"Didn't you?" asked the violinist, surprised.

"No. It says on the program in black and white that you were going to fiddle the *Chaconne*."

Mr. Spalding was overcome.

"My dear man," he replied effusively, "I had no idea that anyone here would know or even care whether I played the *Chaconne* or *Yussel the Muscle*. You are a gem among stones. Please honor me by accompanying me to my hotel. You will be my guest for dinner and afterward I will give you a private concert."

The Bronxite quickly accepted the generous offer and went to the hotel with his new-found friend. After a sumptuous dinner, a liqueur and a good cigar, Spalding picked up his Stradivarius and played the *Chaconne* as he had never before played it in his life.

"Well, well, well," said the honored guest, "so that's the *Chaconne*. Would you believe, Mr. Spalding, that's the first time I ever heard it? I don't like it!"

It was his wife's birthday, so the man went into a pet shop to buy her a canary.

"I'll take that one," he said, pointing to one of the cages where a bird was singing beautifully. "But that sparrow, you'll have to take him out of the cage. Who needs a sparrow?"

"Sorry," said the proprietor, "but the sparrow stays with the canary."

"What for?" demanded the man. "I just want the canary."

"Look, mister, am I charging you for the sparrow? I told you he goes with the canary—free! In fact, if you don't want the sparrow you don't get the canary, and that's final!"

"But this is ridiculous! The canary sings great and I'm willing to buy it. So why do I have to take that scrawny little sparrow?"

"Because," explained the proprietor, "the sparrow's his arranger!"

Among those in the motion picture industry who are truly talented—and they are legion, whatever else you may have heard—David Raskin is among the most gifted. He is best known, perhaps, for his collaboration with Johnny Mercer on the lovely song, "Laura," but he has also written musical scores for dozens of fine films.

Out in Hollywood a few years ago, he was in the 20th Century-Fox commissary having lunch with a group of fellow writers and composers. Raskin happened to mention that his next musical assignment would probably be the scoring of Alfred Hitchcock's latest picture, *Lifeboat*.

"You're not going to get that assignment, Dave," said one of the writers. "Hitchcock is going to release the picture without any music at all."

"That's ridiculous," retorted Raskin.

"Not the way Hitchcock sees it," explained the other. "Just think about it for a minute. All the action takes place in a lifeboat, way out in the middle of the ocean. There really wouldn't *be* any musicians within a thousand miles of the boat. So where would the music come from?"

"Well, if it's a question of logic, let's follow it through to its logical end," suggested Raskin. "You go back to Hitchcock and ask him where his *cameras* come from in the middle of the ocean and I'll tell him where my music comes from!"

Flo, a student of classical music, and Joe, whose taste had never progressed beyond "The Celery Stalks at Midnight," were immersed in a discussion. Somehow the conversation got around to the illustrious Norwegian composer, Grieg.

"Oh, he's my favorite!" cried Flo ecstatically. Edvard Grieg wrote such divine music!"

"Maybe," said Joe, shrugging—"for a guy who couldn't even spell his first name."

British rock 'n roll entertainer Zelig Zeligman, leader of the singing group known as "The London Derrière," arrived in America where he was booked for a huge outdoor concert on the fringes of a small town in upstate New York.

In his hotel room on that first night, he was almost asleep when an eerie hoot sounded just outside his window.

"Don't let that disturb you," said his American manager soothingly. "It's an owl."

"I know," replied Zelig in an uneasy voice, "but 'oo's 'owling?"

Shlomo Baum, the orchestra leader who attained success in Israel with his American-style music, decided to try his luck in the United States. Some members of his band were unwilling to leave Israel, however, so when Shlomo arrived in New York he found it necessary to interview American musicians to fill the vacancies.

The first man he talked with was a rather wild-eyed, slovenly-dressed saxophonist. Shlomo was not impressed with him until he played a few bars of music. The man's talent was truly remarkable. Never had he heard such gloriously beautiful notes.

"You're hired," he said enthusiastically.

"Well, man, I got a confession to make," said the saxophone player. "I got a monkey on my back."

"Dot's all right," said Shlomo, clapping the musician on the back. "In dis bend ve luff enimals!"

Part Three
◆ ◆ ◆
THE STAGE-LEGIT AND ILL-LEGIT

The stage is bad, so rabbis say,
And naught but evil from it springs;
But still it has what angels do
(And rabbis don't) have;
Namely, wings.

Around the turn of the century, the Yiddish Theatre was the main source of entertainment for countless thousands of immigrants. Many of these new arrivals came from obscure *shtetls* in the Pale of Settlement and, as a consequence, knew little or nothing of "quality" stage productions, including those performed in Yiddish. They were, therefore, not always appreciative of the better theatrical fare offered them—at least not in the beginning. As their familiarity with good writing and acting grew, so too, of course, did their critical reactions.

Boris Thomashevsky, actor, playwright and one of the founders of the Yiddish theatre in America won great respect among the Jewish masses after he arrived in the United States in 1881. But he, like many others of that early day, sometimes experienced the hoots and derisive howls of his untutored audiences.

But Thomashevsky, always his own man, not only expected the very best from his actors, he demanded proper respect from his audiences as well. One incident that occurred shortly after he had organized the first Yiddish theatre in New York City, illustrates his individualism.

He was appearing in a play which he himself had written, produced and directed. Months of hard work had gone into the production. But apparently it was somewhat over the heads of the very people he was trying to reach. Only eleven paying customers showed up for the first night's performance. As Thomashevsky's beautiful lines were being delivered, the puzzled spectators at first grew restless, and then came the inevitable hissing.

Thomashevsky's face turned red, but with grim resolution he kept on. The hissing grew louder. He stopped for a moment and the hissing ceased. When he started again, the audience of eleven resumed the hissing, enjoying themselves immensely.

Thomashevsky stopped once more, gathered all the members of his company on-stage and, together, they out-hissed the tiny audience.

Maurice Schwartz, the legendary actor, director and producer, laid the foundation for his future fame when, in 1918, he organized his own dramatic company which became known as the Yiddish Art Theatre. He was also well known for his wit—at repartee he had no superiors and very few equals, in or out of the profession. In the autumn of 1921 he scored on another well-known actor without speaking a word. Yet, Jewish theatrical circles rocked with laughter for many months afterward.

Artistically speaking, this actor was not highly regarded by Maurice Schwartz. He belonged to the old school of ranting scene-eaters for whom Schwartz had a profound contempt. Nevertheless, his merits were valued by at least one individual—his manager, who was also a producer.

The latter was presenting *The God of Vengeance*, by Sholem Asch, with a really distinguished supporting company, featuring

Schwartz's pet aversion, Ossip Leibnitz, his name before he Americanized it when he gravitated to Broadway and then to Hollywood.

On the day when the bills went up for the forthcoming production, Schwartz chanced to pass the Second Avenue theatre where the play was to be presented. In the lobby of the theatre was a large poster which, according to the usual form, read as follows:

MR. ARTHUR JACOBS

presents

The God of Vengeance

by

the brilliant playwright

SHOLEM ASCH

With the Following Notable Cast:

Yussel Nieberg.............................Mr. Carl Dymov
Nudnik......................................Mr. Richard Rosen
Stella Hahn..........................Mrs. Lillian Dienstock
Isaac Himmelfarb ....Mr. Solomon Kauffman
Mrs. Vogel ....Miss Anna Robins

— AND —
MR. OSSIP LEIBNITZ

Schwartz read the announcement through. Then he walked to the corner, entered a hardware store, purchased an extra large carpenter's pencil and, returning to the theatre, he made one single change in the wording:

He crossed out the "AND" and for it he substituted "BUT."

Old-timers will recall the impresario Sid Hirschman, whose publicity stunts often stood New York's theatre-going public on its collective ear. But there was one time when even he was unable to cope with what he described as "an act of Divine intervention."

Sid was producing *World Without Women* when he was forced to cancel the play right at dress rehearsal time.

All seven women in the cast, as well as the cat, were pregnant!

For as long as he could remember, young Rueben Schiff had

nurtured a great love for the theatre. His all-consuming ambition was to become an actor, but his parents, extremely wealthy and acutely aware of their position in the rarefied reaches of upper-class society, would not hear of it. One day, shortly after his 23rd birthday, his parents were killed in a plane crash and, as the only child, he received their legacy of eight million dollars—give or take a few hundred thousand.

Changing his name from Rueben Schiff to Rutherford Shipstead, he organized his own repertory company, hired actors and technicians, and produced his own *Hamlet* with himself, of course, in the starring role. The show was mounted with style and no expense was spared. Never was Shakespeare's play given such an opulent first night. Rueben, or rather Rutherford as we shall henceforth call him, even persuaded some well-known critics to attend the first performance.

But five minutes after the curtain was raised, it became painfully clear that this was to be a theatrical catastrophe—a caricature of Shakespeare's monumental work. Rutherford Shipstead had been unable to engage any actors of repute, and those whom he had hired were as hammy as he. In all the history of the theatre, never had the bard of Stratford-on-Avon been subjected to the hamming now being given to his *Hamlet*. Rutherford wasn't merely bad, he was ludicrous.

The audience not only took the farcical performance with rare good nature, they began to get their money's worth by entering into the spirit of the evening. Catcalls and sundry comments, none of them favorable, reached the ears of the tyros onstage. Jeers, laughter and hissing filled the place. Then a man's shoe was thrown from the audience. A lady's shoe quickly followed, almost hitting Rutherford, who was hamming it up in the leading role. Other articles of clothing, and then pennies flew through the air in a shower around the actors. But, undaunted, they moved relentlessly forward with their play.

Rutherford Shipstead was just getting into the soliloquy, ignoring the rain of missiles from across the footlights, when suddenly a woman's handbag, thrown from the first or second row, struck him full in the face and sent him reeling backwards.

Hamlet regained his balance and ran his hand across his face to see if any blood had been drawn. Then, his anger bubbling to the surface, he looked out into the audience and yelled at the sea of upturned faces before him:

"Are you people crazy or something? What the hell's the matter with you? You oughtta know I didn't *write* this crap!"

From the play, *Lottie Loved Latkehs*, by Milton Karp, 1932:

Cab Driver: Okay, lady, where to?
Passenger: Beth Sholom Maternity Hospital. And, please, to drive like crazy nobody needs. I work there!

Here is another of those delightful anecdotes about Harry Houdini, the ex-Hebrew teacher and son of a rabbi, whose early years as a professional magician were anything but bountiful.

One summer in 1918 or 1919, Houdini was booked into Rose's Resort Inn, a new vacation spot near Lake Placid. Rose was the breath, light and sunshine of the place; her husband, Phil, its nemesis. Rose had the good sense to keep her argumentative, grouchy old man away from the vacationing patrons and the entertainers, so all went fairly well . . . that is, until Houdini appeared on stage. Phil, it seems, was not among Houdini's more ardent admirers.

Sitting in the audience during the magician's opening night performance, Phil glowered as Houdini offered his magic feats. Houdini disentangled himself from a straight jacket within sixty seconds while handcuffed. Phil snorted, "Ridiculous!"

Annoyed, Houdini then had his hands and legs shackled. He was then locked inside a trunk and the trunk completely immersed in a glass tank of water. He would, he announced beforehand, escape from this confinement also within one minute.

"That should put a stop to Phil's insulting comments," he told himself.

But when he emerged in the given time, all Phil could say was "Ridiculous!"

By this time, Harry was determined to impress the man. This time he would again be bound in handcuffs, chains and shackles, and then hanged by the neck with a rope. Once more, he told the audience, he would free himself within sixty seconds. But just as the assistants secured the knot at his neck and left him swinging in mid-air, an ear-splitting explosion sounded in the kitchen adjacent to the backstage. The stoves blew up, smoke filled the place and the panic-stricken audience raced for the exits.

Houdini found himself sprawled in the orchestra pit. Next to him was the irascible Phil, slowly rising to his knees, his face bruised. The man stared at Houdini for a long moment and then rasped:

"Whatsa matter with you? You some kinda *nut*?"

"There's one nice thing about being an actor," observed movie scripter Ralph Goodman—"he doesn't go around talking about other people!"

We have little doubt that this story was first told in ancient Phoenicia, but here is the American version, circa 1913 A.D.— After Dinner. As far as can be determined, it was related at a party by Ed Leopold, later to become nationally known as Ed Wynn.

A traveling repertory company had reached the limit of its endurance. One bad engagement had followed another. The manager was down to his last five dollars. The troupe, practically stranded in a remote corner of Arkansas, was about to disband when a ray of hope shot through the clouds of despair. Word arrived that a theatre had just been completed in an adjoining town. There had been an advance sale up to capacity for the opening night. But at the last minute the attraction booked for the gala occasion had failed to appear, and now the welcome news from the local manager was that if the embarrassed outfit could get there in time, it might give the performance and share in the guaranteed profits.

By superhuman effort, which included the hocking of his watch and fur-trimmed overcoat, the manager raised funds to provide railroad fares for his aggregation to reach the other town. Disembarking from the train, the jubilant thespians climbed into a waiting bus and started along the winding dirt road. In the front seat, alongside the driver, rode the manager.

"Beautiful country you have here," he said. "All nature seems glad. Just look yonder, ahead of us, at that glorious red sunset. I don't think I have ever seen a more magnificent spectacle."

"That ain't no sunset, mister," stated the driver. "That's our new opry house burnin' down!"

Ben Bernie, the "ol' maestro" of fond recollection, used to tell this story on himself.

The Delancey Street Dramatic Guild, a group of local denizens with theatrical aspirations, was putting on a play, *The Nymph in the Lake*, by somebody or other, in Central Park. It might well have been called the Delancey Street Theatre in the Round in the Woods. The stage was a cleared spot at the edge of the woods between 65th and 67th Streets, with the spectators sitting on camp stools in the clearing around the "stage." In those days, the area was almost a forest.

In the audience was Ben Bernie and singer Gertrude Klein, his date for the evening. Young Bernie had been quaffing beer before the proceedings. As the first act was drawing to a close, the beer began to swish around in his inner plumbing, so Bernie politely excused himself, left Gertrude, sought out an usher and asked him the whereabouts of the men's room—or a reasonable facsimile thereof.

The usher gave him careful directions. Bernie was to walk 40 paces to the left until he came to a maple tree, then go right for 32 paces until he came to a triangle of bushes, then turn left again and walk 27 paces. He hurried off and, at length, having completed his mission, finally returned to his seat.

"Has the second act started yet?" he asked Gertrude.

"You ought to know," she hissed. "You were the star!"

A group of fellow comedians were ribbing Jack Benny who had recently passed his 80th birthday.

"I always thought Jack wore a toupee," remarked George Burns between puffs on his ever-present cigar. "Then I realized that he didn't wear a toupee at all. He just had cheap-looking hair!"

"I guess I'll never understand American audiences," complained George Burns. "I tell a joke about Sammy Davis being Jewish and the people become hysterical. Yet, I've been Jewish all my life and it never once got me a laugh."

A respectable number of actors and actresses who had their beginnings in the Yiddish theatre subsequently attained fame on the English-speaking stage. Among them were Paul Muni, Vera Gordon, Edward G. Robinson, Menasha Skulnick, Stella Adler, Luther Adler, Molly Picon, Joseph Schildkraut and many others.

Our subjects for this folksy tale out of the nostalgic early 1920s are Luther Adler and the immortal tenor, Enrico Caruso. Both happened to be in England at the time, and Caruso had just concluded an engagement at the Lyric Theatre in London. Following his final concert, the *signor* gave a farewell party to the friends he had made while in England. The affair began at the theatre and culminated at a fashionable café. Adler, who had become quite fond of the temperamental and sentimental Caruso, was among those present.

He tried to escape, though, when the host insisted on kissing everyone good-bye. But luck was against him. After the singer had thus saluted his manager, his accompanist, the members of his supporting company and everyone else in sight, he insisted that Adler should accompany him in a carriage to his hotel. The hour was now three in the morning and, as a result of the excitement, affection and wine, the Italian was in a highly exhilarated state. As he reached the sidewalk, he disentangled himself from Adler's supporting hand, threw both arms around Adler's neck and implanted a resounding buss on Adler's lips; then fell into a waiting taxi and bade the driver take him to the Garrick Theatre.

The perplexed cabbie turned to Adler.

"Wot's the blinkin' idea in tykin' this cove to the theatre at this time o' the mornin', guv'nor?" he asked.

"I'm not sure, but you better take him there anyway," said Adler. "I think he just remembered that he forgot to kiss the night watchman."

The late film star Edward G. Robinson was a child when he arrived in this country from Rumania. And he was still a very young man when he was bitten by the stage bug. Indeed, his love for the "live" stage continued throughout his life, despite his success in motion pictures. As is the case with so many other actors, it wasn't easy at first. This anecdote concerns his early days, long before he was lured to Hollywood and stardom in the 1933 feature *Little Caesar*.

Young Eddie had been seeking work for many a day, trying to keep up appearances with his one carefully pressed but well-worn suit, and subsisting on little more than bread and beans. When he was down to his last few coins, somebody told him of a vacancy in a small-town stock company thirty miles away, and he borrowed the money to pay his railroad fare thither.

The resident stage manager rubbed his hands gleefully at first sight of the applicant.

"By gosh, I'm glad you turned up," he said. "You're just the man and just the type. We're going into rehearsal today for next week's bill, which is where I'll be needing you."

"Modern play, I suppose?" inquired Robinson, thinking of his one suit and mindful, of course, of the then existing rule that stock actors must furnish their own costumes.

"Sure," said the manager. "A modern society drama."

"That's good," declared the youthful actor, much cheered. "I presume, then, that an ordinary suit of clothes such as I'm wearing will be satisfactory?"

"Hmm, let's see now, just what wardrobe you'll need," said his new boss. "In the first act you will require a suit of tweeds. You are a rich mine-owner. The English syndicate calls you to London and so, in the middle of the first act you have to make a change for a suit you would wear on a train. Also, as you have an ocean trip ahead of you, there must be something characteristic in the way of clothes that're suitable for a voyage—a long overcoat should help. You could wear it and carry a lighter coat on your arm.

"The second act finds you in the smoking room of Lord Basil Metabolism's mansion. You are telling His Lordship about the mine and, as the scene takes place in the evening, you will be in full dress, naturally.

"The third act shows you talking to the Englishman aboard his yacht anchored at Ostend, and here again your dress must be precise. I would suggest white flannel trousers, a blue jacket, white shoes and something classy in the way of a cap.

"Now we come to the fourth act. This time the scene is the breakfast room of a country house. It isn't necessary for me to tell you how to dress for the part for this act. It is simply a matter of looking the part—rich miner and so forth—not letting any Englishman think he can dress better than you—an American."

"Say," demanded Robinson, "who the hell wrote this show—Hart, Schaffner and Marx?"

In June, 1974, George Burns gave a one-man show at the Shubert Theatre in Los Angeles that, in show business parlance, brought the house down. At the age of 78, he displayed all the essentials required of a top-flight comic: good timing, a quick mind, and a style of delivery that was as mellow and slow-burning as his cigar.

"At my age," he told the glittering Shubert audience, "the only thing about me that still works is my right foot—the one I dance with."

George went on to tell about the time he filled in for Karl Betts in a trained seal act called *Captain Betts and Flipper:*

"I used to bribe that seal with a fish so that he'd do his stuff. For two weeks I carried around a dead fish in each pocket, and then I had a date with a girl named Trixie Hart. But those fish didn't bother her at all—even after two weeks. Trixie had just finished a tour with Fink's Mules, and she complimented me on my shaving lotion."

Puffing his cigar, George commented wryly:

"The only thing that gets me excited is if the soup is too hot."

At the start of the show, Jack Benny came on-stage to introduce his old friend, and pouted: "Nobody came out first to introduce *me!*" Then George emerged to do his opening number and several old songs which he delivered with gravelly charm—and even managed to finish a few.

"Sometimes my opening song is so great," boasted George, "people think it's my finish. (Puff.) Sometimes it is!"

Through a cloud of cigar smoke, he concluded, "I'd just as soon you found me funny. But if you don't (puff) I wouldn't disagree with you."

"Seventy-eight or not, he is the most appealing comic in the business," said one critic known for his usually scathing reviews. "He seldom tells ethnic jokes, yet, somehow, one senses a deep-down folk pathos that touches the heart."

And that is what humor—Jewish or other—is all about.

27

Lox Populi

Introduction

We are born red and die bald: what use to holler so? *Lox Populi*—may I be forgiven for coining the expression!—is the humorous Voice of the Jewish People, taking heart in the knowledge that laughter is the solace of the sad, and that happiness is largely a matter of digestion. Jewish man-in-the-street humor, analyze it as you will, is concerned mainly with the important trivia of life. It has a simplistic wisdom of its own.

"Retire?" it asks. "What for? Noah was 600 years old before he built the ark."

It is epigrammatic: The man who says "Money isn't everything" is probably in arrears to his landlord.

It possesses warmth in its nonsense: Thelma is reluctant to marry Joe because she heard that marriage is a gamble—a lottery. And Joe retorts: "If that is so, why don't they arrest the rabbi?"

It does not pontificate: Marriage *a la mode* can become boring in time, but marriage *a la carte*—ach! Goldie baby, pass the noodle soup!

What is a Jew? As if the Jewish people didn't have enough to worry about, this controversial question has been raised with increasing frequency in the past few years, with the Orthodox holding one view and the Conservative and Reform segments of Judaism holding another. Why this should concern an American who can trace his ancestry back to the patriarch, Abraham, is unclear, but a Jew has to be miserable about something or else he's miserable. Lox Populi offers a consensus, to wit:

A modern American Jew is one who smokes Turkish tobacco in his cigarettes, orders Cuban cigars from Canada, drinks Scotch whiskey, drives a German car to an Italian movie, returns to his Mediterranean styled home where he sips Brazilian coffee while enjoying French fries, Spanish olives, English muffins, Danish pastry and Dutch chocolate—and then writes to his congressman with a Japanese ball-point pen, indignantly demanding that he do something about the government buying all that foreign oil from the Arabs.

The jokes passed along through Lox Populi often radiate a cheery hope for the future, as though optimism was a kind of heart stimulant for failure. And when you come right down to it, it is indeed hard to lose faith in humanity, considering the fact that more than 215 million people in the United States have never played you a dirty trick. Agreed, the jokes told by the man-in-the-street aren't profound. Profundities he leaves to the cultured ones. "What is culture," he will snort, "but a matter of buttoning and unbuttoning! . . . Opera, you say? I'd go to the opera, too, if it weren't for the singing!"

Trivia, perhaps, but at least Lox Populi has cast aside its Old World hair shirt. It has abandoned its self-denigration, its subservient whine. The American Jew has long known that it is useless to scratch the back of the professional porcupine in order to secure his good will. The jokes told by your neighbor or member of your family may be a clearer indication of deeper feelings than the intentionally barbed wit of the paid comedian—proof positive that the parrot may be a showy and talkative bird, but it takes the stork to deliver the goods. So it is that your father, watching a political candidate on television, can wryly observe: "That guy's head is getting so big he'll soon need his eyeglasses stretched." And grandpa will add solemnly: "Yeah, the cemeteries are full of people the world couldn't do without." The witticisms will not cause you to fall down laughing, but they do reflect the acerbic thrusts that have characterized Jewish humor down through the ageless centuries.

The field of education is one of the more popular targets of the Jewish American public—a very strange circumstance, considering that the academic world contains a high proportion of Jews and that the Jewish people are among the most highly educated in this country. As Lox Populi sees it, however, education is the art of memorizing things read in books, and things told by college professors who got their education by memorizing things read in books and things told by college professors.

Another area of concern touches on the financial problems associated with higher education. Here is a sample college correspondence course:

Dear Dad:

Thing$ are $well here at $chool, but they could be better. $ome
thing$ are needed mo$t de$perately the$e day$. I'm $uppo$ing
you under$tand what I mean and will $end $ome $oon.

Your loving $on,

$tanley

Dear Son:

NOthing is new here. I kNOw that you are doing better NOw
than you have been. Write aNOther letter soon. I want to get
this off in the NOon mail, so I'll sign off NOw.

Love,

Dad

The traveling salesman joke may be waning in popularity but
its modern counterpart is more sophisticated. It relies for its humor on astuteness rather than an escapade with a farmer's daughter. A good illustration is the office joke about Xavier and Sammy,
two New York shoe salesmen who were sent to Equatorial Africa
to open up new markets.

On the very first day of their arrival in Zululand, Xavier sent a
cable to the home office: RETURNING ON NEXT PLANE. IMPOSSIBLE
SELL SHOES HERE. EVERYBODY GOES BAREFOOT.

Not a word was heard from Sammy until two weeks later
when the sales manager received another cable: PILING UP ORDERS
BY THE BUSHEL. PROSPECTS UNLIMITED. NOBODY HERE HAS SHOES.

Commentaries on the times in which we live need not always
be modern to be current. Many years ago, a rabbinical student approached Sarah Bernhardt after she had just danced *au naturel* on
the stage.

"It seems to me that we Jewish people may be in need of an
Eleventh Commandment," he admonished her gently.

"The hell you say," snorted the divine Sarah. "We have ten
too many now!"

Straight out of Jewish folklore comes another *haimishe* joke
which, for reasons unknown, has never attained wide circulation
although it is, indeed funny. Back in the 1880s, when much of the
United States was still rural, the teacher in a small Hebrew school
near Albany, New York, was surprised to see only one child present. She was aghast when the little pupil told her that the others

were throwing cats into the river.

A few minutes later, her alarm increased when another child wandered into class. "Why are you tardy?" she asked sternly.

"I was throwin' cats in the river," he muttered.

"That's terrible—perfectly horrible!" she gasped. "How could you do such a thing!"

One by one the other students wandered into class, all with the same excuse.

Finally, the smallest pupil of all arrived.

"Well, young man," the teacher demanded coldly, "what is *your* excuse for being so late? Were you throwing cats into the river, too?"

"No, how could I?" said the little boy, wet and sniffling—"I'm Katz!"

• • •

In the spirit of detente and ecumenical brotherhood, it is only fair to give credit where credit is due—in this case to the Arabs. It is said that all jokes can be traced back to six originals which were first told in Egypt during the Sixth Dynasty. If this is really the case, it is the right and duty of every Jew to improve on any old joke he may find lying around loose.

Lox Populi—the people have spoken, and this commandment doth emerge: Do not take thyself too damn serious.

H.D.S.

The kind, dear old lady stopped to give a beggar a coin.

"Oh, my goodness!" she cried, noticing his infirmity for the first time. "You've lost a leg!"

The beggar looked down.

"Well, how about that?" he said coolly. "Damned if I didn't!"

Pat Gold (and never mind the *traife* first name) tells us he was born in a town that was so small everybody knew whose check was good and whose wife wasn't. "If you saw a girl with a man old enough to be her father," said Pat, "he was."

"That town was so small," he continued, "there was nothing doing every minute of the day. All you had to do was use your electric razor and the street lights dimmed. Believe me, the only place that was open all night was the mailbox.

"Can you imagine a town where they have only one traffic light and it changes color once a week? Take it from me, they ring in the New Year at 8:30 P.M. and the excitement is provided by watching an Alka-Seltzer fizz."

A registered member of New York's Liberal Party was discussing former President Richard Nixon, and apparently she was not one of his more enthusiastic followers.

"I don't need a reason," she snapped. "I just don't like him, and from all the things I've said about him, I never will!"

Anna: It's true what I hear about your husband cutting down on his smoking?

Hannah: Yes, now he's smoking only after meals—his meal, my meal, the children's meal, everybody's meal!

Then there's the dog-owner who crossed a basset with a beagle—and got a bagel!

Pretty Rachel Fisher, a model with a figure that called for the once-over twice, had recently moved into the apartment building. Watching her return home from work one evening were her new neighbors, Mrs. Berman and Mrs. Lerner.

"If there's one thing I hate, it's a gossip," commented Mrs. Berman, "but do you believe all those rumors about that Rachel Fisher person?"

"Oh, yes, I certainly do!" breathed Mrs. Lerner. "What are they?"

Back in the days of "twenty-three skidoo," Al Jolson was living at the Academy Hotel in New York. In the suite across the hall lived an amiable couple, and they all soon became friends.

One evening, Al accepted an invitation to have a drink at their place. He was sipping his highball when his eyes fell on a photograph, framed in silver and displayed upon the mantle, of an exceedingly handsome and well-built boy in his early teens.

"Whose picture is that?" he inquired.

"That's our son," explained the matronly woman.

"What's his name?"

"I'll spell it for you: A-e-r-n."

"Rather unusual," said Al. "How do you pronounce it?"

"That all depends," replied the lady. "You see, I happen to be Jewish. My parents were very Orthodox. But my husband is of pure Irish descent. We're both proud of our heritage. So when our son was born we decided to give him a name that would be natural for his family and mine, and still sound familiar and affectionate. After a few conferences we reached a compromise:

"My husband calls him Erin and I call him Aaron."

The traffic cop at the corner held up his hand for the flow of cars to stop, but Miss Peltz, the old maid, sailed right through the intersection.

Enraged, the cop blew his whistle and she pulled over to the curb.

"What's the matter with you, lady?" he barked. "Don't you know what I mean when I hold up my hand?"

"I certainly do," sniffed Miss Peltz in a huff. "I've been teaching school for 30 years."

The Soviet Union's Communist Party Chief, Leonid Brezhnev, following his visit to Washington, D.C. in 1973, decided to spend a day in New York to see the sights of the city. But he lost all interest in the more popular attractions when he caught his first glimpse of Macy's and then Gimbel's.

"You mean to tell me that all the merchandise in those department stores is really available to the American masses?" he gasped incredulously.

"Available!" retorted his State Department guide. "Listen, Macy's and Gimbel's and every other big store in this country has to advertise in the papers and *beg* people to buy!"

"Have you met the new boy next door?" the mother asked her daughter.

"Yes, mom," replied the girl. "His name is Myron, he's 21, and he's one of those sweet, shy, lovable types. You know—a real phony!"

Tonversation heard on a twolley tar:

1st little boy: My daddy met a Jewish man yestiddy an' he said . . .

2nd little boy: Hey, you ain't s'pose ta mention nobody's 'ligion. It's auntie-smetical!

1st little boy: Okay. My daddy met a Chinee man yestiddy . . .

2nd little boy: Yeah, that's gooder.

1st little boy: . . .'an the Chinee man said, "Izzy, where you gonna go for *Pesach?*"

"Mrs. Litvak, for two days I didn't have a bite to eat," whined Shimkus, the *schnorrer.* "Could you spare me please a slice of cake?"

"Cake!" exclaimed Mrs. Litvak indignantly. "What kind of *chutzpah* is that? Bread isn't good enough for you?"

"Today, no," replied Shimkus. "This is my birthday!"

"Mama, what happens to all the beat-up cars when they get too old to run anymore?"

"I thought you knew," replied mama. "Somebody sells them to your father!"

"Whaddyamean I'm a slave to the nicotine habit!" hubby snapped at his wife. "I'll have you know I stopped smoking cigarettes twice as much this year as I stopped last year!"

Ida Kogan entered a recipe contest and won a two-week vacation at Echo Hills in the Catskills—the heart of the Borscht Belt.

She fell in love with the place at once, and above all she wanted a tape recording of the famous echo for which the hills were so aptly named. Accordingly, she set up her equipment, cupped her hands around her mouth and shouted —

"*Haloooooo*—this is Ida Kohhhgaaan!"

And sure enough, there came back a mighty echo:

"*Haloooooo*—this is also Ida Kohhhgaaan!"

The young woman was exceedingly fair to look upon. She entered the auto salesroom and an affable salesman quickly approached the modern Cleopatra.

"This looks like a nice model," she said, after having inspected several cars. "What is it called?"

"That's the Belvedere," replied the salesman.

There ensued a chilly silence. The young woman then drew herself solidly erect, fixed him with a frigid stare, and coldly asked:

"What is the price of the Belva?"

Malka and Marsha, two old maids, were strolling down Lexington Avenue when they came upon a recruiting poster: *The Marine Corps Builds Men.*

"How nice," murmured Malka.

"It sure is!" agreed Marsha enthusiastically. "Let's ask them to build us a couple!"

The fact that a horse and wagon are components of this tale of woe is a good indication of its venerable age. It is a tale that was often told with much gusto and a little water on the side by Sidney Hillman, the great labor leader.

Molly Landau was learning to drive a car. Regrettably, as it turned out, she thought she already knew how, so she dismissed her driving instructor and ventured forth upon the public highway, unaccompanied by either an experienced hand or a driver's license.

As she wobbled in an uncertain course along Southern Boulevard in the Bronx, a milkman driving a well-behaved horse turned a corner. Mrs. Landau tried simultaneously to do several things— apply the brakes, avoid a collision, turn out, turn in, veer left, veer right, speed up, slow down, and who knows what else.

The "what else" was that she banged squarely into the side of the milk-wagon, leaving it turned over on its side in the middle of the street, with the horse and driver entangled in the wreckage.

The lady, losing her head, at the same time lost control of the car. She sped away, swerved out of sight and, on squealing tires she circled the block. A minute later she reappeared at the scene of the accident, still wrestling with the steering wheel. The dairyman, who had managed to extricate himself from the mess, was cutting his struggling horse loose from the twisted harness when he heard the clatter and roar of an approaching, wide-open engine. He looked up to see the same car and the same woman again bearing down on him. Just in time to save himself, he jumped aside.

There was a second crash and once more the green motorist proceeded on her devastating way. But now the capsized wagon was a total loss. The milkman was a natural-born philosopher. As he stood in the midst of the ruins, he shrugged his shoulders and remarked to the curious citizens who had gathered around:

"About that lady's driving, I can't say she's an expert. But you have to give her credit—she's thorough!"

It was the most momentous day in the history of Man. Moses, his face aglow with spiritual fire, descended from Mt. Sinai and pointed to the tablets.

"And now," he thundered to the awe-struck multitude, "a word from the Sponsor."

Cold water from the kitchen cynic:
"You just got married? *Mazel tov!* So tell me, when your new father-in-law dies, what kind of work will you be out of?"

As long as she was in the neighborhood, Mrs. Rifkind decided that she might as well stop in at the synagogue and meet the new assistant rabbi. Inside the temple, she asked the *shammes* where she could find the new rabbi's study.

"I'm sorry," said the *shammes*, "but right now he's engaged."

"Oh, how nice!" said Mrs. Rifkind, beaming. "I hope he'll be very happy!"

When the lights in her house went out for the third time within an hour, grandma called an electrician. It took him only a minute or two to locate the trouble.

"Lady," he informed her, "you got a short circuit."

"*Nu*," said grandma, "so you'll make it a little longer!"

"This drug situation with the younger generation is getting worse and worse every day," muttered the old-timer angrily as he tossed his evening newspaper aside. "It's those doctors. The kids complain to them about a bellyache and right away they get all kinds of drugs—without a prescription, yet!"

"It's not like when I was a young girl," sighed his wife. "In those days we couldn't even buy a brassiere without a prescription!"

"The nerve of that louse!" roared Glasner the glazier. "First he runs into my car against the traffic light; next he gives me a drink it should steady my nerves; then he calls the police!"

"What are your terms for students?" asked the new college freshman.

"I got all kinds of terms for them," snapped the boarding-house landlady: "Loafers, bums, *schnorrers, shikkers* . . . !"

From our Intelligentsia Department:
Tough Guy: Scram, before I knock your teeth in!
Linguist: You mean 'out'!

28

Naughty-Shmaughty

Introduction

We have already discussed the subject, "What is a Jew?" Now, let us address ourselves to the question, "What is sex?" Sex is the means by which reformers, censors, film producers, novelists and psychiatrists make a living. The purpose of sex is to extract a little pleasure out of life without creating a lot of problems for the sexee or sexor. Some of its more participatory aspects are frowned upon by the fastidious, which refers to the Roman, Faustidius, and his modern adherents who are known as Fastidiots.

The reason for Jewish involvement in this popular indoor sport will be found in the people's sacred writings. The Bible exhorts us: "Be fruitful and multiply, and replenish the earth." This is the first of the 613 commandments every pious Jew must observe. In the Talmud, we are admonished: "To refrain from begetting is to impair the Divine image," and it is followed by the rhetorical question, "Was not the world created only for propagation?"

And there you have it! Jews have sex because they're religious!

Not everyone will enjoy this chapter—especially the sexually-oriented type of fellow who determines how many women are at a party by counting the number of breasts and dividing by two. He will be disappointed because this is not a Jewish *Kama Sutra of Vatsametteh*, that curious and informative Eastern manual of erotica. Moreover, this chapter was not designed to meet the community standards of Sodom and Gemorrah, nor does it contain any leering double-entendres: triple, yes—double, no.

Another type who will be sorely disappointed by these pages is the "serious student" of humor. As far as I am concerned, nobody needs some goateed savant to scrutinize, hypothesize and symbolize until our jokes have been analyzed to death. Those professorial types would dress up the family dog in a cutaway suit. The socio-scientist positively slavers when he hears a funny story. ("Egad! The Oedipus complex! Anal regression! The phallic symbol!") In the first place, Jews don't have those naughty things. They just have respectable *tsuris* like decent people are supposed to have. In the second place, if it makes you all that sick you should better stick to Parcheesi.

An American reporter once asked General Moshe Dayan if the rumors about an increase of VD in Israel's army were true. Dayan exploded with a wrathful "That's a lot of claptrap!" The same reply may be reserved for the modern writer of fiction who weaves his spell of mysticism around "Jewish sex"—as though Jews held a patent on some esoteric monkey business unknown to gentiles. Today's children of Israel are an imaginative and resourceful people, but they have yet to invent an intimacy that wasn't at least considered by Abraham, Isaac and Joseph's brothers—and by the Pharaohs and Caesars as well. They just have a funnier way of describing it.

A word about the American-Jewish view of obscenities. Profanity, for the modern Jew, does not consist of such words as hell and damn: they are only profane when they are written h—l and d—n. The "sensitive" writer who is too respectable to use such mild expletives, and causes his character, a barroom brawler, to exclaim "Oh, shucks" instead of a healthy, heartfelt "dammit!"—is an embarrassment. Nevertheless, it is difficult to feel anything but contempt for the writer or storyteller who employs obscenities for no other purpose than their shock value, as though they were communicating with a nation of slobs. Such a word-smith or jokester uses the oath to hide the emptiness in his head, and is often incapable of expressing himself in other terms. But there are occasions—and they are not infrequent—when a play on words—any word—is the actual point of the story rather than an intrusion. Let's say, for instance, that you owned a mare and that you bought a baby donkey for her. You could then quite legitimately and truthfully refer to the colt as a horse's ass without being accused of swearing. After all, the Bible does not hesitate to devote space to the story of Balaam's ass!

There are definite "types" in American-Jewish humor, among them the perennial *shlemiel*. Consider the young fellow who is cautioned against marrying a certain girl. "Everybody in Yonkers has slept with her," the friend warns him. The intended bridegroom thinks it over, and then shrugs. "So what?" he replies. "After all, how big is Yonkers?"

The "outraged husband" is another favorite:

Feinberg came home from a business trip and his wife coolly informed him that she had been unfaithful during his absence.

"What was it?" shouted Feinberg, "that rotten Goldberg?"

"No," his wife replied, "it wasn't Goldberg."

"Was it that crooked partner of mine—that *goniff*, Levy?"

"No, not Levy."

"I know who it was: it was that *momzer*, Shapiro!"

"No, it wasn't Shapiro, either."

Feinberg glowered at his wife. "What's the matter?" he barked, "none of my friends are good enough for you?"

Jokes about the decline of vigor associated with old age form another large body of Jewish humor:

Grandpa and grandma, celebrating their golden wedding anniversary, decided to take a vacation at the same hotel where they had spent their honeymoon. It was a romantic idea, and they agreed to do everything they did in those first few days. Soon they were in the very same hotel and in the very same room. Grandpa undressed in the bathroom, just as he had so many years ago, and then he emerged in his long flannel underwear. Grandma, now wearing nothing but her stockings, and sitting on the edge of the bed, smiled up at him.

"Papa," she cooed, "can you wait until I'm taking off my stockings?"

"Yes, mama," he signed. "I can even wait until you *knit* a pair!"

It is said that men do not vary much in their virtues; they differ only in their vices. On the other hand, the woman who boasts of her virtue is one who probably was tested at an inopportune time by the wrong man. But in Jewish humor, virtue and common sense play an equal role. Let us see how a Jewish girl handled one delicate situation:

Schatz, the marriage broker, called on Lorraine and happily announced that he had found the ideal husband for her.

"There's just one little problem standing in the way," said the *schadchan*. "You see, he's a businessman, and by him everything is business. So he's asking you should first give him a sample of your sexual ability."

"Well, you go right back and tell him that I know a little about business, too," snapped Lorraine. "Samples I'm not giving him. References I'll give him!"

The jokes which follow, of the above and several other types, are guaranteed to be acceptable in Boston, a city so clean that even the birds fly upside down.

H.D.S.

Two housewives were gossiping over the back fence about their neighbor's daughter, Cathy Kanter—otherwise known as Canarsie Kate.

"Oh, what a shame!" chucked the first *yenta.* "She was so sweet when she was small. Even her own family called her 'tateh's little darling.'"

The other woman nodded. "By me her heart still belongs to daddy," she agreed, "but the rest I'm afraid she's renting out!"

Louis Jourdan, the French movie star, was in the United States seeking a good literary script for his next film. He happened to run into Budd Shulberg, the American author and playwright.

"There's a new book out called *Precocious Paula,*" Shulberg suggested tentatively. "It would give you a great co-starring role."

"I nevair hear of zis book," said Jourdan.

"It's something like Nabokov's novel, *Lolita,*" explained Shulberg.

"An' what ees zis *Lolita* about?"

"Well, frankly, it's about a middle-aged man who falls in love with a twelve-year-old."

The Frenchman gave him a blank look.

"I do not undairstan'," he said. "A twelve-year-old *what?*"

Moe and Ike, aged 90 and 92 respectively, had been widowers for many many years. Both were healthy and handsome looking despite their years. The Florida climate agreed with them, and many lovely widows were still after them despite their ages.

One day Moe said to Ike:

"Ike, I'm really lonely. It's been years since I lost my Becky and I've never remarried. But I think now is the time and I'm willing to take another chance at marriage. Even at my age."

"It sounds like a good idea," said Moe. "In fact, maybe I, too, should take a new wife."

Soon thereafter, Moe and Ike both married lovely ladies (89 and 90 respectively) and they both went on honeymoons.

A few days later, Moe and Ike met on the boardwalk.

"Well," asked Moe, "how was your honeymoon?"

"To tell you the truth, Moe, I couldn't consummate our marriage."

"Well," said Moe, "to tell you the truth, I didn't even *think* of it."

In the Jurassic period, when going to Far Rockaway from the Bronx was an event similar to the departure of an astronaut for the moon, there lived a respectable young woman named Miriam Altshuler. Miss Altshuler earned her wherewithal as a piano teacher, attended *shul* regularly and minded her own business. So much for the truth of this story: Now for the *bobeh myseh*:

One summer, Miss Altshuler took leave of her students and decamped for Far Rockaway, in search of two weeks of relaxation on a farm and—O Great *Shadchan* in the Sky—perhaps a husband.

Unbeknown to her, the farmer, a recent widower, had taken a fancy to the young lady, but he happened to be one of those who deems it prudent to taste the milk before buying the dairy. So, with all the subtlety of an Internal Revenue letter, he led our sweet little Miriam Altshuler to his pasture where a herd of Guernseys were peacefully grazing on second-growth clover. With the cows was a prize Black Angus bull. The farmer, it seems, was experimenting to achieve a newer and better breed.

As the farmer and Miss Altshuler watched by the rail, the bull performed his main function in life by servicing a heifer that was in season. The farmer smiled inwardly. All was proceeding as he had planned. He had now reached the point of fail-safe.

"Miriam," he said pointedly, "I think it would be fun to do that."

"Well, who's stopping you?" she replied. "It's your cow!"

The late Ed Wynn enjoyed telling parrot stories.

"I once owned a parrot," claimed Ed, "that laid six-pointed eggs, shaped just like the Star of David. And the parrot could speak only one word —

"'Ouch!'"

Chauncey, a handsome, almost pretty young man, was speaking earnestly with his mother:

"Mumsie, the time has come—it really has—when we must have a heart-to-heart talk about my relationship with Myron. To be quite candid about it, our friendship has blossomed into—how shall I say it without sounding indelicate?—well, into something beautiful and good and even holy. The truth is, Mumsie dear, I love Myron and Myron loves me in return. We want to be married as soon as possible and we both hope you'll give us your blessing."

"But, Chauncey," the mother protested, "do you realize what you're saying? Can you honestly expect me to condone such a marriage? What will people say? What will our friends and neighbors think?"

"Oh, Mumsie, you're going to be dreary—I can feel it in my bones. And after we've been such good pals, too. I never would have believed it of you—of all people. I could just cry!"

"But, son, you can't go against convention like this!"

"All right, Mumsie, let's have it right out in the open like civilized persons. Exactly and precisely what possible objection could you or anyone else have to Myron and I becoming husband and husband?"

"You know perfectly well why I object: He's Jewish!"

In his morning mail, Michael, a bachelor, was surprised to find an invitation to a wedding. His best friend, Bob, a politician, was getting married to Hannah the old maid.

"Well, whaddya know," exclaimed Michael. "The wedding of the humbug to the bum hug!"

Mrs. Leibowitz went into a furniture store.

"I would like please to look at a sexual sofa," she said.

The salesman mulled the request over in his mind for a moment of two and then a smile of comprehension crossed his features.

"Oh, you mean a *sectional* sofa!"

"Sexual-sectional," she retorted impatiently. "All I'm asking is that I should have an occasional piece in the living room!"

Over at Famous Fabrics, Inc., they have a gorgeous model who has everything a man could ask for —

So they're all asking.

It was Eddie's first week in pharmacy school. Outside, the sun was shining warmly, the birds were warbling, the girls were strolling and June was busting out all over.

Eddie's head nodded drowsily and he closed his eyes. But the instructor's sharp voice soon brought him back to scholastic reality:

"Well, sir, we're waiting for your answer!"

"Please repeat the question," muttered Eddie.

"If it doesn't interfere with your slumbers too much," hissed the professor, "please enlighten the class as to the difference between amnesia and magnesia."

"Well," said Eddie uncertainly, "with amnesia you don't know where you're going."

Home cooking: The place where a man thinks his wife is.

Zelda, the Hebrew zebra, was walking down a country lane, someplace in the boondocks of Pennsylvania. Soon she came upon a flock of sheep.

"Yoo-hoo, may I speak to you please?" she called out.

One of the sheep came up to the fence.

"*Nu*, what do you want to speak about?"

"I represent the Hadassah Zebra Association of South Africa. You're Jewish?"

"Oh yes, we're all Jewish here."

"Well, I'm on a fact-finding tour. Our zebras are interested in learning how Jewish animals in America earn a living. Would you mind telling me what kind of work you do?"

"What do I do?" exclaimed the sheep. "What kind of a question is that? I give wool, what else? Every year they shear it off and next season they do the same thing. Is it any different there in South Africa?"

"Oh, no, it's just the same. Well, I must be running along. Ta-ta, and thank you most kindly."

Zelda continued on her fact-finding mission until she met a cow.

"Excuse me, madam, I'm from the Hadassah Zebra Association of South Africa. I'm interviewing Jewish-American domestic animals. Would you be so kind as to describe your work?"

"Glad to," murmured the cow. "I am employed by a strictly kosher dairy, being orthodox myself, of course. My work, you ask?

Well, I'm a purebred Guernsey, and I give Grade A milk. I live up there in that pretty white barn. Sorry I can't ask you in, but we weren't expecting company and the place is a mess."

"That's perfectly all right. Thank you for your information. You've been most helpful. Toodle-oo."

A short time later, Zelda saw a stallion in a pasture, and there was no mistaking *his* Jewishness. He happened to see her at just about the same moment. He charged toward the fence, skidded to a four-footed stop and loomed over the zebra with nostrils flaring.

"And just what is it that *you* do, sir?" she asked demurely.

"Honey, you just slip out of those fancy pajamas," he said, "and I'll *show* you what I do!"

Mr. Shmendrick came home earlier than expected and found his wife in bed with a strange man.

"What are you two doing?" he bellowed.

"See what I mean?" said the wife to her lover. "A *shnook!*"

Harry was scolding his younger brother who had just dropped out of college.

"Every time I see you, you're either all *shikkered* up or running around with wild women—or both!" yelled Harry. "Don't you know what good clean fun is?"

"No," said the brother. "What good is it?"

Howard Rabinowitz, a huge, granite-fisted, super-tough young fellow, was drinking whiskey in a bar when he heard the announcement of the Six Day War on the radio. Filled with excitement and Jewish fervor, he rushed to the airport and took the first available flight to Israel where he was immediately inducted into the army.

But his reception at the military base was rather cool. He wasn't exactly avoided by the Israeli soldiers but neither did they go out of their way to welcome him.

"Listen, what's with you guys?" he complained to his sergeant. "Here I come halfway around the world to help you out and I'm practically ignored. What must an American do to get accepted in this army?"

The sergeant eyed the muscular young giant, glanced around somewhat furtively so that he might not be overheard, and then, in a voice that was almost a whisper, he said:

"Confidentially, and off the record, if you really want to be one of us, there are three things you must do."

"Name them," said Rabinowitz.

"First," explained the sergeant, "you must drink down a whole quart of our strongest Mount Carmel wine without stopping for a breath. Second, you must kill an Arab army officer. Third, you must make love to an Israeli beauty."

So Howard Rabinowitz chug-a-lugged a whole quart of Mount Carmel wine without stopping.

"Now," he demanded, "where can I find an Arab officer?"

"Right across the Suez Canal," said the sergeant. "I'm afraid you'll have to swim both ways; that is, if you're still alive."

"I'll be alive," promised the American as he lurched off. "Hell, I was the roughest, toughest, biggest guy on the East Side. What's a little adventure like this?"

A few hours later he returned, soaking wet from his return swim, his clothes torn and his face scratched and bloody.

"Okay, I took care of that Arab officer," he roared. "Now, where's that Israeli beauty you want killed?"

There is a religious fellow who really believes in the proverb, "Love thy neighbor."

The trouble is, he can't stand her husband.

Over at Chatham Uniform and Work Clothes Manufacturing Company, during their lunch break, a cutter, a sponger and a baster were bemoaning the dilatory ways of the younger generation.

"Mein Harold is so lazy he's getting up at six every morning just so he'll have more time to loaf," moaned the cutter. "Today he told me he's putting popcorn on his pancakes so they should turn over by themselves. *Oy*, is mein Harold lazy!"

"That's lazy by you?" demanded the cutter. "Listen, mein Jerome gets into a rewolwing door and just *waits*! And does he walk in his sleep like a decent Jewish boy? No, he's sticking out his thumb he should hitch-hike!"

The baster gave a deep sigh. "I wish mein Boitram was only so lazy like your boys. Mein Boitram just married a widow with four children!"

Tired of the old fly-in-my-soup jokes? Here's a switch.

Manny sat down in his favorite restaurant and was about to taste his chicken soup when a passing waiter accidentally jostled his arm. To his chagrin, the soup spilled on his lap.

"Now look what you did," complained Manny. "I got a soup in my fly!"

In a Bronxville tavern, Lou was celebrating his one-night-out per week with his bachelor friend, George, who was declaiming on the benefits of blessed singleness.

"It's nice to be a bachelor," George was saying. "I can get in or out of bed from either side; I cook only one breakfast; I have only one set of dishes to wash; I can open my wallet without hiding in the bathroom, and I have all kinds of marvelous faults that nobody tells me about."

"How did you ever manage to avoid marriage in the first place?" asked Lou enviously.

"You have to develop the right frame of mind," counseled George. "To enjoy single bliss there are five principles to guide your steps. First, never make the same mistake once. Second, it helps to know all the ankles. Third, make up your mind that it's better to learn how to mend your socks than your ways. Fourth, you should develop a deep love for the Constitution—especially where it says all Americans are entitled to life, liberty and the happiness of pursuit. Fifth and final, you must strictly follow the Bachelor's Golden Rule—wine, women and so-long."

Lou took another drink, nodded, took still another drink, nodded some more, and let his imagination wander.

"I can see it all," he said dreamily. "A bachelor is a guy with one car, two suits, three girls friends and four all-night parking tickets."

Fifi Flugel of Fairmont Avenue in the Bronx (not to be confused with Fifi *Fliegel* of Fairfax Avenue in Los Angeles) came home one evening and unleashed her tale of woe to her mother.

"Mama, I got took advantage of by my boss," she sobbed. "All he really wanted was my body, and now he's casting me aside like in the movies."

"*Himmel!*" gasped mama, "you're—you're pregnant?"

"Yes, mama, what should I do?"

"I'll tell you what you should do," said mama grimly. "You'll stay home tomorrow from work and I'm going instead to your office I should have a heart-to-heart talk with your *paskudnyak* of a boss."

The next morning, mama barged into the boss's elaborate sanctum and read him the Riot Act in several languages, among them English, Yiddish and Russian. Then, in a voice that had all the metallic resonance of a twanging bronze bedpan, she led into her demands.

"*Nu,*" she snapped as a good negotiator should, "what kind of arrangement you're intending for mine Fifi?"

"You may rest assured, Mrs. Flugel, that your daughter will lack for nothing," said the boss, applying a solid gold lighter to his expensive cigar. "I will get her the best specialist in America so that she has the finest prenatal care possible. She will go to the most exclusive hospital to be found anywhere in the United States and she will have a team of the most experienced, well-recommended doctors and nurses money can obtain. When the baby is born I will set up, in its name, a hundred-thousand-dollar trust fund and, further, I will provide Fifi with $1,000 a week for living expenses while she is bringing up my child."

"Mister," said Mama Flugel after some careful thought, "if it's a miscarriage would you be so kind you should give Fifi another chance?"

Izzie Schwartz, age six, and his little friend, Colleen McGuire, also six, were playing jacks on the sidewalk.

"I'm tired of this game," said Colleen. "Let's play something else."

"Okay, we'll play Daddy and Mommy," suggested Izzie. "I'll be the Daddy and you can be the Mommy."

"Oooh, that sounds like fun! But how do we play it?"

"Well, I'm coming home from work and you make supper and we eat."

So Colleen dutifully went through the motions of cooking and apportioning "supper" on two imaginary plates.

"What do we do now?" asked Colleen.

"Now we watch television."

"So they "watched television," staring vapidly at a spot on the sidewalk.

"Now what?" demanded Colleen, impatient to get on with the game.

"Now it's time to go to bed," said Izzie.

So they stretched out on the sidewalk and pretended they were under the covers.

"What do we do now?" asked little Colleen.

"Now," explained Izzie, "we whisper in Jewish!"

Adam to Eve: "After I eat this apple I'm gonna *what?*"

A minor example of the consequences of censorship occurred in the pages of an English language weekly, *The California Jewish Voice*, a journal subsequently absorbed by the *B'nai Brith Messenger* in Los Angeles. The editor, it seems, was apprehensive when a music critic on his staff wrote a sentence that read:

"The oboe player spent the evening staring at his navel."

The editor apparently considered the word "navel" as too risqué for a nice family paper and ordered the offending word stricken from the sentence. But imagine his horror when, after the edition had been mailed out to the entire list of subscribers, he happened to read the corrected sentence:

"The oboe player spent the evening staring at his —."

Selma the secretary was about to take her annual vacation and was instructing the stunning substitute as to her duties for the next two weeks.

"It's really an easy job," Selma assured the substitute, taking note of her pretty features and curvaceous figure. "All you have to do is continue what I was doing—except with Mr. Yosselov."

"Hey, grandpa, I heard another good one today," shouted young Julius, busting into the house. "What's the difference between a hairdresser and a sculptor?"

"*Nu*, educate me," sighed the grandfather, accustomed to the boy's riddle-of-the-day routine.

"A hairdresser curls and dyes," chortled Julius, "and a sculptor makes faces and busts."

The old man groaned. "All right, you told me your riddle. Now go out and play with your friends like a good boy."

"But I have three more," protested the youngster. "If I can't tell my riddles to you, what'll I do with them?"

"Julius," breathed the old-timer wearily, "if I weren't your very own grandpa, believe me, I'd tell you!"

Bob and Richard, two gentile brothers, fell in love with two Jewish sisters and agreed to become converts to Judaism so that they could marry the girls.

The next day, Bob, the younger brother, showed up at his doctor's office.

"I want to be castrated," he told the medic.

"You *what*! Mister, do you realize what you're saying?"

"I certainly do."

"Well, I'm not sure I want to do the operation," said the good doctor hesitantly. "Castration is a very serious, irrevocable step."

"Then if you won't do it, I'll find another doctor who will."

The doctor shrugged. "In that case, as long as you intend to go through with it anyway, I'll operate."

So he castrated the young man.

The following day, as Bob was about to leave the doctor's clinic, his brother Richard entered the reception room.

"What are you doing here?" asked Bob.

"I came to get circumcised," replied Richard.

"Damn!" exclaimed Bob. "*That's* the word I was trying to think of!"

"I come from a large family," explained Sheldon the druggist. "There were 14 of us kids. We were so crowded I never knew what it was to sleep alone until I got married."

A pregnant silence pervaded the courtroom as the judge considered the paternity suit before him. All at once he looked up from the sheaf of papers he had been studying, reached into the folds of his robe, drew out a cigar and ceremoniously handed it to the defendant.

"Congratulations!" boomed his honor. "You have just become a father!"

The new assistant rabbi, just out of Yeshiva University, was as fervent as any newly-ordained young man of the cloth could possibly be. A real go-getter, he immediately plunged into the task of building up the congregation's membership, but was disappointed when a certain young widow in the neighborhood failed to appear for any of the services.

One *Shabbes*, however, without warning, she attended the synagogue, looking radiant and quite beautiful. The young rabbi rushed over to her, smiling, and extended his hand in greeting.

"I just knew you'd come!" he exclaimed happily. "In fact, I prayed for you last night for a whole hour."

"Why, rabbi," she answered coyly, "all you had to do was give me a jingle. I'd have been over in ten minutes!"

It was a constant battle between Mrs. Levine and her twelve-year-old daughter to keep her room tidy. No matter how much the mother pleaded, cajoled, ranted and raved, the little girl kept her room in a mess.

And then came the day of miracles. Mrs. Levine went into her daughter's room and found it immaculate—everything in its place, the floor swept and the bed made.

"Now this is what I like to see!" she exclaimed. "But what changed you into such a good little girl?"

"The police changed me," replied the girl solemnly. "I heard on the radio this morning that they're gonna arrest anybody who keeps a disorderly house."

Two cutters in the garment district were talking shop in Seventh Avenue luncheonette.

"What I can't figure out," said one, "is all this interest in girls' stretch pants."

"There's lots of reasons," replied the other. "Did you ever see a girl in stretch pants?"

"Sure."

"Well, then you saw two reasons right there!"

For ten years, ever since they were first married, Michael and Tessie Weinberg were content with each other. It was an ideal, happy marriage. Then, following the birth of their third child, Tessie noticed, to her distress, that the pleasure she had always derived from her wifely intimacies had considerably waned. On the other hand, Michael's sexual appetite remained as strong as ever.

Much worried, Tessie decided to consult their family doctor.

"I still love my husband," she explained to the physician, "but I'm afraid I'm not satisfying him any more. I just don't have the same feeling like I used to. Not that Michael complains or anything—he loves me too much for that. Maybe that's why I feel so guilty. Tell me, doctor, have you got something I could take that could help me?"

"Well, as a matter of fact I do have something new that might help your condition," said the doctor. "We don't know too much about it yet, but it seems to produce the desired effect. It's a stimulator imported from Israel where it was recently developed. It is known as Jewish Fly. Unlike Spanish Fly, this is strictly kosher."

"If it will help save my marriage I'll take it."

"Very well, Mrs. Weinberg, I'll give you four tablets. Start off with just half a tablet and see what kind of reaction you get. After that, if you need it, you can take a stronger dose."

A week later, Tessie, obviously distraught, was back at the physician's office.

"Doctor, I came here for only one reason," she cried. "I want you to know that you just about ruined my marriage. That terrible drug you gave me . . . Oh, I'm so ashamed!"

"Now, now, Mrs. Weinberg," the doctor said soothingly, "just tell me what happened. Did you follow my advice?"

"Yes," she wailed.

"You followed my directions exactly?"

"Well, not exactly. I didn't take the tablets at all until last night, about an hour before dinner. I know you said I should take half a tablet, but seeing how I didn't take any all week—ever since you gave them to me—I just thought it would be all right if I caught up by taking all four at once."

"Good heavens!" exclaimed the doctor. "What kind of a reaction did you get?"

"Don't ask. We were right in the middle of dinner when all of a sudden I got this awful compulsion. Not just a normal urge, doctor, but an absolutely *crazy* impulse. I didn't want to just make love to my husband, I wanted to—you should forgive the expression—*rape* him! I jumped up and dragged him out from his chair and practically threw him on the table. Yes, doctor—on the *table*! Just thinking about it makes me so embarrassed. It was terrible. All the dishes fell to the floor and got broken. A bottle of good wine was knocked over and ruined the expensive tablecloth. *Vay iz mir*—in my whole life I never even dreamed of behaving like that! I felt so cheap—like a *kurva*."

"This is dreadful!" said the doctor, his voice shocked. "In a way I feel partly responsible, too; even though you disregarded my instructions. I really shouldn't have given you more than half a tablet to begin with. So let me make amends. You said the dishes were broken, the wine spilled and the tablecloth ruined? All right, I'll pay for the damages."

"Damages? What good will damages do?" she wept. "In a million years they'll never let us into *that* restaurant again!"

Three years ago, Jack Jacobs was struggling along with his little manufacturing concern located in a second-floor loft. Then lady luck smiled on him—he hit on a design for his dress goods and the trade went wild over it. The next season, he created another design that was a fast seller and the third year he did it again. Jack was now a wealthy man. So he decided it was time he became a real 100% American and get himself a young and pretty mistress.

His roving eye soon fell on lovely Miss Bernstein, a model who worked for one of his customers. He immediately began his campaign, plying her with food, drink and glittering promises.

"I'll rent a town house for you," he said, "and you can have your own bank account and credit at all the best shops in the city. I'll visit you a couple of nights during the week and we'll spend all our weekends together. And if we find we've made a mistake, why we can always separate."

Miss Bernstein toyed with the idea and then shook her head.

"It sounds fine, the way you put it," she replied, "but what do we do with the mistake?"

❖ ❖ ❖

The good people of Schenectady, New York, who happen to be more truthful than the bad people of Schenectady, New York, swear and avow that the following eerie occurrence actually happened to the Memel family in that fair city. But, a word of caution: If you do not believe in reincarnation, read no further.

Sol Memel, the very selfsame gentleman who achieved a measure of local fame when he once sold 300 boxes of *yahrzeit* candles to a visiting Arab dignitary on the pretext that they were Sioux Indian mementos, suffered a heart attack a few years after that episode and was cut down in the prime of his life. He couldn't have been much more than forty or so. A pity!

Mrs. Gussie Memel, his adoring wife, was inconsolable. Long after the traditional period of mourning, she was still grief-stricken. Nothing would do but that she contact the departed spirit of her late lamented husband. So she went to a spiritualist and requested a seance. When the medium had gone into his best professional trance, and the table shook a little and a horn blew nice, a voice was heard:

"Gussie, you're there?"

"Sollie! *Oh, Sollie!*" exclaimed Gussie, "It's really you! I'd know your voice anywhere. Tell me, Sollie darling, how's by you?"

"Fine, Gussie. Couldn't be better!"

"It's nice there? You're happy?"

"Take my word, Gussie, I couldn't be happier. It's absolutely gorgeous here. The sky is blue like your eyes when we got married. Everywhere is bright green grass—mine favorite color grass. And such cows, Gussie! If only you could see them! There's brown cows, white cows, black cows, white and brown, brown and black, black and white—such beautiful cows you never saw in your whole life."

"In heaven they got cows?"

"Heaven? Who said anything about heaven? I'm a bull in Argentina!"

Melvin and Miriam were so engrossed in each other as they lay upon the grass that they did not even hear the approach of the policeman.

"Hey, you two," demanded the minion of the law, "what's the idea smooching like that in broad daylight? And right here by the side of the road, too. Ya oughtta be ashamed of yerselves."

"You don't understand, officer," said the quick-thinking Melvin. "I just had a flat tire and my lady friend here is helping me fix it."

"Tire?" echoed the policeman. "What tire?"

Melvin looked around and gasped.

"My God, Miriam, somebody stole the car!"

Sam and Molly Berger, who arrived in this country as impoverished immigrants, had always dreamed that someday they would have their just share of the good life America offered. Through the combination of luck, pluck and hard work, they achieved their goal. Now, many years later, they were wealthy and proud of their *kultur* and "sushel" position.

Came the long-awaited day when their only daughter, Penelope, was ready to go off to finishing school, and the Bergers selected the fashionable Hyannis Port Academy for Young Ladies where, they hoped, their daughter would acquire the grace and manners consistent with the family's station in life. She might also, they hoped, meet eligible, marriage-minded young gentlemen of proper means and background when they came to visit their sisters at the posh academy.

Penelope had not been gone two weeks when Sam and Molly Berger received a letter from their daughter requesting that they airmail a book on etiquette to her.

"Well, well," beamed Sam, "those aristocrat boys she's dating, maybe meeting their families in their fancy homes makes it important she should have good breeding." So he and Molly happily sent her a copy of Emily Post's *Etiquette*.

Six months later, the parents received another request for a book on etiquette and proper social customs. This time the overjoyed father and mother sent her a copy of Amy Vanderbilt's *Etiquette and the Social Graces*.

During her second year at the exclusive school, Penelope arrived home for her summer vacation. Enfolded in her arms was a sweet little infant.

"Penelope," stammered her father, "whose baby is this?"

"Mine, daddy dear."

"And who is the papa, if I may be so bold?"

"I don't know," acknowledged Penelope.

Sam stared at his daughter, his face livid with astonishment and mounting anger. When he finally found his voice, he cried out:

"Two expensive books on etiquette you got and you don't even know how to ask, 'With whom am I having the pleasure?'"

"Theodore, tell us, please," began the professor in the human relations class, "can you love two girls at once?"

"Yes, *sir*!" responded Theodore enthusiastically. "Immediately!"

Teenaged Izzy looked up from the magazine he was reading. "Hey, pop, it says here in *Time* that more student riots are expected next semester. Did they have all these campus protests when you were in college?"

The father shook his head. "No, son," he replied in a nostalgic voice. "In my day, student bodies were interested only in student bodies."

Elsie, in her second year at Roosevelt High School in the Bronx, wasn't exactly the world's champion speller, but her heart was in the right place. In a composition on "The Sanctity of Marriage," she wrote:

"There are millions of nice-looking, lonely women who are unattacked and hungry for love."

Glossary

A klug tsu Columbus: "A curse to (on) Columbus." A hyperbolic term used when things go wrong in America. Also worded: *A klug oyf Columbus.*

A mazel auf Columbus: May Columbus have such luck. Opposite in connotation to the above.

Aleph-Baiz (Aleph-Bess): The first two letters of the Yiddish-Hebrew alphabet, itself called "The Aleph-Baiz" just as the English language alphabet is referred to as the "The ABC's." The Sephardic pronunciation is *Aleph-Bet.*

Alteh: Old one, when referring to a woman; *Altehr* when referred to a man.

Areyngekrokhn in frimorgen: "Crept in at dawn" or "early morning." (From a line of poetry: *Di klayneh fenster vu di zun hot areyngekrokhn in frimorgen*—The little window where the sun came creeping in at morn."

Ashkenazi: Singular form of *Ashkenazim.*

Ashkenazim: A Hebrew word meaning "German." The name applied to the Jews of Germany and North France beginning with the 10th century. In the 16th century, *Ashkenazim* came to include Jews of Eastern Europe as well. They developed their own customs and rituals, in contradistinction to the Jews of the Spanish and Mediterranean countries, who were called *Sephardim.*

Azay: Properly *Azoi.* Just as Americans in the north and south pronounce certain words differently (fire as fahr, cement as *see*ment, Chicago as Chi*cawguh*), Jews in various regions of the diaspora have developed local pronunciations. *Azay* has been used in some of the anecdotes in this book to capture the authentic flavor of the local idiom exactly as told to the author. (See *Azoi,* below.)

Asay es gevayn: "It was like that," or "that's the way it was."

Azoi: This is a type of comment similar to the Japanese "Ah-so!" and its connotation is, "Really!" or "You don't say!" But it can also be used to indicate "This is how"—as in *Azoi dertza-ilt men a vitz?* (Yes, the word *vitz* means "joke.")

Baal ha-bais (bal ha-bos): Pl. *Baal-batim.* An efficient householder. Used in the context of some of the stories in this volume, the *baal-batim* are also those well-to-do members of a *shul* who are generous contributors, and who conduct synagogue affairs with skill and dignity.

Bagel: A hard roll shaped in the form of a ring, resembling a doughnut; the dough is boiled and then baked. Usually sliced down the middle and then spread with cream cheese and lox.

Balabatish: Respectable.

Balaboosteha: See *Baal ha-bais.*

Bar Mitzvah: Literal meaning is "son of the commandment." It is a religious ceremony at which time the Jewish lad of thirteen (actually thirteen years and one day) becomes obligated to observe all religious *mitzvot* (commandments). He becomes a full-fledged member of the Jewish community.

Beblach: Beans. Also see *Bopkes.*

Bissel (Bis'l): Small in amount or of quantity.

Biz a hundert un tsvantzik: "Until a hundred and twenty." (A benediction meaning you should live many years.)

Bleib: As used in these pages, it means "stay" or "remain."

Blintzes: Cheese, *kasha* (groats) or berries rolled in thin dough and fried in fat. The French would call them *crêpes suzettes.* There is no singular form for the word *blintzes* because who eats just one?

Bobeh: Grandmother.

Bobeh myseh: Literally, a grandmother's tale. Actually, it refers to a story that is a complete fabrication; a fairy tale or a lie.

Bopkes: Beans

Borscht: A soup made of beets or cabbage. The beet *borscht* may be eaten hot or cold, with or without sour cream. The cabbage *borscht* is served piping hot and is especially good with pumpernickel bread.

Bris (B'rit): Covenant (of Abraham): the act and ceremoney of circumcision, performed on the eighth day after the birth of the boy, unless it has to be postponed for health reasons.

Broyges: Angry.

Challeh: Rich white bread usually associated with Sabbath or holy day feasts. In our "affluent society" however, *challeh* may be eaten at any time.

Chanukah: Holiday commemorating the victory of the Maccabees in the year 165 B.C.E. It is celebrated for eight days beginning on the 25th day of the month of *Kislev*. One of its traditions is the lighting of candles for eight days as a reminder of the miracle of the cruse of oil which burned for eight days instead of one. It is a festival most popular with children who enjoy lighting the candles, receiving traditional gifts of money (*Chanukah gelt*) and playing appropriate games, especially the *dreidel* which is a top with four Hebrew letters: *Nun, Gimmel, Hay* and *Shin*. These letters stand for *Nes Galol Hayah Sham*, or "A great miracle happened there." *Chanukah* marks what was probably the first struggle for religious freedom in history.

Chasseneh: Wedding.

Chassid (pl. *Chassidim*; adj. *Chassidic*): The word itself means "pious." In actual reference it is a follower or member of the *Chassidic* movement which was founded by Israel Baal Shem Tov in the 18th century. While *Chassidism* has lost its significance as a mass movement, it is still practiced by numerous small groups—some as close as the Williamsburg section of Brooklyn, New York.

Chazan: A cantor.

Cheder (Heder): Jewish parochial school for the teaching of the Bible, Hebrew, history, prayers, etc.

Chochem: A wise man or sage. In the vernacular it is also used sarcastically as a "wise guy." Paradoxically, *chochem* can also denote a simpleton who will believe anything; as in the jeering expression, "Tell that *bobeh myseh* to your *chochem fun Chelm!*"

Cholerya: Cholera; also pronounced *Cholyera*.

Chozzer: Pig, glutton. *Chazir* is the Hebrew word for pig.

Chozzerei: Piggish, piglike, slop.

Chupah, Chupeh: The canopy under which the bride and groom stand during the wedding ceremony.

Chutzpah: Impudence; unmitigated nerve.

Daven: To pray. The origin of the word is not definitely established, though some say it is connected with the Latin *divino*.

Diaspora: Exile; dispersion of Jews after the conquest of Palestine by the Romans in 70 C.E. Also called *Galuth*, or in Yiddish, *Golos*, referring to the collective lands of Jewish dispersion.

Di hoyz vu ich bin gevayn geboyrn: "The house where I was born."

Dinchazzan: "To study" or "to learn" by heart. One may learn by the process of *dinchazzan*, memorizing or absorbing by rote. The word may also be used as a noun: one who learns. (He is a real *dinchazzan*.)

Din Torah: A Hebrew term applied to a trial held in accordance with the principles of Jewish law. A rabbi nearly always presided over the *din torah*.

Dort or *Dorten:* There.

Dreidel: A top which is spun with the fingers. (See *Chanukah*.)

Dumkopf (Dumkup): Literally a "stupid head," a dumb-bell.

Dus: This.

Echot: Also. Often pronounced *oichet*.

Efsher: Maybe, perhaps.

Eppes: Something.

Eretz Yisrael (Eretz Yisroel): The land of origin of the Jewish people: "The land of Israel." The State itself is called *Medinat Israel*.

Ess: Eat. *Ess a bis'l eppes*—"Eat a little something."

Fahrshtunkene: Stinking.

Feeselach: Feet (dim.) The mother who kisses her baby's toes (Jewish mothers are notorious infant-toe kissers) will exclaim, "What pretty little *feeselach*," rather than *feese* (feet).

Feh: An exclamation of disgust or distaste.

Fenaigler: A con man; a conniver.

Folkskeit: That which pertains to the nature or traditions of the masses—the *folk*.

Forvertz: Forward, progress. The anglicized name of the Yiddish daily newspaper in New York, *The Forward*.

Fress: To gobble up one's food; to eat to excess. The difference between *ess* and *fress* is that in the former, one eats in a civilized manner; in the latter, like a *chozzer* at the trough.

Froy: A housewife; wife. Originally the German *Frau*.

Frume Yid: An ultra-religious or extremely pious Jew.

Galernter: A learned one; a scholar. ("He's a regular *galernter!*")

Galitzianer: A Jew from Galicia.

Gan Eden: Heaven.

Gantseh: Whole.

Gedenk: Remember.

Gefilte fish: A variety of fish (usually carp, pike and white fish) fileted, and chopped up fine with spices added. It is shaped in round servable portions and dropped into broth to simmer until cooked. Originally, a Sabbath and holiday delicacy.

Gegent: Neighborhood, district.

Gehakhta leber: Chopped liver.

Gehakhta tsuris: While *gehakhta* means "chopped" and *tsuris* means "trouble," in this case the expression means "utter misery."

Gehenna: Hell.

Gelacht: Laughed. Sometimes pronounced *gelachen.*

Gelt: Money.

Gemara: That part of the Talmud which is an elaboration of the Mishna.

Genz: Geese.

Genzineh gribben: Goose fat, rendered and spiced. Gribben is also referred to as *gribbenes.*

Gevald (Gevaldt): Help!

Gezenge, marshe mit tentze: Songs, marches and dances. The *Gezenge, Marshe mit Tentze:* A social club that flourished on New York's lower east side in the early 1920's.

Goldeneh Medina: "The Golden Land," referring specifically to America.

Golem: A term used in Jewish folklore to describe a robot made of clay or wood and given artificial life with the aid of magic, or the use of the Divine name. The express purpose of these living automatons was to protect the Jews from menacing dangers, and were usually under the spell and control of their creators. They could, however, become destructive if not checked. The *Golem* is mentioned in the Talmud, in medieval folk literature, and in modern stories.

Goniff (Ganeff, Ganev): A thief. The correct pronunciation of this word, which is basically Hebrew, is *Ganav* (pl. *Ganavim*).

Gornisht (Gornit): Nothing.

Gornisht mit leber: An ironic expression, literally meaning "nothing with liver," but actually denoting little or no recompense or reaction. ("For my efforts I received *gornisht mit leber.*")

Gottenyu: The diminutive form for God. (For a further description of the Russian-Polish suffix *nyu*, see listing for *Mamenyu*.)

Gott sie dank: Thank God! Also pronounced *Gott zai dank.*

Gott zol oftn: God forbid!

Goy (pl. *Goyim*): Gentile

Goyishe: That which pertains to gentiles; un-Jewish.

Gribben, Gribbenes: Fat of a fowl that has been rendered and spiced. More precisely, well-browned roasted bits of goose skin.

Griener: A greenhorn; a new arrival to this country, especially one who lacks the most basic knowledge of American ways and customs.

Griven: See *Gribben.*

Haimish, Haimisheh: Homey, friendly.

Hamantashen: A pastry designed specifically for *Purim*, and shaped into a triangle like Haman's three-corner hat. The dough is filled with either a prune paste, a cheese filling, or poppy seeds.

Helzel: Neck of a fowl. In Jewish cookery, *helzel* refers to the neck-skin of a turkey, goose, chicken or duck, and it is stuffed with meal, egg, spices, etc., to make a tasty dish.

Himmel: Heaven.

Hockflaish: Hock means "chop" and "*flaish*" means "meat." Together they spell "chopped meat" or (you should pardon the expression) "hamburger."

Hoyz: House.

Ich (Ikh): The personal pronoun, "I."

Ingelch: Little boy. A boy is an *ingel* (and a girl is a *maidel*), but when the suffix "eh" is added, it is so much more tender and diminutive. Also pronounced *yingel* or *yingeleh.*

Irisher Yontif: An expression attributed to James J. (Jimmy) Walker, Mayor of New York City from 1925 to 1932, to describe an Irish holiday-gathering where "the water flowed like wine and the wine flowed like whiskey." While *Irisher Yontif* is a Yiddish expression for "Irish holiday," it was apparently originated by Irish-American Walker and later picked up by the fun-loving Jewish community.

Kaftan: Long black coat worn by East European Jews.

Kalah, Kaleh: A bride.

Katchkeh: Duck.

Kaynmol gevayn: "Never happened," or "never was," or, "at no time did a specific thing occur."

Kibitzer: A spectator at a card (or other) game who gives uninvited advice; one who jokes and chitchats while others are trying to work or play.

Kimmel (Kiml, Kim'l): Caraway seeds, used in the baking of bread and rolls, and in the distilling of liquor.

Kinderlach: The plural of *kind* (child) is *kinder,* and the affectionate or diminutive form of *kinder* is *kinderlach.*

Kishkeh: Stuffed intestine. On some menus this is listed as "derma."

Klayneh: Small; little. As in *klayneh maidel* (little girl), or *klayneh hoyz* (small house). *Klayneh* refers to small in size; *bissel* refers to small in quantity.

Knaidlach (sing. *Knaidel*): Matzoh-balls.

Knish: A fried or baked turnover or roll of dough with a filling, as of meat, cheese or potato. Usually used in its plural form: *Knishes.*

Kosher: Food prepared according to Jewish ritual law. Relates to the slaughter of animals, preparation of food and dietary regulations. The Jewish dietary laws are based on biblical law and were elaborated upon in the Talmud. These laws distinguish between foods which are *kosher* (permissable) and *traif* (forbidden).

Kreplach: Dough filled with meat and boiled. The Chinese call them *won ton* and the Italians have a version which they call *ravioli.*

Kugel: Noodle or bread pudding usually cooked with raisins.

Kurva: A prostitute.

Lach (Lakh): Laugh.

Landsman (pl. *Landsleit*): Countryman; someone who comes from your home town.

Latkes: (sing. *Latkeh*): *Chanukah* is the time for this delicious pancake. It is made of grated raw potatoes, onion, egg, and seasoning, all mixed thoroughly and fried. The singular form, *latkeh,* is seldom used, although it is a perfectly permissable word, because eating just one is as impossible as eating one potato chip or peanut.

Le'chayim: A drinking toast. Figuratively, "To your health," "Here's mud in your eye," "Bottoms up," etc . . . *Chayim,* literally means "life."

Lekach: A brown honeycake.

Litvak: Lithuanian Jew.

Lokshn: Noodles.

Lox: Smoked salmon.

Luftmentsch: A dreamer, an idealist. A builder of castles in the air.

Maggid: A preacher; usually an itinerant preacher.

Malach: Angel.

Malach-Hamoves: Angel of death; a ghost.

Mamenya: In that inimitable manner of the Jews, the diminutive for mama has the Russian-Polish *nya* added as a suffix to become the very endearing *mamenya.* Similarly, *tateh* (father) becomes *tatenya.* And when *mamenya* raises her eyes to the ceiling and moans *Tatenya* (note the Capitalized "T"), she is of course, addressing God whom she frequently refers to affectionately as *Gottenyu.*

Mashiach: See *Mosheeach.*

Mazel: Luck.

Mazel tov: Good luck!

Megillah: A scroll. Although, technically, there are five scrolls, or *Megillot,* in the Bible, only the Book of Esther is known as **the** *Megillah.* It is read on *Purim* eve and *Purim* morning. In the vernacular, a *megillah* is used freely to indicate a long and complicated story. *Megillah* is a common word, especially around show-biz people.

Mentsch: Man, person. Often used admiringly to denote a gentleman or a decent person. ("He's a real *mentsch!*"). Also, used to describe strength of character ("Be a *mentsch* and stand up for your rights!" or, "If you were any kind of *mentsch* you'd marry the girl!").

Mezuzah (pl. *Mezuzoth*): A small metal or wooden case containing a handwritten piece of parchment on which are inscribed 22 lines from Deuteronomy (6:4–9 and 11:13–21) dealing with the Jew's obligation to love God and to obey His commandments. The reverse side of the parchment bears the name *Shaddai* (Almighty), plus three additional words meaning "God, our Lord, is God." This case is attached to the right doorpost of the house as one enters, and also on the doorpost of each room used for living purposes. Actually, the word *mezuzah* means "doorpost."

Minyon (Minyan): Quorum of 10 adult males required before public religious services may be held. Women are now demanding the right to participate in the *minyon,* but don't hold your breath until it happens.

Mishnah (Mishna): The earliest section of the Talmud consisting of the collection of oral laws edited by Rabbi Judah ha-Nasi, circa 200 C.E. The *Gemara* is an elaboration of the *Mishnah.*

Mishpocheh: Family, relatives.

Mohel: Circumciser.

Momzer: Bastard.

Mosheeach: Messiah.

Nacht: Night.

Nahr: A fool; an ignorant person.

Nahrishkeit: Foolish, foolishness.

Nash: See Nosh.

Noch: As used in some of the anecdotes in this book, it means, loosely, "yet!" as in, "I should have twins, *noch!*" The word has several other meanings, such as "more," "again," etc.

Noch amol: One more time; once more.

Nosh (Nash): There are several variations of this word. Used as a verb, it means to eat something that tastes good. Moreover, it can also mean to "nibble" goodies between meals or at bedtime. To snack. Such a person is a *nosher,* or *nasher.* Used as a noun, a *nosh* is something that appeals to your sweet tooth.

Nu: This is a most versatile non-word. It can be used to urge someone to take action. It is also used to mean "well?" or "so?" or "so what?" and "what about it?" and so on.

Nudgeh: Nagged; goaded.

Nudnik: A bore; a pest. Best illustrated thusly: A *nudnik* is a person who, when asked how he is, really tells you how he is—from his headache to his ingrown toenails.

Oy: An exclamation denoting either pain or surprise, and sometimes even rapture. It all depends on the inflection—and, of course, on how many *oy*'s you say, sigh or scream: *oy, oy!* Or *oy, oy, oy!,* and occasionally, even five or six *oy, oy*'s.

Oysgematert: Tired out. ("How do you feel?" "*Oysgematert!*")

Oy vay: You already know what *oy* means (see above). When you add *vay* to it, you are dding "woe." And if you hear an overprotective mother exclaim: "*Oy vay iz mir!*" she is saying "Oh, woe unto me!" and is probably rushing her mischievous young one to the sink to stop his nose-bleed.

Paskudnyak: A nauseating individual. In plain English, a louse.

Passover: The spring festival which commemorates the deliverance of the Jews from their bondage in Egypt. It lasts eight days, beginning on the 15th day of the Hebrew month *Nisan* (March-April). It is a time when only Passover foods are eaten (matzoh and such), and only on special Passover dishes.

Peltz: A lined, fur coat worn by men.

Pesach: The Hebrew word for Passover. (See above.)

Peyess: Side curls or earlocks, worn by very Orthodox Jewish males, particularly Chassidic Jews.

Peygern zol ehr: The word *payger (payger)* means "perish" or "die." Loosely, as quoted in these pages, the term means, "He should drop dead!"

Pogrom: Organized campaigns of persecution, usually accompanied by robbery, physical injury and sometimes death. *Pogroms* were often instigated or supported by the State, the church, or both. The worst culprits in modern times were Russia and Poland, and of course Nazi Germany.

Pogromchiks: Ruffians who were part of the gangs that pillaged, beat and murdered Jews in Russia, usually under Czarist command or tolerance.

Ponem (Punem): Face. (A pretty girl would have a *shayneh ponem.*)

Poopik (Pippik): Technically, this means a belly-button or navel. But it is used freely in Yiddish to denote something small and insignificant. It is even personalized when the individual referred to is called "Moishe Pippik" and, as such, it means "Mr. Nobody."

Pootehr (Pittehr): Butter.

Potch: A slap or smack.

Purim: Festival of Lots, marking the deliverance of the Jews from Haman's plot to exterminate them as described in the Book of Esther. It is celebrated on the 14th day of the Hebrew month *Adar* (March). Children enjoy Purim carnivals when they can dress up like Ahasuerus or Mordecai, Esther, and even like the villain, Haman. Children and adults participate in "beauty contests" in which the lovely Queen Esther is selected. *Hamantashen* are the traditional delicacy of the holiday.

Pushkes (sing. *Pushke*): Small tin boxes with coin-slots on top. These charity boxes were nailed up on the wall (often whether the apartment or house-dweller liked it or not) by a little old man with a black bag, who emptied the boxes every week. A number of groups and organizations vied with each other for the coins, and many homes were lined with several *pushkes.* The money was collected for Jewish orphans, widows and the desperately poor who had even less than the poverty-stricken

Jews who contributed the coins.

Raycher: A rich man. Also spelled *Reicher.*

Rebbe: Teacher; title given to a learned or respected man. It is also used as the equivalent of "mister."

Rebbetzyn: Wife of a rabbi. Also spelled *Rebbetzn.*

Saichel: Good common sense; good judgment. That common sense is multiplied when it is referred to as *Yiddishe saichel.*

Schmaltz: Usually chicken or goose fat which has been rendered. It has been freely adapted into the English language, particularly in show business, to denote anything well larded with corny sentiment. Schmaltz is delicious when spread on a piece of pumpernickel bread and lightly salted.

Schnapps: Any strong alcoholic beverage. The "aperitif" was very popular among Jewish families who could afford it—but it was called a *schnapps.*

Schvartze: Derived from the German *schwartz*, meaning "black." As used in this book, the word refers to a Negro. There is nothing pejorative in the term, any more than the use of *goy*, which simply means "gentile."

Sephardim: A Hebrew term denoting Jews of Spanish and Portuguese origin. Expelled from Spain by the Inquisition of 1492, the Sephardi Jews were dispersed throughout the Turkish Empire as well as Europe and, later, in North and South America. The customs, language, rituals, traditions and synagogue services of the Sephardim differ markedly from the *Ashkenazim.* The Sephardi pronunciation of Hebrew is basically that which is used today in Israel.

Shabbes: Sabbath.

Shadchan: A marriage broker; professional matchmaker.

Shaigetz: A male gentile; a *goy*, sometimes applied to a Jew who is ignorant of Jewish customs or Judaism in general.

Shalom: Literally "peace." It is also used to denote hello or good-bye.

Shammes: The sexton of a synagogue.

Shandeh: A shame.

Shayneh: A good-looking girl or woman. A handsome man is called a *shayner.*

Shifskart: Ship's passenger ticket. *Shifskart gelt* refers to the passage money for the voyage.

Shikker: A drunkard.

Shikse: The feminine of *shaigetz* (see above).

Shlemiel: One who is clumsy, inept and a dolt.

Shlepper: This is the noun taken from the verb *shlep*, which means "to pull or drag." When used as a noun it is quite unflattering, and means someone who just drags along without ever achieving anything. When used about a woman, it conjures up a total picture of someone whose slip is showing, whose hair is bedraggled, and whose nose is running.

Shmatteh: Rag. The complaining wife will often weep that's all she has to wear. If she steps all over her husband, he becomes a *shmatteh.*

Shnook: In the English vernacular, "a jerk." Somewhere between a *shlemiel* (see above) and a *shlimazl* (the perennial "Hard-luck Harry")—except that the *shnook* has most of the problems of both. Sometimes, it simply means "an ordinary guy."

Schnorrer: A beggar.

Shoichet: Ritual slaughterer.

Shtetl: Small town, village or hamlet.

Shul: Synagogue.

Shund: Trash

Streimel (Shtreimel): A fur hat worn by *Chassidim.*

Talmud: A Hebrew word meaning "study" or "teaching." It is also the name for a library of books (63 volumes) which contain a record of rabbinical comments on the teachings of the Bible. Although dealing primarily with law, the *Talmud* also contains a rich store of historic facts and traditions. In its pages are found scientific discussions, ethical teachings, legends, and profound observations on all phases of human experience.

Tanteh: Aunt

Tateh: Father; papa; daddy.

Torah: Terms variously applied to the first five books of the Bible and the Pentateuch. Also an overall term for Jewish learning and law.

Traif: Food which, according to dietary law, is ritually impure and unfit for consumption. Not *kosher.* Also pronounced *traifa.*

Tsailt mir eppes: "Tell me something." Also expressed as *Der tzailt mir eppes.*

Tsibileh: Onion. Plural: *Tsibiles.*

Tsimmis: A sweet dish in which carrots and prunes are mixed with honey and several other ingredients. It is eaten as a side dish.

Tsuris (Tsouris, Tsorres): Troubles, miseries.

Tuchus: A person's rear end.

Tzaddik: A righteous man. In *Chassidism*, the title given to the leader of a sect.

Umglik: Tragic.

Ver Fahrblunjet: Get lost.

Yahrzeit: The memorial anniversary of the date of death.

Yarmulke: Skull cap worn by religious Jews.

Yenta (Yenteh): Someone who sticks her nose into everyone else's business; a busybody; a gossip and tattle-tale. And Jews, being the wits they are, sometimes give the one they are calling "*Yenteh*" a surname: *Yenteh Tellabendeh.* The surname does little else than rhyme with *yenteh.*

Yeshivah: Rabbinical academy; talmudic college.

Yiddishe saichel: Native Jewish sense. (See listing for *saichel.*)

Yiddishkeit: That which pertains to the nature or traditions of the Jewish people; Jewishness.

Yidden (Yid'n): Jews.

Yingatsh: A young smart-alec; a fresh kid; or, to put it bluntly, a snotnose.

Yom Kippur: Day of Atonement. The most solemn of all Jewish holidays during which time one abstains from all food and drink for twenty-four hours.

Zaftik: Buxom, pleasingly plump.

Zayda: Grandfather.

Zin: Son.

Zun: Sun.

About the Author

HENRY D. SPALDING, a native of New York City, was born in what is now the heart of Harlem. He moved to California in the early 1950s, where he devoted his considerable talents to creative writing, editing, and publishing. Previously, he was a reporter for the *New York Mirror* and the *Journal.* While a member of the National Press Club in Washington, D.C., he was an accredited White House correspondent.

In Los Angeles, where Henry Spalding took up residence, he was a member of the Hollywood Press Club, and, at various points in time, active as editor and publisher of *Deejay, Disc,* and *Top Ten*—all music magazines. For 14 years he served as editor of *Talent News,* one of the major show business trade journals.

Mr. Spalding's *Encyclopedia of Jewish Humor* was issued in 1969 and has since gone through many editions. This was followed by *Encyclopedia of Black Folklore and Humor, Joys of Irish Humor,* and *Joys of Italian Humor and Folklore,* all of which have established him as one of the leading experts on ethnic humor.

Mr. Spalding and his wife, Bert, currently reside in Northridge, California.